ITJOUR
DOC 1
5935

POLICING ECONOMIC CRIME IN RUSSIA

COMPARATIVE POLITICS
AND INTERNATIONAL STUDIES SERIES

Series editor, Christophe Jaffrelot

This series consists of translations of noteworthy manuscripts and publications in the social sciences emanating from the foremost French researchers, from Sciences Po, Paris.

The focus of the series is the transformation of politics and society by transnational and domestic factors—globalisation, migration and the postbipolar balance of power on the one hand, and ethnicity and religion on the other. States are more permeable to external influence than ever before and this phenomenon is accelerating processes of social and political change the world over. In seeking to understand and interpret these transformations, this series gives priority to social trends from below as much as to the interventions of state and non-state actors.

GILLES FAVAREL-GARRIGUES

Policing Economic Crime in Russia

From Soviet Planned Economy to Privatisation

Translated by
Roger Leverdier

HURST & COMPANY, LONDON

First published in the United Kingdom in 2011 by
C. Hurst & Co. Publishers
41 Great Russell Street, London, WC1B 3PL
© Gilles Favarel-Garrigues, 2011
Translation © Roger Leverdier
All rights reserved.
Printed in India

First published in French in 2007 by CNRS Editions as
La police des moeurs économiques. De l'URSS à la Russie (1965–1995)

The right of Gilles Favarel-Garrigues to be identified as the
author of this publication is asserted by him in accordance
with the Copyright, Designs and Patents Act, 1988.

A Cataloguing-in-Publication data record for this book
is available from the British Library.

ISBN: 978-1-84904-065-5

This book is printed on paper from registered sustainable
and managed sources.

www.hurstpub.co.uk

CONTENTS

ACKNOWLEDGMENTS

This book is the product of a long research, fieldwork and research companionship with colleagues in France, Russia and abroad. It would be too drawn-out to name here all the people I have interviewed in Russia and all the colleagues in Russia, Europe and the USA who have helped me to improve my research during the years of fieldwork and in publishing this book first in French, then in English. Some of them, who granted me an access to archives or to interviews, are nevertheless mentioned in the Appendix on sources.

The book itself, and its subsequent translation and editing into English, owe much to a collective process and work. I would therefore first like to thank my research centre, CERI-Sciences Po/CNRS, for its financial support through public funding (DAS). I am also indebted to Christophe Jaffrelot, former director of CERI, and Christian Lequesne, current director of CERI, for their encouragements and support in my research and publication. I would also like to thank the CNRS publishing house for publishing this book in French and helping to translate it into English.

This translation would not have been possible without the diligent work of Roger Leverdier, translator, as well as the unfailing support and patient assistance of Miriam Perier who manages English language publications at CERI-Sciences Po.

Lastly, I would like to thank the publishers, Hurst Publishers and Columbia University Press, for their great professionalism and editing of the current version.

INTRODUCTION

Exploiting the legal vulnerability and social illegitimacy of entrepreneurs has been a feature of political power in Russia since *perestroika*. Russian leaders have frequently attempted to intimidate the business sector by denouncing the illicit nature of its activities. The pioneers of capitalism were exposed to such criticism from the late 1980s, for they had to come to terms with a normative framework that was ill-suited to the development of private enterprise, even though *perestroika* promoted the growth of the private sector. Therefore, and despite the implementation of reforms which reversed the rules of economic activity, the criminal legislation adopted in 1960 remained in place until 1997. The reinvention of capitalist practices[1] led to the exploitation of loopholes in ongoing legislation and to deliberate or inadvertent breaches of the law. There is now a large body of literature—essays, memoirs, novels, etc.—devoted to these methods of capital accumulation and the probability that they were illegal.[2] But efforts to combat economic crime during the late 1980s and early 1990s have received little attention. How were the funds and manpower dedicated to this task actually used? Were law enforcement agencies unable to control rapidly mutating forms of criminal activity? Or did they conform to the government's desire, despite the existence of so many "grey areas", to encourage the primitive accumulation of capital?

The answers to these questions require an understanding of how the fight against economic crime was conducted before *perestroika*, during the Stagnation period under Brezhnev, a period marked by the struggle to control such illegal practices as the "exercise of private enterprise", "speculation" and other

---

[1] J.-F. Bayart, 1994.
[2] See for instance; Y. Dubov, 2002; D. Hoffman, 2002; P. Klebnikov, 2000; R. Sakwa, 2009.

1

"crimes against socialist property," all of which were supposed to represent a "legacy of the capitalist mentality" on Soviet soil. A historical perspective enables us to grasp how the Soviet police, faced with a redefinition of economic crime in the mid-1980s, adapted the professional skills and expertise honed during the fight against the underground economy. The period under examination therefore encompasses three decades, from the beginning of the Brezhnev era in 1965 to the mid-1990s, by which time the first phase of the privatisation process had come to an end, and the impact of economic reforms on the definition of crime and its repression was already clearly apparent.

The fight against economic crime constituted a form of policing that involved not only branches of the Interior Ministry (MVD) and judicial institutions (the Prosecutor's Office[3] and the courts), but also people's control committees, the Party control committees, the People's Volunteer Detachments, and indeed the entire citizenry, whose complaints sustained the hierarchy's critique of local law enforcement agencies. Apart from one seminal book on the subject,[4] our knowledge of the day-to-day activities of this bureaucracy prior to *perestroika* is extremely limited. Studies of its transformation since the mid-1980s have focused principally on the role played by law enforcement agencies in the accumulation of capital—that is, on the commercialisation of policing and the activities of police officers who, along with other "entrepreneurs of violence", have specialised in the use of force, intimidation, extortion and provide protection of private property rights.[5] However, scant attention has been paid to Soviet efforts to counter the development of innovative practices that conflicted with the founding principles of the fight against economic crime.

Given the emphasis on the "totalitarian" nature of the Soviet system, its police have often been regarded as an armed branch of an entity that was itself defined as a "police state." According to this view, the state imposed a social order through agencies which carried out its injunctions to the letter and in a pure top-down manner. Drawing on material which focuses on the "social" history of communism[6] and particularly on the dynamics at work within Soviet society,[7] the current study rejects these premises. It suggests that the Soviet police should instead be seen as social actors who enjoyed some degree of

[3] *Prokuratura.*
[4] L. Shelley, 1996.
[5] V. Volkov, 2002.
[6] S. Kott, 2002.
[7] M. Lewin, 1988 and 2003.

INTRODUCTION

autonomy in the organisation of their professional activities, and that the
"methodological exceptionalism"[8] which typifies so many studies of communist societies may be discarded in favour of a different approach to Soviet policing, making use of the tools developed to comprehend it in other contexts.
The book thus draws its inspiration from Western sociological studies of the
bureaucratic implementation of public policies[9] and of police discretion, the
ways in which police officers select the cases they deal with on a daily basis.[10]
As they are usually tasked with achieving several objectives simultaneously,
regular police officers can neither handle every offence of which they are aware,
nor respond to every call for their services. The Soviet policeman should be
regarded as a "street-level bureaucrat", an agent whose activity was defined by
the constant management of dilemmas arising from the desire to comply with
the orders from above and at the same time to satisfy the demands of the citizenry.[11] To a certain extent his decisions were influenced by personal proclivi-
ties, but they were also influenced by institutional factors linked to the
bureaucratic management of police activity. The policeman's conduct was
guided by the way he was assessed, according to his compliance with the hierarchical injunctions he had to enforce. His priority was therefore to meet the
result-oriented performance criteria. Indeed, Soviet bureaucracies attached
more importance to "goal-rationality",[12] the rationality employed to fulfil the
goals set by the hierarchy, than to adherence to rules and regulations. In the
case of the police, the performance of local Interior Ministry departments was
assessed by matching two indicators—the number of cases recorded and, from
the 1970s, the clearance rate—to the quantified goals set by the hierarchy.

The influence of performance criteria on police activity raises questions
about the Soviet categorisation of criminal behaviour.[13] In this domain, legislation creates the "right to punish":[14] it defines the values and interests that justify the use of legitimate violence by political authority.[15] But the notion of
economic crime based on a "clearly defined category of criminal law"[16] is not

[8] M. Dobry, 2000, p. 580.
[9] E. Bardach, 1977; J. Pressman, A. Wildawsky, 1973; P. Lascoumes, 1990; R. Mayntz, 1980.
[10] D. Monjardet, 1996; R. Reiner, 1997.
[11] M. Lipsky, 1980.
[12] T. Rigby and F. Feher, 1982, p. 10.
[13] J. Carbonnier, 1994, p. 103.
[14] P. Lascoumes, P. Poncela, P. Lenoel, 1989, pp. 10–11.
[15] P. Lascoumes, A. Depaigne, 1997, p. 5.
[16] M. Delmas-Marty (ed.), 1997, p. 13.

3

rooted in any specific context; it generally serves as an umbrella term denoting a wide variety of charges.[17] Moreover, economic crime (*ekonomicheskaia prestupnost*) has never constituted a clearly defined legal category in Russian law, being rather a political and law enforcement construct, which denotes a range of offences spread across several chapters of the Soviet criminal code.[18] Most of these offences were distinguished by their vagueness. A normative framework of this kind enhanced both the degree of autonomy enjoyed by police officers and the discretionary nature of their activity. It became easy for them to develop their own rules of implementation;[19] they were thus able to adapt penal norms to the situations they encountered in the course of their duties and still officially comply with the hierarchy's orders.

The choice of the period under examination (1965–95) reflects the concern to avoid accepting the dissolution of the communist regime in December 1991 and the adoption of the constitution of the Russian Federation two years later as definitive breaks for the purpose of analysis. This standpoint rejects the "transition to democracy" paradigm[20] that dominated analysis of political change in Russia for so long. Academic criticism of this concept is now widespread: the presuppositions attached to the very term transition, its interpretation as a teleological progression from one kind of state ("authoritarian regime" or "planned economy") to another ("democracy" or "market economy"), highlight a normative view of political change[21] which is ill-suited to the Russian case. Moreover, a theoretical reference to preceding waves of democratisation (in southern Europe and Latin America) has proved to be of little relevance when dealing with regimes that, in addition to changing their political structure, have had to renew the rules of economic activity and, on occasion, redefine their national borders.[22] The sociological analysis of post-communist "transformations", a response to the transitological approach, focuses on the ways in which professional skills are adapted to a new institutional environment, create innovative practices and contribute to the formation of social rules,[23] and is therefore of greater relevance here, although the emphasis on "legacies" may in turn foster a form of determinism.[24] Academic controversies

[17] A. Doig, M. Levi, 1996, pp. 248–9.
[18] A.M. Yakovlev, 1988.
[19] On the notion of "secondary rules of application", see P. Lascoumes, 1990, p. 62.
[20] For an account of this approach, see J. Linz, A. Stepan, 1996.
[21] T. Carothers, 2000, pp. 5–21.
[22] C. Offe, 1992, pp. 928–42.
[23] D. Stark, L. Bruszt (eds), 1998.
[24] M. Dobry, 2000, pp. 585–614.

aside, it should be borne in mind that the "transitological" paradigm was also endorsed by Russian political leaders in the early 1990s, notably in order to justify the economic reforms then under way. The privatisation process thus served political ends: its instigators claimed that the creation of a class of small shareholders, which was thought to be the fermenting agent of democracy, would ensure that the exit from communism could not be reversed.[25] On the other hand, the paradigm received little attention when the debate turned to the reform of law enforcement and, especially, of the police. One of the aims of this book is to explain why changes in this domain were restricted to partial institutional measures, and why penal policy generally adhered to the Soviet model long after the collapse of the USSR.

Until the late 1980s, studies of governmental action in the Soviet Union relied upon a limited number of official sources and were mainly confined to analyses of speeches by leading cadres and media treatment of certain policies.[26] The research for this book began in the mid-1990s and has benefited from the partial accessibility of various government sources, including police and judicial statistics and documents held by research centres attached to the Interior Ministry and the General Prosecutor's Office of the Russian Federation, the institutions which for many years monopolised the analysis of crime and penal policy in the Soviet Union. The book has also benefited from the wider variety of sources that became available in the wake of *glasnost*, a policy that stimulated the growth of investigative journalism, non-governmental expertise and collective initiatives to secure the release and rehabilitation of the "convicted managers" tried and sentenced during the Soviet period. Analysis of the implementation of penal policy is based on material housed in regional archives, principally the administrative reports concerning the control of economic crime that all law enforcement bodies submitted to the Sverdlovsk region Communist Party committee between 1965 and 1991.[27] To add to this unpublished archive material, interviews were conducted with serving and retired police officers. Information on the post-Soviet period was derived from administrative reports similar to those consulted in the regional archives, as well as from interviews and personal observation of the privatisation process as it unfolded, and later research on law enforcement reform.

---

[25] V. Bunce, 2000, pp. 633–56.
[26] A. Brown, M. Kaser (eds), 1982.
[27] See Sources, p. 271–2.

The presentation is based on a detailed study conducted in Sverdlovsk *oblast'*,[28] an industrial region in the Urals. Sverdlovsk *oblast'* is rich in natural resources and in the industrial production of military equipment. The capital, Yekaterinburg (formerly known as Sverdlovsk), was closed to foreigners until 1992; it is now one of Russia's major regional cities, with a population of over 1.5 million. Governed by Boris Yeltsin in his capacity as first secretary of the Sverdlovsk Region CPSU Committee from 1976 to 1985, the region became a driving force in the implementation of *perestroika* and the economic reforms of the early 1990s. Besides being one of the few subordinate units of the Russian Federation to contribute to the federal budget, it was also notable for frequent clashes between its governor, Eduard Rossel, an advocate of greater regional autonomy, and federal power during the 1990s. Finally, the Sverdlovsk region, like most of its neighbours, contains a large number of penal establishments. Following a series of spectacular public clashes among criminals in the late 1980s, Yekaterinburg acquired a reputation as a city dominated by "organised crime" and became known as the "Chicago of the Urals."[29]

The first part of the book deals with the period prior to the accession of Mikhail Gorbachev, when political and legal definitions of economic crime reflected some ideological assumptions, directly inspired by Marxist doctrine and designed to protect the fundamental principles of the Soviet economy. Practices regarded as economic offences were particularly problematic for the leaders of the Party-State: they could not acknowledge the progression of such activity in Soviet society, but by the late 1970s they were forced to adapt the law to cover forms of crime that had become a fact of everyday life. By grouping together diverse practices that contributed to the actual functioning of the Soviet economy, the term "economic crime" came close to meaning what Western observers referred to as the "underground" or "second" economy. Most research into economic crime in the USSR employed these terms, but the conceptual association appears to be influenced by existing prejudices concerning the government's approach to this particular form of criminality. In my view, the Foucaldian concept of economic "illegalities" is more appropriate when analysing a policy that fundamentally rested on the selective treatment of illegal practices.

As part of the fight against economic crime, large numbers of personnel were regularly mobilised in campaigns designed to combat specific offences

---

[28] An *oblast'* is an administrative division in Russia.
[29] V.B. Zhitenev, 1993.

(theft of state property, speculation) or broader targets such as "unearned income." However, a study of the implementation of these campaigns highlights the relativity of their impact: they were more or less a permanent feature of police work for many years and, despite their imperative nature, afforded those involved a significant margin of manoeuvre. By and large, the ways in which orders were transmitted and performance assessed enabled "street-level bureaucrats" to define their own objectives once they had met their official targets. During the Brezhnev and Andropov periods, the marked increase in recorded cases, particularly of economic crime, prompted various attempts to adjust police and judicial practices at institutional level. Such efforts highlighted both the confusion experienced by political leaders when confronted with the growth of criminal behaviour and the increasing difficulty of devising appropriate responses to the economic crisis.

In the second part, I explain why political and economic changes occurring in the USSR after 1985 transformed the definition of economic crime and of law enforcement policy in this field. Therefore, this part does not focus on local practices, but rather on the evolving national framework of Soviet crime-control policy after Mikhail Gorbachev came to power. First, the initial privatisation measures triggered by *perestroika* paved the way for economic practices that conflicted with the founding principles of the Soviet regime. Such reforms as the promotion of "individual labour activity", the development of the cooperative sector, the introduction of first measures of "spontaneous privatisation" and finally the adoption of the official privatisation programme in 1992 have almost completely transformed economic offences. The way these reforms were implemented also showed some common features—the role of administrative officials in the development of private firms, the place devoted to entrepreneurs' initiatives, and the political legitimisation of these measures—which have had an impact on the development of economic crime. Second, *glasnost* endowed crime with a sudden media visibility. Partial crime statistics started to be published in the press and it was now possible to write or talk publicly about this issue. Economic crime soon became a political issue, reflecting the historical context of the late 1980s. Hardline Communists pleaded for stronger repression, but entrepreneurs and human rights activists also started to get mobilised and sought to influence the redefinition of economic offences. Finally, the very idea of combating economic crime had to be altered. In the late 1980s and early 1990s, numerous and often incoherent measures were adopted to adapt the crime-control policy to the privatisation challenge. It created growing tension between competing political goals—the defence of individual liberties, including those of entrepreneurs, and the urgent need to tackle new forms of criminality. Measures were taken to strengthen the fight against "economic sabotage" and "organised crime", but control of practices linked to the transfer of property was manifestly weakened.

In the third part, I focus on police activity in such an evolving context. The police were at that time in crisis due to a lack of resources, the departure of personnel, the recruitment of underqualified officers, and the inability to cope with new forms of crime. Budgeting difficulties led to various initiatives in policing at local level, involving municipal or regional authorities, big plants' management and/or workers' leaders, thus complicating the coordination of law enforcement missions. This situation was aggravated by the creation of new governmental police forces in an attempt to deal with new forms of criminality. Within the Interior Ministry, specialist services fighting against organised crime appeared and were given wider autonomy and more funds than the other criminal investigation departments. A new police force, dedicated to tax offences, was also created outside the Interior Ministry.

Observation of the implementation of law enforcement during *perestroika* and afterwards, however, shows clear evidence of continuity with previous police practices. Bound by the obligation to produce results as they engaged with economic crime, police officers responded to the hierarchy's orders by reverting to traditional methods. In doing so, they were able to exploit their position in a much more lucrative way than in the past, as they could use their position to answer the growing demand for private protection. As a result, there was a sharp increase in registered economic offences, but as we will show this reflected an evolving form of differential treatment of illegalities at local level. Police weaknesses were particularly apparent when the privatisation programme was implemented in 1992. As orders from above were often contradictory, local police services tended to find new reasons to explain their weaknesses, pointing out for instance the responsibility of central authorities and of government departments dealing with economic reforms. Finally, the conclusion sums up the main continuities of anti–economic-crime policy during the Soviet and post-Soviet eras, and extends findings to Russian law enforcement in the 2000s.

PART ONE

SOVIET MANAGEMENT
OF ECONOMIC CRIME

INTRODUCTION TO PART ONE

The aim of this part is to understand what exactly the fight against economic crime entailed before Mikhail Gorbachev came to power in 1985. I will show in Chapter 1 that the importance of this fight, within penal policy, was correlated to the ideological challenge this form of criminality posed to Soviet political leaders. According to Marxist-Leninist thought, as criminality was proper to bourgeois societies, it had no reason to survive on Soviet soil. Consequently, its persistence could only be explained through the subsistence of traces of capitalist mentality among Soviet citizens. Although its forthcoming eradication was announced, economic crime remained a target for Soviet penal policy. Therefore, it is necessary to understand how this category was defined in Soviet law. I will show that it designated a series of offences scattered across various chapters of the Soviet criminal code and that this category was not fixed in time. From the end of the 1970s, several institutional changes have showed that in fact there was a real will to adapt social legislation to changing illegal practices.

Development of such practices did not remain totally unnoticed. As Chapter 2 aims to show, they were at the heart of Western research on the Soviet second economy. This field of research that developed from the mid-1970s produced precious knowledge on the real functioning of the Soviet economy but had to face real difficulties understanding the attitude of the public authorities, due to the scarcity of sources available on the issue. The result was a somewhat schematic vision of penal policy that in particular overestimated the law enforcement bureaucracies' capacity to enforce hierarchical orders. I will introduce the Foucauldian concept of "differential management of illegalities", in order to solve this difficulty by analysing the group of factors that may explain why some offenders risked being sanctioned but others did not in the Soviet context.

Chapter 3 presents the actors who contributed to the fight against economic crime. Here, I analyse the role played by the Prosecutor's Office in Soviet penal policy and show the predominant role played by the police in the repression of economic offences. Police agencies specialising in the fight against theft of socialist property and speculation (OBKhSS units) were not the only ones concerned by this form of crime within the Ministry of the Interior, but they were in the front line. Nevertheless, the fight against economic crime was not supposed to be limited to law enforcement agencies, as the population as a whole was expected to engage in the fight. Bodies such as People's Control Committees, Party Control Committees and People's Volunteer Detachments (*druzhinas*) also played an active role. Moreover, any citizen could act as a whistleblower, whose allegations could potentially be taken into account by the authorities.

Chapters 4 and 5 will allow us to examine the fight against economic crime in practice, thanks to the archives I was able to access in the Sverdlovsk region. Chapter 4 shows how the implementation of the never ending mobilisation campaigns was organised at the local level. Local law enforcement bodies had to present results in figures, linked to the number of registered offences and to the clearance rate (*raskryvaemost*). The way law enforcement agencies were evaluated pushed them to find ways to formally respond to hierarchical orders by doctoring statistics. Political authorities, realising the limitations of a strictly quantitative approach, tried to improve the situation by using the results of Soviet criminological research on crime causes. This resulted in an operational model of analysis, encompassing factors linked to the offender's personality or social environment and factors that were supposed to influence the commission of an offence in the economic sphere or working environment. But this did not stop the model being treated as a formality once it was integrated into police reports.

Chapter 5 analyses the way in which archives on the fight against economic crime deal with the responsibility of law enforcement agencies themselves. Suspected of being both incompetent and venal, the police were the first to be blamed. However, the weaknesses of the other institutions concerned are also mentioned in these sources. In the end, observing the fight against economic crime at the local level has revealed the incapacity of law enforcement bodies to deal with evolving criminal activity. Though this incapacity is observable from the mid-1960s, it becomes particularly significant from 1975 onward. The year 1975 seems to represent a break when it comes to analysing both the illegal economic practices and the institutional responses to the phenomenon.

The several attempts made to adapt the penal policy to such "criminal reality" show the dilemmas that political leaders faced in a context of worsening economic crisis. They in no way improved the situation, but prefigured difficulties in reconciling economic reform and social justice that would be even more acute during *perestroika*.

1

THE IDEOLOGICAL AND LEGAL FOUNDATIONS OF THE STRUGGLE AGAINST ECONOMIC CRIME

In our society, the main causes of crime have been eliminated. For the first time in history we can envisage the destruction of this social phenomenon. Criminality has not yet been totally eradicated, for socialism has not rid itself of all its "birthmarks" ... the traces of the past that survive in various sectors of social life as well as in the conscious mind, psychology and daily life of the individual. These causes ... are organically alien to socialist society, in which criminality is a form of regression ... The level of crime is three to four times lower than it was in the 1920s and 30s, and professional criminality has been eradicated.[1]

In the mid-1970s, Soviet propaganda ceaselessly depicted crime as an alien phenomenon to socialism, in reference to the Marxist doctrine which refused to regard it as "a simple violation of rule and law", for these concepts did not reflect the "domination of a general autonomous will."[2] Crime, a product of the exploitation of the masses by the dominant class, represented the "crudest and least fruitful" form of the workers' revolt against the bourgeoisie:[3]

[1] *Bol'shaya Sovetskaya Entsiklopediya. Tom 20.* (The Great Soviet Encyclopaedia. Volume 20.) Moscow, Izdatel'stvo "Sovetskaya Entsiklopediya", 1975, p. 539.

[2] K. Marx and F. Engels, 1982, p. 182.

[3] Most of the quotations from Marx and Engels are from Russian translations of their works. F. Engels. "Polozhenie rabochego klassa v Anglii" ("The Condition of the Working Class in England") in K. Marx and F. Engels. *Sochineniya. Izdanie vtoroe. Tom 2.* (Works. Second Edition. Volume 2). Moscow, Gosudarstvennoe Izdatel'stvo Politicheskoi Literatury, 1955, p. 438. English translations are from Karl Marx and Frederick Engels: *Collected Works*, London, Lawrence & Wishart, 1975–2005.

"We counterpose social peace to social war, we put the axe to the *root* of crime—and thereby render the greatest, by far the greatest, part of the present activity of the administrative and judicial bodies superfluous."[4]

In theory, the dictatorship of the proletariat would lead to the disappearance of antagonism between social classes and, ultimately, of the need for a justice system.[5] Only external factors such as "propaganda of the Western way of life" and the existence of "birthmarks" in society could explain why crime had not completely disappeared from Soviet soil more than fifty years after the revolution. The denunciation of "birthmarks", an omnipresent theme in the rhetoric of Soviet criminology, exculpated the Soviet regime and implied that crime was a temporary phenomenon. Before its programmed decline, criminal law constituted one of the principal tools for achieving the goals that had been set. However, this idea was surrounded by controversy from the earliest days of the Soviet regime. By 1918, some legal experts were arguing that breaches of the law would disappear during the transition to communism, after the elimination of "rudimentary traces of the past."[6] But others regarded this view as unfounded and utopian:

People will continue to kill each other through wickedness, revenge or jealousy; they will set their sights on socialist property rather than private property.[7] Socialism could not claim to eliminate reprehensible frustrations and desires, for "the new social relations" would inevitably produce new forms of offences.[8]

At no point was this argument allowed to influence the official position: in the mid-1970s, the possibility of eliminating crime seemed to be drawing closer; "professional crime", it was announced, had already disappeared.[9] The vocabulary of the Soviet campaigns against various forms of social deviance echoed the terminology employed by Engels: the goal was not simply to curb the growth of reprehensible behaviour, but to "eradicate criminality", "put an end to alco-

---

[4] F. Engels, "El'berfel'dskie rechi" (Speeches in Elberfeld) in *ibid.*, pp. 537–8. The word "root" is italicised in both this and the English edition.

[5] *Ibid.*, p. 538.

[6] This phrase is attributed to M. Yu. Kozlovskii in an article published in the journal *Proletarskaya Revolyutsiya i Ugolovnoe Pravo*, no. 1, 1918. Quoted in L.O. Ivanov and L.V. Il'ina, 1991, p. 120.

[7] These quotations, attributed to Ya. Berman, in an article published in *Proletarskaya Revolyutsiya i Pravo*, no. 2–4, 1919, are reproduced in *ibid.*, pp. 121–2.

[8] *Ibid.*, pp. 121–2.

[9] In the Soviet Union, "professional crime" referred to offences committed by people who adhered to the traditional rules of the underworld. The term had fallen into disuse by the late 1980s, being replaced by "organised crime." See A. Gurov, 1990.

holism" and indeed to "clear up every offence, without exception."[10] Given the absence of facts and figures, these declarations of intent were not open to criticism. Police and court statistics remained secret until 1989. To be sure, such information circulated within the Party, law enforcement agencies and institutes attached to the Interior Ministry and the office of the Prosecutor General, but it was never open to public scrutiny. The Soviet literature on criminology would occasionally reveal a few details—usually in the form of inaccurate percentages—but never offered a full picture of police activity. The degree of control exercised by political leaders enabled them to select the most advantageous comparisons in order to highlight the decline of crime on Soviet soil; they could consequently claim that by the mid-1970s, the level of crime in the USSR was three to four times lower than it had been between 1920 and 1930.[11]

Defending the Fundamental Principles of the Socialist Economy

The law, a "powerful means of social transformation",[12] defined licit and illicit social practices in accordance with prevailing ideological representations. Soviet criminal legislation included many provisions for punishment of behaviour that contradicted the fundamental principles of the socialist economy.[13] In the economic sphere, however, the power of the law had its limits. The Soviet legal system was "conservative by nature"[14] and any code was bound to remain in force for a long period despite the evolution of economic practices.[15] Leonid Brezhnev himself condemned certain legal regulations for their "obsolescence", "unjustified limits" and "overly-detailed clauses."[16] In the 1960s,

[10] A.V. Pokhmelkin and V.V. Pokhmelkin, 1992, p. 49.

[11] W.D. Connor, 1972, pp. 148–62.

[12] V. Chkhikvadze (ed.), 1971, pp. 192–3.

[13] The terms "principle" and "rule" are employed here in a legal sense. A principle is a "general rule or norm of a non-legal character from which legal norms may be deduced." See G. Cornu (ed.). *Vocabulaire juridique*. Paris, PUF, 1994 (4th edn.), p. 631. From our perspective, a rule is above all a rule of law, i.e. "a legally obligatory norm, whatever its source, degree of generality and scope" (*Ibid.*, p. 694).

[14] P.B. Maggs, 1978, p. 117.

[15] *Ibid.*, p. 117.

[16] L.I. Brezhnev. *Vsyo dlya blaga naroda, vsyo vo imya cheloveka. Rech' na vstreche s izbiratelyami Baumanskogo izbiratelnogo okruga goroda Moskvy 14 iyunya 1974 g.* (Everything For the Good of the People, Everything in the Name of Mankind. Speech to the voters of Baumanskaya district electoral constituency, Moscow, 14 June 1974). Moscow 1974, p. 15. Quoted in D.D. Barry, G. Ginsburgs and P.B. Maggs (eds), 1978, p. 119.

some legal experts attempted to address these problems by recommending the adoption of a code of economic relations. One such code was eventually published in 1970, but was never formally adopted.[17]

The role of the law in the regulation of the Soviet economy was intended to fulfil three functions: the protection of "public ownership of the means of production", the definition of the "measure of labour and its remuneration" and the "economic organisation of the socialist state and the activity of enterprises."[18] In the interests of clarity, it is however appropriate to distinguish two functions within the "economic organisation of the socialist state": the definition of property rights and of planning rules.

First, in the Soviet Union the state owned the principal means of production, which it allocated to enterprises. The law prohibited all forms of social relations that were "incompatible with socialist principles", particularly the "exploitation of one person by another in any form whatsoever" and the "appropriation of the results of another person's labour ..."[19]

The second principle in question concerned the definition of the relations between labour and income and was expressed in two well-known rules: "from each according to his abilities, to each according to his needs" and "he who does not work, neither shall he eat." The distribution of national income took the form of a strict correspondence between the amount of labour provided and its remuneration. This equivalence justified the ban on deriving an income from personal assets: "Under socialism, personal property cannot become a means by which one individual can exploit another, or a source of income which is not derived from labour. For example, every Soviet citizen has the right to purchase a car and enjoy the use of it, but they cannot use it to earn money by transporting passengers."[20] Many of the campaigns against economic crime were conducted in the name of this principle. The decision to target practices such as "unearned income", "parasitism" (meaning failure to exercise a "socially useful" activity[21]), and speculation represented a continuation of Leninist thought.[22]

---

[17] *Ibid.*, pp. 120–34.

[18] V. Chkhikvadze (ed.), 1971, pp. 200–1.

[19] *Ibid.*, pp. 200–1.

[20] *Ibid.*, p. 200.

[21] On the significance of this term in Leninist vocabulary, see: D. Colas, 1998, pp. 201–6.

[22] V.I. Lenin, "O "levom" rebyachestve i o melkoburzhuaznosti" ("On 'Left Wing' Childishness and Petty-Bourgeois Mentality"). *Polnoe sobranie sochinenii. Izdanie*

The third principle concerned the protection of socialist property. The 1960 RSFSR Criminal Code was designed to "protect the social regime of the USSR, its political and economic system, socialist property, the person, the rights and freedoms of citizens and the socialist legal order against criminal offences."[23] The priority given to the protection of socialist property, reaffirmed in the text of the 1977 constitution,[24] justified the imposition of harsh penalties for crimes against state property. By the same token, offences concerning personal property were punished less severely. In certain cases, the sanctions even exceeded the penalties for premeditated murder without aggravating circumstances.[25] Moreover, the protection of state property was perceived as a guarantee of the development of personal property.[26] According to the Soviet line, greater productivity would create wealth, stimulate consumption and, ultimately, increase the personal wealth thus "derived" from "state property."[27] The protection of state property was therefore presented as a legitimate imperative, for it served the interests of all citizens.

The fourth principle determined the role of planning in the Soviet economy. The purpose was to break away from the "classic liberalism of the past century [which] envisaged the law as a sort of highway code which indicated the correct procedure but failed to say who should proceed, at what point and with what aim."[28] In the Soviet economic system, the law defined not only the overall planning system, but also the "execution of the plan's tasks by those assigned to them"—which meant the economic activity of all enterprises.[29] This fundamental role justified the definition of crimes directly related to failings in the

---

pyatoe. Tom 36 (Complete Works. Fifth edition. Volume 36). March-July 1918. Moscow, Gosudarstvennoe Izdatel'stvo Politicheskoi Literatury, 1962, p. 297.

[23] Article 1 of the RSFSR Criminal Code. Chapter 1 of the code covered "crimes against the state", Chapter 2 "crimes against socialist property" and Chapter 3 "crimes against the life, health, liberty and dignity of the individual."

[24] See D. Colas, 1997, p. 65.

[25] When aggravating circumstances were present, most forms of theft of state property (articles 89, 90, 91, 92 and 93 of the Criminal Code) were punished by prison sentences ranging from five (or six) to fifteen years, whereas premeditated murder with no aggravating circumstances (article 103) attracted a three- to ten-year sentence.

[26] Soviet law acknowledged "individual property", but not "private property." The adjective "private" was applied only to one charge: "private enterprise activity."

[27] V. Chkhikvadze (ed.), 1971, p. 200.

[28] *Ibid.*, p. 196.

[29] *Ibid.*, pp. 196–7.

plan's implementation. The Soviet state portrayed itself as the defender of the fundamental principles of the economy, and the law was the most powerful of the many means employed to ensure its protection. Soviet criminal law, designed to protect the values upheld by the regime, made definitions and distinctions among economic practices in accordance with their correspondence to the fundamental principles of Soviet society.

The Legal Definition of Economic Crime

Like any similar text, the RSFSR Criminal Code, adopted in 1960, defined the categories forming the basis of the right to punish by setting out the values and interests the political authorities had undertaken to protect. It constructed and classified offences, but its purpose was also pedagogical to the extent that it represented a code of conduct, for the rules that had been formulated were moral as well as judicial.[30] It delimited the space allotted to individual freedoms. Definition of offences meant naming a type of behaviour that in many cases had previously lacked a name. It also meant dividing social space between the licit and the illicit and, more precisely, restricting the space of liberty by a new prohibition.[31]

The concept of economic criminality (*ekonomicheskaya prestupnost*) did not feature as such in the RSFSR Criminal Code. As Leonard Orland noted, it represented a confused legal category that was both "too inclusive and not inclusive enough."[32] Some jurists associated it exclusively with the offences listed in Chapter VI (*khozyaistvennaya prestupnost*) of the RSFSR Criminal Code, which grouped together breaches of the rules of economic activity, for instance speculation, accounting fraud, violations of the rules of commerce and private enterprise activity.[33] But the law enforcement agencies responsible for combating economic crime favoured a much broader definition[34] that encompassed all crimes against state property (Chapter II), certain "abuses of office" involving the offer or acceptance of bribes by "state officials in positions of responsibility"[35]

---

[30] P. Lascoumes, P. Poncela and P. Lenoel, 1989, p. 280.

[31] M. Delmas-Marty, 1992, p. 306.

[32] L. Orland, 1986, pp. 199–200.

[33] M. Ancel and Y. Marx, 1971, p. 2284.

[34] L. Orland, 1986, pp. 199–200.

[35] "Abuse of office" concerned only the *dolzhnostnye litsa*, i.e. "state officials in positions of responsibility", according to the translation in Ch. Kourilsky-Augeven, 1998, p. 1.

(Chapter VII), and, finally, cases involving counterfeiting and currency trafficking that were regarded as "crimes against the state" (Chapter I).[36] This was particularly true of the criminal investigative services responsible for "combating the theft of socialist property and speculation" (the OBKhSS), which, despite their title, dealt with a wider variety of offences. The concept of economic crime was therefore a product of operational concerns, and was used by specialists in criminal law, political leaders and police officers to group together offences that were scattered across various chapters of the RSFSR Criminal Code.

"Economic crime encompasses all crimes against socialist property and the rules of economic activity that are committed for personal gain by persons occupying defined positions in the system of economic relations."[37] This definition is appropriate to the present study, despite the confusion it induces about possible offenders. The expression "occupying defined positions in the system of economic relations" is indeed ambiguous: employed to extend the field to abuses of office, it gives free rein to a variety of interpretations, some narrower than others. In my view, its meaning has to be broad enough to avoid prejudicing the analysis by determining beforehand which segments of the Russian population were singled out in the fight against economic crime. That said, such a definition highlights one of the principal characteristics of economic crime in the USSR: it was always a matter of attacking the interests of the state, whether by appropriating or damaging its property or by contesting its authority to define the rules of economic activity. When the "economic criminal" deceived the state or eluded its control, he caused it actual or symbolic harm. This definition took no account of Chapter V of the Criminal Code, the section covering crimes against personal property (articles 144–151), for the state was not the victim of these offences. Economic crime did therefore not encompass all profit-motivated offences.

Economic offences, especially theft of socialist property and abuse of office, attracted extremely harsh penalties. Capital punishment could be prescribed for certain offences, including the large-scale theft of state property (article 93[1]), aggravated passive corruption (article 173), and crimes against the state such as counterfeiting (article 87) and currency trafficking (article 88). The authors of most economic offences faced long prison sentences, although the law also provided for sanctions such as non-custodial corrective labour and fines.

---

[36] See Table 1 for a list of economic crime offences. All the tables of the volume are in the Appendix.
[37] A.M. Yakovlev, 1987, p. 62.

However, in the post-Stalin context, the penalties for offences defined as crimes against socialist property reflected the desire to mitigate the repression while maintaining the emphasis on protection of socialist property enshrined in Soviet criminal law. Indeed, a decree issued by the Presidium of the Supreme Soviet of the USSR on 4 June 1947 set out extremely harsh penalties for crimes against socialist property, all of which involved prison terms of between five and twenty-five years. The decree also contained an article making it an offence to withhold information concerning the preparation or commission of a theft. By comparison, the 1960 RSFSR Criminal Code set out slightly reduced prison terms: article 89 (simple theft), for example, recommended a maximum of three years imprisonment if there were no aggravating circumstances, and up to fifteen years in cases of recidivism or significant material damage to the state. Moreover, legislators were finally able to balance penalties against the amount of damage caused (article 96 dealt specifically with minor thefts of state property), the character of the accused (recidivist, "parasite", etc.), and the nature of the offence (robbery with or without violence, with or without forced entry). Breaches of the rules of economic activity also continued to attract heavy penalties. Anyone charged with the production or sale of poor quality, sub-standard or incomplete goods, falsification of accounts or production statistics,[38] private enterprise activity, speculation or illegal tree-felling could expect a prison sentence. The three articles relating to bribery all stipulated terms of imprisonment for this offence.

Harsh penalties reflected the importance of the definition of economic crime to the legitimacy of the socialist project and the Soviet regime. However, fluctuations in criminal legislation from the late 1970s onwards demonstrate that far from being set in stone, the definition could be adapted to the changes taking place in Soviet society. These changes brought about modifications in the definition of both illicit practices and the penalties they entailed.

Fluctuations in Criminal Legislation under Brezhnev and Andropov

An examination of the fluctuations in criminal legislation shows that offences are never a matter of "verifiable facts, ahistorical materials or means to defend

---

[38] In Russian, the generic term indicating these practices in the parlance of the time was *ochkovtiratel'stvo*. Etymologically, this term is formed from the verb *vtirat'/vteret'* (to rub, to mix up) and the noun *ochki* (points on a dice or playing card). The most common form of *ochkovtiratel'stvo*, overestimation of activity indicators, is known as *pripiska*. See S. Pomorski, 1978, pp. 291–317.

an atemporal 'natural morality.'"[39] On the contrary, processes of criminalisation, depenalisation and decriminalisation illustrate changes in the perception of illegitimate practices, the social harm they cause at a given moment, and the appropriate judicial response they deserve. In this respect, the Soviet case was no different from any other, even during the period commonly associated with the term "stagnation."

In the late 1970s, the first modifications of articles relating to economic offences gave no indication of an overarching approach to the matter. In 1977, the repeal of the article relating to the changing of small sums of currency (article 154²) clearly reflected the desire to intensify repression, for this offence would henceforth be covered by article 88 and thus become a crime against the state. But other changes suggested a tendency towards greater leniency by providing alternatives to prison terms (corrective labour without imprisonment, and fines) for offences such as petty theft with aggravating circumstances (article 96). This decision inaugurated a move to diversify and reduce penalties for the most common economic offences. In the early 1980s, the introduction of new offences reflected the desire to improve the management of two sectors—commerce and "basic services"[40]—that had hitherto escaped state control and had enabled a large segment of the population to earn extra income. In this case, the criminalisation procedure was aimed at easing penalties for the most common forms of undeclared labour and commercial fraud, which had formerly been covered by more oppressive legal definitions. If there were no aggravating circumstances, the guilty party would in future receive a fine or a short period of non-custodial corrective labour instead of a prison sentence. Legislators wanted to demonstrate vigilance vis-à-vis the actors of the "underground economy" and at the same time avoid a disproportionately repressive response; hence the vagueness of the concept of "illicit remuneration" (*nezakonnoe voznagrazhdenie*) that appeared in the article on "basic services." This all-encompassing concept was defined as "illicit benefit from an asset, in the form of money, foodstuffs or industrial goods... realised by an employee in the basic services sector (shops, food processing businesses, workshops, medical establishments, ticket booths,

---

[39] P. Lascoumes, P. Poncela and P. Lenoel, 1989, pp. 11–2. See also P. Lascoumes, P. Poncela and P. Lenoel, 1992.

[40] This is a matter of "a citizen obtaining illicit remuneration for work involving services to the public" (article 156²) and "violation of the rules of commerce" (article 156³). According to article 156², such work concerns commerce; public catering; basic, communal and medical services; and communal transport. In Russian, the term "basic services" means services such as hairdressing, shoe-repairing, repair of household electrical appliances, etc.

hotels etc.)", for services involving the "sale of goods, railway and airline tickets; the manufacture and repair of clothing; medical consultations..."[41] These lists could not claim to be exhaustive, with good reason: all forms of elementary speculation, corruption, private enterprise activity and theft of socialist property seemed to be concerned. Moreover, as it targeted both monetary and material payments, it included illicit bartering practices.

In my view, all these procedures reflected a fundamental characteristic of Soviet penal policy. As far as economic crime was concerned, the categories were generally broad, often vague, and ensured that diverse practices were punished severely. The desire to relax penalties for the more elementary forms of illicit economic practices resulted in further criminalisation, but did not lead to the repeal of the articles previously used to punish them. Given the existence of several definitions, reprehensible behaviour could henceforth be punished with varying degrees of severity. The political willingness to diversify definitions and ease penalties for more commonplace offences was extended during the Andropov period.

On coming to power in November 1982, Yuri Andropov authorised numerous penal policy measures. Some were aimed at gaining greater control over the leading elite; hence the ousting of the Interior Minister and the neutralisation of the Brezhnev clan.[42] Others indicated that penal policy was seen as a means to enhance the legitimacy of the CPSU's new Secretary General. Andropov demonstrated his intention to break with tradition at the November 1982 plenum, where he set out economic objectives and acknowledged the gravity of the crisis confronting Soviet society.[43] Referring to obstacles to economic reform, he denounced the failure to fully exploit the available means of production, singled out "shoddy work, idleness, and irresponsibility", and called for the intensification of the "fight against all forms of indiscipline ... negligence and waste."[44]

---

[41] *Vedomosti Verkhovnogo Soveta RSFSR*, no. 38, 1981, article 1304.

[42] On these points, see A. Vaksberg, 1992; Yu. Churbanov, 1993.

[43] "In general terms, Comrades, there are many tasks to accomplish in the economic sphere. Of course, I have no instant solution to the problems." Yu. Andropov. "Rech' generalnogo sekretarya TsK KPSS Yu. V. Andropova na plenume TsK KPSS" (Speech by Yuri Andropov, Secretary General of the CPSU CC, at the plenum of the CPSU CC). *Spravochnik partiinogo rabotnika, vypusk dvadtsat tretii, 1983* (Party Militant Handbook, 23rd. edn., 1983). Moscow, Izdatel'stvo Politicheskoi Literatury, 1983, p. 103.

[44] For the November 1982 plenum and on Yuri Andropov in general, see Zh. Medvedev, 1983.

The process crystallised in an initial general reform of the Criminal Code (3 December 1982).[45] Adopted less than a month after Andropov's accession to power, it represented another stage in the adaptation of criminal legislation. The list of measures to repress economic crime was extended and diversified. The desire for fewer prison sentences led to the introduction of fines for all forms of crime against socialist property[46] and greater use of corrective labour without imprisonment. In addition, provision was made for the extensive application of complementary punishments. Penal sanctions for those found guilty of economic crimes could in future be accompanied by the confiscation of assets and/or a ban on engaging in any activity that involved responsibility for material resources. These new sanctions reflected recent developments in Soviet thinking on criminology (cf. Chapter 4). While confiscation was seen as a means of compensating the state, the ban was designed to improve recruitment practices, particularly with regard to jobs involving responsibility for property and commodities. Indeed, it was believed that economic offences often arose from the fact that "profiteers" and "recidivists" were placed in charge of goods in shops and businesses.

Both developments were reflected in amendments to specific articles of the Criminal Code. In future, a person convicted of simple theft (article 89) might receive a fine rather than a prison term or a period of corrective labour. If there were aggravating circumstances, corrective labour could replace imprisonment. These measures could be accompanied by the confiscation of personal assets, an obligatory sanction when robberies were committed in "particularly aggravating" circumstances—that is, by particularly dangerous "recidivists" or on a "particularly large" scale. The amendments extended to certain breaches of the rules of economic activity: *pripiski* (padding of production statistics), for example, now attracted fines or non-custodial corrective labour, often accompanied by a ban on exercising certain functions or activities, as well as prison terms. Prison terms were actually abolished for cases of "buyer and seller fraud" (article 156) if there were no aggravating circumstances, although the maximum period of corrective labour was extended and the possibility of a fine introduced. This article also provided for removal of the right to employment in a commercial business, a public catering business, basic services or municipal

---

[45] *Vedomosti Verkhovnogo Soveta RSFSR*, no. 49, 1982, article 1821.
[46] Before this date, a single article (93^2) provided for such a sanction, when practices relating to articles 89, 92 and 93 were first offences and concerned small sums. The introduction of fines in all Chapter II articles led to the repeal of article 93^2.

management for a period of two to five years. On the other hand, the reform hardly touched upon abuse of office.

The adoption of the RSFSR Code on Administrative Offences[47] in June 1984, several months after the death of Yuri Andropov, maintained the momentum.[48] As in other contexts, the focus was on defining whether an economic crime should entail "an administrative rather than a penal response"— that is, the circumstances in which the administration applied "its own sanction to the author of a crime."[49] This new form of "response" covered a range of practices including unlicensed street trading, minor speculation (involving sums below 30 roubles), unlawful sale or acquisition of petrol and other fuel oils, exercise of a prohibited artisanal activity, use of transport for personal gain and fraud involving communal transport (see Table 2). Anyone convicted of these offences was liable to a fine, but the theft of state property worth less than 50 roubles incurred one to two months of corrective labour.

In one sense, this reform completed the shifts in criminal legislation sketched out during Brezhnev's term in office, which tended to ease sanctions by redrawing the borders between illicit practices through the introduction of new charges and the diversification of definitions and sanctions. Criminalisation in the strict sense of the term was in fact aimed at easing penalties for the most common offences, an effort which continued with the addition, in 1983, of article 156[4] (illegal distribution of petrol and other fuel oils) to the Criminal Code.[50] Although Andropov's position represented a fresh approach in some respects (corruption of leaders, his speech on the state of the economy), the break with past practices accomplished by the end of 1982 should not be overestimated.

This overview of the construction of economic crime in legal terms shows the extent and the imprecision of the categories used in the Soviet penal system and, more generally, the way in which the right to punish was conceptualised in the USSR. Michel Foucault noted—in reference to a very different con-

---

[47] The literal meaning of *administrativnye pravonarusheniya* is "administrative offences." In order to avoid the impression that this means offences committed within administrative bodies, the term is usually translated as "offences sanctioned by the administration", although "administrative offences" is sometimes used to avoid repetition.

[48] *Vedomosti Verkhovnogo Soveta RSFSR*, no. 27, 1984, article 909.

[49] M. Delmas-Marty, 1992, p. 129.

[50] *Vedomosti Verkhovnogo Soveta RSFSR*, no. 33, 1983, article 1203.

text—that "For penal semiotics to cover the whole field of illegalities that one wishes to eliminate, all offences must be defined; they must be classified and collected in species from which none of them can escape. A code is therefore necessary and this code must be sufficiently precise for each type of offence to be clearly present in it."[51] In the Soviet case, criminal offences and their legal definitions were so vague and so conducive to a wide variety of interpretations that they could be used to punish virtually any form of behaviour. Some provisions (on hooliganism, parasitism) enabled the authorities to inflict punishment for a wide range of practices, and a specific offence might be covered by several legal definitions. The few recorded cases of active or passive corruption highlighted the fact that whenever the probity of administrative officials and directors of enterprises was called into question, it was done so in the name of defending state property or upholding the rules of Soviet economic activity.[52] Similarly, the statistical rarity of practices considered as "private enterprise activity" (art. 153) was due to the fact that behaviour of this type was regarded as a diversion of state property.[53] The tendency of criminal law provisions to overlap ultimately gave the investigative officers tasked with implementing Soviet penal policy a considerable degree of latitude.

Concluding Remarks

An examination of the legal definition of economic crime highlights a particular conception of the relation between the law and the economy. In the Soviet system of values, the emphasis on protecting state property was a remarkable specific feature of criminal legislation. But the modifications to the Criminal Code that began in the late 1970s indicated a more lenient approach to the most common forms of economic crime. While their implementation did not significantly reduce the severity of criminal legislation, they could be interpreted as tentative adaptations to obvious social changes. It is therefore likely that what occurred during the 1970s was a qualitative and/or quantitative evolution of the illicit practices that constituted the full range of economic crime, a hypothesis to which we shall return.

At this point, we turn from the law to the practices covered by definitions of economic offences. When examining the conditions for the sociological

[51] M. Foucault, English version, 1977, p. 98.
[52] W.A. Clark, 1991, pp. 75–6.
[53] V. Chalidze, 1978.

treatment of a research topic that is by definition legal, Max Weber distinguished between the approach of the jurist, who ponders the "normative sense" that should logically be attributed to a certain construction of language presented as a norm of law, and that of the sociologist, who seeks to understand what in fact becomes of it in the community. In other words, how do people go about their activities in accordance or non-accordance with legal prescriptions?[54] The adoption of a more sociological perspective enables us to approach a very wide variety of practices, some more common than others, some more diligently repressed than others. And when adopting a sociological approach to a legal topic, it seems more appropriate to employ the term "illicit economic practices" rather than "economic offences." Since the 1970s, much of the knowledge of these practices has come from the study of the "underground" economy in communist contexts.

[54] M. Weber, 1995, p. 11.

2

ILLICIT PRACTICES AND THE "UNDERGOUND ECONOMY"

The enormous variety and occasional complexity of illegal and semilegal activities in production and distribution are ensured by the pervasiveness of controls and the massive number of prohibitions in the state and household sectors of the economy, and appear to be limited only by human ingenuity (...)[1]

A paradox is immediately apparent: while the spread of illicit economic practices in Soviet society throughout the 1960s, 70s and 80s was always abundantly clear—hence the stories Western travellers told about the way they had changed money and sold or exchanged standard consumer goods on the Soviet "black market", the cartoons in Soviet satirical magazines,[2] and Soviet popular comedies[3]—it eluded broader attempts at analysis, for the context gave rise to specific methodological difficulties. Two types of printed matter attested to the growing desire to analyse the spread of illicit economic practices in order to achieve a better understanding of Soviet society: the essays written by dissidents and Soviet émigrés,[4] and academic research papers on the Soviet "underground economy." Academic studies did much to shape Western representations of the illicit practices that constituted, in Soviet parlance, economic

[1] G. Grossman, 1977, p. 29.
[2] M.H. Delorme, 1964.
[3] For instance *Brilliantovaya Ruka* (1968) and *Dzhentelmeny Udachi* (1972).
[4] V. Chalidze, 1978; C. Simis, 1982; K. Simis, 1977, pp. 35–55. On the contribution of émigrés' stories to our knowledge of the Soviet economy, see Z. Katz, 1973, pp. 87–120.

crime. The importance of studies of the "second", "parallel", "informal" or "underground" economy to our understanding of the daily life of Soviet citizens raises questions about the presuppositions they contain and, ultimately, suggests that the most appropriate analytical grid should be based on Michel Foucault's concept of illegality.

Western Problematisation of the Soviet 'Second Economy'

Research into the Soviet second economy originated in the West; the first works on the subject directly published in the USSR did not appear until the second half of the 1980s. Although interest in this field intensified in the late 1970s, a number of studies had analysed illicit economic practices during earlier phases of Soviet history. One notable example used court documents to examine the most common economic offences committed during the New Economic Policy (NEP).[5] As it examines the illicit practices of Soviet entrepreneurs in the 1920s, this text endows the forms of crime that would emerge in the context of *perestroika* with a historical resonance. Empirical research conducted during the Stalin era also highlighted the importance of illicit economic practices in Soviet daily life.[6] Post-war studies of the ways in which the Soviet economy actually functioned ensured that interest in such issues was maintained. Joseph S. Berliner's work on the organisation of labour in factories and the role of managers is a key text: one chapter is devoted to the notion of *blat*, which the author defines as the use of personal influence to obtain favours that are not officially or legally attributed to an enterprise or an individual.[7] During the post-Stalin period, Karl-Eugen Wädekin examined speculative practices in *kolkhoz* markets.[8]

Western researchers became increasingly interested in the subject during the 1970s for several reasons. First, there was an increase in the movement of people between the USSR and the outside world: many Western travellers reported the approaches made to them in a context where foreign currency and standard consumer goods appeared to attract a growing number of "speculators." In addition, the influx of Soviet émigrés into certain countries, especially Israel and the United States, stimulated new research into daily life in

[5] Yu. Larin, 1927.
[6] M. Fainsod, 1958, pp. 195–210 ("Crime in Smolensk"); S. Fitzpatrick, 2002, pp. 52–66.
[7] J. Berliner, 1968, p. 182. (1st. edn. 1957).
[8] K.-E. Wadekin, 1973.

the Soviet Union, much of it based on interviews. On a broader level, studies of the Soviet underground economy were influenced by ideological concerns, the aim being to assert the pre-eminence of liberal democracy. In many cases, the depiction of the Soviet economy's "true face" reflected a desire to prove that the Soviet authorities could not possibly succeed in eliminating individual desires and aspirations, or in stifling manifestations of liberty that contradicted the fundamental principles of the regime. From this perspective, this issue was close to the growing Western interest in Soviet dissident activity, as they both raised awareness that the Soviet regime was unable to satisfy people's economic and political needs. These studies also showed that despite its claims, the USSR was not totally immune to crime. In one sense, the bestsellers dealing with crime in the Soviet Union responded to anxieties related to rising violence and crime in Western societies at that time.[9] Finally, such texts reflected broader epistemological considerations, particularly the development of theoretical and comparative studies of the "informal sector" in "third world" countries.[10]

Researchers believed that a rigorous analysis of the Soviet underground economy was now possible. Gregory Grossman, one of the pioneers in this field, considered he had "enough raw data" to prove the existence of illicit practices in "every sector of the Soviet economy."[11] Grossman relied on official Soviet sources, the press, the observations of visitors to the USSR and the accounts furnished by dissidents, but placed particular importance on the testimony of Soviet migrants to the United States. Inspired notably by works on Soviet Jewish migrants in Israel,[12] he subsequently coordinated a questionnaire-based research project involving former Soviet citizens living in the United States. The information collected would enable analysts to assess the importance of undeclared income in relation to types of employment and household expenditure.[13] Since *perestroika* and the collapse of the USSR, every study of the Soviet economic system has devoted space to developments in the under-

---

[9] Y. Brokhin, 1975.

[10] G. Duchêne, 1981, pp. 256–7.

[11] G. Grossman, 1977, p. 26.

[12] Some economists assessed household income and expenditure in the USSR from interviews with Soviet emigrants in Israel. See G. Ofer, J. Pickersgill, 1980, pp. 121–43; G. Ofer and A. Vinokur, 1983, pp. 158–76.

[13] The results are analysed in the *Berkeley-Duke Occasional Papers on the Second Economy in the USSR*, which began appearing in 1985. The selected methodology is discussed in G. Grossman and V. Treml, 1985, pp. i–ix.

ground economy.[14] Interest in Soviet illicit practices has also nurtured a comparative debate on this phenomenon in contemporary societies.[15]

Grossman began by defining the second economy as any economic practice arising from the quest for personal gain and any practices that contradicts the law.[16] This association was justified by the fluidity of the border between the two phenomena and their conflict with the official economy, although the author later abandoned it and concentrated on the private illegal economy.[17] The latter included, among other things, moonlighting (at individual and group level), undeclared cottage industries, diversion of state-produced goods, clandestine production and corruption.[18]

Despite the "incalculable and inevitably qualitative nature of the unregistered economy",[19] the systematisation of methods for analysing income that occurred in the 1980s, particularly the analysis of questionnaires completed by Russians living in the United States, did result in evaluations. Grossman found that on average, undeclared income increased the remuneration of a Leningrad household by 38 per cent, but this figure rose to 67 per cent in Byelorussia, Moldavia and Ukraine, and 179 per cent in Armenia.[20] The principal bias of this approach was to take immigrants as a representative sample of the Soviet population, whereas permission to leave Soviet territory was frequently obtained through personal resources (access to scarce goods and/or key administrative officials, social capital, cash), and showed the ability to resolve the difficulties of the emigration procedure in an informal manner.

As the "distinction between official and parallel economies, or between first and second economies" could to some extent be applied to "all existing economic systems", many authors attempted to identify the features specific to socialist contexts.[21] In Western countries, the second economy, nurtured notably by underemployment and tax fraud, ran "parallel to the first by producing analogous goods and services." In socialist countries characterised by central planning and shortages, however, it seemed to be a more "complementary"

---

[14] See, for example, G. Duchêne, 1987, pp. 103–10; W. Andreff, 1993, pp. 210–6; B. Chavance, 1989, pp. 146–7; J. Kornai, 1996, pp. 112–36.

[15] M. Los, 1982, pp. 121–37; M. Los, 1983, pp. 39–57; M. Los (ed.), 1990.

[16] G. Grossman, 1977, p. 25.

[17] "Non-respect of regulations by state institutions" constitutes the illegal public economy. G. Grossman, 1979, pp. 834–55.

[18] For this author, the public official acted in a private capacity. *Ibid.*

[19] G. Duchêne, 1981, p. 269.

[20] G. Grossman, 1987.

[21] B. Chavance, 1989, p. 141.

structure.[22] Speculation, corruption, diversion of public assets, moonlighting and accounting fraud in businesses were common amongst all social categories and all economic activities.

Speculation, an offence defined as "the purchase and resale of goods for personal gain", resulted from shortages; it involved a wide range of products as well as foreign currency, and was practiced at all levels of society. Associated with the theft of socialist property, it centred on scarce goods produced legally in the Soviet Union or elsewhere, or goods that had been manufactured secretly. Anyone with direct access to a sought-after resource at work or elsewhere could sell or exchange it by dealing with a client either directly or through recipients of stolen goods. The Soviet press constantly denounced the immorality of the "commercial sector", which was notorious for its permeability to speculative practices.

The analysis of corruption is a more complex undertaking, given the specificities of the Soviet definition. The term *korruptsya* did not appear in the Russian language until the mid-1990s; it owes its existence to external constraints and domestic attempts to justify the disturbing social effects induced by the implementation of major economic reforms in 1992. The generic term for corruption up to that point had been *vzyatochnichestvo*, formed from the word *vzyatka*, meaning bribe. From a penal perspective, corruption was confined to transactions involving the offer and acceptance of a bribe, and acting as go-between in bribery. Other common forms of corruption, notably the diversion of public funds, were a feature of daily life in the Soviet Union, but were treated as crimes against socialist property or other abuses of office.

Many authors, notably Aron Katsenelinboigen, attempted to interpret the systematic "rules" of Soviet corruption. They tried to establish, for example, a correspondence between the position an official occupied in the hierarchy and the proportion of his income derived from corruption.[23] Soviet corruption was linked to the "inadequate supply of goods and services"[24] and was facilitated by factors that were not specific to the Soviet context at all, but particularly accentuated by it. First, the interpenetration of political, administrative and economic elites resulted, at every level of territorial administration, in the formation of horizontal networks that were likely to betray the interests of vertical hierarchies.[25] Second, officials wielded considerable power in economic

---

[22] *Ibid.*, pp. 141–2.
[23] A. Katsenelinboigen, 1983, pp. 233–5.
[24] J. Cartier-Bresson (ed.), 1997, pp. 56–7.
[25] J. Kramer, 1997, pp. 213–24.

and social life: citizens seeking to improve their living standards were often dependent on their goodwill.[26] At the lowest level, "street-level bureaucrats"[27] possessed considerable resources and could easily trade them in a context of widespread shortages. Their activities were monitored in a purely formal manner, by means of quantified indicators that allowed them a margin of autonomy.[28]

Most illicit economic practices were legally defined as crimes against socialist property and prosecuted as such. This notably applied to instances of corruption in state enterprises, where the misappropriation of fuel, equipment, materials and finished goods for personal ends was a mass phenomenon.[29] Some authors argued that the prospect of gaining access to resources that could then be traded illicitly was an important criterion in the choice of a job.[30] Thefts of goods and merchandise from the workplace came as no shock to the general public.[31] Chalidze remarks that the coining of a new word—*nesun*[32]—bore witness to the generally indulgent moral attitude to the authors of petty thefts.[33]

Some crimes against socialist property were more organised than others.[34] Much of the theft was committed by people who did not work for the enterprise or *kolkhoz* and may or may not have had inside help when concealing the traces of their crimes. Illustrating a greater degree of organisation, the term *tsekhovik*—literally a workshop employee—indicated someone running or participating in a clandestine manufacturing process, generally using the premises and/or materials at his disposal, after office hours. This practice contradicted all fundamental principles of the Soviet economy, for it thrived on the theft of state property, privatised the use of the means of production, bent the rules governing the definition of income and obstructed planning objectives. On the increase in the 1970s, it was generally associated with certain regions of the Soviet Union, particularly the Baltic States, Ukraine and the Caucasus.

[26] M. Mendras, 1995, pp. 117–22.
[27] M. Lipsky, 1980.
[28] S. Solnick, 1998.
[29] B. Chavance, 1989, p. 143.
[30] V. Chalidze, 1990, p. 293. This text was written in 1978.
[31] *Ibid.*, pp. 293–4.
[32] The term *nesun*, a noun created from the verb "to take away" (*nesti*), means someone who pilfers property from the workplace—products, means of production, scrap, etc.
[33] V. Chalidze, 1990, pp. 294–5.
[34] G. Grossman, 1977, pp. 29–31.

Undeclared activities were not confined to the *tsekhoviki*. Some citizens used the property at their disposal—an unoccupied room in an apartment building, a car, a plot of land—to improve their living standards. Others—repairers, plumbers, electricians—exploited skills for which demand was high. In some cases, teams were formed to provide services, the *shabashniki* being one notable example. These teams did off-budget work and often supplied the materials as well. For example, they would put up buildings or renovate existing buildings for a *kolkhoz*. The *shabashniki* enabled clients to bypass extremely slow official procedures and were well paid for their work. We shall see later how these productive forms of crime against socialist property benefited from special government treatment.

Finally, another body of illicit practices arose directly from the organisational methods employed by enterprises in order to fulfil planning objectives. "Informal barter agreements between enterprises, mutual loans between production units, the purchase or sale of raw materials or equipment on the black or grey markets, the constitution of excessive reserves of labour, parts or machinery: all these illicit practices were principally aimed at satisfying the *legal requirements* of the plan."[35] In the Soviet system, illicit practices of this type involved three of the leading figures in a state enterprise: the *tolkach*, the director and the accountant. The role of the *tolkach* was crucial: hired to "push" (*tolkat*) the interests of the business, he used every means at his disposal to ensure that it fulfilled its quota obligations, resolving supply problems informally, for example by resorting to more or less corrupt transactions. The director was also under pressure, but the accountant was in an equally sensitive position, as the archives consulted for the present book reveal. The falsification of accounts (*ochkovtiratel'stvo*) usually took the form of padding production indicators in order to claim bonuses for meeting targets (*pripiski*). Forms of *pripiski* diversified and became increasingly sophisticated during the period under review.

The above examples indicate the extent to which the Soviet economy under Brezhnev depended on the interaction between the first and second economies. This symbiosis has been attributed to the "constant articulation between forms of administrative authority and the forms of autonomy exercised by agents",[36] which was subject to a "constant tension between effectiveness and

---

[35] B. Chavance, 1989, p. 142.

[36] J. Sapir, "L'économie soviétique: origine, développement, fonctionnement" in J. Sapir (ed.), 1997, pp. 130–1.

legality, with a remarkable criminogenic potential."[37] When grouped together, however, all the practices associated with the "underground" economy constituted a disparate body which posed severe difficulties in terms of classification.

The Categorisation of Illicit Economic Practices

Classification generally proceeded from legal and/or economic criteria. In the first instance, categories of illicit practices followed the Criminal Code chapters, which implied a perfect equivalence between legal definitions and the operations associated with the "underground" economy.[38] Classification based on economic criteria took into account the practices that had been observed in society: this more realistic approach rejected the official representation of economic crime, but sustained the quarrels among academics. Illicit economic practices were distinguished by the sector in which they occurred ("private" or "state"), the type of operation (production, distribution, etc.), the connection with market or centrally-planned activities, and even by their "systemic or anti–systemic" character.[39] The most common approach was a functionalist analysis based on study of the rationality of economic agents. Aron Katsenelinboigen, for instance, is known for having developed a sophisticated typology in order to understand how the authorities "assessed" the various "markets" in goods and services on Soviet soil.[40] This typology was based on a set of criteria, such as the legality of goods sold, their origin and method of sale, the identities of holders and receivers of goods, the risk—positive or negative—of a sanction, and the short- and long-term development potential of the market for the product on offer. It covered all forms of commerce observed on Soviet soil and distinguished between "legal markets" providing access to scarce goods (reserved stores, commission shops, *kolkhoz* markets, etc.), "semi–legal markets" where accredited asset holders and service providers did not record transactions or pay tax (renting temporary housing, flat repairs, private medical consultations, exchanges of surpluses between enterprises) and "illegal markets" (favouring certain customers in state-owned shops, home-based sale of imported goods, sale of scarce or prohibited goods through specialised intermediaries such as "speculators" and "profiteers").

---

[37] S. Pomorski, 1977, p. 244.

[38] See, for example, F.J.M. Feldbrugge, 1984, pp. 528–43.

[39] "Anti–systemic behaviour is that which does not accord with the legitimacy of the real existing system." See G. Duchêne, 1981, p. 261.

[40] A. Katsenelinboigen, 1977, pp. 62–85.

This typology shows that illicit economic practices are not simply the product of central planning and shortages, but also reflect the attitude of the authorities. By showing that the opportunities for repression are variable, it traces the outline of a differential treatment of illicit behaviour and calls for understanding of the conditions governing the production of distinctive criteria and their political use. Aron Katsenelinboigen affords an insight into only one aspect of this issue in his discussion of the stereotypes constructed by politicians and law enforcement bodies in order to present "profiteers", "speculators" and "plunderers of socialist property" as black market professionals who unscrupulously exploit the dysfunctional nature of the economic system and enrich themselves at the population's expense.

The Limits of Western Analyses

Studies of the underground economy generally assumed that the Soviet Union was a homogeneous entity, so that the phenomena observed could be found throughout its territory. Some authors criticised this approach and stressed the regional specificities of economic crime on Soviet soil, particularly with regard to clandestine production.[41] Moreover, such studies took little account of variations over time in relation to the anti–economic crime agenda. The intensification of police activity during the launch of a campaign against economic crime was itself likely to encourage a reduction in certain illicit practices, or at least drive them further underground. Maria Los has attempted to validate this hypothesis by identifying regular cycles in the battle against economic crime, and their connection with the progress of the five-year plans. According to Los, governmental actors focused on certain breaches of the rules of economic activity, particularly speculation, during the first three years of a five-year plan. During the fourth year, as the pressure on heads of enterprises mounted, law enforcement bodies turned their attention to crimes against socialist property. Falsification of production indicators became the target in the final year of the cycle.[42] However, as we shall see, the archives consulted for the present book do not make it possible to substantiate this hypothesis.

The most systematic analyses of the second economy often concentrated on its social structuring.[43] Here we find the top rung of the ladder occupied by

---

[41] A. Katsenelinboigen, 1983, pp. 233–5; L. Duhamel, 1991a, pp. 21–48.

[42] M. Los, 1983. pp. 52–3.

[43] Maria Los edited a book on the second economy in Marxist states and sought to

"large-scale underground businessmen" running production and distribution operations with the support of members of the "official elite." Below them are the "small-scale private businessmen, moonlighting professionals and full-time black marketeers" who cultivate contacts with mid-level government functionaries. At the bottom stand "those numerous citizens who supplement their meagre incomes through some form of illegal or semi–legal activity."[44] In this case again, the perception of a well-ordered criminal hierarchy, a mirror image of political and social hierarchies, may be questioned.

Some authors argued that besides reflecting rational initiatives to adapt to a restrictive regulatory framework, illicit economic practices were also an anticipated product of the Soviet political economy: "Orders are either ignored or obeyed at the price of illegal behaviour somewhere else. In these circumstances, we can no longer talk in terms of an individual's rational decision to commit an offence, but are compelled to talk in terms of the planned production of economic crime."[45] In Gérard Duchêne's view, this process had several effects: it "invalidated the law", created "widespread tolerance", eroded the "legitimacy which the members of society had accepted" and, ultimately, brought about a "gradual reversal of morality." The priority shifted from duty to self-interest. "Thus we are reduced to a combination of 'selfish' forms of behaviour based not on the idea of a calculating individual, but on the transformation of morality through the influence of ideology."[46] Although the "planned production" theory of economic delinquency enables us to avoid a too legalistic interpretation of the action taken by the authorities, it appears hard to verify. Planning presupposes the existence of a coherent policy, a set of clear orders issued at the highest level of the Party-State, and their scrupulous application by administrative bodies. This top-down view of governmental action, the functioning of bureaucracies and, ultimately, the relations between state and society in the Soviet Union is, on the whole, the chief weakness of studies of the underground economy.

If we consider the Soviet economic system as the conjunction of two elements, the official and unofficial economies, we are obliged to consider the possibility that the Party-State's political leaders and law enforcement agencies

---

determine whether "formal structural similarities can lead to structurally similar informal solutions." M. Los (ed.), 1990, p. 194.

[44] L. Shelley, 1990a, p. 23.

[45] G. Duchêne, 1981, p. 284

[46] *Ibid.*, pp. 284–5.

had no great desire and/or ability to combat economic crime. The tendency of analysts to distinguish between social practices and official discourse and action gave rise to two views of the relations between the Party-State and society. Either political leaders, a privileged social group, had lost touch with reality and were unaware of the growth of the parallel economy,[47] or they were aware of how citizens went about organising their daily life but turned a blind eye to practices that were essential to the regime's survival. The latter view was more widely accepted: "Officials maintained the illegal status of these practices but recognized their necessity."[48] In other words, "the known inefficiency of the centralised model of the state economy" forced leading elites to "accept extensive areas of the second economy" in order to secure "a minimum level of consumer needs satisfaction."[49]

Analysis of the second economy was therefore based on representations of the strength or weakness of the Soviet Party-State. Paradoxically, the existence of the underground economy tended to highlight the power of Soviet leaders, for they were able, after a rational calculation, to decide whether to tolerate practices that were more illegal than illegitimate, or to suppress certain forms of criminality in accordance with their interests. It was also argued that, although the authorities realised the utility of the second economy, they sought to control it "by means of the law enforcement apparatus when they believed that illegal economic activity was stifling the effectiveness of the official economy, or becoming so pervasive as to undermine support for the existing political system."[50] At the conclusion of this analysis, it remains difficult to understand the authorities' "thinking": what information did they refer to, and how did they approach it? Louise Shelley acknowledged that a fundamental question had not been answered. With so many citizens liable to prosecution, who was finally selected and punished for such widespread offences?[51] Furthermore, an examination of local police action is essential if we are to understand whether the management of illicit economic practices corresponded to the policy that was elaborated at the summit of the Party-State.

Some authors have attempted to combine the two representations of governmental attitudes towards the underground economy: "the second economy is believed to contribute to the continuation of the dominant economic rela-

---

[47] See, for example, *Tenevaya ekonomika*, 1991, pp. 28–9.
[48] G. Duchêne, 1981, p. 266.
[49] M. Los (ed.), 1990, p. 6.
[50] L. Shelley, 1990a, p. 22.
[51] *Ibid.*, p. 20.

tionships while at the same time eroding the ability of the bureaucratic party-state effectively to control and manage the society."[52] This contradiction explains the "ambivalent nature" of the policies adopted by the authorities. According to this interpretation, the Party-State was faced with a permanent dilemma, with Soviet leaders torn between the repression of agents of the second economy and accepting that some flexibility was necessary for the survival of the system.[53] In my view, the perception of a constant tension between repression and tolerance lies at the heart of the difficulties posed by the dominant Western view of the Soviet second economy. As there are few sources to describe what information political leaders had at their disposal, or how decisions were made and orders transmitted and implemented, this hypothesis had no firm foundations. Moreover, it lent credence to the view that Soviet law enforcement agencies were efficient, well coordinated and capable of the smooth enforcement of political orders.

This perception needs to be analysed in the light of debates on the nature of the Soviet political regime from the 1960s onwards.[54] The concept of "totalitarianism" implied the existence of disciplined law enforcement agencies, dedicated to achieving the goals set by political leaders and capable of succeeding. The totalitarian analysis created a specific representation of Soviet bureaucracies; these were pure and perfect organisations, devoted to the political regime and, as such, very different from their Western counterparts. The contribution of the Western sociology of organisations or public policy analysis, showing in general that the implementation stage always creates opportunities to reinterpret national norms, while very popular in the 1960s, seemed irrelevant to analyses of Soviet bureaucracies that were as exceptional as the regime they served.

Western academic research into the Soviet second economy seems to suffer from weaknesses linked to the availability of sources—there was no document which would enable researchers to grasp the overall logic of the approach to crime in the USSR—and to the influence of ideological considerations about totalitarianism. Even the most brilliant analyses created a rather schematic impression of Soviet penal policy by reifying the balance between illicit practices and governmental responses. This is particularly evident in the typology advanced by Katsenelinboigen, which virtually ignored the resources individuals used in order to protect themselves from the police and the courts. For

---

[52] M. Los (ed.), 1990a, p. 9.
[53] L. Shelley, 1990, p. 19.
[54] See H. Carrère d'Encausse, 1985, pp. 210–37.

example, a shop assistant who stockpiled goods and priced them according to their scarcity would attempt to reduce the risk by selling them to a specialist intermediary, who would also make a profit. According to Katsenelinboigen, the employee was at risk of losing his job, while the "profiteer", as such people were known at the time, risked prosecution. But in practice the employee could also be prosecuted and punished severely, while the profiteer could avoid the courts if he possessed the necessary resources (money or contacts). Moreover, the idea that sanctions were predictable should be treated with caution.[55] The relation between an illicit practice and a sanction largely depended on the circumstances. The relativity of a legal sanction is, in my view, crucial to an understanding of Soviet attempts to combat economic crime. However, it should not be associated exclusively with the rational calculations of political leaders, but also with the everyday practices of all the actors involved in this task.

Economic Illegalities in the Soviet Context

The spread and visibility of illicit economic practices depend on the chances of their authors being punished. At this point, our analysis of the state's management of such practices may benefit from the concept of illegality. In *Surveiller et punir* (Discipline and Punish), Michel Foucault employs this term when discussing the relation between illegalities and criminality during the *Ancien Régime*, and again when examining the relation between "illegalities of property" and "illegalities of rights" in the second half of the eighteenth century. With regard to the *Ancien Régime*, Foucault shows that "each of the different social strata had its margin of tolerated illegality; the non-application of the rule, the non-observance of the innumerable edicts or ordinances were a condition of the political and economic functioning of society."[56] While noting that this observation is not specific to the context under consideration, Foucault states that illegalities could sometimes assume "a statutory form—as with the privileges accorded to certain individuals and groups", or "the form of a massive general non-observance" of ordinances that were published and revised, but never implemented. He thus posited a "space of tolerance" that for the "least-favoured strata of the population was an indispensible condition of existence."[57]

---

[55] With regard to the predictability of the penal response, one author has developed a typology of illicit practices according to the severity of the sanctions they incurred. F.J.M. Feldbrugge, 1984, pp. 528–43.

[56] M. Foucault, English version, p .82.

[57] *Ibid.*, English version, p. 84.

As employed by Foucault, the concept of illegality can take on two meanings and serve two aims. On the one hand, it illustrates and denounces a particular technique of domination in French society, but it also enables us to avoid a normative view of criminality. The distinction between offences and illegalities gives rise to questions about the relativity of the penal sanction—that is, the chances of avoiding it. Foucault developed the first aspect by contrasting "illegalities of property" and "illegalities of rights", but said little about the way in which the "space of tolerance" that illegalities constitute is constructed. Pierre Lascoumes developed this analysis some years later, when applying the concept of illegalities to major economic and financial crimes in France. Lascoumes found the concept appropriate when "the practice in question resists or escapes the application of the judicial code because it was invisible, or because no social actor had the ability or knowledge required to apply the code; because of the resistance of the author or the difficulty of finding and implementing an adequate definition. Illegality rests on the relativity of the judicial definition."[58]

Although the causes suggested in the French case are not entirely applicable to the present study, we shall take economic illegalities to mean those illicit economic practices that contradict existing law but "escape the application of the judicial code." Following on from Foucault and Lascoumes, our study of the organisation and implementation of the campaign against economic crime will focus on "the differential management of illegalities", that is, the treatment of illicit practices in accordance with certain considerations: the nature of the offence, the modalities of its detection and the identity of its author. In my view, the heuristic value of this concept is not confined to denunciation of the variable treatment of illicit economic practices in accordance with their authors' social status. A comparison of the sanctions imposed on the *nomenklatura*, Party members and ordinary citizens would certainly be of interest, but such contrasts, widely denounced for reasons of principle,[59] are difficult to explore for want of sources.

Concluding Remarks

Western analyses of the Soviet second economy have helped to understand the diversity and the growing importance of illegal economic practices in the

---

[58] P. Lascoumes, 1985, pp. 15–6.
[59] M. Voslensky, 1980.

Soviet economy. Major works have attempted to describe these practices and to analyse their function in the Soviet economic system. They have showed that a wide range of markets, more or less accessible to the entire population, existed in Soviet society in order to satisfy people's consumer needs. However, they were less relevant for understanding how the fight against these behaviours was organised in practice. As they focused systematically on the Soviet economy as a whole, they assumed that governmental responses were decided on the top, according to the varying degree of seriousness and social usefulness of illegal practices.

In fact, the construction of a "space of tolerance" for economic illegalities was a way of dealing with a composite body of constraints, and was far more complex than a simple admixture of repression and tolerance prescribed by Soviet leaders and faithfully applied by the relevant bureaucracies. Analysis of the differential management of illegalities in the Soviet context should highlight the involvement of a variety of political and administrative actors (federal, regional and local political leaders, law enforcement agency cadres and "street-level bureaucrats"). The relativity of the legal sanction was linked not only to the choices offered by economic and penal policy, but also to their interpretation by regional leading elites, and to the ways in which the police in the field selected the cases they dealt with on a daily basis.

3

LAW ENFORCEMENT IN THE SOVIET UNION

The principal policing tasks—maintaining security, combating crime, intelligence gathering—were never entrusted to a single institution. In the Soviet system, several law enforcement services possessed their own criminal investigation departments, which dealt with a list of offences defined in the Code of Criminal Procedure. The Prosecutor's Office (*Prokuratura*), the Interior Ministry and the KGB thus handled most economic crimes between them, according to the nature and gravity of the offence (see Table 3). Within the Interior Ministry, several criminal investigation services were in charge of the struggle against economic crime, but the services for combating the theft of socialist property and speculation were supposed to be the most competent. The loose definitions of some offences and the fact that many practices were covered by several definitions increased the possibility of institutional rivalry.[1]

Besides judicial actors, other inspection and control bodies such as People's Control Committees, Party Control Committees and People's Volunteer Detachments (*druzhinas*) were also involved in combating economic crime. Citizens, for their part, could play a direct role in this policy by reporting offences or serving as *druzhinniki* (unpaid auxiliary citizen policemen).

Criminal Investigation Departments

The Prosecutor's Office occupied a pre-eminent but ambivalent position in Soviet criminal procedure. It took responsibility for initiating legal proceed-

---

[1] Some police and Prosecutor's Office services, responsible for maintaining order and combating transport crime, particularly on the railways, were largely independent.

ings against the authors of criminal offences, and also had to check on the legality of the activities of enterprises, organisations, administrations, officials and citizens.[2] This general oversight extended to the work of police services and courts at every stage of criminal procedure. The Prosecutor's Office could raise doubts about Interior Ministry investigations and the probity of police officers, and also contest the decisions of the courts. At the same time, it investigated files relating to certain offences (see Table 3). It had sole responsibility for cases involving corruption, the production of substandard goods and *pripiski*,[3] and could also take charge of cases that would normally be handled by the police, according to the gravity of the offence. In practice, investigations were usually conducted by the Interior Ministry. Some authors claim that the ministry also handled *pripiski* cases, although it had no official responsibility for this offence.[4] The arrangement nevertheless placed the Prosecutor's Office in a situation of institutional rivalry with the Interior Ministry.

This ambiguous relationship meant that the Prosecutor's Office was in a position to criticise the activities of the police. In fact, its reports are the richest source of information concerning the shortcomings observed in the implementation of penal policy. However, the spontaneity of such criticism should not be overestimated. The Prosecutor's Office had its own hierarchy at both regional and federal level and, in keeping with the principle of double subordination, was also accountable to the Party's Department of Administrative Organs. It was therefore required to record any dysfunctional aspect noted in the work of law enforcement bodies when compiling activity reports. These constraints obliged Prosecutor's Office agents to maintain a delicate balance. References to dysfunctional aspects could not exceed certain limits, for the report's author might suffer repercussions. For example, a fundamental critique of the way in which Soviet penal policy was organised was out of the question. The institution's role as a coordinating body thus encouraged it to ensure that police performance indicators matched the requirements of the hierarchy.

The fight against economic crime constituted one of the principal tasks assigned to the police. The statutes adopted in 1973 placed the maintenance of order in public places above the protection of socialist property and the rights and interests of citizens, enterprises and organisations; crime prevention came third on this list.[5] As we have noted with regard to the architecture of

---

[2] M. Lesage, 1981, p. 133.

[3] RSFSR Code of Criminal Procedure, article 126.

[4] L.I. Shelley, 1996, p. 70.

[5] Law of the USSR, 19 July 1973: "On the Fundamental Rights and Duties of the So-

the Criminal Code, the protection of socialist property, as a fundamental value, took precedence over the rights and interests of citizens. Most police services were involved in the fight against economic crime to some extent, the state vehicle inspectorate and the passport division being two examples.[6] Within the criminal investigative apparatus, however, criminal investigative services (*ugolovnyi rozysk*) and those assigned to combat the theft of socialist property (OBKhSS) were chiefly responsible for the more common forms of economic crime that fell outside the remit of the Prosecutor's Office and the KGB.[7]

Both services were empowered to conduct preliminary inquiries and, in some instances, a full investigation. For serious crimes, their role was limited to urgent inquiry procedures (arresting suspects, local inspections). The information they collected had to be forwarded to a judge within ten days. For less serious offences, police forces conducted the preliminary inquiry to the point at which suspects were formally charged (if necessary, the case would be sent to court via the Prosecutor's Office), or continued their inquiries until the case was closed.[8] A decree issued in 1963 extended responsibility for criminal investigations to all Interior Ministry regional directorates and local departments.[9] Their activities were coordinated at national level by a main investigative directorate that was theoretically obliged to work in close collaboration with the Prosecutor's Office. Competent police services were responsible for investigating most crimes against socialist property; certain crimes against the life, health, liberty and dignity of the individual; most crimes against citizens' personal property; and certain breaches of the rules governing economic activity, such as speculation.[10] Shelley estimates that after 1965, the MVD investigated most (80 per cent) cases of recorded

---

viet Militia with Regard to the Protection of Public Order and the Fight against Crime." *Svod zakonov SSSR, tom 10* (Collected Laws of the USSR, vol. 10), Moscow, Izdatel'stvo "Izvestiya", 1986, pp. 230–5.

[6] See figure 1 in the appendix.

[7] The KGB had responsibility for investigating crimes against the state (smuggling, currency trafficking, counterfeiting), diversion of state property by public officials and major thefts of socialist property.[7] It specialised in sensitive cases and did not feature in the archives consulted for this book.

[8] K.F. Gutsenko, 1991, pp. 185–7.

[9] Decree of the Presidium of the USSR Supreme Soviet, 6 April 1963: "On the Distribution of the Right to Conduct Investigations among Services for the Protection of Public Order." *Vedomosti Verkhovnogo Soveta SSSR*, no. 16, 1963, Article 181.

[10] K.F. Gutsenko, 1991, pp. 187–8.

crime, economic or otherwise, while the Prosecutor's Office concentrated on homicide, rape and corruption.[11]

The structure of the principal police services comprised a federal main directorate, regional directorates and local departments at municipal and district (*raion*) level. The criminal investigative unit (*ugolovnyi rozysk*) was the most important element, for it handled most criminal offences, combated recidivism and professional crime and was also involved in prevention.[12] However, the OBKhSS, the service combating the theft of socialist property and speculation, took the leading role in fighting economic crime.

This specialised investigative body was created on 16 March 1937 as part of the main directorate of the Workers' and Peasants' Police of the People's Commissariat of Internal Affairs (NKVD). Its creation derived from the text of the 1936 constitution, which enshrined socialist property as the economic foundation of the USSR. It was given the task of "combating the theft of socialist property in state-owned organisations and commercial establishments, consumer cooperatives, warehouses and savings banks, and combating speculation."[13] The OBKhSS was also responsible for investigating counterfeiting operations, although in practice KGB units dealt with most of these cases. Its development reflected the need to "professionalise" police officers in order to ensure "respect for the law in the economic sphere."[14]

After the Second World War, the OBKhSS was used to enforce the draconian decree "On Penal Responsibility for Crimes against State and Socialist Property" issued by the Presidium of the USSR Supreme Soviet in 1947. This document called for the pettiest theft to be punished with extreme severity.[15] The organisation underwent a transformation following the adoption of the RSFSR Criminal Code in 1960, which was designed to promote the "principles of legality and equity."[16] Its powers were no longer restricted to the recording of economic offences and preliminary inquiries, but were extended to judicial investigations, preventive action and supervision of the uses to which state resources were put. Unlike other services, it did not simply react to recorded instances of crime, but conducted proactive inquiries triggered by its

---

[11] L.I. Shelley, 1996, p. 70.

[12] K.F. Gutsenko (ed.), 1991, p. 182.

[13] NKVD Order (*Prikaz*) no. 0018, cited in Ministerstvo Vnutrennikh Del RF. OBEP UVD Sverdlovskoi oblasti, 1997, p. 5.

[14] A.V. Vlasov (ed.), 1987, p. 151.

[15] N. Werth, 1992, p. 346.

[16] A.V. Vlasov (ed.), 1987, p. 230.

own observations of suspect behaviour, an order from the hierarchy, or a denunciation. It also mounted undercover operations.[17] In the 1960s, OBKhSS services were ordered to focus more closely on three elements: crime prevention, research into the causes of crime, and its clearance,[18] notably after a joint resolution from the CPSU Central Committee and the USSR Council of Ministers in December 1965: "On measures to improve investigations by the Prosecutor's Office and public order protection services."[19]

OBKhSS organisational charts varied according to the local economic environment, but generally included specialist sections dealing with theft, speculation, corruption, currency trafficking and, in the 1970s, counterfeiting. Other sections dealt with all offences committed in economic sectors such as commerce, food processing, light industry, construction and agriculture.[20]

As police work became more technical and the need for specialised skills increased, OBKhSS officers were expected to proceed like "economists and engineers."[21] During the period under review, OBKhSS officers represented about 2 per cent of Interior Ministry personnel, which also included the fire service and prison staff. The 300 officers deployed in the Sverdlovsk region in the 1970s were joined by another 200 at the beginning of the 1980s. On 1 January 1986, a total of 20,532 people were employed by the Interior Ministry in the Sverdlovsk region; 2,408 worked in prison administration, 4,712 in the fire service and 12,758 as regular police officers. Of the latter group, 863 were exclusively attached to criminal investigative services, 248 to the state vehicle inspectorate and 445 to the service combating the theft of socialist property.[22]

---

[17] For the role of undercover operations in Soviet police activity, see L. Shelley, 1996, pp. 118–19.

[18] A.V. Vlasov (ed.), 1987, p. 231.

[19] The USSR Interior Ministry was abolished in 1960, then re-established as the Ministry for the Protection of Public Order in 1966. It reverted to its original name in 1968. In the Soviet republics, the Interior Ministry was not abolished, but was known as the Ministry for the Protection of Public Order between 1961 and 1968. See M. Lesage, 1971, p. 229.

[20] Interviews with the head and deputy head of the economic crime department at the Interior Ministry's Sverdlovsk regional directorate. Both men were members of the services combating the theft of socialist property respectively from 1973 and 1968. Yekaterinburg, June 1997.

[21] *Informatsionnyi byulleten' shtaba Upravleniya Vnutrennikh Del Lenoblgorispolkomov*, no. 24, 1973, p. 119.

[22] Interior Ministry regional directorate report: "On Organisational and Management Work in 1985", 7 February 1986, 5 pages. Fond 4, opis 115, delo 3, list 3.

The vast majority of OBKhSS officers held high ranks in the police hierarchy. In the Sverdlovsk region, these services comprised 5 per cent of the cadres of all regional police forces.[23] The people interviewed for this book often insisted that all OBKhSS investigators were CPSU members, but this is not confirmed by the archive material: Communist Party members accounted for no more than 40 per cent of staff in 1981, with the figure rising to 55 per cent in 1985.[24] On the other hand, most of the investigators were well-educated: 76.5 per cent possessed a higher degree in 1981, 89 per cent in 1985. Most were lawyers, economists, agronomists or product experts (*tovaroved*): "Many police officers worked in the Soviet economy after graduating. When they joined our services, they underwent five years of training with a focus on perfecting their knowledge of the law. They became fully-fledged officers after this training period."[25]

A job with the OBKhSS became a much more attractive proposition in the 1960s, when salaries in the various branches of the Interior Ministry were levelled. But there were several motives for joining the fight against economic crime: "A decent salary, a qualified and interesting position which was less physically demanding and more intellectual than the requirements of other criminal investigative services and, finally, direct access to numerous products and commodities."[26] As we know, social distinctions in the Soviet Union depended less on the level of income than on the ability to obtain access to relatively scarce goods and services such as food, standard consumer goods, shops reserved for the elites, medical benefits and travel abroad. In this context, working for the OBKhSS was particularly advantageous, for the job entailed permanent contact with shops and warehouses—that is, with food and high-demand consumer goods. It thus attracted people who sought to improve their living standards and enhance their social capital. However, not all reasons for

---

[23] Interview with the head of the economic crime department at the Interior Ministry's Sverdlovsk regional directorate, a member of the services combating the theft of socialist property since 1973.

[24] Interior Ministry regional directorate report: "On the Work of Organizing and Managing the Services Combating the Theft of Socialist Property", 21 April 1986, 6 pages. Fond 4, opis 115, delo 42, list 3. Unfortunately, we have no information on these figures at central level.

[25] Interview with the head of the economic crime department at the Interior Ministry's Sverdlovsk regional directorate, a member of the services combating the theft of socialist property since 1973, Yekaterinburg, June 1997.

[26] Interview with a former regional OBKhSS officer, in post from 1978 to 1983. Yekaterinburg, July 1997.

joining were purely opportunistic, for the prospect of access to scarce resources and the desire to serve one's country were not always incompatible.

The sociologist Yuri Levada has drawn our attention to the duality of "ordinary Soviet man", who supported the fundamental principles of the Soviet regime but contradicted them on a daily basis by resorting to what were regarded as illicit practices.[27] It appears that such behaviour was also characteristic of the police. The former OBKhSS officers I spoke to often distinguished between those who improved their living standards in a legitimate but not entirely legal way and those who devoted all their energy to the accumulation of scarce resources. One went as far as saying, "Of course I sometimes accepted gifts and arranged things for people, but I never neglected the tasks I was entrusted with. I did come across colleagues who were basically dishonest and bad-minded, who thought only of their own good and blackmailed people."[28] Another claimed to have "left the service in disgust in the mid-1980s, when I realised that most of my colleagues were behaving like racketeers."[29] As we shall see, CPSU regional leaders frequently condemned OBKhSS officers for their dishonesty (cf. Chapter 5). The reputation of these services therefore suffered from the contrast between quality and venality, both of which tended to inspire fear. As a former regional cadre remarked, "There's no doubt that in the old days, when you picked up the phone and said 'hello, OBKhSS,' you could tell that the recipient was intimidated."[30] It would however be interesting to ascertain exactly what the recipient feared: the discovery of his illicit activities or the greed of the investigator.

Judges played a crucial role in the penal chain but were not autonomous actors. The proclaimed independence of the courts should be treated with great caution, for they were closely tied to the administration, the soviets and the Party. The Justice Ministry was responsible for the "organisational leadership of the courts (preparing legal texts, organising elections, compiling judicial statistics)", while the "USSR Supreme Court reported its activities to the USSR Supreme Soviet."[31] Moreover, the courts almost always followed the advice of

[27] Y. Levada, 1993.
[28] Interview with a former OBKhSS officer based in the city of Sverdlovsk, in post from 1978 to 1988. Yekaterinburg, June 1997.
[29] Interview with a former regional OBKhSS officer, in post from 1978 to 1985. Yekaterinburg, July 1997.
[30] Interview with the deputy head of the regional services combating economic crime, in post since 1968. Yekaterinburg, June 1997.
[31] M. Lesage, 1981, p. 135.

the prosecution service, a practice highlighted by the extremely low acquittal rate (less than 1 per cent). A judge could jeopardise his chances of professional advancement if acquittals exceeded this percentage. In court, judges had very little room for manoeuvre, for they had to comply with the position adopted by the Prosecutor's Office and meet the expectations of the administration and the Party. The focus on quantified indicators when assessing the performance of judges and courts encouraged compliance.[32]

The principal local actors involved in penal procedure (police, Prosecutor's Office, courts) were accountable to the CPSU Regional Committee's Department of Administrative Organs. This department monitored and coordinated the activities of all three bodies.[33] It convened meetings of judicial, police and security services, evaluated their work, issued directives, participated in internal police meetings, and examined letters containing allegations against the police. Although it did not exercise financial control, the Department of Administrative Organs had primary responsibility for assessing the performance of law enforcement agencies and their compliance with the demands placed upon them by the leaders of the Party-State. The meetings it organised also enabled local leaders to exchange information on the state of crime in the region, which they could then collate and present to their superiors when visiting Moscow.[34]

Inspection Bodies, Druzhinas *and Citizen Vigilance*

The archives relating to campaigns against economic crime in the Sverdlovsk region reveal the involvement of a large number of social and economic surveillance bodies with the power to intervene on public highways and in the workplace.[35] The documents also contain numerous references to the letters citizens sent to political authorities in order to complain, express concern or denounce illicit practices.

People's volunteer detachments (DND or *druzhinas*)[36] helped to maintain order and public safety, notably by combating hooliganism. Institutionalised

---

[32] P.H. Solomon Jr. (ed.), 1997.

[33] M. Lesage, 1971, pp. 266–9.

[34] Interview with an agent of the Perm region Prosecutor's Office, in post in the early 1980s.

[35] The archives consulted do not mention the activities of people's courts in residential buildings.

[36] *Dobrovol'naya narodnaya druzhina* (People's Volunteer Detachments).

in 1959 and coordinated from municipal and district headquarters (*shtaby*), these detachments were formed on a geographical basis and operated in enterprises, neighbourhoods, residential centres and villages. They were authorised to check identity papers, confiscate materials that might be used to commit an offence, guard convicted prisoners and hand over to the police or DND headquarters individuals who had committed an offence or were preparing to do so.[37] The *druzhinniki* were portrayed as exemplary citizens, individuals who actively assisted the police. Although only 2 per cent of them had received any specialised training in combating crimes against socialist property, they participated directly in the suppression of economic crime by arresting thieves and patrolling streets and markets in order to tackle the most visible forms of speculation.[38] The number of individuals registered as *druzhinniki* seems remarkably high: there were more than seven million in 1971, serving in 173,000 detachments! These figures should be treated with caution, however, for many registered *druzhinniki* were not active members. Anne Le Huérou notes that factory managers were required to compile lists of *druzhinniki*, in compliance with orders issued by the Party's control bodies. One of the main reasons for joining may have been the two days leave granted in return for taking part in a patrol. Some members probably regarded a policing role as the best way of improving their access to certain food products and standard consumer goods.[39]

People's Control Committees (KNK) were less visible than the *druzhina*s, and operated at the various levels of territorial organisation as well as in *kolkhoz*es, *sovkhoz*es and enterprises. Besides alerting managers and directors to any dysfunctional aspects, professional shortcomings and illicit practices they may have noted, they could also instruct managers to take steps to remedy the situation or involve the workforce and the Party in a discussion of the problem. The committees usually issued public reprimands, but sanctions extended to ruling that an enterprise was in debt to the collectivity, suspending an official and referring certain cases to the Prosecutor's Office.[40] Their presence within enterprises and *kolkhoz*es gave them access to internal information—material that the police and Prosecutor's Office could obtain only with difficulty— which they forwarded to Party leaders.[41] These details could be used to pro-

---

[37] K.F. Gutsenko, 1991, p. 229.

[38] DND regional headquarters report on the protection of public order, 10 July 1983; 3 pages. Fond 4, opis 106, delo 209, list 119.

[39] A.M. le Huérou, 2003, pp. 99–103.

[40] M. Lesage, 1971, p. 237.

[41] Interviews with a Russian Federation Interior Ministry agent, a specialist in the

duce highly informative summaries regarding matters such as stock protection or the output of an entire branch of the regional economy. They also helped to define prevention policies, particularly at regional and local level.[42]

Party Control Committees (KPK) were empowered to inflict disciplinary sanctions (a severe warning noted on the Party card, dismissal, etc.) on CPSU members. They were also authorised to refer the cases handled to the Prosecutor's Office, but seldom did so. These committees, non-penal bodies dealing with economic offences, were directly involved in the differential treatment of economic illegalities. In effect, they enabled Party members to avoid criminal responsibility for offences committed while at work.[43]

Other organisations, supposed to be responsible for monitoring the activity of economic actors, played some part in the managing of economic illegalities. The Finance Ministry's Control and Revision Department,[44] for example, audited the accounts kept by enterprises. This service did not seem to inspire much fear among factory and *kolkhoz* managers,[45] even though its decisions could result in harsh economic and financial sanctions.

The institutional information providers mentioned above had no monopoly on the flow of material concerning economic crime. Certainly they were the only bodies to provide a quantified analytical view of the phenomenon, but the media and the citizenry were also able to express their views. The readers' letters published in Soviet newspapers and magazines reflected public anxiety over the growth of the second economy and the shortcomings in police capabilities and methods.[46] Serials in the daily press[47] and cartoons in the weekly *Krokodil*[48] took a humorous look at shortages, speculation and the probity of police officers. The weekly *Literaturnaya Gazeta*, which had a more limited

---

analysis of economic crime since 1975, and a Perm region Prosecutor's Office agent, in post at the beginning of the 1980s.

[42] Ibid.

[43] Interviews with a former Sverdlovsk region OBKhSS officer, in post from 1978 to 1983, and a former official of the People's Control Committee at the Uralkhimmash factory. Yekaterinburg, June 1997.

[44] In Russian: *Kontrol'no-Revizionnoe Upravlenie Ministerstva Finansov* (KRU MinFina)

[45] The interviewees expressed amusement, and indeed contempt, when recalling the authority of the Finance Ministry's Control and Revision Department.

[46] C. Revuz, 1980.

[47] V. Jobert, 1991.

[48] M.-H. Delorme, 1964.

circulation, fostered critical debate on Soviet economic activity in the 1970s with its "Morality and the Law" column.

Many citizens attempted to alert the authorities to practices they had observed as they went about their daily business, which was far removed from the world of the Kremlin. Soviet legal terminology distinguished between "suggestions" for modifying the law, "requests" for it to be applied, and "complaints" concerning illicit acts.[49] Nicholas Lampert, the author of a book on "whistleblowing", notes that under Brezhnev, citizens were given every encouragement to contact the relevant authorities: these rights were set out in several legislative texts and in two articles of the new (1977) constitution. Article 58 stated that every Soviet citizen had the right to lodge a complaint against the actions of officials and state and public bodies. Article 49 referred to the right to criticise the shortcomings of state bodies and public organisations, and to submit proposals for enhancing their efficiency. The state thus called upon the citizen to "act as an auxiliary" in the application the law.[50] The leaders of the Party-State stressed the value of citizens' letters, a "vital source of information which is indispensible to decisions affecting both the short- and long-term development of the state and its economic and socio-cultural infrastructure."[51] These letters, together with the emphasis on their importance and their contribution to policy decisions, helped to legitimise the political regime in general and Soviet leaders in particular.[52] Embodying one of the principal forms of "popular participation in the administration of state affairs", they evoked the original legitimacy of the Soviet regime.[53] Moreover, Soviet leaders tended to interpret them as reflecting an "identification of citizen's concerns with those of the state."[54] The letters showed that "the people" and their "leaders" shared common values, and had to overcome the same obstacles in order to

[49] M. Lesage, 1971, pp. 257–8.

[50] N. Lampert, 1985, pp. 7–8.

[51] Decree of the Presidium of the USSR Supreme Soviet, 4 March 1980: "On the Rules for Examining Citizens' Suggestions, Requests and Complaints", *Vedomosti Verkhovnogo Soveta S.S.S.R.*, no. 11, 1980, p. 173.

[52] Legitimacy "ensures that a political regime and its leaders receive a variety of support, from habitual consensual docility to the mobilisation of specific groups for the defence of a power under threat. It guarantees acceptance of political domination by social agents over which this domination is exercised ..." J. Lagroye, 1993, p. 394.

[53] Resolution of the CPSU Central Committee, 29 August 1967: "On the Reinforcement of Work Regarding the Examination of Letters and the Organisation of Workers' Reception." *Spravochnik partiinogo rabotnika. Vypusk vosmoi. 1968*, p. 298.

[54] N. Lampert, 1985, p. 66.

fulfil their aspirations. They highlighted the damage caused by "bureaucrats" when trying to achieve the goals of socialism: "citizen's requests enable the people to strengthen their control of state and social services activity and combat administrative sluggishness, bureaucracy and other shortcomings noted in their work."[55] They sustained the idea that governing elites and citizens alike were dogged by the selfish acts of unscrupulous "bureaucrats" and attributed social problems to the tendency of officials to form cliques.

Beyond the attempt to use the letters to enhance the legitimacy of the state, the precise impact of this correspondence on penal practice is hard to grasp. Nicholas Lampert tends to accept that they enhanced the "effectiveness" of law enforcement bodies.[56] According to the people interviewed for this book, their impact depended on the identity of the author, the target of the criticism, the interests of the recipients and the political priorities of the day. Leaders of the Party or the Interior Ministry's Main Directorate could decide to conduct an inspection if the performance indicators were abnormal, or if public opinion, in the form of a series of related complaints, denounced serious failings on the part of police officers. A single complaint could even trigger a major operation if it drew attention to the activity of a police station that had already attracted criticism from regional authorities.[57] But as a rule, the police services responsible for processing the complaint simply acknowledged its receipt and closed the file.

Concluding Remarks

Fighting economic crime in the Soviet Union was supposed to concern a wide range of institutions and virtually every citizen. The role of the Prosecutor's Office in the coordination of law enforcement agencies was crucial. Within the police, economic crime was considered as a priority, and all criminal investigation services had to participate in tackling it. The growing importance of specialist OBKhSS services showed the government's attempt to adapt law-enforcement institutions to more frequent and more sophisticated forms of

[55] Decree of the Presidium of the USSR Supreme Soviet, 4 March 1980: "On the Rules for Examining Citizens' Suggestions, Requests and Complaints." *Vedomosti Verkhovnogo Soveta S.S.S.R.*, no. 11, 1980, p. 173.

[56] N. Lampert, 1985, p. 66.

[57] Interview with the head of the economic crime department at the Interior Ministry's Sverdlovsk regional directorate, an OBKhSS officer since 1973. Yekaterinburg, June 1997.

economic offences. Motives for working in OBKhSS services reflected the agents' willingness to deal with complicated investigations but at the same time to get access to scarce goods and services.

This apparent paradox might be explained by a detailed analysis of everyday police activity. Police archives show that this activity was chiefly defined by the ability to follow the hierarchy's orders, whether confidential or expressed publicly, during the implementation of anti–crime campaigns. Implementing the fight against economic crime meant in the first instance meeting planning objectives, which was compatible with more personal goals.

4

PRACTICAL RESPONSES
TO PERFORMANCE TARGETS

How visible was the fight against economic crime? In Western countries, the ritual presentation of statistics usually influences the evaluation and reorientation of policy, but Soviet police and judicial statistics were never made public. In the USSR, announcements and forecasts linked to the goal of eradicating crime on Soviet soil took precedence over assessments of the fight against economic crime. This explains the crucial role of anti–crime campaigns, which were designed to publicise the state's determination to mobilise the population under the banner of a common objective. Some general campaigns against crime also targeted economic offences, such as the 1966 drive against hooliganism (*khuliganstvo*). Specific campaigns against economic crime were launched in 1968, in 1975, at the end of the 1970s and in late months of 1982, after Andropov had come to power.

The archive material consulted for this book highlights the scale of these governmental priorities, but also shows that their implementation did not automatically produce the desired effect in terms of statistics. While encouraging local police services to crack down on certain forms of delinquency, the campaigns reflected how the orders were transmitted and how their implementation was checked. From the mid-1970s, reports also included data about crime causes. This novelty reflected the contribution to law enforcement policy by criminologists, who were asked to help explain the persistence of crime on Soviet soil. However, the causes they had identified could not question the principles of the Soviet economy. For street level-bureaucrats, crime explanation soon became a new routine.

Mobilisation Campaigns

Prior to the Gorbachev era, the battle against economic crime was punctuated by campaigns. CPSU governing bodies would announce their desire to crack down on some practice or other, order regional leaderships to act accordingly, and expect results.[1] These offensives had up to four different functions: the repression and prevention of certain offences, the transmission of new political priorities to law enforcers and citizens, the collection of information on regional crime and the encouragement of citizen involvement in state action.[2] A study of the archive material relating to the implementation of campaigns in the Sverdlovsk region leads to a focus on two principal functions. The desire to mobilise the citizenry was abundantly clear, but there was no monitoring system to assess contributions at individual level. Above all, the campaigns intensified the activity of law enforcement bodies, which were obliged to demonstrate their commitment to the task by presenting their hierarchies and the Party with satisfactory statistical results. Further motivation was provided by the exposure the campaigns received in the media, for citizens might be encouraged to inform the authorities of any shortcomings they had noted. Campaigns also tended to reinforce the legitimacy of Soviet leaders, who were always keen to promote their role as defenders of the regime's fundamental principles. Throughout the period under review, the appointment of a new secretary general was inevitably accompanied by the launch of a new campaign: Leonid Brezhnev targeted hooliganism (*khuliganstvo*) in 1966, Yuri Andropov focused on indiscipline in the workplace in 1983, and in 1986 Mikhail Gorbachev announced his intention to put an end to "unearned income."

Five campaigns to intensify the fight against economic crime were launched during the period under review: in 1966, 1968, 1975, 1979–81 and 1982–83. Not all of them were explicitly dedicated to repression of this type of crime. The 1966 campaign, for example, targeted hooliganism,[3] which was defined as "any deliberate behaviour which violates public order and expresses explicit disrespect towards society."[4] A legal definition of this sort authorised the

---

[1] A.V. Pokhmelkin, V.V. Pokhmelkin, 1992, p. 64.

[2] G.B. Smith, 1979, p. 143 and p. 162.

[3] This campaign was initiated by a CPSU Central Committee and USSR Council of Ministers resolution issued on 23 July 1966—"On Measures to Reinforce the Fight against Crime"—and also by a decree of the Presidium of the Supreme Soviet (26 July 1966) "On the Reinforcement of the Responsibility for Hooliganism."

[4] Article 206 of the 1960 RSFSR Criminal Code.

repression of a broad range of illicit practices, for it erased "the usual distinctions between property crime, violent crime and political crime."[5]

The following campaigns were explicitly related to the fight against economic crime. On 18 March 1968, the CPSU Central Committee's political bureau adopted a resolution "On the Eradication of Embezzlement and Theft of State Property." A new offensive was launched in 1975 in order to combat the "embezzlement and squandering (*razbazarivanie*) of socialist property."[6] As we shall see, this campaign had a considerable impact at regional level. More targets were announced in the late 1970s, with a particular emphasis on speculation, which the CPSU Central Committee denounced in a 1979 resolution and again in a "sealed letter" that circulated at Party meetings and conferences in 1981. The letter targeted crimes against socialist property, *pripiski* and corruption, and introduced a new element by referring to the devious practices of the *shabashniki* and *tsekhoviki*.[7] Finally, reform of the Criminal Code in 1982, accompanied by Yuri Andropov's pronouncements on indiscipline in the workplace, marked the opening of another campaign with a variety of targets including parasitism, theft of socialist property, *pripiski*, speculation and corruption.[8]

This chronology calls for a remark on the differential treatment of illegalities in the USSR. Some of the more common illicit practices were virtually ignored. This was true of *shabashniki* and *tsekhoviki* activities, which received a single mention in the sealed letter mentioned above, a document the public would never see. These criminal enterprises were highly productive; the relative lack of official interest in them tends to support the view that Soviet leaders based political regulation of the second economy on a judicious combination of repression and tolerance. But as we shall see, the policies applied were much more complex than a strictly "top down" view of government action suggests.

The campaigns were used to establish benchmarks in the fight against crime: quantified goals were set for every level of police bureaucracy. According to

---

[5] M. Los, 1988, p. 252.

[6] CPSU Central Committee resolution, 20 February 1975: "On Measures to Reinforce the Fight against the Embezzlement and Squandering of Socialist Property."

[7] Department of Administrative Organs report, 23 October 1981: "On the State of the Fight against Theft of Socialist Property, Corruption and Speculation in the Sverdlovsk region"; 7 pages. Fond 4, opis 100, delo 119, lists 73–80.

[8] Unlike its predecessors, this campaign was not launched by a resolution. See Zh. Medvedev, 1983, p. 134.

interviewees who were in post before 1985, the personnel involved received verbal instructions as to the priorities and the targets they were expected to meet. These informal "activity intensification" (*aktivizatsiya deiyatelnosti*) procedures were accompanied by warnings: disappointing results would expose local officials to reprimands or withdrawal of their Party membership cards, which would affect their chances of future employment.[9] As a general rule, the hierarchy's demands (*tverdye zadaniya*, or "firm orders") resulted in the determination of objectives related to the number of recorded cases and, in the 1970s, the clearance rate.[10] It was in the interests of OBKhSS services to submit high indicators.[11] The intensification of police activity was linked less to the publication of a decree or resolution than to the more or less emphatic informal orders that characterised its implementation. An analysis of Sverdlovsk region police statistics supports this hypothesis and highlights the relative impact of campaigns on police activity.

The Statistical Presentation of Results

The crime statistics that appear in reports are intrinsically flawed, but they provide an insight into the way the campaign against economic crime was conducted. Many researchers are rightly suspicious of this type of data, regarding it as "inconsistent and inaccurate ... erroneous given the incompetence of the personnel responsible for this task ... scattered across different services" and "based on the poor classification of different offences."[12] As in other countries, it naturally tends to reflect police activity rather than the actual level of economic crime. In France, for example, the police and gendarmerie tend "to see in every figure an element designed to monitor their activity and their results."[13] A similar attitude prevailed in the USSR, where statistics were the

---

[9] Interviews with the head and deputy head of the Sverdlovsk region economic crime department, OBKhSS officers since 1973 and 1968 respectively. Yekaterinburg, June 1997.

[10] Interviews with two former Sverdlovsk region OBKhSS officers, in office between 1984 and 1989 and between 1985 and 1990 respectively. Both men are now officials in the security department of a regional bank. Yekaterinburg, June 1997.

[11] It was in the interests of criminal research services, however, to tone down the increase in recorded cases, except when the hierarchy issued injunctions to the contrary. Interviews with the head and deputy head of the Sverdlovsk region economic crime department, OBKhSS officers since 1973 and 1968 respectively. June 1997.

[12] P. Juviler, 1976, p. 133.

[13] P. Robert *et al.*, 1994, p. 31.

only means by which local forces could prove they were conscientiously fulfilling the demands made by the hierarchy. Despite their flaws, statistics were regarded as sensitive and confidential and were made available only to "governing bodies and criminologists."[14] They were processed by the CPSU Central Committee's Department of Administrative Organs before being forwarded to Party leaders.[15] Their impact on policy decisions is hypothetical, but I was able to establish that regional political leaders used them as the basis for analysing local crime.

According to Erik Hoffmann, awareness of the need for more detailed information on the implementation of policy decisions emerged during the Brezhnev era, in the context of rationalising bureaucratic procedures. But given the impossibility of questioning established priorities, change was limited to marginal adjustments.[16] What was the situation with regard to penal policy? What kind of information did Soviet leaders have at their disposal as they sought to combat economic crime?

Recorded Economic Offences: the Predominance of Theft of State Property until the mid 1970s. The reports consulted for the present work continued to describe crime as a "trace of the past" until the mid-1980s, but recorded crime rose steadily during the period under review. It became increasingly difficult to claim, let alone believe, that crime was a form of deviance that socialism would eventually wipe out, as shown by the gradual disappearance of the word "eradication" from police reports.

A comparison of recorded case totals in regional and Russian statistics reveals an overall increase during the period under consideration and a sharper increase in the Sverdlovsk region (see Table 4). In 1984, recorded crime (all offences) in the Sverdlovsk region was 350 per cent above its 1965 level, whereas in Russia the increase amounted to 290 per cent. During the same period, the Sverdlovsk region's share of crimes recorded in the RSFSR rose from 3.3 per cent to 4.0 per cent.[17] The statistics also indicate a steady increase of the number of economic crimes in the overall totals. This trend reflected the rise in crimes against socialist property during the period under review, as well as a rise in speculation cases that began in the late 1970s. On the eve of Mikhail Gorbachev's accession to power, the Sverdlovsk region was clearly fail-

---

[14] P. Juviler, 1976, p. 133.
[15] P.H. Solomon Jr., 1978a, p. 173.
[16] E.P. Hoffmann, 1978, pp. 63–87.
[17] In 1975, the Sverdlovsk region represented 3.2 per cent of the federal population.

ing to combat crime effectively, with 1,208 recorded offences for every 100,000 inhabitants as opposed to a national average of 987.[18]

The fight against economic crime centred on the theft of socialist property. In 1966, this type of offence accounted for 7.5 per cent of all offences, economic or other, recorded both in Russia as a whole and in the Sverdlovsk region. By 1984, the figure had risen to 9.3 per cent at federal level and 8.3 per cent in the *oblast'*. Recorded thefts of socialist property tripled during this period (see Table 5). The category encompassed a wide variety of practices involving a range of high-demand goods and methods associated with their misappropriation, but some offences were more specific to the Sverdlovsk region. The *oblast's* natural wealth made it a prime target. Luc Duhamel noted that in the 1980s, one of the central routes of the illegal timber trade in the USSR ran south from the Sverdlovsk region.[19] The archives for the early 1960s reveal the existence of networks specialising in the theft and resale of timber. A 1961 document describes three cases in blunt detail: the diversion of timber worth 50,000 roubles to the territory of Krasnodar between 1958 and 1962; a scheme devised by a *tolkach* to divert over 10,000 m³ of timber to *kolkhoz*es and *sovkhoz*es in Krasnoyarsk territory and Orenburg *oblast'* after bribing managers in the Sverdlovsk region and officials at the Agriculture Ministry in Moscow; and the transportation of timber to Georgia by six Georgian nationals after they greased the palms of timber company directors and, probably, the railway police as well.[20] This period saw the rise of networks specialising in the theft of raw materials. They were formed by employees of state-owned enterprises with access to scarce resources, and administrative officials who were prepared to assist them in selling the commodities. Such networks could also include underworld figures, professional criminals who would take charge of the more delicate operations (transport, resale, etc.), particularly when the thefts concerned the region's natural resources: "Rubies are being stolen from an enterprise by employees who send them to accomplice gem cutters. The stones are cut and passed on to fences. Seventeen people are involved in the organisation of this traffic."[21] According

---

[18] USSR Interior Ministry inspection service report, 19 December 1985: "On the State of Criminality and the Results of Sverdlovsk Region Interior Ministry Services' Activity between 1980 and 1985"; 6 pages. Fond 4, opis 111, delo 88, list 16.

[19] L. Duhamel, 1989, p. 85.

[20] Report of the Sverdlovsk region Prosecutor's Office, 25 September 1961: "On a Series of Major Cases of Property Theft and Corruption"; 5 pages. Fond 4, opis 64, delo 114, lists 83–87.

[21] L. Duhamel, 1989, p. 85.

to several Sverdlovsk region police reports, the presence of companies extracting and refining metals and gemstones facilitated the development of increasingly sophisticated diversion circuits.[22]

The theft of socialist property was one of the principal targets for police action in the late 1960s, notably with the launch of the campaign against hooliganism in 1966. Some of the administrative reports produced by law enforcement agencies in the early 1970s continued to refer to this governmental priority. Although the campaign was initially successful in repressing various practices, particularly property crime, it was marking time by the following year, as the reduction in recorded cases of hooliganism indicates. The archives of the Sverdlovsk region, which contained a large number of penal institutions, mention the concern expressed by prison directors over the rise in the prison population in the last six months of 1966. Other documents reflect the anxiety felt by municipal leaders when confronted with a massive influx of ex–convicts. The Soviet authorities appear to have been faced with a genuine dilemma, hence the wide-ranging amnesty declared in 1967; while it was essential to crack down on all forms of delinquency, it was now thought that incarceration should be reserved for criminals regarded as a danger to the public. In one sense, these concerns announced the forthcoming modifications to criminal legislation.

The impact of the 1968 campaign against the theft of socialist property and *pripiski* was much more discreet: while recorded cases of robbery (*grabiozh*), robbery with violence (*razboi*), the use of state-owned transport for personal ends and petty property crime[23] increased, thefts of socialist property declined and stimulated less police activity than in 1966. By the very early 1970s, few reports were specifically devoted to the outcomes of the 1968 campaign, whereas several documents continued to refer to the anti–hooliganism offensive. The remarkable flexibility of this target enabled local police services to crack down on a wide variety of illegal practices, but the Sverdlovsk region Prosecutor's Office expressed doubts as to the "public danger" posed by some of the characters arrested, who were not "hooligans in the true sense."[24]

---

[22] Sverdlovsk region OBKhSS report, 17 September 1976: "On Economic Offences between 1971 and 1975 and their Causes"; 10 pages. Fond 4, opis 87, delo 161, list 60.

[23] Respectively articles 145, 146, 94[1] and 96 of the Criminal Code in force at that time.

[24] Sverdlovsk region Prosecutor's Office report, 12 December 1968: "On the Application of the Joint Resolution of the CPSU Central Committee and USSR Council

Many of the reports produced in the 1970s highlighted the increase in thefts of socialist property. Regional authorities openly criticised the way the 1968 measures were being applied: "The campaign against thefts of socialist property is unsatisfactory."[25] Their criticism extended to *pripiski*, another target of the 1968 campaign.[26] The battle recommenced in 1975, with the launch of another campaign. This had a spectacular impact in the Sverdlovsk region: a massive increase in the number of activity reports for more than a year, and a sharp rise in recorded offences, especially those involving hooliganism and all types of property theft. The most significant change in the regional evolution of crime during the period under review occurred at that time. Regional leaders relayed their concerns to law enforcement officials: "I repeat once again that the situation is alarming: get down to work and expect to receive firm demands from us."[27] Numerous inspection committees were dispatched to Yekaterinburg in 1975 to discover why the results of the region's offensive against the theft of socialist property had failed to match the national average for several years. They were particularly concerned about the total number of recorded crimes involving state-owned property for 1974, which was far lower than the Federal total. The 1975 campaign was therefore pursued assiduously, the aim being to bring the Sverdlovsk region results up to federal level.[28] The focus on crimes against socialist property was maintained throughout the period under review. Yuri Andropov's pronouncements on indiscipline in the workplace in late 1982 and early 1983, together with the appointment of a new Interior Minister, resulted in a marked increase in the recording of this category of crime at both federal and regional level.

---

of Ministers of 23 July 1966 on Measures to Reinforce the Campaign against Crime." Fond 4, opis 73, delo 102, list 3.

[25] Sverdlovsk region statistics office report, early 1970: "On Shortages, Theft and Wastage of Material Goods in the Sverdlovsk Region in 1969"; 9 pages. Fond 4, opis 74, delo 261, list 155.

[26] Rises and falls in the number of *pripiski* cases, which were often recorded as thefts of state property, cannot be ascertained. Department of Administrative Organs report, 23 October 1981: "On the State of the Campaign against the Theft of Socialist Property, Corruption and Speculation in the Sverdlovsk Region"; 10 pages. Fond 4, opis 100, delo 119, list 74.

[27] Concluding remarks by the secretary of the CPSU Regional Committee at a meeting of Party leaders, police forces and commerce, food and supply officials, 10 June 1975; 12 pages. Fond 4, opis 87, delo 164, list 62.

[28] Interview with the head and deputy head of the Sverdlovsk regional directorate's economic crime department, OBKhSS officers since 1973 and 1968 respectively. Yekaterinburg, June 1997.

Diversification of Recorded Cases from the mid-1970s. By the second half of the 1970s speculation, and to a much lesser extent corruption, had begun to feature more frequently in police reports (see Table 5). These offences seldom appeared in regional statistics until the early 1970s. The number of recorded cases of speculation began to rise in 1973–74, and continued to increase sharply until the end of the period under review. Reports devoted specifically to this form of economic crime began to appear in the late 1970s. In the Sverdlovsk region, the increase in recorded instances of speculation did not correspond to the launch of anti–economic-crime campaigns, as shown by the steep increase in 1977–78 and, conversely, a marked downturn in the years that followed, despite the central willingness to intensify the fight against this type of offence. While federal statistics indicate an increase in thefts of socialist property in 1979 and in speculation in 1981, the results for Sverdlovsk *oblast'* are harder to assess. Very few archive documents refer explicitly to the texts that provided the framework for this campaign. The recording of speculation seems to have been due more to continuous pressure from the hierarchy than to the specific orders that accompanied the campaigns. In 1984, speculation cases recorded in the region represented 3.57 per cent of the Russian total, as opposed to 1.85 per cent in 1966. This increase prompted regional police to hone their skills by dedicating entire reports to the type of goods that attracted speculators, their sales outlets and their levels of organisation: "In 1975, speculation was a matter of two people who combined to commit the offence, but the tasks (purchase, delivery, sale) are now shared between several individuals."[29]

However, efforts to crack down on the practice were hopelessly inadequate, given the number of transactions conducted in public places. In 1980, one of Sverdlovsk's leading daily newspapers noted that "many readers are infuriated when police forces take no action against people who sell scarce consumer goods in the central market, on the city's main street and in the area around the station."[30] As for corruption, it certainly featured in police statistics but no reports were specifically devoted to it, probably because the Prosecutor's Office dealt with most cases of this type. Despite the increase in recorded cases, the

---

[29] Regional OBKhSS report, 15 February 1979: "On the State of the Campaign against Speculation and the Measures Aimed at Eliminating Conditions that Give Rise to this Offence"; 5 pages. Fond 4, opis 95, delo 116, list 30.

[30] Report by the editor of *Uralskii Rabochii* (The Urals Worker), 1980: "On the Characteristics of Letters to the Editor Concerning the Activities of the Region's Law Enforcement Agencies (Police, Courts, Prosecutor's Offices) During the First Eight Months of 1980"; 5 pages. Fond 4, opis 98, delo 248, list 60.

figures remained low, notably because corruption was often prosecuted on the basis of other articles in the Criminal Code.[31]

The *tsekhoviki* and other *shabashniki* referred to in the sealed letter of 1981 received several mentions in the speeches made by regional leaders in the very early 1980s. The annual statistics indicate a very small number of cases involving "private enterprise activity", and the offence features only twice in the available regional archives, in 1981 and 1984:

Private enterprise activity is causing considerable damage to the state. Between August 1979 and September 1980, for example, two employees of the Sverdlovsk Institute of Mines were permanently engaged in private enterprise activity: repairing glasshouses for various organisations during their working hours. One of these individuals earned 22,000 roubles and the other 4,000 roubles.[32]

Despite scarcity of evidence, the OBKhSS regional directorate reported that the discovery of a clandestine shirt factory that had opened in 1983, along with two similar cases, was characteristic of the type of offence the service had to deal with in 1984.[33] Activities of this sort appear more frequently in the later archives, and particularly during the 1986 campaign against unearned income. Clandestine workshops, while rarely mentioned, were certainly not uncommon in the Sverdlovsk region. The police were not required to justify their efforts in this particular field, whereas they were compelled to produce results when combating offences with a higher priority. It is highly likely that the police used arrests of *tsekhoviki* to inflate the statistics on speculators and "squanderers of socialist property." Moreover, the scandals that came to light during *perestroika* confirmed that clandestine workshops could not have been organised without the support of administrative officials or members of the local elite, who could facilitate the provision, production and sale of goods at no great risk to themselves.

It is not unreasonable to assume that the *shabashniki* also flourished in the Sverdlovsk region in the 1970s, given the plentiful supply of timber for the construction industry. But they are mentioned only once in the archives for

---

[31] W.A. Clark, 1991, pp. 73–76. The articles on theft of socialist property, private enterprise, speculation and illegal commerce were frequently employed.

[32] Sverdlovsk region Prosecutor's Office report, 21 October 1981: "On the State of Legality in the Campaign against Theft, Speculation and Corruption." Fond 4, opis 100, delo 214, list 77.

[33] Regional OBKhSS report, 11 May 1984: "On the Characteristic Offences Recorded by the Regional Directorate for Combating the Theft of Socialist Property"; 4 pages. Fond 4, opis 107, delo 201, list 53.

the 1970s, and on only three occasions in those covering the years 1980 to 1984. In 1973, the police inspected several construction firms and discovered numerous breaches involving "the payment of unjustified wages to certain brigades of employees" and the "embezzlement of funds through the fulfilment of building contracts."[34] The term *shabashniki* first appeared in an official document in 1981. As with the *tsekhoviki*, the reference to a new practice was not confined to the description of one particular case, and emphasised its widespread nature from the outset:

It is not uncommon in the region that thefts of socialist property are committed by brigades known as *shabashniki*. The engineer L., for example, formed a brigade of workers, people he knew well, and struck a deal with firm T. to construct several buildings. He registered the brigade as a detachment of students, which attracts various benefits and bonuses. The misappropriation of bonuses and raw materials, not to mention the avoidance of taxes, cost the state more than 60,000 roubles.[35]

The archives consulted indicate that tolerance of this form of illegality had its limits. In 1981, for example, the members of one brigade were prosecuted for the theft of socialist property and received long prison terms.[36]

The Clearance Rate. The clearance rate was one of the most important indicators during the period under review. Prior to the mid-1970s, it rarely appeared in police and Prosecutor's Office reports, which at that time were more concerned with the amount of material damage sustained by the state and the compensation it was able to secure through the recovery of stolen goods, imposition of fines (or deductions from wages) and, in some cases, confiscation of the assets of those convicted.[37] From 1975 onwards, law enforcement agencies

---

[34] Interior Ministry directorate report, 20 September 1973: "On the Results of the Activity of Sverdlovsk Region Interior Services in the Campaign against the Theft of Socialist Property, Breaches of the Rules of Economic Activity and Abuse of Office During the First Six Months of 1973." Fond 4, opis 80, delo 222, list 151.

[35] Material compiled by the Party Regional Committee prior to a discussion of the CPSU Central Committee confidential letter "On the Reinforcement of the Campaign against the Theft of Socialist Property, Corruption and Speculation", 6 November 1981; 17 pages. Fond 4, opis 100, delo 213, list 10.

[36] Administrative Organs Department report, 23 October 1981: "On the State of the Campaign against the Theft of Socialist Property, Corruption and Speculation in the Sverdlovsk Region"; 10 pages. Fond 4, opis 100, delo 119, lists 76–77.

[37] From the second half of the 1970s, the courts increasingly resorted to the confiscation of assets.

were obliged to include economic crime clearance rates in their activity reports. This was followed by a decline in clearance rates, which stood at 89 per cent (all recorded crimes) in 1980 and 78 per cent in 1984. The regional Prosecutor's Office had begun expressing its dissatisfaction with the clearance rate for thefts of state property (66 per cent of recorded cases) in 1975.[38] Unfortunately reports do not give details about the way such figures, which are remarkably high when compared with the performances of Western police forces,[39] were actually reached. The insistence on inclusion of clearance rates nevertheless demonstrates the limitations of attempts to professionalise law enforcement agencies by introducing a new performance indicator. As the authorities were reluctant to acknowledge the existence of crime on Soviet soil, they could hardly be expected to tolerate indicators that tended to prove that crimes were left unpunished. The introduction of the clearance rate was therefore accompanied by orders to achieve the desired results.[40] Instead of improving police performance, it simply created new requirements to meet by all means.

Criminology and the Causes of Crime

The compliance of local police services was not restricted to recording crimes and clearance rates. Their reports also devote considerable space to the explanation of crime; they refer to a catalogue of causes that reflected the evolution of Soviet thinking on criminology. From the 1930s onwards, criminologists and specialists in penal law constantly sought to exert greater influence over the organisation of anti–crime measures. Their contribution was institutionalised in the 1960s,[41] although even then some of their work—meetings with law enforcement officials, restricted dissemination of research results, participation in the drafting of legislation—remained confidential. Academics and scientists working in the field of penal policy were chiefly concerned with prevention of crime, which in the Soviet sense meant discovering its causes.[42] This

---

[38] Sverdlovsk region Prosecutor's Office report, 22 December 1975: "On the State of the Campaign against the Theft of Socialist Property"; 6 pages. Fond 4, opis 87, delo 161, list 66.

[39] For example, the clearance rate for theft in France reached 14.3 per cent in 1992. P. Robert *et al.*, 1994, p. 71.

[40] Interview with an Interior Ministry agent, a specialist in analysing economic crime since 1975, Moscow, April 1997.

[41] P.H. Solomon, Jr., 1978b.

[42] P.H. Solomon, Jr., 1978a, p. 171.

aspect of penal policy became increasingly important during the 1960s, hence the creation in 1963 of an institute for the study and prevention of crime within the USSR Prosecutor's Office[43] and the introduction in 1963 of courses on crime and its causes in university law departments.[44] Meanwhile, empirical research into the causes of crime, effectiveness of criminal law and relevance of its reinforcement continued.

Police typology of crime explanation was restricted to a catalogue of ideologically acceptable causes. As Peter H. Solomon Jr. noted, criminologists were enlisted to improve the effectiveness of penal policy, to rationalise government action and penal policy rather than question its fundamental principles.[45] Their endeavours enriched the language traditionally employed to explain the causes of crime (traces of the capitalist mentality and influence of the imperialist camp).[46] Much of the Soviet criminological literature produced in the 1960s posited three sets of explanatory factors. The first comprised causes that contributed to the "moral formation" of the criminal's personality and the presence of "traces of the capitalist mentality." Family background, education and type of employment were important here, but there were a number of other factors including alcoholism, the quest for gain, contempt for socialist property and the rejection of "socially useful" labour. Criminologists often openly expressed their irritation at the absurdity of such reasoning: "How can the past survive in an adolescent born in the fourth decade of Soviet power?"[47] The second set listed factors that were likely to encourage the passage to a criminal act—drunkenness, inadequate protection of goods, encounters with disreputable characters, etc. The third set comprised the circumstances that could influence the chances of success when committing a crime, such as poor accounting systems in businesses and the infrequency of police patrols in certain areas. In contrast to the second set, the criminal would not necessarily be aware of such circumstances, but they increased his chances of getting away with the crime.

This typology, established by Soviet criminologists and often taken up by Western researchers, was not exactly reflected in police activity reports, for it was difficult to apply, the difference between alcoholism and a state of drunkenness being one example. In practice, the police approached explanatory fac-

[43] P.H. Juviler, 1976, p. 130.
[44] E.A. Weinberg, 1974, p. 77.
[45] P.H. Solomon, Jr., 1978a, p. 174.
[46] P.H. Juviler, 1976, p. 145; W.D. Connor, 1972, pp. 161–75; V.N. Kudryavtsev, 1968.
[47] N.A. Struchkov, 1971, p. 100.

tors with the aid of more operational distinctions. Their activity reports singled out factors linked to the delinquent's personality or social environment (parasitism, alcoholism, recidivism), before turning to those that influenced the commission of an offence in the economic sphere or working environment (lack of supervision, indiscipline in the workplace, flawed accounting practices, technical problems). The third set of factors directly implicated the actors responsible for implementing penal policy (the shortcomings of police forces, judicial services and organs of social control).

Each factor called for responses selected from a vast range of preventive and repressive measures. In drawing up an inventory of these responses, Walter D. Connor suggested distinguishing between repressive measures, preventive activity and all decisions taken to "eradicate the causes of criminality." Repressive measures included penal, administrative, disciplinary and medical (psychiatric confinement) sanctions as well as those imposed collectively, as when a case was tried in a comrades' court. Preventive measures included gathering intelligence on potential criminals and proactive measures to forestall the commission of an offence. Finally, governmental approaches to the causes of crime encompassed a variety of measures: organisational (improvement and rationalisation of the campaign against criminality); economic (restrictions on the sale of alcohol in order to combat hooliganism); judicial (modifications to existing legislation); technical (tightening surveillance, enhancing stock security); and ideological (organisation of public conferences at which judges and police discussed crime, use of the media to inform the public).[48]

The analytical framework outlined above features in most of the administrative reports consulted for this book. Local law enforcement bodies were obliged to provide information on the causes of crime. However, this new form of compliance had little influence on police activity because its application presented no challenge to the bureaucratic logic governing enforcement of the hierarchy's orders. Although employed to enhance the effectiveness of police services, criminology's main contribution to Soviet penal policy was to create another set of administrative formalities. Police were thus able to refer to an officially endorsed catalogue of causes and responsibilities when explaining the difficulties they encountered.

Soviet Figures for Delinquency

Given the tendency to associate criminal acts with "traces" of the old regime, the construction of figures for delinquency was of crucial importance when

[48] W.D. Connor, 1972, pp. 190–3.

attempting to explain the persistence of crime on Soviet soil. The challenge posed by criminal behaviour was restricted to the irresponsible behaviour of three types of "antisocial" individual—the parasite, the recidivist and the alcoholic. These were figures of delinquency in the Foucauldian sense: "The delinquent is to be distinguished from the offender by the fact that it is not so much his act as his life that is relevant in characterising him ... he is not only the author of his acts ... but is linked to his offence by a whole bundle of complex threads ..."[49] The construction of such figures is one of the main features of treatment of illegalities in a given society. By creating a distinction that focuses not on the acts committed but on the personality of those who commit them, it forms the basis of penal policy: "No doubt delinquency is a form of illegality; certainly it has its roots in illegality; but it is an illegality that the 'carceral system', with all its ramifications, has invested, segmented, isolated, penetrated, organised, enclosed in a definite milieu, and to which it has given an instrumental role in relation to other illegalities."[50]

The reports have little to say about the family background and education of adult delinquents, but the documents dealing specifically with juvenile delinquency are more informative as to education, especially when they touch upon the relation between crime and time spent at vocational and technical schools (*professionalno-technicheskoi uchilishche*). In the case of adults, the working environment was evoked only when police officers lamented the tendency of "workers' collectives" to ignore the scheming of a colleague.

In fact, references to a criminal's occupation featured in reports devoted to the activities of the "parasite", the person who did not engage in a "socially useful activity." The repression of parasitism intensified in 1961, with the publication of a decree emphasising its importance when combating economic crime.[51] At the time, it was considered important to stem the increase in crimes related to certain post-war social phenomena, particularly urbanisation and workforce mobility.[52] However, the reports dealing with the decree's enforcement reflected the various ways in which police services exploited this amorphous catch-all category, presenting a hotchpotch of results that encompassed begging, prostitution, private enterprise, speculation, the diversion of state trans-

---

[49] M. Foucault, English version, pp. 251–3.

[50] *Ibid.*, p. 277.

[51] Decree of the Presidium of the RSFSR Supreme Soviet, 4 May 1961: "On the Reinforcement of the Campaign against People who do not Exercise a Socially Useful Activity and Lead a Parasitic Way of Life."

[52] About these phenomena, see M. Lewin, 1988.

port for personal ends, and illegal religious sects![53] In one case, police issued a warning to:

A resident of Sverdlovsk, aged fifty, unemployed and living in a detached house, who constructed a hothouse with lighting and a water supply on his plot of land in order to grow food and sell it in the market. He bought himself a Volga with his earnings and spends money like water.[54]

The flexibility of the concept of parasitism, which was specified "less in accordance with the law than with the norm",[55] meant that it could also be used against dissidents thanks to the modification of its meaning in 1965.[56] The conviction of the poet Joseph Brodsky[57] was a notorious example of this practice, but no cases appear in the archives consulted for this book. Police and judicial reports used the category to explain the overall increase in criminality by indicating the percentage of "parasites" in relation to the total number of individuals arrested or convicted. However, the significance of parasitism as an explanatory factor gradually diminished. "Parasites" represented 23.6 per cent of those brought to trial (all crimes) in 1973,[58] but the figure fell to 20.3 per cent in 1975,[59] 20.2 per cent in 1979 and 19.1 per cent in 1983.[60] In 1981, the number of thefts of socialist property attributed to parasites stood at less than 17 per cent;[61] the category also accounted for 10 per cent of convictions for speculation in 1981.[62] But the

---

[53] Interior Ministry report, 15 June 1961: "On the Measures Taken to Fulfil the Decree of the Presidium of the RSFSR Supreme Soviet of 4 May 1961 'On the Reinforcement of the Campaign against People who do not Exercise a Socially Useful Activity and Lead a Parasitic Way of Life.'" Fond 4, opis 64, delo 215, lists 1–9.

[54] *Ibid.*

[55] M. Foucault, English version, p. 253.

[56] M. Los, 1988, pp. 78–93.

[57] See *Brodski ou le procès d'un poète*, 1988.

[58] Report on the implementation by the Sverdlovsk region tribunal of CPSU Central Committee resolutions, "On Measures to Reinforce the Campaign against Crime" (23 July 1966) and "On Measures to Improve the Work of Justice and Prosecutor's Office Services" (30 July 1970), 1974; 7 pages. Fond 4, opis 80, delo 218, list 30.

[59] Untitled Sverdlovsk region Prosecutor's Office report, 9 December 1975; 6 pages. Fond 4, opis 87, delo 163, list 86.

[60] Sverdlovsk region CPSU Committee Department of Administrative Organs report, 1984; 1 page. Fond 4, opis 107, delo 201, list 49.

[61] Sverdlovsk region Prosecutor's Office report, 21 October 1981: "On the State of Legality in the Campaign against Theft, Speculation and Corruption"; 9 pages. Fond 4, opis 100, delo 214, list 76.

[62] *Ibid.*, list 79.

causal relationship between parasitism and delinquency had not been abandoned.[63] In one sense, the campaigns against "indiscipline in the workplace" and "unearned income" in the 1980s represented its continuation.

The figure of the recidivist was particularly apparent in regions with a large number of penal institutions, Sverdlovsk *oblast'* being one example. Recidivists were constantly denounced during the period under review, and consistently made up about one third of the prison population. The evocation of this particular stereotype led to two forms of criticism of weakness. First, there was criticism of the police, who were accused of failing to fulfil two of the tasks assigned to them: keeping ex–prisoners under surveillance and assisting their reintegration into society. This criticism extended to neighbourhood police inspectors (*uchastkovye inspektora*), who were supposed to work closely with ex–prisoners, and also to workers' collectives, which were responsible for keeping an eye on colleagues with criminal records. Second, those in charge of hiring staff were criticised for giving too much responsibility to recidivists. Reports fulminated against the practice of giving jobs with "material responsibility" (direct contact with goods and commodities) to people who had been convicted of or sacked for economic offences. "If we were more careful about hiring personnel, there would be no more thefts and embezzlement."[64] Examples included low-level employees, like the buffet waiter with five convictions and twenty-three years in prison behind him; the chief accountant of a *kolkhoz*; and a senior inspector in a district branch of the state insurance agency (*Gosstrakh*), employed after serving a ten-year sentence. The recidivist category was finally useful for combating members of the Soviet underworld, shaped by their experience in the prisons and camps, before the term "professional crime", the forerunner of "organised crime", appeared in the 1970s.

The alcoholic constituted the third figure in this delinquency troika. The alcoholic was not, as might be assumed, used simply to explain the increase in hooliganism. To be sure, the two categories tended to overlap: a report on the 1966 campaign notes that "95 per cent of those convicted of hooliganism

[63] "Officially registered at a workplace as guards or concierges, a group of "parasites" paid others to stand in for them and were thus able to devote all their time to gambling." Sverdlovsk city Interior Ministry report, November 1985:"On its Activity in the Campaign against People who Devote their Time to Gambling and Leading the Life of a Parasite"; 2 pages. Fond 4, opis 111, delo 198, list 35.

[64] Remarks by the president of the Sverdlovsk region tribunal at a meeting of Party leaders, police forces and commerce, food and supply officials, 10 June 1975; 12 pages. Fond 4, opis 87, delo 164, list 59.

[were] drunk when they committed the offence."[65] But alcoholism also served to explain much of the theft of socialist property: "In 1980, 50 per cent of thefts of state property were committed in a state of inebriation ... The repression of theft is therefore directly linked to the fight against alcoholism, parasitism and recidivism."[66] However, denunciations of this supposedly self-evident link rarely relied on percentages. Only three reports (1975, 1980 and 1981) mention the percentage of thefts committed in a state of inebriation (46%, 50%, and 53%, respectively). In most reports, alcoholism was associated with homicide, rape and assault but not with economic crimes involving state property. Its mention in relation to economic offences probably corresponded to the existing situation, but even so it often seemed automatic. For example, one report begins by declaring that "Thefts of socialist property increased during the first eight months of 1982. This phenomenon is directly linked to alcoholism, but also to shortcomings in the campaign itself."[67] The body of the report contains no information concerning the links between alcoholism and crimes against state property, but the weaknesses of local police forces are subjected to detailed scrutiny. At the close of the period under review, the campaign against indiscipline in the workplace reflected the determination to target alcoholics and parasites: "Everybody knows that the alcoholic and the idler are potential criminals and disrupt production."[68]

An examination of the three Soviet figures of delinquency enables us to highlight a specific feature of the case under review. According to Michel Foucault, the contrast between illegalities and delinquency is based on distinguishing the offender's social origin. In the Soviet case, delinquency tended to reflect a life choice which disregarded socialist values, or a personality characterised by a degraded view of its "social utility", rather than membership of a particularly criminogenic social milieu. The differentiation strategy the Soviet regime

[65] Report "On the Execution of the Resolution Issued by the Sverdlovsk Region CPSU Committee and the Executive Committee of the Regional Deputies and Workers Soviet, 12 August 1966, 'On Measures to Reinforce the Campaign against Crime in the Oblast'", 27 January 1967; 13 pages. Fond 4, opis 69, delo 99, list 37.

[66] Sverdlovsk region Prosecutor's Office report, 21 October 1981: "On the State of Legality in the Campaign against Theft, Speculation and Corruption"; 9 pages. Fond 4, opis 100, delo 215, list 76.

[67] Report of the Verkh-Isetskii district (Yekaterinburg) Prosecutor's Office, 8 September 1982: "On the State of Crime"; 5 pages. Fond 4, opis 101, delo 201, list 28.

[68] Concluding speech by Boris Nikolayevich Yeltsin, first secretary of the CPSU Regional Committee, at a conference on public awareness of the action undertaken by police forces, 7 February 1983; 5 pages. Fond 4, opis 106, delo 209, list 23.

applied to illegalities could hardly rely on the denunciation of a "dangerous class" or a social milieu that was conducive to crime: "traces of the capitalist mentality" were noted at individual rather than collective level. Even so, this specificity did not prevent the establishment of a distinction between offenders and delinquents. Although all Soviet citizens broke the law or operated on its margins on a daily basis, the regime discerned personality traits that constituted aggravating factors. In one sense, the numerous comedy films of the 1960s, in which an honest man—or rather an honest offender—becomes suddenly enmeshed in the world of delinquency, support this observation.[69]

Analysing the Circumstances of Crime

In addition to "subjective" factors, there were several so-called "objective" factors that favoured passage to an offence in the delinquent's working environment. These were mainly shortcomings in the management of resources— capital, means of production, production assets, raw materials and finished products—in the enterprise, shop or *kolkhoz* in which the offence was committed. There were three main areas of concern: surveillance of goods and commodities, recruitment and management of personnel, and resource-related accounting practices. This catalogue of causes diminished in importance from 1976 onwards, but police services readily resorted to it, and provided examples, when compiling activity reports.

Monitoring access to the property of enterprises and *kolkhoz*es was a central concern; measures were introduced to tighten identity checks at the point of entry. One judge justified such measures on the grounds that "80.8 per cent of those convicted of theft of socialist property [were] not part of the organisations in which they committed their offences."[70] Access to warehouses and production units could be restricted, and electronic alarms installed, but the distribution and use of the equipment provided for this task also required monitoring: "We know perfectly well that you are not installing the special locks you have been given for your sheds and stock. You are selling them to the public! In the Alapaievsk district, you have installed only 241 of the 513 provided. You have sold the others!"[71]

---

[69] The film *Brilliantovaya ruka* is typical of this genre.

[70] Regional tribunal report, 19 December 1975: "On the State of Judicial Practice and the Activity of the Regional Tribunal in the Implementation of the CPSU Central Committee Resolution of 25 February 1972 Relating to Issues in the Campaign against the Theft of State Assets"; 7 pages. Fond 4, opis 87, delo 161, list 35.

[71] Call to order issued by the secretary of the Party Regional Committee to a Consum-

Police reports also highlighted weaknesses in the employment procedures followed in production, distribution and retail units. As noted earlier, references to this particular factor helped to explain recidivism by stressing the culpability of personnel managers who employed ex–convicts and gave them jobs with access to scarce resources. This failing also sustained a broader critique of the way production units managed their personnel:

Theft in the commercial sector is facilitated by the employment in positions of material responsibility of individuals who have been convicted of or sacked for economic offences—alcoholics or people with no experience in the commercial sector. These individuals are often transferred to other enterprises within the sector after committing another offence, or are allowed to resign instead of being sacked for professional misconduct.[72]

In terms of identifying the causes of crime, senior managers of businesses in which offences had been committed were a favourite police target throughout the period under review. Their irresponsibility and negligence continued to arouse criticism in the early 1980s: "Some business executives and managers have lost their sense of responsibility: they do not monitor the protection, utilisation and distribution of material resources."[73]

Shortcomings in accounting practices in shops and enterprises were another leitmotiv in the presentation of the causes of crime, although they had become less important by the late 1970s. They explained why thefts had not been spotted and why their authors were likely to go unpunished. In the food sector, for example, "The absence of rigorous accounting practices with regard to raw materials, foodstuffs and sales receipts"[74] ensured that offences remained unde-

---

ers Union official in: Meeting of Party Leaders, Police Forces and Commerce, Food and Supply Officials, 10 June 1975; 12 pages. Fond 4, opis 87, delo 164, list 56.

[72] Special communication from the regional directorate for the maintenance of order, 27 February 1967: "On the Inadequacy of the Protection of Socialist Property in the State and Cooperative Commerce Sector"; 12 pages. Fond 4, opis 61, delo 101, list 31.

[73] Presentation by the first secretary of the Sverdlovsk region CPSU Committee, Boris Nikolayevich Yeltsin, 16 June 1981: "On the Tasks to be Accomplished in order to Improve Communist Education and the Reinforcement of Legality and Order in the Light of the Decisions Taken at the 21st CPSU Congress." Fond 4, opis 100, delo 72, list 20.

[74] Interior Ministry regional directorate report, 16 May 1972: "On the State of the Protection of Socialist Property in Food Enterprises"; 5 pages. Fond 4, opis 79, delo 227, list 169.

tected. Moreover, flawed accounting practices extended to specific types of fraud such as the falsification in weighing. In a 1975 report detailing the causes of crime in a number of economic sectors (commerce, agriculture, construction, forestry, food, etc.), the issue of checking accounts relating to resources was singled out in every instance. The problem eventually led to the denunciation of "immoral accountants ... who turn to crime when their duty is to protect socialist property."[75]

In the absence of a wide-ranging critique of the Soviet economic system, research into the causes of crime was doomed to failure; at the most, it could pinpoint those responsible for it. This approach led to the imprisonment of numerous accountants in the 1970s and 1980s, many of whom remained behind bars until the charges against them were quashed in the wake of *perestroika*. In effect, the search for the causes of crime was a formal exercise, a show of compliance with orders from above. It imposed few restraints, and indeed offered law enforcement agencies new possibilities for justifying their performance despite the rise in crime. But the very fact that it gave rise to these strategies for self-justification tells us something about the extent of the difficulties confronting Soviet society as a whole.

By 1975, the importance that police reports placed on the causes of crime had begun to diminish, an indication that it was becoming increasingly difficult to conceal factors linked to the overall organisation of the Soviet economy. The attempt to explain economic crime was extended to more general considerations, with a particular emphasis on finding solutions for the dysfunctional aspects that had been noted. Some proposals were not restricted to penal policy but encompassed economic policy as well. By doing so, they constituted a twofold critique: of economic regulation and of the Soviet approach to penal policy.

The critique of the ways in which Soviet enterprises managed state property prompted the police to suggest modifications to the assessment criteria applied to such establishments. For example, they advocated withdrawing bonuses and privileges for enterprises and employees when there was evidence of "negligence, falsification of production indicators, theft of socialist property, and misappropriation of funds, wages and raw materials."[76] The level of protection

---

[75] Sverdlovsk region Prosecutor's Office report, 1972: "On Violations of the Law on the Protection of Socialist Property in the Region's *Sovkhozes* and *Kolkhozes*"; 4 pages. Fond 4, opis 79, delo 227, list 171.

[76] Interior Ministry regional directorate proposals, 14 March 1975; 3 pages. Fond 4, opis 87, delo 161, lists 27–28.

of socialist property should be taken into account when "awarding prizes for socialist emulation, given the diffusion of economic offences."[77]

Criticism of supply systems and shortages of material goods also emerged in 1975. With one exception, these malfunctions were never referred to in police reports, but they did arise at conferences and meetings, and had featured in the archives of the regional statistical office since 1970.[78] The sudden addition of supply problems to the debate on the causes of crime came about through the denunciation of alcoholism. The police were in effect concerned about the negative social effects of kiosks and buffets, which they regarded as dens of vice because they offered their customers nothing but alcohol. Supply problems helped to explain why these outlets had turned into drinking dens: "Buffets should stock more confectionery, cakes and pastries so that people go there for something to eat rather than just to drink."[79] "As for vodka, you can find it anywhere, while the shops are empty. You can't buy a bun, but getting hold of brandy is no problem at all."[80]

This argument sometimes led to an explicit, if timid, denunciation of the supply problems afflicting the Soviet economy:

Speculation arises from shortages of certain industrial goods in the commercial sector, failings in the supply chain, flawed assessments of supply and consumer demand by state chambers of commerce and consumer cooperatives, and from the grossly inadequate number of second-hand shops (*skupochnie*) and commission shops (*komissionnie*).[81]

By the late 1970s, OBKhSS services in the Sverdlovsk region were not afraid to make the link between speculation and shortages of high-demand goods:

---

[77] Information on the progress made by Interior Ministry services in the reinforcement of the campaign against theft, abuses of office and breaches of the rules of economic activity, 26 January 1977; 2 pages. Fond 4, opis 89, delo 47, list 15.

[78] Sverdlovsk region statistics department report, early 1970: "On Shortages, Theft and Wastage of Material Goods in the Sverdlovsk Region in 1969"; 9 pages. Fond 4, opis 74, delo 261, lists 146–155.

[79] Remark by a food official at a meeting of Party leaders, police forces and heads of commerce, food and supply, 10 June 1975; 12 pages. Fond 4, opis 87, delo 164, list 58.

[80] Remark by an unidentified author, *Ibid.*, list 60.

[81] Interior Ministry regional directorate report, 27 August 1976: "On the State of Crime in the Sverdlovsk Region between 1971 and 1975 and the First Seven Months of 1976"; 15 pages. Fond 4, opis 88, delo 65, list 85. Commission shops are shops where individuals can leave goods to be sold or resold on payment of a commission.

Despite some improvement in the quality and variety of products, the light industry sector in the city of Sverdlovsk and the region as a whole cannot respond to the general market situation ... high-demand industrial products are stored in commercial premises for long periods, which creates an artificial shortage ... the network of commission shops is extremely inadequate ... food and goods markets are not properly monitored.[82]

By the end of the 1970s, almost all OBKhSS reports contained passages on the progress made by certain economic sectors in "satisfying consumer needs."[83] Children's items, furniture and electrical goods were offered as examples.

However, problems of supply had little influence on the traditional explanations inspired by Soviet criminology. The Interior Ministry's regional directorate did not include the observations of specialist departments when it reported on its efforts to combat economic crime, nor did the CPSU Regional Committee's Department of Administrative Organs, when it evaluated the work of regional law enforcement agencies. Attempts to draw attention to these dysfunctional aspects of the Soviet economic system were ignored in favour of more acceptable explanations of the causes of crime: "Why aren't they selling bread? Why are they selling vodka instead? Because cadres are poorly trained, poorly recruited and poorly organised: they do not look into the background of the vendors they employ. They hire people with a string of convictions!"[84]

Criminology's contribution to penal policy enabled high-ranking officials to avoid difficult questions about the way the Soviet economy functioned, while encouraging conformity of local law enforcement agencies. The conclusion of a lengthy report on the problems of supplying high-demand goods illustrates this systemic blockage: "We should bear in mind that it is not the living conditions in our country which produce thieves, speculators and corrupt individuals, but the retardation of consciousness, the fondness for the tradition of individualism and private property."[85]

---

[82] Regional OBKhSS report, 15 February 1979: "On the State of the Campaign against Speculation and the Measures to Eliminate its Causes"; 5 pages. Fond 4, opis 95, delo 116, lists 33–34.

[83] Material compiled by the Party Regional Committee prior to a discussion of the CPSU Central Committee confidential letter "On the Reinforcement of the Campaign against the Theft of Socialist Property, Corruption and Speculation", 6 November 1981; 17 pages. Fond 4, opis 100, delo 213, list 17.

[84] Concluding remarks by the secretary of the Party Regional Committee at a meeting of Party leaders, police forces and heads of commerce, food and supply, 10 June 1975; 12 pages. Fond 4, opis 87, delo 164, list 61.

[85] Material compiled by the Party Regional Committee prior to a discussion of the

Concluding Remarks

As a rule, sociologists reject the view that police bureaucracy is a "mechanically ordered universe" or a "bulldozer travelling down the slope of the hierarchy, driving before it the general policies decided at the summit, which become increasingly fragmented as they approach the base."[86] This position is relevant to the implementation of Soviet anti–crime campaigns. Their implementation, more zealous in some instances than in others, was a response to orders from Moscow and varied according to each regional context. While it appears that the latitude available to regional leaders when defining the general thrust of penal policy on their own territory was severely reduced, they had nevertheless the possibility to intervene in the handling of certain cases and to intensify the fight. Thus the results of the 1975 campaign in the Sverdlovsk region, which were clearly better than the national average, intended to show initiative after a series of inspections by high-ranking MVD and Party officials. This call to order, designed to correct shortcomings noted in the fight against the theft of state property, took place a year before the first secretary of the Party Regional Committee was sacked and replaced by Boris Yeltsin. At meetings to discuss the anti–crime campaign, Yeltsin made a point of alluding to the failings of his predecessor: "It is clear that not everything has been done to eliminate this scourge."[87]

Moreover, the intensification of regional police activity did not always correspond to the launch of a national campaign. The sudden increase in recorded cases of speculation in 1977 led to its greater prominence in activity reports. Yet the focus on speculation was not a response to a decree or resolution issued by the central authorities, at least not until 1979. Conversely, the campaigns did not automatically bring results in terms of the fight against crime. Their impact depended on the informal commands from the hierarchy that accompanied their implementation in a given region, where the specific features of the local crime situation were taken into account. If need be, they could serve as a stimulus: the recording of targeted crimes would suddenly increase and be

---

CPSU Central Committee confidential letter "On the Reinforcement of the Campaign against the Theft of Socialist Property, Corruption and Speculation", 6 November 1981; 17 pages. Fond 4, opis 100, delo 213, lists 22–23.

[86] D. Gatto, J.-C. Thoenig, 1993, pp. 19–20.

[87] Statement by Boris Yeltsin, first secretary of the Sverdlovsk region CPSU Committee, at a conference on crime in the Sverdlovsk region, December 1976. Fond 4, opis 88, delo 62, list 3.

maintained at the higher level (hooliganism in 1966 and thefts of socialist property in 1975). In these cases, campaigns enabled police in a "backward" region to adjust their performance to national standards.

Launching regular campaigns did not help to tackle economic crime. From the mid-1970s, many facts showed the authorities' willingness to improve the quality of policing. Police officers were asked to pay more attention to the causes of crime—that is, to the factors that might help to explain why an offence was committed and why it eventually succeeded. The contribution of criminologists to this new policy orientation was therefore crucial. On the one hand, it helped to define the differential treatment of economic illegalities in defining three types of delinquents: the parasite, the alcoholic and the recidivist. Unlike other offenders, these delinquents were supposed to commit offences because of some particular things happening in their lives. On the other hand, criminologists also emphasised factors that pointed to the responsibility of state enterprises' cadres and law enforcement agencies. However, this interest in crime explanation has rapidly been integrated into police reports as mere new requirements to comply with routinely.

The disturbing evolution of economic delinquency eroded the influence of the orthodox explanatory factors favoured by Soviet criminology. Faced with the difficulty of challenging Soviet methods of economic organisation, the local actors responsible for implementing penal policy, governed by an internal logic that focused on satisfying the demands of the hierarchy, increasingly and systematically justified their performance by denouncing the shortcomings of the other actors with whom they shared their task.

5

CRITIQUE AND REFORM

When confronted with the problem of defining the effectiveness of police action, Western sociologists emphasise the danger of relying exclusively on statistics relating to recorded cases and clearance rates. As Dominique Monjardet notes:

all police action is always likely to be flawed, either because by standing firm on the issue of restricted resources the police officer does not obtain the results the hierarchy expects of him, or because he has taken liberties with the resources allocated in order to achieve them. The first instance will highlight his passivity and lack of motivation; the second is the most certain source of police 'blunders'.[1]

Given the tendency of the Soviet authorities to conceal increases in crime and stress the obligation to produce results, they were unlikely to be satisfied by police efforts. Local forces were prisoners of paradoxical constraints, no matter what goals were set for them. Obliged to prove their effectiveness by means of statistics, they were exposed to criticism as soon as their performance indicators exceeded the hierarchy's expectations. Their indifference to crime offenders was often denounced, as well as their probity, but they were probably the most obvious scapegoats within law enforcement agencies for Soviet authorities.

Facing worrying trends in the evolution of economic crime, Soviet authorities however attempted to promote institutional changes that were not restricted to the police but also affected other law enforcement agencies, enterprises and local political leaders. These changes reflected a discussion within

---

[1] D. Monjardet, 1998, p. 27.

the political elite and high-rank officials in the MVD, between those who endorsed a comprehensive view of the crime issue and the need to change law enforcement policy and those who called for stronger repression. However, institutional changes that occurred from the mid-1970s were not sufficient to deal with this issue in a context of worsening economic crisis.

The Police on Trial

The remarkable increase in recorded crime in the Sverdlovsk region in 1975 rapidly turned against police forces. The *oblast'* acquired the status of a territory "strongly affected by criminality." It "topped the national list for certain types of offence" and was a matter of "particular concern to the competent authorities in the CPSU."[2] On the other hand, local OBKhSS units came under fire for not working hard enough: "Services in some areas remain passive as speculation spreads throughout the region ... Not one single case of speculation has been brought before the courts in towns like Revda, Irbit and Krasnouralsk!"[3] OBKhSS units were accused of ignoring the information on illegal activity in the workplace submitted by People's Control Committees.[4] Once called to order, police officers endeavoured to embellish their activity reports and thus demonstrate compliance with the hierarchy's orders. They tampered with the results by tracking down petty thieves but neglected more serious offences, which went unpunished.[5] Boris Yeltsin, first secretary of the Sverdlovsk CPSU Regional Committee, vehemently denounced such practices:

With regard to the activity of OBKhSS units, I will speak frankly: few people are satisfied with it! Their work is restricted to a preoccupation with statistics: they cannot be allowed to fall below the previous year's level! If performance indicators decline, a team of inspectors rushes off to check shops: where are the scarce products hidden? Are the scales properly balanced? And there you are! The statistics are good; the few criminal

[2] CPSU Regional Committee's Department of Administrative Organs report, 1976; 4 pages. Fond 4, opis 89, delo 86, list 24.

[3] Sverdlovsk region Prosecutor's Office report, 21 October 1981: "On the state of Legality in the Campaign against Theft, Speculation and Corruption"; nine pages. Fond 4, opis 100, delo 214, list 79.

[4] Sverdlovsk region Prosecutor's Office report, 18 June 1975: "On the State of the Campaign against the Theft of Socialist Property in the Sverdlovsk Region"; five pages. Fond 4, opis 87, delo 161, list 16.

[5] Sverdlovsk region Prosecutor's Office report, 21 October 1981: "On the State of Legality in the Campaign against Theft, Speculation and Corruption"; 9 pages. Fond 4, opis 100, delo 214, list 80.

cases required have been discovered! But in fact they mask the inactivity of certain investigators.[6]

The critique of police activity was also influenced by increasing demands for a better clearance rate from 1975 onwards. Given the authorities' desire for all offences to be cleared up, any variation in this indicator tended to cast doubt on the efficiency of police services. "The poor clearance rate is chiefly due to delays in implementing penal action and badly organised investigative and inquiry procedures ..."[7] Although the authorities were dissatisfied with the results, they largely exceeded Western performances: "The principal causes of the rise in recorded crime and the ineffectiveness of prevention measures are linked to serious inadequacies in the practical activity of Interior Ministry services. See for yourselves: in five years, the clearance rate fell by 6 per cent and stood at only 78 per cent in 1983."[8]

The belief that the police left offences unpunished and criminals at large formed the basis for assessing their performance. The Prosecutor's Office rebuked law enforcement agencies for closing too many cases after a perfunctory investigation; it often refused to accept such decisions and in many instances demanded a full and proper inquiry.[9] Some of the other institutional actors took a similar line; the regional trade directorate, suspected of lax employment procedures, blamed the police: "In shops, we are frequently obliged to defend ourselves against crooks. Now when we hand them over to the police, they are released almost immediately. Their entourage, at work or at college, doesn't know what they're up to."[10]

The Prosecutor's Office also reproached the police for failure to conduct the analysis necessary for an "objective" understanding of the causes of crime. In 1975, the Interior Ministry responded by proposing a review of the "quality

---

[6] Meeting between the first secretary of the CPSU Regional Committee, Boris Niko-layevich Yeltsin, and the heads of Interior Ministry municipal departments, 22 May 1984; 42 pages. Fond 4, opis 107, delo 202, list 56.

[7] Sverdlovsk region Prosecutor's Office report, 9 December 1975; 6 pages. Fond 4, opis 87, delo 163, list 88.

[8] Meeting between the first secretary of the CPSU Regional Committee, Boris Niko-layevich Yeltsin, and Interior Ministry officials, 20 April 1984; 18 pages. Fond 4, opis 107, delo 202, list 10.

[9] Sverdlovsk region Prosecutor's Office report, 7 December 1978; 7 pages. Fond 4, opis 92, delo 142, lists 56–57.

[10] Remarks by the head of the Sverdlovsk region commerce directorate at a meeting of Party leaders, police forces and heads of commerce, food and supply, 10 June 1975; 12 pages. Fond 4, opis 87, delo 164, list 52.

of and deadlines for investigations conducted by the OBKhSS, as well as its efforts to obtain compensation for losses resulting from the theft of socialist property." The Ministry also suggested "increasing the participation of Prosecutor's Office agents in investigations."[11] The police, for their part, found fault with the other actors involved in penal policy, particularly the control committees operating in enterprises and the *druzhina*s. Their final line of defence was the lack of resources and personnel, but this argument tended to backfire, for Party leaders expected better results as soon as they agreed to increase funding.[12]

Another critique of police performance focused on the probity of police officers. It appears in the archives for the 1960s, but has become more pronounced by 1975. Shortcomings in professional conduct were noted, especially various forms of abuse of power and the falsification of performance indicators. Reference to "offences involving the abuse of position committed by police officers" emerged from the analysis of cases of abuse of office and passive corruption. A 1969 report highlighted the relative impunity enjoyed by offenders and lamented the "unwarranted laxity" of the sanctions applied in three-quarters of cases (eighteen out of twenty-four).[13] During the 1970s, disciplinary sanctions gave way to prosecution for criminal practices. Forty-four police officers were prosecuted in 1974 and seventy-five the following year. Of the latter group, forty-three were found guilty of corruption or abuse of office.[14] Twenty-six policemen were tried and sentenced for such practices in the first nine months of 1978.[15] In 1981, 25 per cent of all those sentenced for passive corruption were police officers (no judge or Prosecutor's Office agent was found guilty of this offence). The cases brought before the courts involved attempts to shield suspects from prosecution by terminating an investigation

---

[11] Proposals by the Interior Ministry directorate, 14 March 1975; 3 pages. Fond 4, opis 87, delo 161, list 28.

[12] Presentation by the first secretary of the CPSU Regional Committee, Boris Nikolayevich Yeltsin, 16 June 1981: "On the Tasks to be Accomplished in order to Improve Communist Education and the Reinforcement of Legality and Order in the Light of the Decisions Taken at the 21st CPSU Congress." Fond 4, opis 100, delo 72, list 23.

[13] Administrative Organs Department report, 1969; 6 pages. Fond 4, opis 73, delo 161, lists 12–13.

[14] Sverdlovsk region Prosecutor's Office report, 9 December 1975; 6 pages. Fond 4, opis 87, delo 163, list 89.

[15] Sverdlovsk region Prosecutor's Office report, 7 December 1978; 7 pages. Fond 4, opis 92, delo 142, list 60.

or destroying evidence in return for material gain (money, food or standard consumer goods). In several cases, suspects were helped to escape.

Doctored police statistics aroused the ire of the Prosecutor's Office and the CPSU Regional Committee's Department of Administrative Organs. The practice is mentioned in the archives for 1969, but it is not known whether the falsifications noted—the destruction of judicial evidence—reflected a desire to improve performance indicators or to conceal the failings of certain police officers.[16] In 1970, ministerial authorities were so concerned by the problem at national level that they issued guidelines for strengthening disciplinary sanctions. By 1975, the reasons for altering statistics had become clearer: according to the Prosecutor's Office, police in Nizhnii Tagil, the second largest city in the Sverdlovsk region, were not recording all offences, because they were trying to "create an illusion of success in the fight against crime."[17] Such practices were so common that a drive to stamp them out was launched in the mid-1970s: suspects henceforth ran the risk of prosecution as well as disciplinary sanctions. In 1978, 20 per cent (six out of thirty) of the police officers found guilty of "falsifying statistical indicators" appeared before a court.[18] The regional Prosecutor's Office denounced these practices, which seemed to be taken for granted, whenever it conducted an inspection. It singled out the strategies employed to produce a satisfactory number of recorded crimes, and expressed alarm at the tendency to "invent" or "conceal" cases accordingly, "select the most appropriate definition of an offence", neglect non-priority offences and overestimate the seriousness of offences committed.[19] The compilation of clearance rates was equally misleading: it was quite common to attribute a crime to a fictional culprit and claim he had fled the area.[20] Simply knowing the identity of an offender was enough to state that a crime had been solved. In 1982, the Prosecutor's Office counted 593 cases in which statistical indicators had been concealed or falsified in order to "create the illusion of an exemplary approach."[21]

---

[16] Sverdlovsk CPSU Committee's Administrative Organs Department report, 1969; 6 pages. Fond 4, opis 73, delo 161, list 14.

[17] Sverdlovsk region Prosecutor's Office report, 9 December 1975; 6 pages. Fond 4, opis 87, delo 163, list 89.

[18] Sverdlovsk region Prosecutor's Office report, 7 December 1978; 7 pages. Fond 4, opis 92, delo 142, list 60.

[19] Sverdlovsk region Prosecutor's Office report, 11 December 1979: "On the Results of Verifying the Observation of Legality in the Serov Interior Ministry department"; 3 pages. Fond 4, opis 95, delo 198, lists 77–79.

[20] *Ibid.*, lists 77–79.

[21] Sverdlovsk region Prosecutor's Office report, 13 July 1962: "On Inadequacies and

These practices highlighted the importance of the principle of hierarchical inversion, as defined by Dominique Monjardet, in the way the Soviet police bureaucracy operated. The fact that police performance was assessed on the basis of the indicators they submitted placed middle-ranking officials in an ambiguous position, for while obliged to pass on ministerial orders, they also had to justify the action taken at local level in order to guard against possible repercussions.[22]

The room for manoeuvre available to local police services was limited: unusual fluctuations in the statistics could lead to sanctions. In the early 1980s, for example, the Interior Ministry's inspection office placed police services in Sverdlovsk *oblast'* "under permanent supervision" in order to "help" them to improve their performance, which was still held to be "mediocre" despite the reprimand administered to the regional police chief two years earlier.[23] An unsatisfactory figure could trigger action at the top, with potentially serious consequences for officials on the lower rungs of the ladder. The best option was to submit performance indicators that appeared to comply with orders. Police officers were thus able to avoid checks and inspection procedures and also increase their autonomy. Satisfying the hierarchy's demands at the least cost (by doctoring statistics, focusing on less serious offences and inventing cases and culprits), allowed the police officer more time to use his position for personal ends. The obligation to produce results was undoubtedly a powerful formal constraint on local law enforcement agencies but, paradoxically, it also fostered opportunistic behaviour[24] by enabling police officers to exploit the resources with which they came into contact in order to improve their living standards.

This obligation also provided the basis for a critique of the other actors involved in combating economic crime. The *druzhina*s, for example, had to submit statistical evidence of their activity. Their regional director boasted of having arrested "300,000 [*sic*] offenders" in 1979, including "more than one thousand thieves and almost one thousand people who had breached the rules of commerce."[25] Despite such figures, *druzhinniki* still attracted criticism for

---

Offences in the Work of Interior Ministry Services"; 4 pages. Fond 4, opis 101, delo 201, lists 6–9.

[22] D. Monjardet, 1996, p. 89

[23] USSR Interior Ministry inspection service report, 19 December 1985: "On the State of Crime and the Results of the Activity of Sverdlovsk Region Interior Ministry Services between 1980 and 1985"; 6 pages. Fond 4, opis 111, delo 88, list 15.

[24] G. Favarel-Garrigues, 2005, pp. 63–82.

[25] Presentation at a regional seminar for heads of municipal and district *druzhina*s, 26

their low profile in public places and poor contribution to crime prevention. Supervisory bodies like the People's Control Committees also came under fire, their performance never matching the standards expected by regional leaders. The regional hierarchy took a dim view of the work carried out by judicial authorities and often condemned municipal Prosecutor's Office services for their inability to monitor the legality of police activity, coordinate the fight against crime and maintain the flow of propaganda.[26] The regional picture that emerged from this situation contained both good and bad elements.[27] Courts were attacked more frequently for their "inactivity." It was easy to reproach them for not dealing with every instance of economic crime, for an examination of their performance reports was bound to reveal shortcomings. In 1975, they were ordered to punish offenders convicted under Article 92 (theft of state property through the abuse of office) with greater severity.[28] In 1978, the Prosecutor's Office expressed surprise that nobody had been sentenced under Article 156[1] (violation of the regulations concerning the sale of alcoholic drinks).[29] The following year, it asked the courts to strengthen the application of Article 152[1] (*pripiski*).[30] And in 1981, it denounced the inability of judicial services to deal with all cases of speculation. Given the circumstances, the courts concentrated on satisfying short-term demands.

The Limits of Institutional Change

The desire for a new conceptual and practical approach to combating economic crime became apparent in the mid-1970s. This period saw the development of

---

June 1980: "On the Tasks of *Druzhina*s Following the CPSU Central Committee Resolution 'On Improving the Work of Maintaining Order and Reinforcing the Campaign against Offences'"; 21 p. Fond 4, opis 98, delo 248, list 173.

[26] Joint report by regional law enforcement bodies (Prosecutor's Office, tribunal, police), 1968: "On the Results of Verifying the Execution of the CPSU CC Political Bureau Resolution of 18 March 1968"; 10 pages. Fond 4, opis 72, delo 129, list 132.

[27] Sverdlovsk region Prosecutor's Office report, 22 October 1979; 10 pages. Fond 4, opis 95, delo 198, list 69.

[28] Sverdlovsk region Prosecutor's Office report, 22 December 1975: "On the State of the Campaign against the Theft of Socialist Property"; 6 pages. Fond 4, opis 87, delo 161, lists 66–67.

[29] Sverdlovsk region Prosecutor's Office report, 7 December 1978; 7 pages. Fond 4, opis 92, delo 142, list 59.

[30] Regional Justice Department report, 17 September 1979: "On the State of Judicial Practice." Fond 4, opis 95, delo 198, list 135.

institutional measures to professionalise specialist police forces and adapt penal categories to reflect the increase in crime. In addition, various initiatives were launched in an attempt to raise the public's awareness of its responsibilities in relation to the problem. However, as neither the fundamental principles of the Soviet economy nor the logic governing the evaluation of police performance could be called into question, the impact of such efforts was relatively small.

Soviet leaders believed that OBKhSS personnel should be equipped with the skills of "engineers." This became possible in 1975, with the opening in Gorky of the first police academy specialising in the fight against economic crime.[31] All OBKhSS cadres would receive their training in this college in future. The courses focused on new approaches to economic crime and, as the creation of a chair of "economic and legal problems" indicated, took into account the relations between the law and the economy. This somewhat abstruse terminology was typical of other institutional innovations, notably the creation within the MVD's Moscow headquarters of a "central laboratory for scientific research into the economic and legal problems relating to the protection of socialist property" in 1977.[32] The new establishment was "a consequence of the increase in economic crime and the inability of leaders to understand the phenomenon ... The laboratory was supposed to adopt an objective approach to legal measures. It studied the way in which the economy actually functioned in order to improve its regulation."[33] This retrospective assessment is in line with the laboratory's mission statement as it appeared in late 1970s documents. The need for a new approach was justified by alarming evidence of increasingly sophisticated illegal activity; it was reported that "Crimes against socialist property are often committed by talented and technically proficient individuals who are familiar not only with the overall production process, but also with the details of how its branches actually function. They do not act alone, but as part of secret, organised groups ..."[34]

The tasks entrusted to the laboratory reflected the desire to break away from the traditional criminological viewpoint: it was no longer a matter of identify-

---

[31] Now known as Nizhny Novgorod.

[32] In Russian: *Tsentral'naya Nauchno-issledovatel'skaya Laboratoriya* (TsNIL) MVD SSSR *po Ekonomiko-pravovym Problemam Okhrany Sotsialisticheskoi Sobstvennosti.*

[33] Interview with the laboratory's former deputy director, working at the MVD Russian Scientific Research Institute in Moscow at the time of the interview, April 1997.

[34] G.K. Sinilov, 1980, pp. 2–3.

ing the causes of crime and improving the security of state property, but of updating police knowledge of economic matters, enhancing the ability of inspectors to deal with complex fraud cases, and helping to develop legal norms in order to combat such crimes.[35] The branches established in forty-one regions of the RSFSR employed a total of 280 agents, many of them OBKhSS officers, but there were also a number of lawyers, criminologists, sociologists and economists. All regional branches were jointly managed by operational officers and economists.

In practice, the laboratories produced overviews of the crime situation in a given sector, taking into account the rationality of the actors operating in the underground economy. For example, they advocated legalising the activities of the *shabashniki*, a group which "in many respects showed signs of a rational economic process", and also refined the assessment of latent crime in order to counterbalance police indicators. Directly subordinate to the Deputy Interior Minister, the laboratories were accountable to the OBKhSS main directorate, which had to be convinced of the feasibility of their proposals. Possessing no operational legitimacy or authority, they were unable to disseminate their ideas within the policing apparatus. They did not survive the change of CPSU General Secretary and were closed down by the Interior Minister Vitaly Fedorchuk in 1983. The academics were posted to MVD research institutes and the inspectors integrated into operational branches. In the final analysis, the fate of the laboratories illustrates the fragility of institutional bodies if their understanding of the issues surrounding economic crime diverges from the position adopted by the state.

As noted earlier, legal sanctions were diversified in the late 1970s. The courts were told to extend the use of complementary sanctions by confiscating the property of convicted offenders and barring them from posts involving material responsibilities. The courts and the Prosecutor's Office began submitting information on the implementation of such sanctions in the late 1970s. One report states that almost 25 per cent of those convicted of economic offences were barred from certain jobs in 1980.[36] Following the penal reforms of 1982, all activity reports produced by criminal justice services contained this type of information, which was expected to include accurate figures. A 1983 Prosecutor's Office report claiming that "courts were using additional sanctions against

---

[35] *Ibid.*, p. 5.

[36] Sverdlovsk region Prosecutor's Office report, 21 October 1981: "On Respect for Legality in the Campaign against Theft, Speculation and Corruption"; 9 pages. Fond 4, opis 100, delo 214, list 78.

squanderers of socialist property and speculators with increasing frequency" was not good enough for the head of the regional Department of Administrative Organs, who demanded figures.[37]

The courts also attempted to adapt the legal arsenal to deal with the rise in certain forms of delinquency. In the early 1980s, speculation was rife in every area of Soviet daily life and it was clear that a strictly penal response could not be envisaged for everyone found guilty of this offence. Consequently, there was a tendency to take the speculator's character into account when passing judgement. The courts advocated disciplinary sanctions for mothers of families, exemplary workers and those with no criminal record. On the other hand, "inveterate speculators" continued to be punished heavily.[38] The implementation of a differential approach highlighted the massive scale of forbidden practices in Soviet society and the inability of the criminal justice system to cope with it. However, it is not possible to establish whether this strategic difference of approach resulted from orders from the top or from local initiatives.

From the mid-1970s onwards, most initiatives were designed to mobilise society in an attempt to stem the increase in economic delinquency. As mentioned earlier, bonuses and privileges awarded for achieving planning objectives were adapted to reflect the degree to which enterprises protected "the integrity of state property" against theft, negligence and waste.[39] Regional authorities also attempted to promote a more responsible attitude on the part of municipal leaders: following the decree of 2 August 1979, they declared that "highly criminalised towns" would be downgraded in the "socialist emulation" rankings.

Such measures were seldom enforced but reflected the central premise of the campaign against economic crime: increasing delinquency was due to the indifference of all those responsible for combating it. It was not simply a matter of exhorting law enforcement agencies to "intensify their activity"; all those in

---

[37] Report of the Sverdlovsk region Prosecutor's Office report, 20 October 1983: "On the Execution of the CPSU Central Committee Resolution of 16 October 1981 on the Reinforcement of the Campaign against the Theft of Socialist Property, Corruption and Speculation"; 2 pages. Fond 4, opis 106, delo 209, list 88.

[38] Sverdlovsk region Prosecutor's Office report, 2 November 1981: "On the State of the Campaign against Speculation in the Chuvakinskii Clothes Market"; 4 pages. Fond 4, opis 100, delo 214, lists 35–38.

[39] Information addressed by the Interior Ministry regional directorate, 26 January 1977: "On Assessing the Activity of Interior Ministry Services in Reinforcing the Campaign against Theft, Breaches of the Rules of Economic Activity and Abuses of Office"; 2 pages. Fond 4, opis 89, delo 47, list 15.

positions of responsibility at municipal and administrative level, as well as in enterprises, workers' collectives and social organisations, were expected to do so. By extension, all citizens were supposed to contribute to the effort: despite their numbers, the *druzhinniki* were often criticised for their inactivity. This basic premise enabled the authorities to explain the failure of both ideological and technical measures. In the latter case, they pointed to the failure to monitor the use of means—padlocks, alarm systems—provided to improve security. Similarly, ineffective institutional measures could be explained by the inability of senior managers to supervise subordinates.

The problems encountered in attempting to reinforce anti–economic-crime measures therefore revealed the inability of Soviet leaders to think of crime as requiring anything other than a broad policing operation by all the actors involved in law enforcement. As noted earlier, leaders were challenged by two factors: bureaucratic practices that prevailed in law enforcement bodies, and the actual implementation of the Soviet economy's founding principles. Their inability to face the facts was ultimately compounded by political manipulation of the anti–crime campaign—that is, the exploitation of penal policy for political purposes.

The Political Exploitation of Repression

From the Soviet political leaders' point of view, the campaign against economic crime was more than a response to increasing delinquency. There were other goals, which varied according to the context. For example, the issue could be used to strengthen the legitimacy of a new leader.[40] We have already seen that every new secretary general appointed during the period under review began his period in power with a repressive campaign, and that when Boris Yeltsin took over the leadership of the Sverdlovsk region CPSU, he repeatedly announced his intention to re-establish order. But it should be stressed that another highly important political use, which influenced the interplay between economic and penal policy at the end of the period under review, emerged at the beginning of the 1980s.

In Russia, Yuri Andropov is still regarded as a dedicated reformer who died before he was able to implement all the measures he considered necessary to overcome the "stagnation" induced by the Brezhnev regime. Most studies argue that the former head of the KGB possessed more authority and a greater capac-

---

[40] L. Holmes, 1993.

ity for action than his predecessors. According to Medvedev, the police and other law enforcement and inspection bodies began a real offensive against illegal economic activities in the workplace and in the streets.[41] The belief in the effectiveness of Andropov's penal policy is linked to the liquidation of the Brezhnev clan, and notably to the sacking of the former Interior Minister Nikolai Shchelokov, who was replaced by a former KGB head, Vitaly Fedorchuk, after more than fifteen years in the post. The new Secretary General also attempted to place the MVD under the surveillance of the KGB: 150 KGB cadres were seconded to the Interior Ministry in order to dismantle the local and regional allegiances that had been forged within the police bureaucracy.[42] This action was taken in the name of the campaign "against thieves, corrupt individuals and speculators."[43] Andropov also created inspection services within the MVD; by making them accountable to the CPSU Central Committee, he hoped to improve control of the Party's administration and its regional and local sections.[44] During the *glasnost* period, Fedorchuk was frequently attacked for employing KGB tactics—surveillance, denunciations, unjustified arrests—at the MVD in order to replace many of its staff. His sacking of over 160,000 personnel[45] deprived the Interior Ministry of many competent professionals.[46] For Fedorchuk, the suppression of economic crime was an undeniable priority, as demonstrated by the increase in OBKhSS personnel (up by 57 per cent in the Sverdlovsk region) and the promotion of its director to the rank of Deputy Interior Minister. The closure of the central laboratory for scientific research, and staff cuts in the ministry's other research centres, highlighted the overwhelming desire to strengthen operational resources. The ministry's new executive took the view that the fight against economic crime would gain nothing from an understanding of its role in the broader economic context.

As we have seen, efforts to overcome the Brezhnev–era "stagnation" did not lead to radical changes in the Soviet approach to penal policy. In fact, the strengthening of internal bureaucratic controls in the hope of enhancing repression did very little to impede the growth of economic crime that had been noted during Brezhnev's period in office. The reports submitted by law

[41] Zh. Medvedev, *Andropov*, 1983, p. 132.

[42] See the MVD website: www.mvdinform.ru/index.php?docid=370

[43] *Pravda*, 10 August 1983.

[44] P. Kruzhin, 1983.

[45] A. Vlasov, 1988a, p. 47.

[46] N. Kipman, 1990, p. 22.

enforcement ceased to systematically include passages on the progress they had achieved, but Andropov's slogans seem to have had little impact on the practical activities of local police forces.

These continuities may be explained by the new leaders' stated desire to use penal policy as a tactic to address more general problems. The invocation and implementation of the campaign against crime and indiscipline in the workplace assumed an instrumental character, for management of a critical economic situation was an absolute priority. There was an explicit link between Andropov's decisions on penal policy and the Soviet socio-economic context. The campaign against indiscipline in the workplace was considered as "a demand dictated by life. We cannot make rapid progress if we do not impose discipline in the workplace, the planning system and the state. The establishment of order does not require capital investment, and produces considerable effects."[47] This logic is echoed in studies of the action taken by Andropov:

[Reinforcing discipline] may be the simplest and cheapest method to stem the decline in productivity in the short term, but it is unlikely to work in the long run without proper economic incentives. Such measures are acceptable only if they are temporary, designed to gain time so that real economic reforms can be developed and tested and so that bureaucrats can be replaced by genuine experts. But if stricter discipline backed up by administrative pressure is seen as the only cure for the ailing Soviet economy, positive results can hardly be expected.[48]

The fight against economic crime was no longer perceived as a social requirement, an element of the overarching communist project, but as a temporary political resource, a means of buying time to devise a more effective economic policy, for experimentation was a slow process.[49] From this perspective, penal action represented an expedient, a stopgap measure while waiting for a solution to the enigma of a large-scale economic reform which would not jeopardise the edifice of the Soviet state.

Concluding Remarks

The bureaucratic organisation of police activity, based on the obligation to deliver quantified results, put the achievement of planned objectives beyond

---

[47] Remark by Yuri Andropov from "Draft of a Concluding Speech by the First Secretary at a Sverdlovsk Region CPSU Committee Meeting", 9 February 1983; 5 pages. Fond 4, opis 106, delo 209, list 23.

[48] Zh. Medvedev, 1999, pp. 373–4.

[49] See O.S. Ioffe, 1986, pp. 3–28.

reach. Moreover, it encouraged police officers to adopt a variety of practices in order to comply with the hierarchy's orders: they invented, concealed or redefined offences, and concentrated on the most visible and minor infringements committed by the most vulnerable people. The contribution of criminologists to the definition of penal policy simply maintained the status quo: when police officers were asked to explain crime by referring to a catalogue of accepted causes, they rapidly resorted to stereotypical responses which enabled them to blame other law enforcement actors for the problems they encountered. Although it was a formal constraint, the obligation to meet performance targets ultimately enabled police officers to exercise a considerable degree of autonomy when deciding which cases to investigate, and also allowed them to use their positions for personal advantage.

This autonomy was a prominent feature of the differential management of illegalities in the Soviet Union. The risk of a sanction largely depended on the resources available to the offender and the motivations of the police officer with whom he was confronted. Despite the claims advanced by studies of the Soviet second economy, action against illegal activities could not be reduced to a decision by top level politicians and police bureaucrats to establish a skilful balance between repression and tolerance, although offences involving clandestine production units were of less concern to the authorities than property crime, speculation and *pripiski*. Another side to dealing with illegalities concerned the social status of the author of an economic crime; Party members with responsible positions in enterprises did not appear in court, but were dealt with by the Party's internal disciplinary or professional control bodies. Finally, the possibility of a sanction depended on the attitude of regional political leaders. While they were not in a position to influence the general direction of penal policy, they could alert law enforcement agencies or intervene in legal procedures if they regarded them as unjust.[50]

The principal modifications to the campaign against economic crime began in the mid-1970s, when it had become clear that the police were unable to get to grips with more visible and increasingly sophisticated forms of delinquency. Targets were extended to include speculation, legal sanctions were diversified, the clearance rate was adopted as one of the main criteria for assessing the work of law enforcement services, and changes to policing methods were introduced. But given the impossibility of challenging the principles of Soviet economic policy and the organisation of law enforcement, the impact of such measures

[50] B. Yeltsin, 1990, p. 54.

was likely to be minor. The problem was exacerbated by the political exploitation of crime. Leaders looked for ways in which to satisfy the population's need for consumer goods without contradicting the founding principles of the Soviet economy; the announcement of greater repression and the creation of accepted figures of delinquency ("parasites", recidivists and alcoholics) therefore tended to bolster their legitimacy. As Andropov stressed, the crackdown constituted a stopgap measure while the search for a hypothetical solution to a critical economic situation continued. However, the political resources of the campaign against economic crime were finite: when employed as emergency measures, they delayed the development of a proper policy to tackle the very real threat posed by economic crime to the survival of the Soviet economic system. The tension between economic and penal policies reached a critical level shortly after Mikhail Gorbachev came to power, when the crackdown on "unearned income" coincided with the development of "individual labour activity."

PART TWO

PERESTROIKA, GLASNOST AND PENAL POLICY

INTRODUCTION TO PART TWO

It would be wrong to think that the organisation of the fight against economic crime changed suddenly when in March 1985 Mikhail Gorbachev became General Secretary of the Central Committee of the Communist Party of the Soviet Union. Until 1987, his policies in fact extended his predecessors' moves, particularly when it came to the way the penal policy was conducted, through measures against alcoholism and unearned incomes. This said, two pillars of his politics profoundly modified the way the fight against economic crime was conducted in USSR: *perestroika* and *glasnost*.

Chapter 6 focuses on economic reforms and recalls the stages of privatisation and accumulation, from the enactment of the law on individual labour activity in 1986 to the development of the cooperative sector, measures of "spontaneous privatisation" and then the implementation of the government's privatisation programme in the early 1990s. This chronological description is completed by an analysis of three crucial issues at stake in all these reforms: first there was the role of government departments in the implementation of the various stages of privatisation; second, the space given to private entrepreneurs and their initiatives for the reinvention of Russian capitalism; while the third issue is linked to the way the government legitimised all these measures vis-à-vis the population.

Chapter 7 analyses how the context of *glasnost* fostered a debate on the issue of economic crime in Soviet Union. Suddenly, information and opinion on crime and penal policy poured forth in the media. Statistics on the fight against crime started being published and commented on. Criminal violence became more visible. All kinds of experts were asked to give their opinion on the subject: politicians, police officers, journalists, scholars and even some criminals (anonymously). The newly highlighted crime problems, linked to the deepening of the economic crisis, led to the multiplication of opinion polls about the

103

fear of crime in the Soviet society or about the perception of police activity. The fight against crime also became a political issue. To answer the hardliners who pleaded for undifferentiated repression, defenders of economic reforms started to get mobilised. Cooperative officials sought for instance to improve their image among the population by showing they were not offenders. Meanwhile, an association took the initiative of rehabilitating and helping managers convicted for offences that should not exist in a "normal" liberal economy. Then, in 1990, the idea started to develop that capital of illegal origin could be usefully invested in a legal economy that was in turmoil at that period.

As will be shown in Chapter 8, in such a context the fight against economic crime lost all coherence. Following the fight against unearned income launched in 1986, the Soviet government initially let the cooperative sector develop. But measures were rapidly adopted—in December 1988—to limit its expansion. The fight against organised crime, which developed at the same time, aimed, among other goals, at gaining control over the private economy. Soviet authorities even tried, in vain, a final riposte by launching a campaign against "economic sabotage." But they faced a better-organised business milieu, able to get mobilised in order to defend its interests. The launching of the privatisation process marked the temporary success of reformers and of businessmen: almost no repressive measure was adopted to control the transfer of state property to the private sector.

6

THE RULES OF PRIVATISATION

The privatisation of the Russian economy was implemented in several stages, beginning with the enactment of the law on individual labour activity in 1986. Although the effects of this piece of legislation were minimal, it paved the way for the development of cooperatives (1987–88), which had a far greater impact. A raft of measures designed to privatise and facilitate the acquisition of privileges in the commercial sector was introduced between 1988 and 1991. In the 1990s, the term "spontaneous privatisation" came into use as a retrospective description of all the measures adopted during that initial period. The launch of the actual privatisation process occurred in the context of the collapse of the USSR in 1991. These measures undermined the founding principles of the Soviet economy described earlier.[1]

The present chapter does not offer a detailed description of the process, which is easily available elsewhere,[2] but focuses on similarities in the formulation, justification and implementation of these measures and their contribution to the reorientation of penal policy.

First, all these reforms were implemented by state officials, who at local level thus gained an access to valuable administrative resources, allowing private managers to develop their activity. Second, once the access to competent state officials was secured, entrepreneurs could innovate. In the late 1980s and early 1990s, regulation of economic activity was dual, between national legislation

---

[1] The abandonment of central planning is not discussed here. Criticism of this method first emerged in 1987, but the twelfth five-year plan was completed despite the collapse of the economy. See B. Chavance, 1997, pp. 153–4.
[2] A. Aslund, 1989; T. Cox, 1996.

and local initiatives. New private economic practices could even influence national legislation. Third, most of these reforms were legitimised as measures meant to ensure not only economic well-being, but also social justice.

Stages of Accumulation

The law on individual labour activity was adopted on 19 November 1986.[3] The activity in question, defined as "socially useful and exercised by citizens with the aim of producing goods and providing paid services",[4] was intended for wage-earners looking for an additional income, housewives, invalids, retired people and students. The employment of full-time staff was forbidden, but the means of production could belong to the producer, supplier or vendor. All such work had to be authorised by the local administration and required a registration license. The income derived from it was liable to tax. Legislators targeted three sectors for the development of individual activity: small-scale production units, basic services and the "socio-cultural sphere."[5]

This measure had little effect, for it did not provide adequate guarantees for those who wished to take advantage of it. Licenses were restricted to a five-year period and many prospective candidates were reluctant to apply for them, fearing that the law would be repealed. Moreover, there was confusion over the social rights to which "individual workers" were entitled. In fact the reform suffered from its presentation as a necessary evil, a means to boost the socialist economy's ability to meet consumer needs.[6] Tolerated but never really encouraged, it provided no incentive to approach the administration, which was thought to be capable of reprisals.

Cooperatives. Some of these difficulties were resolved by the introduction of the law on cooperatives. The 1977 constitution had advocated expansion in this area,[7] but no steps had been taken prior to *perestroika*. Cooperatives were mentioned in the very first speeches delivered by Mikhail Gorbachev, and pro-

[3] "USSR Law on Individual Labour Activity" in *Spravochnik partiinogo rabotnika. Vypusk 27. 1987.* (Party Militant Handbook, 27th. edn., 1987), Moscow, Politizdat, 1987, p. 499.

[4] *Ibid.*, p. 500.

[5] *Ibid.*, p. 503.

[6] A. Aslund, 1989, p. 163–6.

[7] See article 12 (chapter 2) of the Constitution in *Spravochnik partiinogo rabotnika. Vypusk 18. 1978* (Party Militant Handbook, 18th. edn., 1978). Moscow, Politizdat, 1978, pp. 21–2.

moted by means of sector-based resolutions. The initial texts, including the resolution on consumer cooperatives,[8] were published at the beginning of 1986 but had little impact. The sector really started to expand in 1987, with the adoption of new resolutions by the USSR Council of Ministers. Designed to promote public catering establishments, basic services and the production of consumer goods,[9] these texts offered greater incentives.[10] The early cooperatives did not attract people in large numbers (55,000 employees had registered by 1 July 1987), but they fuelled the debate on the sector's eventual expansion.

The law on cooperatives (26 May 1988)[11] was designed to replace the prevailing approach to sectorial activity with a comprehensive regulatory framework. Its definition of the spheres open to cooperatives was vague, but it provided a legal framework for a group of practices that had hitherto been associated with the underground economy. These included the preparation, processing and sale of agricultural produce and certain consumer goods; the repair of appliances and equipment; the construction of private accommodation; the retail trade; public catering; basic services; organised leisure; the manufacture of wooden objects; the extraction of precious metals and other natural resources; and medical services. The possibility of forming cooperatives offering legal advice was also mentioned.

A cooperative had to have at least three members and could be either an independent entity or part of a state-owned enterprise or organisation. In other words, it could create an entirely new business or exploit the resources of a state-owned enterprise. This distinction should be borne in mind, for one type had a higher public profile and aroused more hostility than the other. A Cooperative's directors could remunerate employees on the basis of a labour contract that listed the conditions agreed upon by both parties. Those with convictions for property crime, corruption and other offences involving personal gain were barred from executive positions, managerial duties and jobs involving material

---

[8] CPSU Central Committee and USSR Council of Ministers resolution, 9 January 1986: "On the Measures Adopted to Develop Consumer Cooperatives" in *Izvestiya*, 1 February 1986.

[9] *Sobranie postanovlenii SSSR* (Collected USSR Resolutions), no. 10, articles 41, 42 and 43.

[10] See, for example, Gorbachev's report to the CPSU Central Committee Plenary Assembly, 27 January 1987. *Pravda*, 28 January 1987.

[11] Published in *Spravochnik partiinogo rabotnika, vypusk 29, 1989* (Party Militant Handbook, 29th. edn., 1989), pp. 382–431. For an analysis of this law, see M. Lesage, 1988, pp. 49–60. In English: A. Aslund, 1989, pp. 167–71; A. Jones and W. Moskoff, 1991.

responsibility.[12] Finally, cooperatives were legally obliged to pay taxes on their profits and on the earnings of their members and employees.

Cooperatives played a pioneering role in the development of the private economy: they transformed the definition of ownership of the means of production, the employment of workforce and the setting of pay rates. They constituted one of the first legal sources of personal enrichment and stimulated the emergence of the first entrepreneurs. As Albert Hirschman noted in another context, this new-found wealth aroused the hostility of the public.[13] Discontent crystallised around the most visible cooperatives, which were often entirely new ventures (cafés and restaurants which charged exorbitant prices were a favourite target). The less visible cooperatives created within enterprises or organisations prospered by taking advantage of the opportunities afforded by "spontaneous privatisations." Measures to impede the cooperative sector's growth were adopted in late 1988 (see Chapter 8), but their number continued to rise until 1990, by which time entrepreneurs were seeking other forms of ownership.

"Spontaneous Privatisation" and the Acquisition of Privileges. An analysis of "spontaneous privatisation" is hampered by a twofold problem: the lack of reliable documentation and the conditions surrounding the formation of the concept itself. The term *spontannaya privatizatsiya* emerged in 1991, with the launch of the privatisation process, and was used as a retrospective denunciation of the injustice of the early phase, from which only the elites had benefited.[14]

By 1988, entrepreneurs had devised a range of strategies for personal enrichment based on the use of public resources.[15] In comparison with the other reforms studied, all these practices escaped close public scrutiny. Certainly they were often supported by legislative texts, but they also relied on more discreet authorisations or derogations granted by administrative officials. For example, an entrepreneur might seek to engage in international trade, thereby earning foreign currency and exploiting the difference between Soviet and world market prices.[16] By the end of the 1980s, the opening of foreign bank accounts and the creation of joint-venture and companies abroad had become viable options but required administrative support.

[12] M. Lesage, 1988, p. 54.

[13] A. Hirschman, 1983, pp. 81–106.

[14] In 1991, the terms "spontaneous privatisation" and "nomenklatura privatisation" (*nomenklaturnaya privatizatsiya*) were interchangeable.

[15] S. Johnson, H. Kroll, 1991, pp. 281–316.

[16] On opportunities for foreign trade, see E.A. Hewett and C.G. Gaddy, 1992.

The growth of cooperatives within state-owned enterprises, which often constituted the initial phase of spontaneous privatisations, divided up available assets according to their profitability. Cooperatives within state enterprises were permitted to lease the means of production,[17] which would be formally privatised at a later date thanks to the law on "small-scale enterprises",[18] for example. Legislation on the leasing of enterprises, stipulating that "the profits belonged to the producer who had the right to use them as he saw fit",[19] was drafted in 1989.[20] Moreover, contracts took the form of leases with an option to purchase. These practices constituted one of the principal methods for privatising the means of production, particularly within state-owned enterprises. In case of litigation during the span of a contract, the case would be submitted to an arbitration tribunal. In practice, litigation was largely concerned with the price at which the leased asset was sold. As there was no clearly established market in this sphere, property values were frequently underestimated. And as the set price took little account of inflation, many enterprises and shops were acquired for a derisory sum.[21] Their profits were lightly taxed, and they did not arouse as much hostility as their more visible counterparts. The sector experienced rapid growth: by the middle of 1991, 4.2 million people were working in leased enterprises.[22]

The creation of "small-scale enterprises" (*maloe predpriyatie*) in 1989[23] also made fragmentation of state enterprises' assets possible. These new concerns

---

[17] S. Johnson, H. Koll and S. Eder, 1994, p. 151.

[18] One case study describes the structural changes that occurred in the various workshops of a Moscow factory in the late 1980s. It was clear that far from acting as a single unit, the management of the factory was divided. Workshop managers competed with each other to privatise the most productive assets. M. Burawoy and K. Hendley, 1992, pp. 371–402.

[19] Remarks by Yu. Trushin, then president of the entrepreneurs and enterprise leaseholders association, at a round table to discuss "K privatizatsii cherez arendu" (Towards Privatisation by way of Leasing) in *Ekonomika i Zhizn'*, no. 26, June 1991, p. 15.

[20] *Vedomosti Verkhovnogo Soveta S.S.S.R.*, no. 15, 12 April 1989. Article 105, *Vedomosti S'ezda Narodnykh Deputatov SSSR i Verkhovnogo Soveta SSSR*, no. 25, 29 November 1989. Article 481. On this legislation, see B.V. Perestyuk, 1990, pp. 137–9.

[21] Interviews with two judges of the Sverdlovsk region arbitration tribunal, June 1997.

[22] P. Rutland, 1992, p. 44.

[23] See the "Declaration on the Organization of Small-Scale Business Activity", drafted by the USSR Council of Ministers commission for improving the economic system, headed by the economist Leonid Abalkin. *Sobranie postanovlenii pravitel'stva S.S.S.R.*, no. 18, 1989. Article 59.

were permitted to keep their own accounts, sign commercial agreements and set wages. "State enterprises enthusiastically took advantage of this opportunity and rapidly set up hundreds of small businesses internally or from available financial and material resources."[24] In 1990, the state offered further encouragement in the form of subsidies, loans and tax breaks; it also helped to obtain supplies and authorised citizens to seek employment in the sector.[25] This measure gave incentives to many cooperatives, which had previously been subject to high taxes, restrictions on their activities and greater interference by bureaucrats,[26] to turn themselves into "small-scale enterprises."[27] Small concerns consequently began to multiply; more than 10,000 were registered by October 1991,[28] mostly within state enterprises.[29] Finally, this period also saw the development of joint-stock and limited liability companies inside state enterprises, following approval by the relevant ministry.[30] Shares were distributed among the staff but could not be purchased by outside investors.[31] The various laws adopted from 1986 onwards changed the status of property in the socialist economy, as was highlighted in 1990 by the inclusion of the concept of "collective" property (ownership of leased enterprises, collective enterprises, cooperatives, joint-stock companies, and other entities) in the Soviet Constitution.[32]

The other forms of "spontaneous" privatisation are well known. The structures responsible for controlling economic activity and organising production were transformed in the late 1980s.[33] Ministries, like the state planning units

---

[24] B. Dudenkov, 1991, p. 70.

[25] "USSR Council of Ministers Resolution, 8 August 1990: 'On Measures to Create and Develop Small Businesses.'" *Sobranie...*, no. 19, 1990. Article 101.

[26] A. Jones and W. Moskoff, 1991, pp. 54–77.

[27] *Ibid.* p. 71.

[28] *Ekonomika i Zhizn'*, no. 49, December 1991, p. 13.

[29] "Eighty-six percent of small businesses are state-owned; 13% are in mixed ownership (state and cooperative, for example)." *Ibid.*, p. 13.

[30] "USSR Council of Ministers Resolution, 19 June 1990: 'On the Regulation of Joint-Stock and Limited Liability Companies.'" *Sobranie...*, no. 15, 1990, pp. 333–56.

[31] S. Johnson, H. Kroll and S. Eder, 1994, pp. 151–2.

[32] Articles 11, 12 and 13 of the USSR Constitution. Modified by the "USSR Law 'On the Institution of the Function of President of the USSR and on the Introduction of Modifications and Supplements to the USSR Constitution.'" *Vedomosti S'ezda...*, no. 12, 21 March 1990. Article 189.

[33] "This is what this latent stage of privatisation looks like: the ministry is suppressed and replaced by a *kontsern* in the form of a joint-stock company (in the same building, with the same furniture and managers). The minister is then sacked. Most of

(*glavki*, the relays between ministries and enterprises), were often carved up in order to create commercial structures (economic coordination bodies, commodities exchanges, etc.).[34] The banking sector was also privatised during this period: independent establishments sprang up in the cooperative sector, the financial departments of ministries,[35] and regional branches of the state banking sector.[36] Party organisations, especially those of the Young Communists (Komsomol), began creating internal commercial and banking structures in 1988.[37] Consumer cooperatives, commodities exchanges, semi–public companies with foreign partners and banks such as Menatep and Inkombank thus saw the light of day. Komsomol Centres for Scientific and Technical Creativity of the Youth (Tsentry Nauchno-Tekhnicheskogo Tvortchestva Molodyozhi) were permitted to engage in commercial activities and provide services. This opportunity enabled young cadres to acquire wealth, familiarise themselves with the new rules of economic activity and join the ranks of the Russian elite.[38]

Opinion was divided as to the merits of "spontaneous privatisations." Some denounced the transfer of ownership as unjust[39] and claimed that it amounted to a "privatisation of the state by the state" which enabled those in power to seize capital and maintain their social status.[40] Others believed that such measures were a necessary apprenticeship in the transition to a market economy, and would also ensure that the process of emerging from communism could not be reversed;[41] by enabling elites to convert their power into wealth, they acted as a "socio-political stabiliser."[42] In one sense these teleological views, formulated after the event, chimed with the official discourse that accompa-

---

the shares are transmitted to the state, while the rest are divided between the heads of the ministry. The number two or three at the former ministry becomes the head of the *kontsern*. That's how the famous Gazprom was born." O. Kryshtanovskaya, 1996. See also S. Fortescue, 1992, pp. 15–8; *Voprosy Ekonomiki*, no. 7, 1991, pp. 3–71; *EKO*, no. 10, 1991, pp. 6–68.

[34] S. Fortescue, 1992, pp. 15–8.

[35] For example, Neftekhimbank (petrochemical bank) and Promradtekhbank (radio technology industry bank). O. Kryshtanovskaya, 1996.

[36] L. Freinkman, 1994, p. 6.

[37] S. Solnick, 1998.

[38] N. Chmatko, M. de Saint Martin, 1997, pp. 88–108; S. Solnick, 1998, pp. 60–124.

[39] M.J. Peck and T.J. Richardson (eds), 1991, p. 160.

[40] O. Kryshtanovskaya, 1995, pp. 94–106.

[41] J.D. Sachs, 1991, pp. 317–21; S. Johnson, H. Kroll and S. Eder, 1994, pp. 147–73.

[42] N. Lapina, 1995, p. 19.

nied the launch of the privatisation process: in effect, reform drew its legitimacy from the need to regulate social practices and provide an institutional framework for spontaneous privatisations.

The Privatisation Process (1991–94). I would like to focus here on the first phase of the privatisation process, the period from 1991 to 1994.[43] Generally known as "mass privatisation" because of the vouchers distributed to all Soviet citizens, it may be distinguished from a second stage during which shares in state enterprises were acquired for cash.[44] The idea of a mass privatisation of businesses and shops took shape in the late 1980s.[45] The Law on the Privatisation of State and Municipal Enterprises in the RSFSR, adopted by the Supreme Soviet on 3 July 1991, established the basic framework: it defined privatisation, appointed the agencies responsible for the process (Committees for the Management of State Property working within federal, regional and local administrations; Property Funds in the corresponding soviets) and prescribed an annual privatisation programme.[46] The following year, the State Programme for the Privatisation of State and Municipal Enterprises in the Russian Federation for 1992[47] defined the practicalities of ownership transfer and marked the beginning of its implementation.[48] Among other things, the reform's instigators aimed at creating a stratum of private property to assist the development of a socially beneficial market economy; boost the efficiency of enterprises; improve social security and expand the social infrastructure (with the receipts from privatisation); stabilise the financial situation; create a competitive economic environment; break up monopolies, and attract foreign investment.[49]

---

[43] For a focus on the success of the reform, see M. Boycko, A. Shleifer and R. Vishny, 1995; A. Aslund, 1995. For a more critical analysis see L.D. Nelson and I.Y. Kuzes, 1995; J. Sapir, 1996, pp. 106–17.

[44] This phase opened with the adoption of the "Fundamental Principles of the Programme for Privatising State and Municipal Enterprises in the Russian Federation after 1 July", enacted by presidential decree on 22 July. The text is presented in two parts in *Ekonomika i Zhizn'*, no. 31–32, July 1994.

[45] V. Shlapentokh, 1993, pp. 19–31.

[46] *Vedomosti S'ezda...*, no. 27, 4 July 1991. Article 927.

[47] *Vedomosti S'ezda...*, no. 28, 16 July 1992. Article 1617.

[48] Regional and Municipal Committees for the Management of State Property were responsible for drafting their own annual programmes.

[49] Introduction to the "State Programme for Privatising State and Municipal Enterprises in the Russian Federation for 1992" in *Vedomosti S'ezda...*, no. 28, 16 July 1992. Article 1617.

In short, the privatisation process was seen as the answer to most of the ills afflicting the Russian economy.

Legislation set out the procedures for "small-scale" and "large-scale" privatisations. The former involved business and manufacturing units employing fewer than two hundred people or whose book value on 1 January 1992 did not exceed one million roubles. The transfer of business ownership rights took place by means of competitive tenders, auctions or lease-buyouts. Auctions ensured that the asset went to the highest bidder, but competitive tenders benefited the most persuasive—that is, the parties that guaranteed to preserve the profile of the enterprise, maintain staff levels, pursue an investment programme, etc. Buyouts were ruled out if the lease had been signed after 3 July 1991. In theory, all these variants should have allowed the staff of the establishment undergoing privatisation to benefit from the procedures.

This was also true of the "large-scale privatisation" model applied to enterprises employing more than one thousand staff or whose book value exceeded 50 million roubles. These enterprises would be converted into joint-stock companies, but the transfer could take several forms. Two of the variants allocated 40 per cent of the shares to the workforce, while a third allotted 51 per cent The 51 per cent option was the most popular. Some 30 per cent of the remaining shares would be acquired by means of vouchers held by the staff of the enterprise undergoing privatisation or by an outsider. Auctions (*chekovye auktsioni*) were organised to this effect. In practice, the private investment funds that collected the vouchers in order to place them in enterprises often gained control of the remaining 30 per cent The remaining shares would ultimately be sold at investment auctions (*investitsionnye torgi*) marking the second phase of privatisation, the "cash privatisations" introduced in 1994. Potential buyers were also required to submit an appropriate investment strategy for the enterprise.[50]

According to this framework, the privatisation process should have benefited the workforces of enterprises and the Russian population as a whole. However, the priority given to factory workers in "large-scale" privatisations should not be overestimated. In many cases, the solidarity of "workers' collectives" was a fiction. Moreover, the anonymity of the vouchers did not encourage people to hold on to them. In order to emphasise the "popular" character of the first phase, every citizen, including minors, received a privatisation

[50] The property of enterprises employing between 200 and 1,000 staff, or with a book value of between one and fifty million roubles on 1 January 1992, could be transferred according to the modalities devised for small or large-scale privatisations.

cheque with a nominal value of 10,000 roubles. This measure helped to legitimise the reform, but did not produce the expected outcomes. A voucher could be exchanged for shares or placed with an investment fund, but it could also be sold on the street at a fluctuating rate.

The privatisation process may be considered as a reform in perfect continuity with the first *perestroika* property transfer measures, because the way they were all conceived and implemented reflects common features in terms of economic policy. In all these reforms, the role of administrative officials, the latitude left to innovative practices, and the way political discourse legitimised them were often similar.

The Influence of Administrative Officials

Officials of the local executive committees responsible for economic issues acquired a crucial role in the implementation of all these reforms. As they were dealing with entrepreneurs who were eager to take advantage of the opportunities on offer, they had some margin for manoeuvre. Administrative officials were accustomed to loose or purely formal supervision, and benefited from the hierarchical inversion mechanism noted earlier in relation to police bureaucracy; they regarded their prerogatives as sources of power and/or profit. The allocation of resources resulting from implementation of the reforms was therefore conducted on an arbitrary basis that owed much to personal interaction between entrepreneurs and local administrative officials.

As noted earlier, the law on individual labour activity had had little impact since the future of this sector was shrouded in uncertainty. The administration was supposed to issue registration licences, but was not required to meet defined, quantified targets. The law on cooperatives did not impose significant constraints on the role played by bureaucrats in the growth of the private economy. Although cooperatives were no longer subject to an administrative authorisation procedure, they were still obliged to register with the local executive. Despite the imposition of a deadline for processing applications and the establishment of an appeal procedure, a private arrangement with a bureaucrat was still the best way to obtain a licence. The level of dependency was even greater in the case of entirely new ventures, for local officials were supposed to make available "at no cost or by means of a lease with an option to purchase, land and buildings for production and other activities, as well as plants and facilities."[51]

[51] M. Lesage, 1988, p. 55.

The central role of the bureaucrats in the creation of cooperatives explains the variations in the sector's growth on Soviet territory. Some officials were more favourable to the proliferation of cooperatives than others and were in a position, at least initially, to encourage or impede the aims of the reform. As Pierre Lascoumes noted with regard to the bureaucratic implementation of government decisions, the application of the law on cooperatives was a "continuous process of secondary normative creation", in which the rules derived from legislation could be used as "shields", "coffers" or "scourges",[52] depending on the internal logic of a given administrative department. Local officials were also influenced by other factors such as public attitudes towards cooperatives or permanent legislative changes.

"Spontaneous privatisations" were by definition based on the existence of collusion between the economic and administrative spheres, or on overlapping positions within them. Access to the principal sources of wealth that became available in the late 1980s required the solid support of administrative bodies. An export business, for example, could purchase raw materials at the local market price, persuade an official to grant an export license and then sell the commodity at the going price on the world market. This method was particularly widespread in the Urals, a region rich in natural resources (metals, minerals). With regard to imports, the Russian government encouraged the purchase of foreign food products by providing enterprises with currency at very favourable rates. As no formal control was exercised over the selling price, the profits were considerable.[53] "Spontaneous privatisations" consolidated the influence of administrative authorisations and derogations on the development of the Russian economy.

The launch of the privatisation process at the beginning of the 1990s did little to alter this situation. Initially, management of the reforms was shared between the executive and legislative sectors, as much at regional and municipal level as at central level. The confrontational stance adopted by both sectors persisted until late 1993 and rapidly hindered the process. Privatisation procedures were finally redefined following President Yeltsin's assault on the Russian parliament in October 1993. The Committees for the Management of State Property (*goskomimuschestvo*, or GKI) were given sole responsibility for

---

[52] P. Lascoumes, 1990, p. 52–3.
[53] This analysis could nevertheless respond to the desire to minimise the role of the privatisation process in the illegitimate accumulation of personal wealth in Russia in the early 1990s. See the article written by former adviser to Yegor Gaidar in 1992: A. Aslund, 1996.

the transfer of ownership; local and regional government departments thus acquired all the prerogatives linked to the organisation and implementation of the reforms.

In many respects, the way the committees operated recalled the planning of Soviet bureaucratic activities. In keeping with the principle of double subordination, they were accountable to the federal hierarchy and also to local or regional political authorities. Moreover, they were required to meet targets. By comparison with previous economic reforms, the orders in this instance were precise. The committees were expected to privatise a set number of businesses and shops each month. Local committees were subjected to additional pressure in the form of exhortations to accelerate the tempo (*vysokie tempy*) of privatisations, thus ensuring that the exit from communism could not be reversed.[54]

When confronted with targets, local bureaucracies were more willing to assist the growth of the private economy, but local officials were still able to exercise considerable autonomy in this area. Because of the emphasis on performance targets, criteria such as the calculation of the price at which an asset was privatised, the identity of the new owners, the observance of legal procedures, the advertising of such procedures, and the impact of the ownership transfer on the privatised enterprise's output were marginalised. The obligation to deliver results was matched by poor control of the opportunities for enrichment and/or acquisition of power open to local officials. Bureaucrats provided the coveted signatures, stamps, authorisations and derogations, which they could offer arbitrarily by creating "their own privatisation code."[55] As with previous reforms, privatisations furthered collusion between entrepreneurs and administrative officials, and ensured that local networks commanded greater loyalty than the vertical hierarchy.

In such circumstances, the privatisation process worked to the advantage of those with financial and administrative resources, in other words the people with privileged access to the government officials responsible for implementing

---

[54] In September 1993, the deputy director of the Sverdlovsk region State Property Fund complained that "The region is certainly behind with regard to the speed envisaged by the administration in Moscow, but what does that mean? The absolute and exclusive priority given to speed could become dangerous. Our experience tells us that the more we privatise enterprises in the region, the more new problems we see emerging. We prefer a slower privatisation speed so that we can prepare for the second phase, which is potentially fraught with problems." Interview with the director of the Sverdlovsk region GKI investment department. September 1993.

[55] E.G. Animitsa and N.M. Ratner, 1993, p. 36. See also R. Lotspeich, 1995, p. 588.

the reforms. In most cases there was a third resource: contacts with specialists in the use of force (police and security agents, private security firms, the internal security departments of large-scale enterprises, criminals), for the reforms made no provision for the protection of property on an institutional basis.[56] We shall see to what extent the role of violent entrepreneurs[57] in protecting property rights contributed to changes in policing tasks in the late 1980s (see Chapter 9).

The Reinvention of Entrepreneurial Practices

The degree of autonomy exercised by the administrative officials responsible for the resources created by economic reforms did not simply lead to their allocation in an arbitrary manner; it also offered entrepreneurs the possibility of developing initiatives that were often highly innovative. By 1988, the rules of the game had been twisted to form a dialectical opposition between the prescription of formal objective norms at federal level and the practices invented by local entrepreneurs.

The first measure to privatise the Russian economy ushered in by *perestroika* encouraged entrepreneurs to devise, individually or collectively, practices which in turn influenced the objective norms being decided at federal level. Privatisation of the economy had originally been envisaged as a "top down" process,[58] in accordance with legislative texts adopted at federal level. But by 1987–88, cooperatives had begun to innovate. In a context of "divergence between two rules",[59] the prescription of objective norms had two aims: to eliminate certain rules in force in the business world and to adapt the legal

---

[56] On the conduct of auctions and competitive tenders, see Chapter V, B, 4, a, ii.

[57] V. Volkov, 2002

[58] This refers to the distinction made by Jacques Commaille, although he reserved it for Western countries, between regulation from the top, which bases its legitimacy on the legal-rational mode of state domination, and "regulation from below ... which stems less from an imposition that is accepted by citizens than from multiple participation which sometimes contradicts the construction of the fundamental principles of customary law" (p. 205). According to this latter ideal type, norms can notably be conceived "by individuals or social groups engaged in innovative social practices which are likely to constitute new models of behaviour or new ways to organise social life, and finally result, following this confrontation between 'juridical reasons', in a juridical change in the 'imposed' legal system." (*ibid.*). J. Commaille, 1994. See also J. Commaille and B. Jobert, 1998, p. 19.

[59] J.-D. Reynaud, 1997, p. 98.

framework to accommodate innovative social practices. The importance given to innovation recalls Schumpeter's definition of the entrepreneur, whose role is to "reform or revolutionise the pattern of production by exploiting an invention or, more generally, an untried technological possibility by producing a new commodity or producing an old one in a new way, by opening up a new source of supply of materials or a new outlet for products, by reorganising an industry and so on."[60]

The emphasis on the ability to innovate enables us to exclude ethical considerations which are inappropriate to the Russia of the late 1980s, although many entrepreneurs sought to acquire legitimacy by defending a Weberian view of their vocation and professional ethos.[61] From this perspective, the term entrepreneur denotes both those who engage in productive activity and those who simply exploit available resources, even to the extent of acquiring wealth through illicit practices. The thinking behind the choice of allocating resources to "productive" or to largely "unproductive" activities such as the quest for unearned income or criminal activities varies according to the institutional context under consideration.[62] When property rights are not sufficiently guaranteed, as in Russia in the late 1980s, high transaction costs encourage entrepreneurs to opt for predatory or protective, but not productive, strategies.[63] When extended to "activities involving the search for a legal or illegal income",[64] a definition of this type enables us to avoid distinguishing entrepreneurs by means of their social milieu, whether that of the *nomenklatura* or the underworld.[65]

While the government had initially supported cooperatives with repeated statements to the effect that "everything that was not forbidden was authorised", Russia became "an innovator's paradise."[66] Entrepreneurs with access to financial and administrative resources began devising strategies for economic growth that Soviet legislation had not yet taken into account. "When we

---

[60] J. Schumpeter, *Capitalism, Socialism and Democracy*, London, Allen & Unwin, 1976, p. 132.

[61] Mark Masarskii, one of the pioneers of the cooperative movement, often mentioned Weber's work on the relation between the Protestant ethic and capitalism. See *Stolitsa*, no. 36, 1992.

[62] W.J. Baumol, 1990, pp. 893–4.

[63] E.L. Feige, 1997, pp. 21–34.

[64] J. Cartier-Bresson, 1997b, pp. 74–5.

[65] On the entrepreneurial paradigm in the analysis of Russian organised crime, see F. Varese, 2001, pp. 6–17.

[66] M. Robertson, 1994, p. 138.

founded 'Interquadro', there was no law on joint-ventures. When we turned it into a limited company, officials had no idea what that meant. To be ahead of one's time: that's what enterprise means."[67]

Such practices did not imply a total rejection of existing legislation or a turn to economic delinquency. On the one hand, they often involved exploring the opportunities that forthcoming reforms might present. It was therefore important to possess information on these innovations, on the allocation of special authorisations and derogations to certain Soviet enterprises. Personal contact with officials of federal ministries, leading politicians, lawyers and the businessmen's associations that were springing up was of particular value. On the other hand, new practices exploited flaws in existing legislation (loopholes, contradictory texts) and the sluggish pace of the legal reform agenda. This required a good grasp of legal issues: "By definition, the entrepreneur is someone who undertakes something. He is a creator, an innovator. He is not restrained by existing legislation, he bypasses it, identifies the loopholes. That is his nature."[68] The point is illustrated by countless examples. Here is just one, concerning the practices of investment funds which exchanged citizens' vouchers for shares in enterprises:

According to existing legislation, investment funds do not have the right to hold more than 10 per cent of the shares in an enterprise. This arrangement does not suit us! There are a thousand and one ways to acquire more than 10 per cent of the shares in an enterprise. It just takes a little thought. For example, I can organise it so that five investment funds follow the same course, each buying 10 per cent of the shares of five different enterprises and informally dividing up the management of 50 per cent of the shares of one of these five enterprises.[69]

The need for a detailed understanding of the law—"a system of potentialities which enables the deployment of specific activities for mobilising rules"[70]—in order to identify the opportunities afforded by existing legislation encouraged the rapid emergence of a new professional specialisation. Many lawyers set up consultancies to advise entrepreneurs on development issues. The law of 1988 thus fostered the growth of legal services cooperatives. Their existence indicated the determination of entrepreneurs to organise, guarantee the future of

---

[67] Interview with businessman Lev Veinberg, shortly after his arrest on a corruption charge, *Kapital*, 1 November 1995.

[68] *Ibid.*

[69] Interview with the director of an investment fund, Yekaterinburg, September 1993.

[70] P. Lascoumes, 1990, p. 50.

their companies by adhering to the legal framework, and bolster the legitimacy of the new rules they were in the process of creating. Indeed, at that time lawyers already played an important role in private enterprises; for instance, they proved to be able to manage the legal transformation of cooperatives into small businesses as soon as Soviet legislation afforded that possibility. "Once hired by cooperative X, my role, along with two other lawyers, was to track developments in legislation on a daily basis and draw up the most relevant strategies for the enterprise. My employers wanted to be irreproachable from the legal point of view."[71]

Although entrepreneurs generally tried to keep on the right side of the law, they could not avoid committing offences, particularly in the area of taxation. By inventing their own rules, they exposed themselves to violent clashes with governmental authorities. Their attempts to join forces, to which we shall return, indicated the extent to which legal vulnerability affected the business world's political and social legitimacy.

Legitimising the Reforms

A comparison of the way in which the reforms adopted between 1986 and 1992 were presented—with the exception of discrete "spontaneous privatisations" and the acquisition of privileges—highlights some common features in the legitimisation process. The privatisation of the Russian economy was undertaken in the name of two interdependent factors: economic well-being and social justice. From this perspective, it represented the continuation of attempts to modify Soviet economic policy that dated back to the 1960s.[72]

The law on individual labour activity was associated with the simultaneous achievement of three objectives: to "improve satisfaction of the population's consumer needs; increase the employment of citizens in socially useful activities; and offer them the possibility of earning extra income, in accordance with the labour provided."[73] The goals reflected an implicit desire to legalise certain forms of economic activity that had traditionally been associated with parasitism. The law on cooperatives extended this argument by stressing that the

---

[71] Interview with a lawyer recruited by a cooperative in 1988–89, now head of a business law consultancy, Yekaterinburg, June 1997.

[72] On the history of Soviet economic reforms, see E.A. Hewett, 1988.

[73] "USSR Law on Individual Labour Activity" in *Spravochnik partiinogo rabotnika. Vypusk 27. 1987.* (Party Militant Handbook, 27th. edn., 1987). Moscow, Politizdat, 1987, p. 499.

eventual enrichment of cadres and employees in the cooperative sector would help to satisfy the needs of all consumers and provide jobs for the inactive. From this perspective, the law on cooperatives was designed to represent a continuation of the new economic policy (NEP) introduced by Lenin in 1921.[74]

The arguments deployed during the privatisation process did not differ greatly from those of the past. In a context where a large segment of the population expressed hostility to the *"nouveaux riches"* and resented the prices charged by cooperatives, social justice was clearly a matter of concern to the authorities, hence the distribution of vouchers to all citizens and the development of variants on the transfer of property reserved for "workers' collectives." Indeed, the reformers claimed that "unlike the liberalisation of prices and monetary constraints, privatisation was seen as the only reform from which the population could benefit." The process thus "rallied the vote, reduced the influence wielded by the reforms' opponents and had an undeniable impact on politics."[75] As indicated earlier, the new legislation was designed to create an objective regulatory framework to replace unofficial arrangements based on social capital, collusion and overlapping positions of power and accumulation. This apparent determination to put an end to the selfish behaviour of those who had been surreptitiously acquiring a monopoly on state assets since the late 1980s led Boris Yeltsin to declare that the country did not need "dozens of millionaires, but millions of shareholders."[76] By mid-1992, some experts were noting that the closure of spontaneous privatisation channels had already cast the reforms in a more favourable light.[77]

There is little point in denouncing the gulf between the aspirations expressed during the privatisation process and the actual effects of this reform.[78] Indeed, that would lead us to neglect goals that while less apparent were nonetheless regarded as priorities, and also to underestimate the eminently political nature of the reform agenda.[79] The privatisation process was not simply a matter of transferring property rights, it was also designed to democratise the regime. Russian leaders constantly stressed the link between the diffusion of ownership rights and the creation of a "middle class", which they portrayed as the ferment

---

[74] On the reference to Lenin and the NEP, see A. Brown, 1996, pp. 119–20.

[75] M. Boycko, A. Shleifer and R. Vishny, 1993, p. 147.

[76] Yeltsin's famous statement was delivered at a press conference. See *Izvestiya*, 24 August 1992 and *Rossiiskaya Gazeta*, 22 August 1992.

[77] D. Vasilev, 1992, p. 11.

[78] V. Kouznetsov, 1995, p. 23.

[79] B. Hibou, 2004.

of democracy. The privatisation process constituted the cornerstone of a two-fold transition, both economic and political, which would guarantee that the exit from communism was irreversible.[80] This was the reason for the absolute priority given to the speed of its implementation when assessing the local bodies managing the transfer of ownership. Like Anders Aslund, economic adviser to Prime Minister Yegor Gaidar, who claimed that the privatisation of "half the economy in two years" was an "extraordinary achievement" that created "tens of thousands of new property owners",[81] the reformers judged its success by the speed of its achievement.

Concluding Remarks

From 1986 to 1992, all privatisation stages shared common features regarding their conception and their implementation. First, the implementation of economic reforms relied on state officials. At the local level, the reinterpretation of national norms and policy goals often led officials to manage their "own privatisation code." This was already the case during the development of the cooperative sector, as many authorisations were required in order to start and develop a business. During the spontaneous privatisation phase, between 1988 and 1992, their importance was obvious as most business strategies and strategies of enrichment relied on access to confidential or reserved information within state administrations, making it possible to get special authorisations and derogatory rights. The privatisation process did not reverse this trend: after a brief period of dual authority (administration and soviets) over the implementation of the reform, the executive sector has monopolised this competence, and GKI officials became sole responsible for managing the transfer of property.

Second, connections and collusions with key-officials allowed entrepeneurs to innovate and to invent new capitalist practices, entering into dialectical opposition with top-down economic rules. These practices could sometimes be illegal, but in many cases they were just ahead of the legislation. Hence a complex relationship between law and capitalism from the beginning. Lawyers first became needed in private firms when the cooperative sector expanded. They helped to give a legal framework to business operations, but also to identify new opportunities within permanently evolving legislation.

---

[80] V. Bunce, 2000, pp. 633–56.
[81] A. Aslund, 1995, p. 264. See also M. Boycko, A. Shleifer and R. Vishny, 1995.

Third, most of the privatisation stages were legitimised in the same way, except for spontaneous privatisations that were discreet by definition. The balance between economic well-being and social justice was difficult to find. The development of the cooperative sector was justified by the need to answer people's consumer needs, but soon the government paid attention to the resentment of most of the population against *nouveaux riches*. The privatisation process in 1992 was presented as an answer to unjust spontaneous privatisation or "*nomenklatura's* privatisation." Workers' collectives and citizens in general, considered as potential shareholders through the possession of a voucher, were supposed to benefit from the reform. But the privatisation process was an economic *and* a political reform. As a symbol of rupture with the communist regime, it had to be implemented urgently and by all means, in spite of possible negative social consequences. The focus on justifying the reforms ultimately reflected the way in which criticism of government action had become a feature of everyday life since the advent of *glasnost*.

7

THE PROBLEMATISATION
OF ECONOMIC CRIME

On more than one occasion, our editorial staff have wondered where to place the dividing line between commerce and speculation, between sabotage and negligence. And how do we shed light on the scale of the shadow economy? There are many points of view about this, and no common conception has ever been arrived at.[1]

To the Western mind, the term *glasnost* reflects the sudden freedom of speech that resulted from the removal of various forms of censorship. While the watchword did not stimulate open discussion of all the difficulties confronting Soviet society, it did provoke debates on a number of "social problems"—situations of serious concern whose formulation pitted different groups of actors against each other and which called for a response from the authorities. The crime issue was one of the most debated. The publication of crime statistics, however partial, together with an increasing concern over the development of crime, gave rise to a range of interpretations which reflected the disparate interests of different groups, each of which strove to secure the adoption of the courses of action they presented as solutions.[2] Experts were called to explain the rise of crime in the media, and research into the fear of crime became popular amongst sociologists. Political debates on crime soon became polarised. Some political actors argued that managers were "exploiters" and that the private sector should not get rid of state control, while others called for more

---

[1] Comment by a journalist during an interview with Interior Minister Boris Pugo. *Pravitel'stvennyi Vestnik*, no. 17, April 1991.
[2] M. Edelman, 1991, p. 42.

liberalisation and asked law enforcement agencies to let the business sector expand. The constitution of the crime "problem" was shaped by a context in which entrepreneurs, emboldened by the opportunities afforded by *perestroika*, attempted to mobilise in order to defend their interests. As defenders of economic freedom, some human rights activists also joined them in the fight.

The Unveiling of Crime Statistics

After two years of hesitation, the first statistics on police activity were published in the Soviet press at the beginning of 1989.[3] An article in *Izvestiya* presented relatively consistent information (totals in relation to the previous year) on twelve categories of offences,[4] including certain types of property crime (theft, robbery, robbery with violence, deception[5]) and speculation. These were the most common, or at least the most widely recorded, forms of economic crime. The statistics aroused concern, particularly as recorded cases of certain types of crime had risen sharply in 1988; robbery, for example, had increased by 44 per cent The publication of these figures had a considerable impact on the conception and construction of the problem of crime.[6] In future, crime statistics would be published at regular intervals, usually every six months.

Some criminologists criticised the limitations of this exercise in *glasnost* and denounced the Interior Ministry's monopoly of sources of information concerning police activity.[7] This argument, often advanced in the West, was of particular importance in the Russian context given the informal mechanisms for applying hierarchical orders described in Part One. We read for example, "Ilyumzhinov, President of the Kalmyk Republic, declared recently that juvenile delinquency had been eradicated in his republic! Absurdities of this kind arise from the fact that statistics are compiled by the body which is at the same time combating crime."[8]

---

[3] With regard to judicial statistics, the publication of partial data on convictions began in 1988. The deputy USSR Justice Minister returned to this point in "Prestupnost' v zerkale glasnosti" (Crime in the Mirror of Glasnost). *Novoe Vremya*, no. 9, 1989, pp. 30–1.

[4] *Izvestiya*, 14 February 1989.

[5] Apart from cases of simple theft, the distinction between "state property" and "personal property" does not appear in statistical tables.

[6] A. Gurov, 1995, pp. 28–9.

[7] Obshchestvennyi tsentr..., 1997, p. 47.

[8] *Ibid.*

Criminologists argued that crime statistics provided information on the activities of law enforcement agencies but not on the development of crime. They urged the authorities to conduct surveys of victims; this would foster further understanding of the ways in which crime developed by supplementing crime statistics with an estimate of unrecorded offences. Similar surveys conducted in other countries reveal the gap between recorded and overall crime, but do not give a comprehensive picture of the evolution of delinquency. They focus on offences harmful to individuals (burglaries, assaults, etc.), but ignore those involving less visible victims, such as tax fraud. Moreover, they suffer from "errors of memory, difficulties in describing the facts of the case [and] the retention of information."[9] When Russian sociologists began conducting such surveys in the 1990s[10] they found that many respondents were suspicious and did not like telling strangers—possible informers—why they had not alerted the police to a particular crime.[11]

Revelations in the Press

Glasnost boosted coverage of crime in the Soviet media, especially from 1988 onwards.[12] A study of the print media highlights the pluralisation of discourses on crime: leading politicians, law enforcement agents, criminals (either anonymously or openly), entrepreneurs, journalists, investigators, researchers, academics and victims all began to publish their analyses, observations and opinions, offering definitions of the problem and suggesting ways to deal with it.

The launch of the "campaign against unearned income" in May 1986, several months before the adoption of the law on individual labour activity, stimulated press criticism of Soviet penal policy. This offensive was aimed at all the illicit practices regarded as economic crimes, even the most harmless forms (see chapter 8). Early in the summer of 1986, angry letters denounced the abuses committed by local law enforcement agencies, which were accused of "distorting" the spirit of the legislation.[13] This perception was swiftly followed by ques-

---

[9] Ph. Robert *et al.*, 1994, p. 26.

[10] I. Mikhailovskaya (ed.), 1995, pp. 32–40.

[11] Obshchestvennyi tsentr..., 1997. p. 48.

[12] A. Nivat, 1997, chapters 2, 3 and 4.

[13] The campaign against unearned income began with a police crackdown on *kolkhozes* which supplied fruit and vegetables to the markets in large provincial towns, thus creating shortages of these products. See "Vinovat li ogurets?" (Is the Cucumber Guilty?), *Pravda*, 14 July 1986.

tions related to the definition of the goals that had been announced. "Does the law regard my income as licit or illicit; does it come from a job or not?"[14] This recurrent question illustrated the bewilderment of the Soviet citizen: if all extra income was henceforth to be regarded as illicit, everyone had cause for worry. The campaign ran counter to social representations of the relative legitimacy of income derived from sources other than conventional employment. For example, a woman who had rented one of her two rooms to students expressed astonishment at the hostility such practices aroused in the press, in the context of the campaign against unearned income. She argued that she was not getting rich through idleness as she continued to live modestly and also had more housework to do. She concluded: "I am sure most people share my opinion: unearned income means speculation, corruption, using your position for personal gain. It certainly does not mean the small sums accumulated by honest people who are trying to supplement their meagre wages by the sweat of their brow and ensure they have just enough to live on."[15]

A letter from a group of *sovkhoz* employees complained about the hostile attitude adopted by local administrative officials following the launch of the 1986 campaign: "Each of us is regularly accused of making a profit on the fruit and vegetables we grow. We are all supposed to be greedy speculators ... After the decree on unearned income, these accusations turned into threats and then into action. Fines of 50 roubles are now imposed for 'irregular use of a plot of land'. They have even confiscated plots of land!"[16]

The critique of the implementation of penal policy distinguished illicit behaviour according to its social legitimacy. This denunciation heightened the fear arising from the increase in crime from 1988 onwards, for it suggested that "real criminals", those belonging to criminal organisations, the economic elite or spheres of government, could break the law with impunity.

In 1988, the press began to focus on the Soviet underworld, which it described as "organised crime", "professional criminality" or "the mafia."[17] The first articles on the structure of the Soviet criminal milieu created a considerable stir. One notable case concerned an interview with a police officer, Lieutenant-Colonel Alexandr Gurov, in the weekly *Literaturnaya Gazeta*. Gurov

---

[14] *Literaturnaya Gazeta*, no. 46, 12 November 1986.

[15] *Ibid.*

[16] *Izvestiya*, 28 September 1986.

[17] For example: *Sotsialisticheskaya Industriya*, 16 January 1988 (on the "mafia" run by speculators to control currency exchange outlets); *Moskovskaya Pravda*, 16 July 1988 (on racketeering); *Ogonyok*, no. 48, 1988 (on the underworld).

referred to the presence of a mafia in the Soviet Union and defined it as a hierarchy of professionals with close contacts in state agencies.[18] By revealing the existence of a new social actor—the mafioso obeying his underworld rules— the article broke with the way the term had been used in the past. It now denoted something more than the misappropriation of public assets orchestrated by regional elites in areas such as Central Asia, the Caucasus and the southern provinces of the RSFSR,[19] although the publicity surrounding the "Rostov–on-Don gang" in 1986 stemmed from a similar attempt to come up with a label.[20] In future, it would also be associated with those "violent entrepreneurs" who had nothing to do with law enforcement administrations. The article generated a considerable response[21] and contributed to the creation within the Interior Ministry of a department to combat organised crime. Alexandr Gurov was appointed as its leader.[22]

Once associated with the existence of a criminal milieu, the term "mafia" was applied to a range of practices. A single page of responses to the Gurov interview in *Literaturnaya Gazeta* contained references to shoot-outs between rival gangs, racketeering in cooperatives, gambling and the criminal hierarchy, as well as more common forms of delinquency.[23] An interview with a head of a criminal investigation department, published in the same issue, provides an

---

[18] "Lev prygnul. Diagnoz: organizovannaya prestupnost'" (The lion sprang. Diagnosis: organised crime), *Literaturnaya Gazeta*, 20 July 1988.

[19] On major "political mafia" affairs in the Soviet Union, see A. Vaksberg, 1992.

[20] In July 1984, a network specialising in the diversion of food products (theft, speculation and corruption) was dismantled in Rostov-on-Don. Seventy-six people were involved, including Boudnitskii, the head of the regional trade department. Two of the accused were sentenced to death, while Boudnitskii received a fifteen-year sentence and died in prison in 1986. After an elaborate funeral service, he was buried in the Avenue of Heroes section of the central cemetery. Journalists protested at the honours bestowed on this "godfather": "Beware! They are on the attack. It's not Boudnitskii in that grave; it is everything new that happens in our lives. It is us they buried!" See V. Fomin, "Kak oni khoronili nas" (how they buried us). *Literaturnaya Gazeta*, no. 2, 7 January 1987; E. Myslovskii, 1989, p. 39.

[21] See for example V. Sokolov, "Bandokratiya" (the gangocracy). *Literaturnaya Gazeta*, 17 August 1988, and readers' reactions in "Pryzhok l'va na glazakh izumlennoi publiki" (the lion pounces while the public is stupefied). *Literaturnaya Gazeta*, 28 September 1988.

[22] A. Gurov, 1995, pp. 19–27.

[23] On the traditional criminal hierarchy in Russia and the Soviet Union, and particularly on "thieves-in-law" (*vory v zakone*), see A. Gurov, 1990; A. Gurov and V. Ryabinin, 1995; V.S. Razinkin, 1995.

insight into the uses to which concepts as flexible as "organised crime" and "mafia" can be put: "Between 1986 and 1988, hundreds of highly dangerous criminal gangs operating in the economic sphere, committing thefts, robberies and robberies with violence, and running rackets, were rendered harmless."[24] The term "gangs" could encompass isolated agreements between three individuals who went on to commit occasional crime. The term "mafia" was simultaneously associated with the thefts committed by political and administrative elites, speculative commercial practices and the actions of the Russian underworld. The word's polysemic nature helps explain the confusion that characterised social representations of organised crime in the 1990s.[25]

Television channels began depicting the most sensational forms of crime in the late 1980s. Programmes like Alexandr Nevzorov's *600 Seconds*, broadcast on the St Petersburg channel, thrilled and horrified viewers with their graphic portrayal of local scandals, corruption cases, swindles, serial killings, conjugal crime, drug trafficking, prostitution and score-settling. The programme helped to foster widespread hostility to the unscrupulous, predatory elites formed by corrupt politicians, greedy entrepreneurs and underworld figures.[26]

This was the background to media treatment of the "feeling of insecurity" (*sentiment d'insécurité*).[27] In 1989, *Pravda* ran a headline declaring that "rising crime is causing widespread concern", and published extracts from letters to support its claim.[28] The increasing use of opinion polls sustained such views.

[24] *Literaturnaya Gazeta*, 28 September 1988.

[25] Numerous surveys showed that Russians believed the "mafia" and "organised crime" were responsible for most of their problems. Yuri Levada's polling centre, noting that this was true of 51 per cent of the respondents, asked another question: "What do you understand by mafia?" The answers were: parallel economy activity (43 per cent), bureaucrats in the ministries and administrations (36 per cent), the Party-State apparatus (34 per cent), criminals (25 per cent), cooperative members and individual workers (18 per cent). See Y. Levada, 1993, p. 41.

[26] "*600 Seconds* exploits a simple but effective formula: it reveals the hidden face of Soviet society. One segment, for example, revealed that the former first secretary of the Leningrad Party used his contacts to buy a Mercedes limousine at far below the going rate; another unmasked a meat processing plant which made sausages from old carcasses; a third described in all its sordid detail how the labels were removed from insecticide sprays, which were then sold in state shops as deodorants!" A. Nivat, 1997, p. 263.

[27] The notion of a "feeling of insecurity", the subject of much debate in France, is highly controversial. According to Hugues Lagrange, it is both "a genuine fear of the risk of being personally robbed or assaulted, and a preoccupation with security that takes the form of a vague anxiety concerning crime and its alleged causes, without necessarily feeling that one is the victim of it." H. Lagrange, 2003, p. 54.

[28] *Pravda*, 11 May 1989.

The Russian surveys, sometimes unfairly compared with similar surveys carried out in other countries, enabled commentators to advance certain arguments: Muscovites, for example, were more afraid of being alone in the streets than the inhabitants of Detroit, Boston and San Francisco![29] The concern over personal safety was reflected in the Russian media, in which advertisements for home security devices (armoured doors, fences) and martial arts courses proliferated. Every newspaper introduced a crime column, and publishers brought out specialist magazines.[30]

The multiplying of sources of information on criminal issues included the many interviews with underworld figures that appeared in the press. Despite their dubious authenticity, they also contributed to the formulation of the problem of crime. Moreover, testimony of this sort appeared in what were known at the time as "reforming" publications, organs that advocated a market economy for Russia. Proponents of liberalisation thus tended to adopt a tolerant attitude towards "underground" entrepreneurs and denounced the absurdities of the normative framework applied to entrepreneurial activity:[31]

It's not me who needs this interview; it's you, the servile citizens of the empire. Interior Ministry officers and university professors deceive you every day by churning out rubbish about us on television and in the newspapers ... If our respectable functionaries can strut around like experts and hold forth on what they call the mafia and the shadow economy, then why can't we have our say on these matters as well? Everything they say about such matters, all these so-called scientific studies that create so much confusion in citizens' minds, all this propaganda about combating organised crime—it's all nothing more than stupidity, deception and pretence.[32]

The arguments employed by "underground entrepreneurs" to justify their actions often highlighted the contrast between existing legislation and the morality of the action taken by those in power, the leaders who resorted to

[29] "Boyus' vykhodit' iz doma" (I'm afraid to leave the house). *Moskovskie Novosti*, no. 21, 1989.

[30] Examples include Moscow's *Kriminal'naya Khronika* (Chronicle of Crime) and Yekaterinburg's *Syshchik* (the detective).

[31] L. Yur'ev, 1991, *Ogonyok*, no. 30, 1991, *Nevskoe Vremya*, 5 April 1994, *Novyi Z.E.S.*, no. 4, 1990, no. 5, 1990. See also the comments of entrepreneurs who openly and regularly resorted to illicit practices in the course of running their businesses, e.g. Lev Veinberg (*Kapital*, 1 November 1995) and Malik Gaisin, the "clandestine entrepreneur" who founded an industrial empire before being elected to the State Duma in 1995 (*Kommersant*, 22 June 1995).

[32] L. Yur'ev, 1991, p. 4.

terms like "organised crime" and "mafia" in order to create ill-defined but acceptable scapegoats. These labels were used to legitimise a vast enterprise of political domination, but could also be applied to the conduct of leaders themselves: "Frankly, I am sick of being blamed for the worst crimes on earth. OK, we break the law, but it would never occur to us to steal from an impoverished engineer or a poor old man, which is the kind of odious crime our Prime Minister, Valentin Pavlov, commits. There he stands, the great specialist in plundering poor and honest people!"[33]

Whether true or false, such testimony highlights the difficulty of defining criminal behaviour when the rules of economic activity are undergoing a transformation. On the one hand, the entrepreneurs who emerged from the underground economy—criminals according to Soviet law—complied with *perestroika* requirements and market economy behaviour. On the other, they were quick to challenge the state over the categorisation of illicit practices. The references to "university professors" and "so-called scientific research" into organised crime highlight the extent to which views with a claim to scientific rigour influenced dominant representations of the evolution of crime.

Scientific Expertise

Glasnost helped to diversify and publicise the work of the social sciences on criminal issues. Several highly respected sociologists focused on the fear of crime, including Tatyana Zaslavskaya, a director of the Centre for the Study of Public Opinion (VTsIOM) at the time. In 1990, Zaslavskaya coordinated a survey using a sample of 3,000 people.[34] The survey revealed that the respondents regarded crime as one of their chief concerns, coming just after "the future of [their] children" and "nuclear war", but before the "death of a close friend or relative" and "poverty." More than half the respondents thought the crime situation had "deteriorated" recently; only 15 per cent believed it would improve in the near future. There was a pronounced fear of being assaulted: 60 per cent of respondents said they did not feel safe when walking the streets after dark and 30 per cent admitted feeling afraid when inside their own buildings. When asked to rank repressive measures in order of priority, they put the fight against speculation at the top of the list, followed by serious crimes

---

[33] Interview with a racketeer, *Ogonyok*, no. 30, 1991.
[34] VTsIOM, 1990.

(homicide, rape), organised crime, hooliganism and public order offences. More than half of those who expressed concern over speculation defined it as it was defined in criminal law. Finally, when asked to rank forms of criminality according to the danger they presented, respondents placed the mafia at the top of the list, followed by homicide, juvenile delinquency, rape, corruption, theft in enterprises, speculation and hooliganism. The fear of crime was not linked exclusively to the fear of physical assault, but was also induced by the fall in purchasing power, the difficulty of obtaining standard consumer goods and, finally, increasing evidence of personal enrichment through means that were perceived as illegitimate.

Numerous questionnaire-based surveys were conducted in the early 1990s. They revealed that public anxiety stemmed less from personal prejudice than from rumours, unverified information and first-hand accounts. In 1992, most respondents cited the fear of crime as their greatest anxiety, but only 20 per cent admitted that they had been direct victims of a crime. The fear of crime seemed to be linked to two factors: official recognition of the problem of crime in the late 1980s, and media coverage of the most violent and spectacular criminal acts.[35]

Studies of economic crime often focused on the shadow economy and organised crime, for these aspects had escaped the confines of a narrow circle of specialists in Soviet law and had triggered broader debates. During *perestroika*, researchers with a self-proclaimed expert knowledge of the underground economy often alleged that their work in this field dated back to the 1970s, although this could not be verified. The economist Tatyana Koryagina, for example, cited her work on the provision of basic services at the Scientific Institute for Technochemical Research, a branch of the RSFSR Ministry of Basic Services[36] which had been given the task of determining the true level of household consumption of basic services, including those provided by individuals. Koryagina subsequently continued her work at Gosplan's economic research institute, which attempted to identify the scale of illegal service provision in order to improve the assessment and prediction of consumer needs.[37] Moreover, economists had access to Western theoretical literature on the second economy. Researchers at the Central Institute of Mathematical Economy

---

[35] I. Mikhailovskaya (ed.), 1995, p. 41.

[36] "Basic services" is a translation of *bytovoe obsluzhivanie*. It can also be translated as "everyday services."

[37] T.I. Koryagina, "Analiz, otsenki, prognozy" (analysis, evaluations, predictions) in *Tenevaya ekonomika*, 1991, p. 29.

of the USSR Academy of Sciences claimed a special interest in this field dating back to the early 1980s, but published nothing on it until 1987.[38]

With the advent of *perestroika*, the underground economy attracted the attention of lawyers, criminologists, economists[39] and, more rarely, sociologists.[40] The subject was in phase with the period and, while hard to grasp, had aroused considerable public interest:[41] "A wide variety of adjectives has been employed to define [the shadow economy]. It may be underground, second, unregistered, destructive, criminal, minor, fictive, non-state, market, private, defective, parallel, black, unofficial, illegal, outside the law—the list goes on."[42]

Most studies sought to arrive at an appropriate definition of the "shadow economy" by highlighting its principal forms, calculating its scale and predicting its evolution. This undertaking placed economic crime at the centre of a political debate. On the one hand, the inclusion of the most common types of illicit transaction and their association with flaws in the Soviet regulatory framework promoted a more tolerant view of such practices. On the other hand, denunciations of their illegality which ignored the environment that gave rise to them led to calls for greater repression.

The concept of "organised crime" also contributed to pseudo-scientific debates on economic delinquency during *glasnost*. Like the "shadow economy", it was vague, had no legal meaning and could easily be manipulated for political ends. After the controversial *Literaturnaya Gazeta* interview with Alexandr Gurov, the media began seeking out experts on organised crime—police officers, judges, members of the underworld, investigative journalists, scholars. Scientific journals, particularly legal periodicals, began discussing organised crime in 1988.[43] Like specialists in the shadow economy, experts justified

---

[38] M.I. Nikolaeva and A.Yu. Shevyakov, 1987, p. 53.

[39] See O.V. Osipenko, 1989, 1990, 1991; S. Golovin and A. Shokhin, 1990; V. Felzenbaum, T. Kuznetsova and L. Nikiforov, 1991. For an overview, see *Tenevaya ekonomika*, 1991; V. Rutgaizer, 1991.

[40] One sociologist, for example, studied the practices of a group of workers specialising in building dachas. A. Goryanovskii, 1990, pp. 56–64.

[41] The cover of the principal study of the subject illustrates the confusion of registers that characterised the argument: a badly drawn but repugnant rat with a sack on its back scurries into its hole; on the back, a seductive young woman squeezes a wad of banknotes between her breasts (*Tenevaya ekonomika*, 1991).

[42] K.A. Ulybin, "Znakomaya neznakomka" (a familiar unknown) in *Tenevaya ekonomika*, 1991, p. 18.

[43] A glance at the contents pages of the main Soviet legal journals supports this obser-

their grasp of the subject by emphasising the length of their professional acquaintance[44] with "professional crime", "organised criminal groups" (*organizovannye prestupnye gruppy*) and the "organisational nature of crime" (*organizovannost v prestupnosti*)[45]—in other words, all forms of group preparation of illicit acts.

The first study with a claim to approach organised crime in a scientific manner set out to demonstrate its advance on Soviet soil. Once its existence had been accepted, the principal task was to identify the symptoms and causes and then help to devise an appropriate political response. This project encouraged the use of a pseudo-scientific argument to support ideological convictions. Some commentators insisted that organised crime had been rife during the communist period, even in the darkest days of Stalinist repression, while others linked it to the reforms introduced in the second half of the 1980s.[46]

Academic and scientific literature continued to associate the thefts committed by local elites with "mafias." The definition proposed at a round table on organised crime was clearly influenced by such views, for it stressed factors such as conspiracy, stability and the extent of territorial control. As it omitted resort to violence for personal gain, such a definition could just as well have been applied to predatory elites as to criminal organisations in the strict sense of the term. Moreover, it favoured a culturalist approach to organised crime: a "mafia" could be distinguished first by the consistency of its ethnic make-up, and secondly by its choice of criminal activities. Finally, the fondness for the term "conspiracy" sustained the idea of a plot to destabilise every element of Russian society.[47]

The first texts on Russian organised crime highlighted the permeability of the boundaries between scientific, political, police and legal discourse. The leading experts in the field worked in law enforcement agencies' research insti-

---

vation. See, for example, *Sotsialisticheskaya Zakonnost'*, no. 6, 1988, pp. 25–7; no. 9, 1988, pp. 34–7; no. 4, 1989, pp. 34–7; no. 6, 1989, pp. 45–7; *Sovetskoe Gosudarstvo i Pravo*, no. 5, 1988, pp. 128–33; no. 7, 1989, pp. 66–7. See E. Myslovskii, 1989, pp. 4–12.

[44] A 1979 reference is available: B. Vodolaszkii and Yu. Vakutin, 1979.

[45] See A.I. Dolgova and S.V. D'yakov (eds), 1989, p. 101.

[46] G. Khokhryakov, 1989, pp. 11–9.

[47] A.I. Dolgova, S.V. D'yakov, 1989, pp. 16–8. A conversation with one of the two round table coordinators rapidly turned to the relations between criminal conspiracies, the machinations of Freemasons and political power in Russia in the early 1990s (Moscow, April 1997).

tutes or training centres, notably those attached to the General Prosecutor's Office and the Interior Ministry. The formation of an academic community to support a repressive approach to crime was illustrated by the creation in 1991 of the Criminological Association under the aegis of Azaliya Ivanovna Dolgova, a researcher at the General Prosecutor's Office research institute who had coordinated the first published work on organised crime. The Association set out to influence the definition of penal policy by raising public awareness on the issues surrounding crime.[48] Legislators welcomed its input when drafting certain laws, despite the controversial conspiracy theories advanced by some of its members.

In 1986, some researchers began to focus directly on "economic crime." One of the pioneers in this field, Alexandr M. Yakovlev, combined legal and criminological perspectives but remained open to sociological considerations.[49] Yakovlev argued that economic crime represented a distinct field of inquiry that highlighted the flaws in traditional Soviet management and validated *perestroika*. This analysis did not challenge the fundamental principles of the socialist economy, but advocated the encouragement of "desirable, socially useful and economically effective" behaviour, as well as the removal of obstacles to the "worker's desire to increase his remuneration through honest labour."[50] The concept of "economic crime" gave rise to a large body of scientific research.[51] The need to redefine the category's boundaries resulted in the emergence of three competing views, thus provoking arguments that persisted until the mid-1990s. Some authors argued that the current legal definition should be extended to three chapters of the Soviet Criminal Code,[52] while others advocated restricting it to breaches of the rules of Soviet economic activity.[53] A third group dismissed this approach on the grounds that it ignored the offender's personal situation, and claimed that economic crime was a matter

---

[48] Presentation by the Criminological Association, in *Izmeneniya prestupnosti v Rossii*, 1994, p. 312.

[49] A.M. Yakovlev, 1986, 1987, 1988 and 1990. Alexandr M. Yakovlev was appointed President Yeltsin's representative at the State Duma in the 1990s.

[50] A.M. Yakovlev, 1988, pp. 236–40.

[51] I.I. Rogov, 1991; V.V. Kolesnikov, 1994; G.K. Mishin, 1994; A.A. Tolkachenko, 1994; A.A. Aslakhanov, 1997.

[52] A.M. Yakovlev, 1988. p. 50; N. Kirichenko *et al.*, 1995, p. 17.

[53] I.I. Rogov, 1991, p. 52; A.A. Tolkachenko, 1994, p. 5; Russian Federation Federal Programme for Reinforcing the Campaign against Crime in 1994 and 1995. *Sobranie zakonodatel'stva Rossiiskoi Federatsii*, no. 5, 30 May 1994. Article 403.

of "white collar" crime[54]—that is, offences committed by those with positions of responsibility in the economy, the administration and politics.[55] However, a broad legal definition of economic crime seems most appropriate for the purposes of this book, for the desire to differentiate offences according to the offender's identity was seldom reflected in police activity, which remained almost exclusively dedicated to repression of the more common illicit practices. The mid-1990s were marked by the failure to establish a legitimate definition of economic crime, despite the circularity of the discourse advanced by journalists, experts and politicians. Political and social actors interpreted the concept in the light of the interests they sought to protect and the goals they were intent upon pursuing.

The Politicisation of Crime

The population, bewildered and distressed by the economic crisis and the spectacle of new wealth, generally supported greater repression, as did many politicians, scholars and journalists. Business leaders and proponents of economic reform required an alternative presentation of the crime problem, and began looking for new ways to protect economic freedoms from government intervention. Entrepreneurs attempted to restore their image by disassociating themselves from the criminal environment. Once they had achieved this, the task of organising and defending the cause of economic freedoms could be delegated to human rights activists, many of whom came from dissident backgrounds. In the name of the emergence of civil society and shared liberal values, entrepreneurs and human rights activists formed a temporary alliance to combat the repression of illicit economic practices. In the very early 1990s, the idea of legalising illicitly acquired capital began to influence political debate.

A Crackdown on Economic Crime? There were many calls for greater repression, for it was commonly believed that offenders operated with impunity because the policing and judicial infrastructure had not been adapted to deal with the problem. The prevalence and strength of this belief in the late 1980s was apparent from the language used by leading politicians, journalists, experts and public figures. The analysis of the impact of the law on coopera-

---

[54] V.V. Kolesnikov, 1994, pp. 15–6.
[55] *Prestupnost'—ugroza Rossii*, 1993, p. 31.

tives was decisive in this respect. Its critics regarded cooperatives as opportunities for the illicit acquisition of wealth, and interpreted subsequent reforms as further opportunities for illegal activity and further stages in the criminalisation of the economy. They also tended to ignore the distinction between economic crime and the underground economy. The Govorukhin case provides a good illustration of this position. Stanislav Govorukhin, a popular Soviet film maker, began making documentaries about Russia in the late 1980s, and was eventually elected to the State Duma in 1993. His first documentary, *We Can't Live Like This (Tak zhit' nel'zya)*, shot in 1989, was a great success, for it depicted a society blighted by poverty, violence and injustice:[56]

No, there are no serious crimes and petty crimes: they are all equally dangerous to society. There are no petty thieves and master thieves, no minnows and big fish. A thief is a thief: he should rot in prison.[57]

Govorukhin favoured the type of discourse that associated cooperative members and businessmen with criminals: "I maintain that 90 per cent of today's entrepreneurs are criminals."[58] Confronted with the spectacle of illegitimate wealth, indignation would give way to "terror", to "the most extreme measures" imposed by an "iron hand."[59]

Some political figures claimed to embody such social aspirations, Alexandr Rutskoi being one example. On becoming head of an interdepartmental committee for the fight against crime and corruption, Rutskoi announced his intention to wage a "decisive and uncompromising" war against this "threat to the Russian state." A range of "both repressive and preventive" measures[60] designed to "strengthen the state and protect society and the individual"[61] would be introduced. According to the rhetoric, which became increasingly intense, the focus on the interests of the state meant that democratisation would depend on the government's ability to impose respect for the law in

---

[56] Synopses of his first three documentary films can be found in S. Govorukhin, 1994.

[57] *Ibid.*, p. 43.

[58] *Ibid.*, p. 164.

[59] *Ibid.*, p. 19, pp. 33–4, p. 84.

[60] Speech to the Interdepartmental Committee for the Campaign against Crime and Corruption, Moscow, 19 January 1993. *Neizvestnyi Rutskoi*, 1994, pp. 209–10.

[61] Speech delivered at a meeting about the organisation of the All-Russia Campaign against Crime and Corruption, Moscow, 12 February 1993. *Ibid.*, p. 211.

Russian society. The "relentless offensive" against crime was presented as a justifiable response to the "anarchy and chaos that certain people, acting in their own interests rather than those of the state, are trying to depict as a manifestation of democracy."[62]

Public acceptance of Rutskoi's rhetoric was enhanced by his career as a Red Army officer and hero of the war in Afghanistan. He never missed an opportunity to highlight the "looting of national assets": far from benefiting all citizens as foreseen, the privatisation process worked to the advantage of a "handful of speculators" and "cosmopolitan compradors who were ready to subject the country to foreign interests."[63] Rutskoi's hardline approach relied on analyses from policing sources and the literature produced by experts. Many researchers agreed with this approach, arguing that the only solution to avoid the criminalisation of the Russian state was to accept repression.[64]

In the early 1990s, the various social actors hostile to economic reform justified their positions by relying on different sources of legitimacy that tended to validate each other: experience of war, social proximity, access to confidential material, scientific evidence, etc. Stanislav Govorukhin made films that resembled investigative journalism and featured expert testimony. His documentaries thus became a source of reference for works with a claim to scientific rigour, as illustrated by a quotation from him in the introduction to a legal text on organised crime.[65] Moreover, Govorukhin recognised a kindred spirit in Alexandr Rutskoi, a politician who shared his diagnosis of Russian society and had the power to implement the most appropriate repressive measures.[66] When taken together, these legitimising factors constituted a regime of truth based on the partial revelation of opaque, if not secret, sources. The most common source was police documents, but the arguments employed by the hard-liners were often nothing more than allusions to their access to unpublished information.

---

[62] *Ibid.*, p. 211.

[63] *Neizvestnyi Rutskoi*, 1994, p. 445.

[64] After having supported Boris Yeltsin, the economist Tatyana Koryagina rejoined the Communist camp. She regarded the Gaidar reforms as a "diktat of the West and the criminal milieu." *Rabochaya Tribuna*, 7 February 1992. See also the work of Anatoly Lar'kov, a researcher at the Russian Federation Prosecutor's Office General's Institute of Scientific Research (A. Lar'kov, 1994, p. 38).

[65] V. Yarochkin, 1995, pp. 3–4.

[66] S. Govorukhin, 1994, pp. 303–4 & 355–6.

Collective Action by Cooperative Members and the Definition of Economic Crime.
Cooperative members, the first entrepreneurs to actively defend their interests
on the political stage, could hardly adopt at the outset a tolerant position on
illicit economic practices.[67] They were generally regarded in a negative light,
and were keen to acquire social legitimacy and respectability. Their support
for a new penal policy which could be adapted to the exigencies of *perestroika*
exposed them to widespread hostility. The first cooperative associations,
founded in 1988,[68] sought to create mutual aid networks in order to resolve
the practical problems faced by entrepreneurs. The development of legal assistance, creation of lending banks and provision of managerial training were
given priority.[69] The sector's institutional fragility provided its representatives
with an incentive to participate in defining the legal framework surrounding
their activities.[70]

The adoption in December 1988 of government measures to restrict the
scope of the cooperative sector strengthened this mobilisation.[71] The first few
months of 1989 saw the emergence of several forums for cooperative members.
During the summer of that year, the Pan-Soviet Congress of Production and
Services Cooperatives received a goodwill message from the government in
the form of a telegram from the USSR Council of Ministers. The sector was
encouraged to continue its work and also to predict and combat the "negative
phenomena" observed within it.[72] The congress, held in June-July 1989, was
also a public relations exercise. Seeking to avoid labels such as "speculators"
and "profiteers" in future, cooperative members denounced non-productive
methods of personal enrichment. In addition, they stressed their own vulnerability to racketeering, a move which enabled them to distance themselves
from "organised crime." They argued that they did not oppose harsh penal
measures, but simply sought to homogenise the laws governing their activities,

---

[67] On the emergence of entrepreneur mobilisation, see A. and W. Moskoff, 1991,
pp. 110–20; D. Slider, 1991, pp. 797–821.

[68] *Pravda*, 7 July 1988.

[69] *Izvestiya*, 4 November 1988.

[70] *Ibid.*

[71] "That new year present, the famous USSR Council of Ministers resolution of 29
December 1988, was in fact merely a trial run for a massive, well-organised attack
on the cooperative sector." V. Tikhonov, 1996, p. 177–8. See also the appeal for assistance from entrepreneurs faced with the "legal vulnerability of the cooperative
sector." *Moskovskie Novosti*, no. 5, 29 January 1989.

[72] *Ekonomicheskaya Gazeta*, no. 27, July 1989.

particularly with regard to taxation, and to curb the latitude enjoyed by the officials charged with their implementation.[73] In order to achieve their objectives, the participants agreed to create a base for political representation. This decision resulted in the creation of the Union of United Cooperatives (*Soyuz Ob'edinennykh Kooperativov*), led by key figures in the movement such as V.A. Tikhonov[74] and A. Tarasov.[75]

In his writings, Vladimir Tikhonov argued that economic offences were the product of a centrally planned economy, particularly in relation to the status of property in the socialist system.[76] However, he mounted no direct challenge to penal policy. He did emphasise that speculation was not an economic offence "in the context of a normal market economy",[77] but he called for its continued repression in the Soviet Union. Since the absence of free competition and the maintenance of artificial prices so greatly disturbed the equilibrium of the market, speculation should be regarded as a form of theft, for it was based on the misappropriation of money the state paid the producer in order to maintain artificially low selling prices. When discussing the social illegitimacy of entrepreneurs, Tikhonov did not criticise existing criminal categories but instead used them to create a strategic contrast between two types of economic actor—the honest cooperative member and the criminal—and condemn the conflation of the cooperative sector and organised crime. His portrayal of the sector in terms of a capitalist ethos—hard work, honesty, humility and a contribution to the public good[78]—broke with the discourse

---

[73] *Izvestiya*, 10 July 1989.

[74] At the time, Vladimir Tikhonov was a USSR people's deputy and a member of the Academy of Agricultural Science. After running several research and study institutions, he began to construct an image as a reformist economist and an intellectual. A staunch supporter of cooperatives, he promoted the image of a "civilised" entrepreneur, i.e. responsible, honest, humble and pious. See his public blessing at the Union's inaugural congress, *Izvestiya*, 10 July 1989. On his death in 1994, Boris Yeltsin eulogised him as an "eminent scholar, eminent social actor, authentic Russian citizen and man of goodwill." See V. Tikhonov, 1991, 1996.

[75] Artyom Tarasov was one of the most high-profile members of the Soviet cooperative movement. He was elected as a deputy in 1989 and again in 1993, and his name and fortune often featured in the news. Some of his companies were searched when the decree on economic sabotage was enacted, as he accused Mikhail Gorbachev of making money out of the Kurile Islands (*Izvestiya*, 1 February 1991).

[76] V. Tikhonov, 1996, p. 181.

[77] *Ibid.*, p. 188.

[78] During the 1990s, some entrepreneurs claimed their views were derived directly from

of deception, tricks of the trade, networking skills and capacity for coercion employed by other Russian entrepreneurs at the time.

But the denigration of cooperatives showed no signs of abating, and scandals involving leading political figures were exploited in order to tarnish the sector's image.[79] The severity of fiscal constraints encouraged attempts to circumvent them by illegal methods. Moreover, cooperatives were still dependent on local authorities' goodwill. In the final few months of 1989, their activities were banned in many Russian towns and regions, and indeed in some of the USSR republics such as Uzbekistan. These local decisions were justified by the need to combat speculation, and extended to all cooperatives, not just those engaged in buying and selling food and standard consumer goods.[80] Furthermore, public resentment over severe food shortages sometimes led to assaults on cooperative members.[81] Against this background, central authorities were quick to demonstrate their own hostility. In December 1989, the Interior Minister Vadim Bakatin denounced the sector as a haven for crooks and profiteers seeking to legalise illegally acquired capital. In Bakatin's view, cooperatives were the driving force behind the increase in theft, speculation, racketeering and corruption in the Soviet Union.[82]

The options available to cooperatives seemed extremely limited given the intensity of the offensive. At the 1990 Union Congress, Tikhonov advocated a strategy of civil disobedience and called upon members to refuse to fill in their tax returns.[83] There were also calls to restrict the activities of local authorities and government departments and place cooperatives on an equal footing with state-owned property.[84] On the eve of the March 1990 elections (local soviets and republics), the idea of creating a political party took shape and an

---

Weber. See the interview "Ne po Marksu, a po Maksu" (not according to Marx but according to Max) with Mark Masarskii in *Stolitsa*, no. 36, 1992, p. 12.

[79] In February 1990, the KGB denounced a scheme by the ANT cooperative to sell twelve tanks to a foreign country. It was later revealed that Nikolai Ryzhkov, then head of the USSR Council of Ministers, had been involved in the contract. On the ANT affair, see D. Slider, 1991, p. 809.

[80] The vice-president of a Krasnodar neighbourhood executive committee informed a journalist that "We have decided to do away with cooperatives. You must know why: we are sick of these speculators, these *shashlyki* [grilled meat] sellers." See *Izvestiya*, 11 February 1990.

[81] V. Tikhonov, 1996, pp. 172–5.

[82] *Trud*, 23 December 1989.

[83] *Kommersant'*, no. 5, February 1990.

[84] *Izvestiya*, 18 February 1990.

appeal went out to all the economic actors in favour of a more rapid transition to a market economy.[85] The programme, expressed in very broad terms, was based on the defence of economic and political freedoms, as well as the rights of the individual. Given their championing of liberal values, entrepreneurs supported the activities of certain human rights campaigners.

The Defence and Rehabilitation of Convicted Managers. Viktor Sokirko declared in an editorial in 1993, "We hope that our publication will awaken the reader's desire to restore the honour and good name of those who created the business sector in the Soviet Union. Many of those convicted were not criminals at all, but victims of economic repression. Indeed, they were pioneers of human, market and contractual relations in the economy."[86] Sokirko had been fighting for economic freedoms in the Soviet Union since the late 1970s. This vocation had already won him a marginal position in dissident groups campaigning for social and political freedoms. While employed at the Moscow Institute of Economics, Sokirko had contributed to *Poiski*, a clandestine magazine. Using a pseudonym,[87] he founded his own *samizdat* periodical, *In Defence of Economic Freedoms*, and published eight issues between 1978 and 1979.[88] Denounced by the Institute's director, he was arrested by KGB agents in 1980 and given a three-year suspended sentence plus probation for "knowingly making false assertions which defamed the social and state regime of the Soviet Union" (article 190[1] of the Criminal Code).

Sokirko returned to the fray in the early days of *perestroika* and campaigned for the release of the "convicted managers" (*osuzhdennye khozyaistvenniki*). He argued that the governmental denunciation of "speculators" and other "profiteers" was irresponsible and counter-productive: the Soviet Union had committed itself to sweeping economic reforms but had deprived itself of its best entrepreneurs, whom it had imprisoned for practices that would not have been penalised in other contexts.[89] His association, formed to provide con-

---

[85] *Ibid.*
[86] Editorial in *Zashchita Ekonomicheskikh Svobod i Kommercheskoi Deyatel'nosti*, no. 2, 1993.
[87] The pseudonym, K. Burzhuademov, has its own eloquence. The "K" stands for Kommunist, so the name actually means "communist bourgeois." At the time, the author was convinced of the need to "reconcile communist ideals and the bourgeois way of life."
[88] The *samizdat* published forthright comment and reproduced extracts from unobtainable books and articles, including work by I. Zemtsov, A. Katsenelinboigen, V. Chalidze and K. Jaspers.
[89] See the article by V. Sokirko in *Literaturnaya Gazeta*, no. 15, 8 April 1987.

victed managers with legal aid and influence political decisions, became known as the Society for the Defence of Convicted Managers and Economic Freedoms.[90] In November 1990, the Society began publishing *The Voice of Convicted Managers*.[91]

Sokirko asked qualified lawyers to re-examine the files of convicted managers and begin appeal proceedings. By the end of 1990, the Society had achieved its first success:[92]

G. was tried by the Kalinin regional court for abuse of office and *pripiski*. As director of a poultry slaughterhouse, he signed a contract with a construction brigade [i.e. *shabashniki*] for the erection of two buildings. G. was charged with abusing his position, and committing a gross breach of remuneration regulations by subtracting 30,000 roubles from the budget, which were paid to the brigade. The intervention of the Society for the Defence of Convicted Managers resulted in the quashing of the court's decision and the abandonment of criminal proceedings. It was acknowledged that G. had acted in the best interests of his enterprise and that the work had been carried out properly.[93]

Within the space of a few years, the organisation took on 700 cases and helped to secure the release of almost 350 convicted businessmen. It was finally accepted as a legitimate intermediary by the Interior Ministry, the Prosecutor's Office and judicial services.

The defence of the collective interests of convicted businessmen entailed the construction of a network that encompassed everyone working towards similar ends. The public and political leaders also had to be sensitised to the issue. The Society was openly in favour of repealing certain articles of the Criminal Code which "ran counter to economic reforms",[94] including those relating to private enterprise activity, commercial intermediation, speculation,[95] theft of socialist property, corruption[96] and *pripiski*. Its members were in no doubt as to the hostility these proposals might arouse: "as soon as this idea

---

[90] The society was founded in May 1990 and registered by the October district executive committee in Moscow in October 1990, thus acquiring the status of an autonomous entity.

[91] This bulletin appeared between 1990 and 1993.

[92] *Golos Osuzhdyonnykh Khozyaistvennikov*, no. 1, November 1990, p. 19.

[93] *Golos Osuzhdyonnykh Khozyaistvennikov*, no. 2, December 1990, p. 50.

[94] *Golos Osuzhdyonnykh Khozyaistvennikov*, no. 1, November 1990, pp. 33–4.

[95] "The current view of speculation dates from wartime communism." *Ibid.*, p. 34.

[96] "Who amongst us has not slipped a surgeon a banknote so that his son can have an operation in the right place?" *Ibid.*, p. 34.

appears in the press, they will treat us as accomplices of the mafia and corrupt police officers."[97]

Once these arguments had appeared in the press,[98] they began to attract the attention of the nascent business community. Sokirko began receiving support from the early entrepreneurs' associations. The Society's first grants came from foreign foundations such as the Cultural Initiative, founded by Georges Soros, and from Russian associations,[99] including the USSR Association of Business Leaders,[100] headed since 1990 by Mark Masarskii. A philosopher by training and a former journalist, Masarskii had begun working for Pechora, a road-building cooperative run by Vadim Tumanov,[101] in 1982. In 1987, he created his own cooperative in the Novgorod region,[102] before developing interests in property construction, the banking sector and mineral extraction. Masarskii, a favourite with the media, was keen to nurture an intellectual image of the business world that promoted a capitalist ethos based on hard work, honesty and humility.[103] Armed with a reputation as one of the

[97] *Ibid.*, p. 34.

[98] Accounts of the meeting were published in *Izvestiya*, 19 May 1990 and *Literaturnaya Gazeta*, 27 June 1990.

[99] In 1990, the Cultural Initiative Fund donated 12,000 roubles, a computer, a printer and a fax machine. The USSR Association of Business Leaders contributed 20,000 roubles. The Society's accounts were published in *Golos Zashchity Osuzhdyonnnykh Khozyaistvennikov*, no. 1, November 1990.

[100] Initially created under the aegis of the Central Committee of Komsomols, this association was led from 1989 to 1990 by G. Popov, at that time president of the Moscow Municipal Soviet. Mark Masarskii directed it from 1990 to 1992. It trained managers for the coming market economy and had some political influence thanks to members who also served as deputies. It openly supported Boris Yeltsin in the August 1991 putsch. A year later it criticised Gaidar's policy, expressing concern over the consequences of a predatory and criminal capitalism for Russian society. V. Sirotkin, 1994, pp. 114–22.

[101] "In Pechora, I felt like a city-dweller who had fallen in with Cossacks! I was surrounded by people who did not tremble at the words 'regional committee' and 'central committee'; who did not hide their opinions; who were confident and independent." Interview with Mark Masarskii in *Kommercheskii Vestnik*, no. 3–4, 1994, p. 2.

[102] Cf. *Izvestiya*, 16 February 1988; *Sovetskaya Rossiya*, 11 March 1988, 13 May 1988, 6 September 1988, 6 December 1988.

[103] Masarskii readily recalls his early days in the cooperative sector: "I kept 150 of the people I had already worked with at Tumanov's, the ones who lasted longest. With these people, we started from nothing. I lived in my mother's house, I ate what grew in my garden, I received no salary. We tightened our belts to the last notch. Why?

richest men in Russia,[104] he took a critical view of the 1992 reforms[105] but contributed financially to Boris Yeltsin's re-election campaign in 1996.[106]

At the beginning of the 1990s, many leading businessmen supported Sokirko's campaigns, either openly or through the intermediary of recently formed associations, in the hope of extending economic freedoms and reducing government intervention in their activities. They believed that denouncing Soviet repression of rational economic behaviour would strike a chord with the public and strengthen the legitimacy of a programme of radical reforms. The Society for the Defence of Convicted Businessmen came to embody the hopes of the former dissidents campaigning for individual rights and freedoms, as well as the aspirations of ardent supporters of neo-liberal economic reforms: "Only the union of human rights campaigners and businessmen can guarantee the progress of economic freedoms and the emancipation of the individual, liberated at last from the yoke of socialism."[107]

The coalition of interests was further strengthened in 1992, when Konstantin Borovoi, a prominent businessman and director of the Russian raw materials and commodities exchange, founded the Economic Freedom Party.[108]

Because we were all convinced that work is the father of all wealth." *Kommercheskii Vestnik*, no. 3–4, 1994.

[104] "I don't have many consumer goods. On the other hand, I am rich in production assets: I manage capital that runs into tens of millions. But it's not liquid capital: it's factories, roads, shares in private companies. I drive a Volga, although I have foreign cars." Interview with Mark Masarskii in *Kommercheskii Vestnik*, no. 3–4, 1994, p. 4.

[105] See M. Masarskii, "Gde sidit pravitel'stvo reformatorov? V lokomotive ili v pritsepnom vagone?" (Where does the reforming government sit? In the locomotive or the carriage?). *Nezavisimaya Gazeta*, 21 November 1992.

[106] When I met him, Masarskii was running a "federal consultation bureau" which acted as an interface between the president of the Russian Federation, the presidential entourage and the business world. In response to an interview question about corruption, he pointed to one of the many telephones, a *vertushka*, a direct line to the presidential office: "If an official causes me a problem, I call his minister. If a minister causes me problems, I call the President. That's why I never have to resort to corruption." Interview conducted in Moscow, 20 June 1996.

[107] Remarks by a former detainee and member of the Society for the Defence of Convicted Businessmen. *Golos Zashchity Osuzhdyonnykh Khozyaistvennikov*, no. 5, March 1992.

[108] The Economic Freedom Party's programme was published in *Golos Zashchity Osuzhdyonnykh Khozyaistvennikov*, no. 7, June 1992, p. 81.

Svyatoslav Fedorov, a doctor and well-known businessman, became the new party's co-president. Its secretary general was none other than Irina Khakamada, a businesswoman destined for a long career as a deputy representing the Union of Right-Wing Forces. The two organisations quickly issued a joint statement setting out the need for an amnesty for convicted businessmen. This was followed by another statement, on prison conditions in Russia, signed by two representatives of the Economic Freedom Party, Konstantin Borovoi and Gennadii Zhavoronkov,[109] and two celebrated human rights campaigners, Elena Bonner and Larisa Bogoraz.[110]

Disillusion soon set in, however, for it became apparent that the goals pursued by the two organisations were almost incompatible. Economic Freedom Party leaders were disappointed by the poor response to the joint effort to raise public awareness of the fate of convicted businessmen, which had been expected to achieve swift and noticeable results. By 1993 their interest had waned: financial contributions to the Society diminished and eventually dried up completely; the presentation of concrete cases of unjust detention also ceased; plans for a joint declaration on the economic freedoms of the individual came to nothing. "The Party cannot restrict itself to assisting convicted businessmen: it must concern itself with society as a whole, but it does not have the means."[111] Moreover, the Society's decision to merge with its partner had proved unpopular with some of its members and sponsors, who accused it of serving Borovoi's political ambitions by handing him the support of former dissidents. One opponent of the merger, the Association of Business Leaders, headed by K. Zatulin, stopped paying its subscription.[112]

Despite these setbacks, the Society for the Defence of Convicted Managers gradually acquired an undeniable solidity thanks to the financial support of entrepreneurs, some of whom it had helped to get out of prison. It also benefited from the contacts it had cultivated in journalistic, legal and political circles. The editorial committee of its new journal, *ZEK*,[113] was a diverse body

---

[109] A journalist on *Moskovskie Novosti*, Gennadii Zhavoronkov was noted for articles promoting cooperatives and businessmen. See in particular his interview with Artiom Tarasov: "Ispoved' sovetskogo milionera" (Confessions of a Soviet Millionaire), *Moskovskie Novosti*, no. 9, 26 February 1989.

[110] *Golos Zashchity Osuzhdyonnykh Khozyaistvennikov*, no. 11, February 1993, p. 321.

[111] *Ibid.*, p. 326.

[112] *Ibid.*

[113] In Russian, *zek* means detainee. In this instance, the initials stand for *Zashchita*

and contained several well-known figures including Sokirko himself, the human rights campaigner Valerii Abramkin, three leading journalists (Valerii Agranovskii, Gennadii Zhavoronkov and Otto Latsis), the respected lawyer Genrikh Padva, a Prosecutor's Office agent (Andrei Pokhmelkin), a celebrated business figure (the surgeon Sviyatoslav Fyodorov), and a lawyer specialising in economic crime (Alexandr M. Yakovlev). Some of these figures held important positions in political life.[114]

Viktor Sokirko likes to think that his campaign played a decisive role in the State Duma's adoption on 23 February 1994 of a resolution "On the Declaration of a Political and Economic Amnesty."[115] The amnesty, linked to the repeal of most of the articles in the Criminal Code covering breaches of the rules of the Soviet economy, meant that the Society for the Defence of Convicted Businessmen had achieved its principal goal by the end of 1994. It subsequently struggled to define new missions. It continued to denounce the suppression of economic freedoms, but by this time other campaigning organisations had entered the field. Once the Soviet businessmen had been released, it campaigned for the establishment of assize courts in the Russian judicial system.[116]

The defence of economic freedoms was not simply a matter of rehabilitating Soviet entrepreneurs; it was also aimed at protecting cooperatives from the law enforcement agencies which attempted to exploit their legal vulnerability. The possibility of legalising illicitly acquired capital, which had proved highly unpopular when first broached, moved in 1990 to the forefront of political debate, where it helped to polarise attitudes to the issues associated with economic crime.

Ekonomicheskikh Svobod i Kommercheskoi Deyatel'nosti (Defence of Economic Freedoms and Commercial Activity).

[114] Svyatoslav Fyodorov was elected to the State Duma in 1993; Andrei Pokhmelkin headed the State Duma Committee for Legislative Reform from 1994 to 1996; Alexandr M. Yakovlev was appointed presidential representative to the State Duma in 1994.

[115] The amnesty covered detainees convicted before 1991 for "violation of the rules of currency transactions" (article 88), "crimes against state property in the form of theft, damage or abuse of office" (article 92), "theft of state property by means of embezzlement" (article 93), "abuse of official power or position" (article 170), "negligence" (article 172), and "crimes committed in the exercise of an official position" (article 175) if there were no aggravating circumstances. *Zashchita Ekonomicheskikh Svobod i Kommercheskoi Deyatel'nosti*, no. 3, 1994, pp. 2–3.

[116] In the second half of the 1990s, the Society, aided by George Soros's Open Society foundation, regularly organised experimental assize courts.

Integrating Illegally Acquired Capital into the Economy—an Acceptable Measure?
This option first appeared in 1990, when Gorbachev and Yeltsin asked the economist S. Shatalin to present an economic programme, *The Transition to the Market*, drafted by a team of economists who would often feature prominently in the promotion of the 1992 reforms.[117] The programme placed ambitious reforms to privatise and liberalise the Soviet economy on the political agenda and was thus a radical document. One section dealt specifically with the underground economy.[118] "Many people mistakenly link the increase in underground economic activity to the transition to the market. The shadow economy is an indispensible compliment to the Soviet economy. The more the state intervenes in the distribution of goods, the more the shadow economy's field of activity expands. The transition to the market is the most effective way to liquidate it."[119]

This argument rejected the dominant interpretation of the "shadow economy" while at the same time espousing the governmental rhetoric that called for its "liquidation." Echoing the Soviet line on crime, it claimed that there was no reason why the shadow economy should survive in a market economy. But the programme's authors warned that distinctions should be made between practices relating to the "criminal economy", the "fictitious economy", the "informal economy" and the "non-legalised second economy."[120] This semantic distinction served two purposes: it stressed the rationality and legitimacy of most of the economic behaviour under consideration, and also justified giving incentives to those in possession of illicitly acquired capital to invest it in the legal economy: "The scale of the underground economy[121] assumes a particular

---

[117] *Perekhod k rynku. Kontseptsiya i programma* (The Transition to the Market: Conception and Programme). Moscow, Arkhangel'skoe, 1990, two volumes.

[118] *Ibid.*, pp. 135–40. This chapter was inspired largely by the work of Golovin and Shokhin (S. Golovin and A. Shokhin, 1990, pp. 51–57; A. Shokhin, 1989. p. 69).

[119] *Ibid.*, p. 135.

[120] According to the authors, the criminal economy comprised economic offences, economic transactions involving illicit goods and services, and crimes against individual property. The fictitious economy was essentially a matter of accounting fraud. The informal economy comprised all economic exchanges based on personal relations and replacing the state regulations designed to govern such exchanges. Finally, the non-legalised second economy comprised all cooperative and individual activity forbidden by law or not officially registered. The Programme's authors attached great importance to the distinction between the criminal economy and the other three forms. *Ibid.*, p. 136.

[121] The Programme's authors calculated that revenue from the shadow economy represented 20 per cent of GNP. *Ibid.*, p. 138.

importance, for the logic of the transition to the market anticipates using underground capital in order to serve the interests of the country's entire population. This is a major resource for guaranteeing the reform's success."[122]

The Shatalin group argued that introducing market mechanisms would enable 90 per cent of "underground" capital to be integrated into the official economy.[123] This belief strengthened the legitimacy of the privatisation measures adopted in the early 1990s. Although they were intended to clarify the rules of economic activity, they took little account of the origin of the capital invested in property transfers, for ultimately the entire population would benefit from the process.[124]

The idea that "underground" capital could be integrated into the official economy became one of the leitmotifs of Russian political debate during the 1990s. It proceeded from an argument that distinguished practices according to the degree of legitimacy attached to them. According to V. Ispravnikov,[125] the inefficiency of the economy's regulatory framework obstructed the development of a "normal" market economy and forced rational economic actors to conceal their activities. This uncomfortable situation of legal vulnerability led to calls for the "legalisation of illicitly acquired income, i.e. the modification of existing laws and norms",[126] in order to counter capital flight and money laundering. Legalisation was presented as a relatively simple way to attract the investment needed to emerge from the crisis; it offered reliable opportunities to deposit dormant capital in Russia or elsewhere. Legalisation of the "underground" economy provided a domestic response to national economic concerns.[127]

---

[122] *Ibid.*, p. 136.

[123] *Ibid.*, p. 139. For a critique of the impact of this proposal, see V.V. Kolesnikov, 1994, p. 106.

[124] See also O.V. Osipenko, 1991, pp. 78–88 (chapter entitled "Individual Labour Will Evict the Shadow Economy").

[125] V.O. Ispravnikov, an economics professor, was elected as an RSFSR deputy in 1990 and served as deputy president of the Supreme Soviet of the Russian Federation from 1991 to 1993. He was a major influence on the Russian Federation Law "On property" (1990). He subsequently headed a pressure group concerned with the direction of Russian economic policy—the Russian Independent Economic Society (*Vol'noe Ekonomicheskoe Obshchestvo Rossii*). For his position on the shadow economy, see "Tenevoi kapital: konfiskovat' ili aministirovat'?" (Shadow Capital: Amnesty or Confiscation?). *Ekonomika i Zhizn'*, no. 24, June 1996, p. 29.

[126] V.O. Ispravnikov, 1996, p. 11.

[127] *Ibid.*, p. 11. To support his argument, Ispravnikov took the example of the *chelnoki*,

The controversy this position aroused throughout the 1990s is hardly surprising. In Russia, there was a widespread belief that attempts to legalise the shadow economy amounted to collusion between liberal reformers and criminals, and indeed the manipulation of the former by the latter. Hostility to the business world certainly contributed to this view, but in addition advocates of legalisation were unable to present a coherent argument. The idea they were defending was based on a fundamentally subjective and arbitrary view of economic virtue. They had their own way of distinguishing between delinquents and entrepreneurs who were forced to contravene the law in order to work in decent conditions. Everyone knew that the law was being broken, but some regretted it more than others! It was therefore appropriate to establish a clear legal distinction between the capital held by criminals and that of entrepreneurs.[128] Given the difficulty of applying this distinction, it amounted to little more than a call to redefine the way in which the differential treatment of illegalities was conducted in post-Soviet Russia: certain actors should be treated more leniently, while all "criminals" and "delinquents" should continue to be punished.

Advocates of an amnesty for the underground economy accepted that assessing the origin of capital in accordance with the identity of its holder would prove difficult, but argued that national interests were more important than moral scruples about the origin. Once a moratorium on repressive action had been declared, a new regulatory framework for economic activity could be established. Some leading political figures welcomed the idea. Eduard Rossel, governor of the Sverdlovsk region, publicly advocated an amnesty for illicitly acquired capital, which could then be invested in the manufacturing sector. Rossel argued that the measure would assist the recovery of the industrial sector and improve regional living standards, as well as offering holders of illicit capital a chance to earn respectability.[129] This approach enabled him to justify

---

who travel between Russia and countries like China, Turkey and Finland in order to buy goods and resell them in the markets. He claimed that the *chelnoki* were responsible for between 20 per cent and 25 per cent of imports. While they helped to "create employment in the countries where they buy their goods", these entrepreneurs could represent "a significant internal source of investment in Russia's small- and medium-size businesses."

[128] *Kommersant'*, 17 April 1994.

[129] Appearance on NTV, 6 May 1997. For Rossel's position on economic crime, see also T. Frisby, 1998, p. 46. At the beginning of the 2000s the Russian government, noting the decision taken by Kazakhstan, considered urging Russian citizens to repatriate capital placed abroad, but asking no questions as to its origin.

the understanding between his administration and the criminal world. "If I learned that so and so was a mafioso, I would invite him to discuss the matter and suggest that he worked legally."[130] Rossel took the view that in Russia, "economic crime" reflected phenomena that would always arise in a context of primitive accumulation of capital. He used the term "mafia" only when referring to the security services or the country's leaders.[131] His opponents were quick to argue that the economic reforms already in place had led to the *de facto* legalisation of numerous "underground" practices, but had not resulted in a reduction in the number of economic crimes recorded.[132]

Concluding Remarks

What is crime—an always relative social phenomenon—in a suddenly evolving society? *Glasnost*, by definition, fostered a debate on the definition of criminality. First, people were more and more contesting the relevance of Soviet crime definitions, suggesting that illegal economic practices should not always be considered as offences and calling for a shift in the differential treatment of economic illegalities. Secondly, facing a deep economic crisis, people feared crime more and more. Considering that they had lived safer lives before *perestroika*, they started to develop resentment towards entrepreneurs and *nouveaux riches*. The new expression "organised crime", vague by definition, seemed at that time to crystallise this resentment. Gangsters soon became new figures of delinquency, replacing "parasites" and "recidivists."

There was a huge demand in the media for crime expertise. Law enforcement officials, organised crime groups' members, lawyers and victims started to voice their opinion on this issue. Scholars also answered this demand, carrying out polls on the fear of crime or gathering knowledge on organised crime or underground economy. Their analyses fed political discourse, which became soon polarised. The debates reflected a dilemma between on the one hand the desire to develop economic initiatives and, on the other hand, the desire to

---

[130] Remarks by Eduard Rossel reported in *Nezavisimaya Gazeta*, 20 April 1999.

[131] *Ibid.*

[132] "The idea of a moratorium on the fight against the shadow economy has become a political slogan. The ineffectiveness of measures to integrate shadow economy actors into the legal business world clearly indicates that legalisation does not reduce the factors underlying the existence of these practices, even in a context marked by the equality of all forms of property and the encouragement and support provided for businesses." B.S. Bolotskii, 1996, p. 41.

crack down on economic crime and to control the emerging private sector in the name of social justice. Entrepreneurs started to defend their interests by themselves, seeking to benefit from a better image among the population. They later started to call for policy incentives in order to integrate illegally acquired capital into the official economy, but they have never obtained any result in this field. They had little support from human rights activists, who did not especially focus on the promotion of economic freedom, except from the Society for Defence of Convicted Managers. In this case, the existence of a temporary alliance between entrepreneurs and human rights activists showed the difficulties for these two groups to find common interests and join forces against state power. Their split also announced that these misunderstandings would last a long time during post-Soviet Russian history. *Glasnost* triggered a profusion of competing claims linked to the imposition of a legitimate definition of crime. These were also apparent in the debates on penal policy from 1986 onwards.

8

REDEFINING PENAL POLICY

Initially, the measures adopted to combat economic crime represented a continuation of traditional Soviet campaigns, as with the offensive against "unearned income" launched in 1986. However, the introduction several months later of the law on individual labour activity complicated its implementation. This contradiction represented the first explicit manifestation of the fundamental tension between economic and penal policy since the mid-1980s.

The growth of cooperatives from 1987 onwards transformed the struggle against economic crime. Economic initiatives started to develop at a pace that exceeded the penal policy reform agenda. Soviet authorities tried to reverse the trend by taking measures to stem the expansion of the cooperatives and to control their activity, but it was too late as entrepreneurs had already found new legal opportunities to develop their business. Soviet leaders also attempted to revive the traditional conception of penal policy by creating comprehensive new targets, such as organised crime or "economic sabotage", but these attempts fizzled out. The fight against economic crime would in future be of secondary importance. In spite of announcements, few measures were adopted to control crime during the privatisation process, and decisions made in this domain had little impact. The discrepancy between economic practices and legal rules was increasingly blatant. The 1960 RSFSR Criminal Code was at that time permanently subjected to suppression, modification or addition of articles, but it would be replaced as a whole only in 1996.

The Campaign Against Unearned Income [1]

Mikhail Gorbachev's Political Report to the 27th Congress of the CPSU set out his main economic goals—"acceleration", "restructuring", "autonomy of accounting in Soviet firms", "activating the human factor", etc.—and also contained several references to the problem of unearned income. Resorting to the customary rhetoric, the report denounced the vast range of illicit practices employed by the "*nesuni*, who pilfer anything they can lay their hands on in the workplace", the "corrupt", the "profiteers of all kinds who exploit their position for personal gain", "parasites" and "anybody who follows a course alien to our hard-working society."[2] The campaign against unearned income was portrayed as a response to the population's growing resentment at social injustice and the frustration caused by shortages of consumer goods.[3] According to Gorbachev, the emergence of groups of individuals "with property owners' motivation and a stated contempt for the public good" was due to the "weakening of control."[4]

The concept of "unearned income" stood at the intersection of three principles of the Soviet economy which theoretically guaranteed economic well-being and social justice: the integrity of socialist property, collective ownership of the means of production, and an income determined by the amount of labour accomplished. The denunciation of illicit income was part of an exercise to enhance the government's legitimacy, based on its perception of citizens' expectations and their attachment to common values. It was indeed a question of belief: exploited for its symbolic value, the term "unearned income" encompassed all forms of economic illegality. Within this new category, the traditional figures of economic delinquency—profiteers and parasites[5]—rubbed shoulders with the ordinary Soviet citizen, the *nesun* who pilfered indiscriminately from his workplace. According to this view, the population condemned all forms of economic illegality regardless of the offender's character, the method of enrichment, the frequency of a criminal practice or the amount of organisation it required. Gorbachev thus appeared to renounce one of the main political resources mobilised by his predecessors: the strategic opposition between illegalities and economic delinquency.

---

[1] In Russian, *netrudovyi dokhod* signifies "an income not derived from labour."

[2] M.S. Gorbachev, 1986, p. 89.

[3] *Ibid.*, p. 85.

[4] *Ibid.*, p. 85.

[5] The third figure of delinquency—alcoholics—was managed apart, during the notorious campaign against alcoholism that began in 1985.

However, Gorbachev did distinguish between those possessing unearned income and those in receipt of "extra income" derived from an individual labour activity that satisfied the demand for goods and services.[6] The almost simultaneous crackdown on unearned income and promotion of individual labour activity resulted from a new analysis of economic illegality. Although crimes of this nature could not be excused, they should be interpreted in the light of the difficulties encountered in meeting the needs of the population. Therefore, it was considered appropriate to increase supply by encouraging the involvement of individuals, while at the same time punishing anyone who took advantage of shortages to acquire wealth by illicit means.[7] This logic explains why both measures were initially presented as the two sides of a single project. But the campaign against unearned income, boosted by the repeated references to it in the Political Report, was launched six months before the adoption of the law on individual labour activity. Moreover, it was the first time since the 1966 anti–hooliganism offensive that a campaign had been backed by three official pronouncements: a resolution of the CPSU Central Committee, a resolution of the USSR Council of Ministers and a decree issued by the Presidium of the USSR Supreme Soviet.[8]

All citizens were exhorted to "express contempt" for those in receipt of unearned income and combat the "indifference" to them.[9] Academics and journalists were enlisted; artists were urged to create "films, shows and other artistic works" which promoted "respect for hard work and honesty, as well as an uncompromising attitude towards parasitism and other forms of behaviour which are antithetical to communist morality."[10] One of the aims was to improve social control; the public indignation aroused by these practices would be channelled into much closer surveillance of activity in enterprises, streets and buildings. Faced with the unscrupulous exploitation of shortages by "speculators", "profiteers" (*rvachy*) and "egoists", the population would unite

---

[6] *Ibid.*, 1986, p. 89.

[7] S. Shatalin, 1986, p. 60. See also T. Zaslavskaya, 1986, pp. 61–73.

[8] The three texts were published in *Pravda*, 28 May 1986. The Central Committee and the Council of Ministers resolutions appear in slightly abridged form in *Spravochnik partiinogo rabotnika. Vypusk 27. 1987* (Party Militant Handbook, 27th. edn., 1987), Moscow, Politizdat, 1987, pp. 522–9. The decree of the Presidium of the USSR Supreme Soviet was published in *Vedomosti Verkhovnogo Soveta S.S.S.R.*, no. 22 (2356), 28 May 1986, pp. 369–73.

[9] M.S. Gorbachev, 1986, p. 89.

[10] *Ibid.*

to defend the socialist principle of redistribution in accordance with the amount of labour provided.[11]

The campaign's implementation was supported by the introduction of new criminal offences—"illegal use of transport, machines and mechanisms" (art. 94[1]), "violation of the regulations on the domestic use of energy and gas" (art. 94[2]), "refusal to provide a declaration of income" (art. 162[1])[12]—and offences covered by the Administrative Code: "refusal to compensate an enterprise or organisation following the commission of an offence" (art. 49[1]), "violation of the regulations on the domestic use of energy and gas" (art. 95[1]), "violation of the regulations on the acquisition of building materials" (art. 150[1]), "refusal to provide a declaration of income" (art. 156[1]), etc.[13] In keeping with a trend established in the late 1970s, most of the sanctions provided for took the form of increasingly heavy fines. In addition, a set of measures was designed to reinforce prevention and eradicate the causes of the targeted practices. This involved the recruitment of people with responsibilities for goods and materials, the surveillance of premises, assets and materials, accounting regulations and the monitoring of expenditure. This last point was something of a novelty: citizens were now obliged to declare any cash transaction that exceeded a set value, and also had to justify the origin of the money.[14] As we shall see, this ambiguous government programme proved extremely difficult to interpret and apply at local level.

The Framework of the Cooperative Sector

Russian leaders encouraged the development of a cooperative sector before a legal framework had been drafted to deal with the forms of criminality that might emerge from it, the only exception being the article that barred people with convictions for economic offences from occupying certain positions. Moreover, the law of May 1988 did not clarify how its application should be monitored. Cooperatives were naturally expected to conform to accounting regulations but did not face severe penalties if they failed to do so, for the powers of the competent authority, the Finance Ministry's control and revision department,[15] had not been extended.

---

[11] *Ibid.*
[12] *Vedomosti Verkhovnogo Soveta R.S.F.S.R.*, no. 23, 5 June 1986. Article 638.
[13] *Ibid.*
[14] *Ibid.*
[15] *Kontrol'no-Revizionnoe Upravlenie Ministerstva Finansov* (KRU MinFina).

Interior Ministry and Prosecutor's Office services were also expected to take note of internal directives that recommended a hands-off approach to the development of cooperatives: entrepreneurs were to be encouraged to display initiative, creativity and dynamism. As "everything which was not prohibited was allowed", entrepreneurs were invited to exploit loopholes in the legislation and devise strategies for circumventing it. In the early days, moreover, the authorities attempted to protect the sector against racketeering[16] by extending the article on the extortion of state and social assets (art. 95) to cooperative property.[17] Fines for this offence were replaced by prison terms and corrective labour. The fact that the crime had been committed by an "organised group" rather than "a group of people on the basis of a prior understanding" would in future constitute an aggravating circumstance and attract a mandatory prison sentence. However, this protective attitude was swiftly replaced by a more repressive approach.

The first resolution to restrict the scope of the sector was issued on 29 December 1988. Cooperatives were henceforth barred from publishing or distributing cultural, scientific and medical works. These restrictions affected the rapidly expanding sector which screened imported videocassettes and charged an admission fee. Certain other activities were henceforth exclusively reserved for cooperatives that had been created within an enterprise or any other organisation. Enterprises created from scratch could no longer organise concerts, dances or variety shows, or become involved in the publishing, printing and distribution of books, records and cassettes. Cooperatives which contravened the new legislation were given one month to restructure their activities.[18]

The sector sustained further blows in the autumn of 1989, with the publication of three pieces of legislation. The first tightened the fiscal regulations

---

[16] In late 1988, newspapers began advising cooperative members who had been victims of racketeering. One *Trud* reader commented: "Newspapers publish alarming articles about racketeering. The mafia extorts money from cooperative members, and the law does nothing for them. How long do we have to wait before a new article penalising these practices is added to the Criminal Code?" *Trud*, 30 November 1988.

[17] Decree of the Presidium of the RSFSR Supreme Soviet, 12 January 1989: "On the Introduction of Modifications and Additions in the RSFSR Criminal Code." *Vedomosti Verkhovnogo Soveta R.S.F.S.R.*, no. 3, 1989. Article 50.

[18] USSR Council of Ministers resolution, 29 December 1988: "On the Regulation of Certain Aspects of Cooperative Activity in Conformity with the Law on Cooperation in the USSR." *Spravochnik partiinogo rabotnika, vypusk dvadtsat' devyatyi, 1989.* Moscow, Izdatel'stvo politicheskoi literatury, 1989, p. 475.

governing cooperatives and their well-paid employees.[19] The second was designed to improve the way they set the prices of their products. Local Soviets were authorised to restrict the selling price of consumer goods (whether made in Russia or imported) and services provided by cooperatives.[20] From now on, anyone running a business exclusively based on the purchase and resale at a higher price of products and goods in the state commercial sector was forbidden to do so, and was given six weeks to restructure the business or go into liquidation. Similarly, state-owned businesses lost the right to sell their stock to cooperatives. Financial control bodies, the police and the Prosecutor's Office were ordered to take immediate steps "to ensure that cooperatives obeyed the law and to protect consumer rights."[21] In June 1990, a third law was introduced to regulate the creation of subsidiary companies, entities that had previously escaped the obligation to declare their income. The government also granted itself new powers to restrict the registration of cooperatives and force them to cease their activities.[22]

Despite these restrictions, more than 245,000 cooperatives were registered by the beginning of 1991, as opposed to 193,000 in 1990; over six million people (up from nearly five million in 1990) were employed in the sector. Repressive measures did not prevent entrepreneurs from developing their own rules of activity, even if that meant transforming their establishments into "small-scale businesses", "leasehold" businesses and, eventually, joint-stock companies. In the final analysis, the measure to repress the cooperative movement introduced between 1988 and 1990 did not weaken entrepreneurs, but rather nurtured their ability to defend their interests.

---

[19] USSR Supreme Soviet resolution, 26 September 1989: "On Measures Concerning the Regulation on Augmentation of Expenditure on Remuneration by Production and Services Cooperatives, Tenants' Organisations and Enterprises of Other Social Organisations." *Vedomosti S'ezda...*, no. 16, 27 September 1989. Article 316. The tax position of cooperatives had already been reviewed in February 1989, in a Presidium of the USSR Supreme Soviet resolution (23 February 1989) "On the Taxation of Cooperative Revenues." For an analysis of fiscal legislation, see A. Jones and W. Moskoff, 1991, pp. 70–7.

[20] "USSR Supreme Soviet resolution, 17 October 1989: "On the regulation of the Commercial Activity of Cooperatives and the Prices of the Goods sold by Cooperatives to the Population and Organisations." *Vedomosti S'ezda...*, no. 19, 18 October 1989. Article 353.

[21] *Ibid.*

[22] USSR Law, 6 June 1990, "On the introduction of modifications and additions to the USSR law 'On Cooperation in the USSR.'" *Vedomosti S'ezda...*, no. 26, 27 June 1990. Article 489.

The Search for New Targets

From 1988 onwards, the fight against economic crime was marked by ambivalence: campaigns were launched, but the authorities were reluctant to hamper the growth of the private sector. Government measures reflected the desire to devise categories that could cope with the changing nature of criminal behaviour.

In April 1988, the CPSU Central Committee issued a resolution designed to reinforce respect for legality in the context of economic reform. The Committee pointed to the successes achieved in combating crime between 1985 and 1987, which owed much to implementation of the "dry law" and the offensive against unearned income, and called for a mobilisation against economic crime, with an emphasis on property crime. The April 1988 resolution denounced the ineffectiveness of purely repressive methods and called for a "detailed study" in order to stimulate innovative responses and improve coordination between the various actors involved in fighting crime. This discourse echoed the positions adopted by the "laboratory for scientific research into the economic and legal problems relating to the protection of socialist property", created within the Interior Ministry in the late 1970s. Moreover, the context was favourable for denunciation of the severity of the Soviet penal regime. *Glasnost* had provoked furious debates on the issue, and the amnesty of 18 June 1987, declared to commemorate the seventieth anniversary of the October Revolution, seemed to fulfil the aspiration to "humanise penal policy." However, the amnesty aroused considerable disquiet among law enforcement officials, political leaders in regions with high concentrations of prisons, and a certain segment of the population.[23] The CPSU Central Committee believed a more humane penal policy would actually be accompanied by greater social control: "the reduction in the number of detainees increases the responsibility of workers' collectives and state and social bodies with regard to crime prevention and the re-education of offenders."[24] As we shall see, the resolution had little impact at local level, although regional leaders seized the opportunity to decry the shortcomings of traditional penal policy, with its vague objectives

[23] See, for example, the indignation expressed by the readers of *Ogonyok*, 4 September 1987.

[24] CPSU Central Committee resolution, 2 April 1988: "On the State of the Campaign against Crime in the Country and Supplementary Measures to Prevent Offences." *Spravochnik partiinogo rabotnika, vypusk dvadtsat' devyatyi, 1989.* Moscow, Izdatel'stvo Politicheskoi Literatury, 1989, p. 490.

and texts couched in general terms. In such a context, the creation of new categories of criminal offences ("organised crime", "economic sabotage") in order to meet the challenges arising from *perestroika* swiftly became a priority.

The series of orders on "organised crime" reflected official "anxiety" over its "sudden increase"[25] and the determination to "rise to the challenge" that this presented to "Soviet society."[26] This new generic term enabled the authorities to recycle tried and tested arguments in an attempt to create a new stereotype, an acknowledged internal enemy that would arouse universal indignation and prompt law enforcement agencies to mobilise and reorganise their approach:

Criminals are banding together in organised groups; their technical equipment and weaponry are becoming increasingly sophisticated, as is their collusion with corrupt public officials ... Police forces and judicial bodies are ill-prepared and cannot combat organised crime effectively; the regulatory and material resources at their disposal do not correspond to the demands of the current situation.[27]

As elsewhere, the evocation of "organised crime" was more about responding to the need to stress the seriousness of a threat than clarifying its nature. Inevitably, insoluble conflicts arose over its definition—what degree of structure or number of participants indicated a criminal "organisation"? The category also highlighted the extent to which illicit trafficking relied on networks of corruption—the combination of various types of offence and various professional bodies in the quest for mutual gain. The need for corrupt relations with bureaucrats, whose decisions influenced the flow of commodities and capital, corresponded to the eagerness of criminals to profit from the opportunities afforded by economic reform and possibly exploit them at international level. Whereas instances of corruption had previously been associated with economic crime, by the late 1980s they tended to be associated with organised crime. The presidential decree of 4 February 1991, which authorised the creation of a "main directorate for combating the most dangerous crimes, organised crime, corruption and drug trafficking" within the Interior Ministry, signalled this change of approach.[28]

---

[25] USSR Supreme Soviet resolution, 4 August 1989: "On the Decisive Reinforcement of the Campaign against Crime." *Vedomosti S'ezda...*, no. 9, 9 August 1989. Article 222.

[26] USSR Congress of People's Deputies resolution, 23 December 1989: "On the Reinforcement of the Campaign against Organised Crime." *Vedomosti S'ezda...*, no. 29, 27 December 1989. Article 576.

[27] *Ibid.*

[28] Decree of the President of the USSR, 4 February 1991: "On Measures to Reinforce

Economic crime and organised crime were indeed, by definition, closely linked.[29] But while the former constituted a body of offences, organised crime as a new form of delinquency was above all defined by the identity of the authors of certain types of offence.[30] It seems that in the 1990s, Russian researchers gradually reached agreement on some of the characteristics of "organised crime." The term tended to denote a group with a hierarchical structure, whose members had long-term interests and regularly engaged in illegal economic activities, resorted to violence and established corrupt relations with officials.[31] This definition was of little practical use in operational terms, and generated numerous conflicts over its interpretation: in the final analysis, the police on the streets were responsible for deciding which of the cases they dealt with fell into the category of "organised crime." Unsurprisingly, police forces were therefore subjected to a constant barrage of criticism from the General Prosecutor's Office during the 1990s, particularly over their tendency to apply the organised crime label to gangs composed mainly of three or four adolescents and young adults which committed occasional theft. This practice was justified on the grounds that the members had been together for some time and had formed a hierarchy.

In 1991, the authorities once again resorted to a category that had no proper legal definition in order to enhance the effectiveness of law enforcement agencies. On this occasion, a presidential decree targeted "economic sabotage" and called for a guaranteed supply of food and standard consumer goods to meet the needs of the population. This text compared entrepreneurs to criminals and considerably reinforced the powers of Interior Ministry and state security services. The latter were authorised to enter an enterprise at any time, even in the absence of its owners, in order to conduct checks and searches. Offices and other premises containing money, valuables and documents could be sealed and, when this was required, "subjected to other measures in order to guarantee their security."[32]

The decree revived a definition that had formed part of the Criminal Code established under Stalin, and thus outraged many lawyers. Its opponents

the Campaign Against the Most Dangerous Crimes and Their Organised Forms." *Izvestiya*, 5 February 1991.

[29] N. Queloz, 1999, pp. 21–39.

[30] *Organizovannaya prestupnost'*, 1989, p. 14.

[31] A. Gurov, 1995, pp. 280–3; Ya. Gilinskii, 1996, p. 4.

[32] Decree of the President of the USSR, 26 January 1991: "On Measures to Ensure the Achievement of the Campaign Against Economic Sabotage and Other Offences in the Economic Sphere." *Vedomosti S'ezda...*, no. 5, 30 January 1991. Article 155.

argued that the classification of economic sabotage as a crime was unconstitutional, for the definition of offences was the sole preserve of criminal legislation. They also feared that law enforcement bodies would use the decree in an arbitrary manner.[33] In fact, it led to "brutal searches" of cooperatives run by some of the movement's key figures, the entrepreneurs who had openly criticised Mikhail Gorbachev.[34] However, the victims were able to defend their interests with the aid of businessmen's associations, which had by this time acquired a certain amount of experience. One cooperative owner, Artiom Tarasov, boasted that it had taken only two days to rally several hundred opponents of the decree,[35] which was finally repealed in October 1991.[36]

The offensive against economic sabotage, launched several months before the August 1991 putsch, illustrated the conservative turn taken by Gorbachev and Soviet leaders in the late 1990s[37] when confronted with the more radical economic reform agenda pushed by Russian political elites. The heavy-handed policing of economic reforms reflected in the implementation of the campaign against "economic sabotage" actually gave an argument to admit the idea of distancing law enforcement agencies from the privatisation process.

Penal Policy During the Privatisation Process

Soviet criminal legislation remained in force until 1997. Pending its renewal, changes were implemented in poorly coordinated stages. The transformation of the nature of economic crime gave rise to the simultaneous development of several procedures: criminalisation, decriminalisation, depenalisation, redefinition of offences and penalties.

---

[33] See, for example, the round table composed of lawyers and police and KGB representatives in *Soyuz*, no. 8, February 1991. See also the monitoring of the decree's application and press treatment of the topic in "Luchshie epizody bor'by s ekonomicheskim sabotazhem" (The Finest Episodes in the Campaign against Economic Sabotage). *Golos Zashchity Osuzhdyonnykh Khozyaistvennikov*, no. 3, April 1991.

[34] B. Quinton, 1991, p. 42.

[35] A. Berelowitch and M. Wieworka, 1996, pp. 168–9.

[36] Decree of the President of the USSR, 21 October 1991, "On the Repeal of the Presidential Decree of 26 January 1991 'On Measures to Ensure the Achievement of the Campaign against Economic Sabotage and Other Offences in the Economic Sphere'", *Vedomosti S'ezda...*, no. 44, 30 October 1991. Article 1224.

[37] I. Klyamkin, 1990, pp. 4–7.

The Chaos of Criminal Legislation. The transformation of economic crime triggered by the reforms of the early 1990s began with several decriminalisation procedures that have been described as "the retreat of the penal system" and "the absence of answers in terms of substitution."[38] These procedures principally affected private business activity (December 1991)[39] and *pripiski* (April 1993).[40] The more numerous depenalisation measures—"the replacement of a penalty with an extra-penal sanction"[41]—applied to most breaches of the rules of economic activity. After considerable procrastination[42] the first wave, in February 1991, involved speculation and violations of trade regulations.[43] In future, such offences would attract administrative sanctions.[44] However, this decision was partially reversed following a period of confusion, and violations of trade regulations reappeared in the Criminal Code on 1 July 1993 (article 156[5]). In April 1993, some of the charges created during the campaign against unearned income seven years earlier—articles 94[1], 94[2] and 156[1]—were depenalised[45] and redefined in the Code of Administrative Offences.[46]

In a context of rising prices, economic change required not only the redefinition of offences, but also the creation of new benchmarks to assess the damage caused by criminal behaviour. This was especially necessary in relation to theft of socialist property, where "aggravating" and "particularly aggravating" circumstances were assessed according to the amount of damage caused. Both factors were adapted so that the former applied if the sum of the assets stolen was more than fifty times higher than the minimum monthly remuneration

---

[38] M. Delmas-Marty, 1992, p. 319.

[39] *Vedomosti S'ezda...*, no. 52, 1991, article 1867.

[40] *Vedomosti S'ezda...*, no. 22, 1993, article 789.

[41] M. van de Kerchove, 1989, pp. 17–18.

[42] Two months before their depenalisation in February 1991, the penalties for speculation and violations of trade regulations had been reinforced by a USSR law designed to establish order in the "consumer market." See *Izvestiya*, 3 November 1990.

[43] *Vedomosti S'ezda...*, no. 9, 1991, article 204.

[44] With regard to violation of the rules of commerce, we should also note the existence in the Code of Administrative Offences 149 (violation of the rules of commerce in *kolkhoz* markets). Administrative sanctions also targeted street hawkers (article 150: *torgovlya s ruk v neustanovlennykh mestakh*).

[45] *Vedomosti S'ezda...*, no. 22, 1993, article 789.

[46] Article 94[1] of the Criminal Code was replaced by several articles in the Code of Administrative Offences, which devoted an entire chapter to "offences in the sphere of transport, traffic and communications" (Chapter 10).

set out in labour legislation; the latter applied if it was one hundred times higher.[47] In the case of "petty" property theft, the sum was fixed at the minimum monthly remuneration.[48]

The economic background also gave rise to new methods for calculating fines. Fines, along with imprisonment, corrective labour and complementary penalties, had been one of the main punishments for economic offences since the late 1970s.[49] Until the early 1990s, amounts were set out in the Criminal Code. In December 1991, the article concerning "petty theft of state or social property" was modified and the maximum fine set at five times the amount stolen. But in 1992, penal and administrative sanctions were altered and a new scale introduced: multiples of the minimum monthly remuneration. This measure affected most of the articles relating to the theft of socialist property and breaches of the rules of economic activity.[50]

Some definitions of offences were adapted to changes in the economic system. In July 1993, "buyer and seller fraud" was replaced by "consumer fraud";[51] the "production of poor, sub-standard or unfinished goods" was renamed "production or sale of goods, or provision of services that fail to meet safety standards." In the Code of Administrative Offences, "violation of commercial law by employees in the commercial sector and public catering establishments" was altered to the more general "violation of commercial law."[52]

On 1 July 1994, the entire chapter on crimes against socialist property was repealed. In future, property crimes would no longer be distinguished according to the victim (the state or the individual), but would be grouped together in the name of protecting the "property of others" (*chuzhaya sobstvennost*).[53] At the same time, article 88, relating to "violation of the rules on currency trading", regarded as a crime against the state, was also repealed and replaced by article 162[7]—"illicit currency transactions"—and included in the chapter on economic offences.[54] The measures adopted on 1 July 1994 overturned the hierarchy of values the Criminal Code was designed to defend. The order of

---

[47] *Vedomosti S'ezda...*, no. 52, 1991. Article 1867.

[48] *Ibid.*

[49] The death penalty for major crimes against socialist property (article 93[1]) and accepting bribes (article 173) was abolished in December 1991. *Ibid,.*

[50] *Vedomosti S'ezda...*, no. 47, 1992. Article 2664.

[51] *Vedomosti S'ezda....*, no. 32, 1993. Article 1231.

[52] *Ibid.*

[53] *Ugolovnyi kodeks RSFSR* (Criminal Code of the RSFSR), Moscow, Kodeks, 1994.

[54] *Sobranie Zakonodatel'stva Rossiiskoi Federatsii*, no. 10, 1994, p. 1109.

the chapters is worth noting: crimes against the state; crimes against the life, health, liberty and dignity of the person; crimes against political rights and freedoms (relating to a citizen's work or other spheres); and crimes against property.

The privatisation process was marked by four successive waves of criminalisation which completely altered the chapter of the Soviet Criminal Code dealing with "breaches of the rules of economic activity." The first, in March 1992, was designed to strengthen the powers of the recently created anti–monopoly commission;[55] it added violation of anti–monopoly legislation to the Criminal Code (art. 175[1]) and provided for administrative sanctions in case of non-compliance with the commission's injunctions.[56] The second, several months later, concerned fiscal matters. Two articles of the Criminal Code would henceforth address "the concealment of income, profits and other resources subject to taxation", as well as "non-compliance with the injunctions of fiscal services" (art. 162[2] and 162[3]).[57] The third, dealing with practices that had arisen from the liberalisation of prices in January 2002, created a series of offences: "illegal increase or maintenance of prices", "violation of the rules of commerce",[58] "violation of state price discipline", "illegal enterprise" and "illegal enterprise in the commercial sector" (art. 154[3], 156[5], 156[6], 162[4] and 162[5]). These measures were supported by new articles in the Code of Administrative Offences, most of which were designed to protect consumers (art. 146[3]-146[6] and 150[3]).[59] The final wave, in July 1994, penalised "refusal to pay customs duties", "violation of the customs laws of the Russian Federation", "illegal currency transactions", and "concealment of foreign currency" (art. 162[6], 169[1], 162[7] et 162[8]).[60] These measures reflected the desire to create a regulatory framework for the import and export of goods and prevent the concealment of funds.[61]

---

[55] On the anti–monopoly policy, see A. Aslund, 1995, pp. 152–6.

[56] *Vedomosti S'ezda...*, no. 16, 1992, article 838.

[57] *Ibid.*, no. 33, 1992, article 1912.

[58] This article in fact replaced the old article 156[3], repealed in February 1991. The title remained unchanged, but the entire content was replaced.

[59] *Vedomosti S'ezda...*, no. 32, 1993, article 1231.

[60] *Sobranie Zakonodatel'stva Rossiiskoi Federatsii*, no. 10, 1994. Article 1109.

[61] At the beginning of 1992, Russian political leaders associated capital flight with money held abroad by former leaders and Party members. In March, the Russian government went as far as employing an American detective agency to track down these funds. Capital flight was later used to denote the practices of entrepreneurs and citizens in general. V. Tikhomirov, 1997, pp. 591–615.

As we can see, the criminalisation of certain commercial practices sometimes occurred more than five years after they had emerged. And even by 1995, some were still not covered by criminal legislation: fraudulent bankruptcy; insider trading (despite its prevalence in the organisation of auctions and competitive tenders during the privatisation process); money laundering; misleading advertising; and the corruption of employees in private enterprises. These offences would not be made punishable until the publication of the new Criminal Code of the Russian Federation in 1997.

Legislative Inertia. There was no legislation specifically devoted to combating the economic crime arising from the context of privatisation. Until the dissolution of the Supreme Soviet and the adoption of the Constitution of the Russian Federation in late 1993, announcements on the issue were few and far between.[62] The decree on "combating corruption in the public service system"[63] was an exception in this respect, at least for a short period. Designed to prevent collusion between public officials and economic actors, it barred the former from entrepreneurial activity (either directly or through an intermediary), from assisting the entrepreneurial activity of a physical or moral entity, and from participating in the management of a private limited company, a limited liability company or any other form of enterprise. However, the decree, aimed at "restricting the commercialisation of administrative bodies",[64] had little impact, for there were many ways to circumvent it, the penalties envisaged were slight and, finally, it was seen as a provisional measure, the precursor to an anti–corruption law which never materialised despite many announcements.[65]

---

[62] Decree of the President of the RSFSR, 9 November 1991: "On Immediate Measures to Combat Crime" (*Vedomosti S"ezda...*, no. 46, 14 November 1991. Article 1565); Decree of the President of the Russian Federation, 8 October 1992: "On Measures to Defend the Rights of Citizens, Maintain Lawful Order and Reinforce the Campaign against Crime" (*Ibid.*, no. 42, 22 October 1992. Article 2373); Congress of People's Deputies resolution, 14 December 1992: "On the State of the Legality of the Campaign against Crime and Corruption" (*Ibid.*, no. 51, 24 December 1992. Article 3018).

[63] Decree of the President of the Russian Federation, 4 April 1992: "On the Campaign against Corruption in the Public Service System." *Ibid.*, no. 17, 23 April 1992. Article 923.

[64] V. V. Trubin, 1993, p. 70. On this decree, the hopes it aroused and the ensuing disappointment, see V. Luneev, 1996, pp. 79–80.

[65] For the saga of anti–corruption law in the 1990s, see G. Satarov, M. Levin and M. Tsirik, 1998, pp. 10–1.

Legislative activity in the field of penal policy remained weak following the political events of 1993. The laws to "combat corruption" and "repress organised crime"[66] adopted by the State Duma were subjected to a presidential veto. Other texts focused on organisational measures, notably the redefinition of the responsibilities of the actors involved in combating crime (law on inquiry and investigation procedures, August 1995; law on the modification of the responsibilities of the Prosecutor's Office, February 1992 and November 1995;[67] law on the imprisonment of suspects and guilty parties, August 1995; law on the protection of judges, law enforcement officers and inspectors, April 1995).[68] The law on the modification of the powers of the tax police merits attention. The responsibilities acquired by the tax police, tasked with investigating cases once criminal proceedings were under way, were on a par with those of Prosecutor's Office, the Interior Ministry and the security services. The powers of this newcomer to the campaign against economic crime were constantly increased during the 1990s[69] (cf. *infra*, chapter 9). Finally, the State Duma voted through the aforementioned "political and economic amnesty" on 23 February 1994.[70]

---

[66] In both cases, the proposed legislation was adopted by the State Duma but rejected by the Council of the Federation. When re-adopted by the State Duma, the President of the Russian Federation used his veto. Source: *Parlamentarizm v Rossii...*, 1996, p. 98.

[67] In conformity with the law of February 1992 (see "RSFSR Law on the Prosecutor's Office", *Rossiiskaya Gazeta*, 18 February 1992), the Prosecutor's Office retained most of its prerogatives and continued to act as a public prosecutor while monitoring the legality of the work of the various administrative bodies. The 1992 law nevertheless introduced several changes. For example, it banned party-based political activity in the Prosecutor's Office. The November 1995 modifications made it clear, for example, that the Prosecutor's Office would not be involved in monitoring the implementation of presidential decrees (cf. "Law on the Introduction of Modifications and Additions to the Law 'On the Russian Federation Prosecutor's Office.'" *Sobranie zakonodatel'stva Rossiiskoi Federatsii*, no. 47, 20 November 1995. Article 4472). On the evolution of the Prosecutor's Office up to 1996, see G.B. Smith, 1997, pp. 348–73. See also P.H. Solomon, Jr., 1997, pp. 50–6.

[68] *Parlamentarizm v Rossii...*, 1996, pp. 93–8.

[69] Federal Law "On the Introduction of Modifications and Additions to the Law of the Russian Federation on the Federal Organs of the Tax Police and the RSFSR Code of Criminal Procedure", adopted by the State Duma on 15 November 1995. *Sobranie zakonodatel'stva Rossiiskoi Federatsii*, no. 51, 18 December 1995. Article 4973.

[70] On this amnesty, see *Zashchita Ekonomicheskikh svobod i Kommercheskoi deyatel'nosti*, no. 2, 1993, pp. 8–9.

Of the few presidential decrees on penal policy, some defined what action should be taken in this sphere. The "programme of measures to reinforce the maintenance of law and order and the protection of the rights and personal safety of citizens and their property" set the legislative agenda in terms of combating crime. It introduced measures to combat hooliganism, alcoholism, begging and the carrying of weapons, but did not single out economic crime as such. Consideration was given to a decree on commercial freedom, with input from the Interior Ministry.[71] The more detailed state programme for reinforcing the fight against crime in 1994–95, adopted in May 1994, established guidelines for combating the various forms of crime that had emerged in the two years since the launch of the privatisation process.[72] The programme aimed to "break up"[73] the conventional approach to fighting crime by "ensuring effective protection of the life, health, property and rights of citizens, and of social and state interests in the context of social reform."[74] The hierarchy of values defended and the term "social reform" illustrated the stated desire for a different approach.

According to the state programme, privatisation encouraged "criminal structures to infiltrate the economy and politics and consolidate their positions."[75] It led to unequal access to information concerning the opportunities afforded by the reforms and, more broadly, to dysfunctions in the implementation of market economy. Privatisation also placed many citizens in a "vulnerable" position which could easily be exploited by anyone with a good knowledge of the mechanisms involved,[76] a view borne out by the innumerable and widely-discussed swindles that made headline news in Russia in the early 1990s: the pyramid schemes, expropriation of property, and theft of vouchers by investment funds and other actors. The first two arguments linked the crimes emerging in the wake of privatisation to the disastrous influence of the underworld and the "profiteers" who sought to exploit its opportunities and thus discredited its "social" aspect. But the text of the programme moderated this traditional position:

[71] *Sobranie aktov Prezidenta i Pravitel'stva Rossiiskoi Federatsii*, no. 47, 22 November 1993. Article 4586.

[72] *Sobranie zakonodatel'stva Rossiiskoj Federatsii*, no. 5, 30 May 1994. Article 403.

[73] The Russian term employed is *perelom* (fracture).

[74] "Federal Programme of the Russian Federation for Reinforcing the Campaign against Crime in 1994 and 1995." *Sobranie zakonodatel'stva Rossiiskoi Federatsii*, no. 5, 30 May 1994, p. 671.

[75] *Ibid.*, p. 669.

[76] *Ibid.*

The implementation of economic reforms has reinforced social differentiation within the population. The inadequacies of state structures in terms of social assistance, education and employment have confronted the young, the unemployed, ex–military personnel and former detainees with difficult choices. The sudden change in status of those who have not managed to adapt to the new conditions has engendered a widespread resort to crime and violence in order to resolve social contradictions.[77]

According to this view, economic reform itself produced social effects that helped to explain the changes in the nature of criminality. However, the paradoxical return to the Marxist explanation of crime relied heavily on the evocation of figures of delinquency linked to recidivism and inactivity, the avatar of "parasitism."

In order to resolve these problems, the authorities devised a set of "emergency measures" to be imposed during the first six months of 1994. These would be accompanied by more vaguely defined "secondary measures." The former involved the adoption of twenty legislative texts and eighty-five organisational measures, while the latter were outlined in fifty-four points! The emergency "legislative package" comprised the Criminal Code, the Code of Criminal Procedure, basic legislation on offences sanctioned by the administration, and laws on organised crime, public service, corruption, terrorism and banditry, the formation of illegal armed groups, public participation in the maintenance of law and order, etc. In addition, there were plans for four laws relating to economic crime: on "legalisation of criminal income", illicit financial transactions, commercial activity in other countries and control of the mineral and precious metals markets. Further measures were envisaged to tackle economic offences occurring during the privatisation of economic activity. As the project avoided the customary denunciation of the opportunism of "profiteers" and the voracious greed of the criminal milieu, these measures reflected the desire to modify the conception of the reforms by harmonising the rules of economic activity and ensuring that they applied to all actors. According to the rhetoric (which had been well-honed in the context of cooperatives), it was a matter of protecting "honest businessmen" while cracking down on "unfair competition, dishonest business practices, fraudulent bankruptcy, misleading advertising, the appropriation of loans, violations of tax and customs legislation, illegal alliances and computer crime."[78]

It would be somewhat pointless to assess the programme's impact, for apart from a few measures, it was not implemented.[79] As far as privatisation was

---

[77] *Ibid.*, p. 669.

[78] *Rossiiskaya Gazeta*, 25 February 1994.

[79] This is clear when comparing the programme with its successor, the "Federal Pro-

concerned, the campaign against economic crime was ultimately restricted to programmes and declarations of intent. Their implementation was entirely hypothetical, for they required rational, effective cooperation among the various holders of political power at federal level, and competent administrative services to relay the hierarchy's orders and monitor their application in the regions.

However, the magnitude of the crime problem was a constant theme during this period. In his 1994 annual speech to the Federal Assembly, the Russian President stressed the need to strengthen the state in order to address what he regarded as the "most important problem of the year."[80] While waiting for new criminal legislation to be drafted, he planned to introduce "special" anti–crime measures which the population expected and would understand.[81] The deputies, for their part, believed that "restoration of order in the country" should henceforth take precedence over economic reform. In their view, the prevalence of crime highlighted the inefficiency of the executive sector: above all, steps should be taken to strengthen every level of the top-down power structure in order to ensure that decisions were followed by appropriate action.[82] The two goals—"restoration of order" and "economic reform"—were extremely difficult to reconcile, and represented a continuation of the dilemmas which Yuri Andropov and Mikhail Gorbachev had faced before.

The Debate on the 1996 Criminal Code

The RSFSR Criminal Code, adopted in 1960, therefore remained in place until 1997, but arguments for a completely new version, rather than modification in accordance with changing economic practices, emerged with the advent of *perestroika*. In 1987, a group of experts from Moscow's Institute of State and Law had published a project for the Fundamental Principles of Criminal Legislation. The document recommended replacing the general section of the

---

gramme for Reinforcing the Campaign against Crime in 1996 and 1997", adopted on 17 May 1996 by decree of the government of the Federation of Russia (*Rossiiskaya Gazeta*, 24 July 1996). See also the Russian Federation Interior Ministry report "On the State and Measures to Reinforce the Campaign against Economic Crime and Corruption in the Russian Federation", *Nezavisimaya Gazeta*, 17 January 1997.

80 *Rossiiskaya Gazeta*, 25 February 1994, p. 2.

81 *Ibid.*, p. 2.

82 *Rossiiskaya Gazeta*, 1 March 1994.

Criminal Code,[83] thus placing reform on the political agenda.[84] The principal aim was to remove redundant articles from the Criminal Code, along with others which the experts regarded as matters best dealt with by other bodies, whether disciplinary or administrative. Once this had been achieved, the wider goal of reducing and diversifying penalties could be pursued. The reform was justified by the desire for a "more humane" Soviet Criminal Code, but there was no question of modifying the prevailing order and hierarchy.

The new plan for the Fundamental Principles of Criminal Legislation appeared at the end of 1988 and followed the same logic.[85] It proposed a new system for classifying offences in accordance with their gravity.[86] It called for the abolition of penalties such as the ban on living in a specified area and internal exile, and also recommended new types of sanction. For example, petty criminals could be sentenced to a maximum of three months detention in "strict isolation" to counteract the influence of the "professional criminals" who made up the bulk of the prison population. According to article 26 of the plan, a breach of the law could not be considered as a criminal offence if it resulted from a "justified professional or economic risk." This extremely vague formulation was based on considerations that the plan's authors sought to clarify: "the diligent decision-maker who takes an economic or commercial risk for the general good, and by doing so violates irrelevant legal norms, should not be regarded as a criminal."[87] The desire for a more lenient approach to illicit economic practices, particularly those involving accountants and the *tolkachi*, was accompanied by a pledge, aimed at entrepreneurs, to increase the flexibility of the penal framework surrounding economic activity. This chimed

---

[83] *Ugolovnyi zakon. Opyt teoreticheskogo modelirovaniya* (Criminal Law: A Theoretical and Experimental Model). Moscow, Nauka, 1987. According to one of the book's authors, work on the new Fundamental Principles of Criminal Legislation began in 1982. S.G. Kelina, 1991, p. 12.

[84] *Izvestiya* published an interview with Vladimir Kudryavtsev, the director of the Institute of State and Law and a member of the authors' collective, on 26 August 1987. Sofia Kelina, a specialist in criminal law at the Institute and also a member of the authors' collective, was interviewed that same week in *Moskovskie Novosti* (Moscow News), no. 34, 23 August 1987.

[85] *Izvestiya*, 17 December 1988.

[86] On the principles underlying the classification of offences, see P. Lascoumes and A. Depaigne, 1997, p. 15.

[87] Interview with I. M. Gal'perin, a research fellow at the Scientific Research Institute; a specialist in the problems of reinforcing the legal order and one of the authors of the Fundamental Principles. *Izvestiya*, 18 December 1988.

with the principle that "everything which is not directly prohibited by law is allowed."[88]

In the very early 1990s, debates on the new Criminal Code involved a reassessment of the values that had been upheld in the past. The protection of the person—the rights of the victim as well as those of the accused—would henceforth constitute one of the priorities of new criminal legislation.[89]

The new Fundamental Principles of Soviet Criminal Legislation were adopted by the USSR Supreme Soviet on 2 July 1991. They were supposed to take effect twelve months later, but the timetable was disrupted by the collapse of the Soviet Union. The drafting of a new criminal code commenced in 1992 and continued for four years, exhausting the energies of several committees and hindered by a rejection from the Council of the Federation and a presidential veto.[90] The text of the sixth criminal code in Russia's history was finally voted through by the State Duma on 24 May 1996 and promulgated by the President of the Russian Federation on 13 June 1996, a few days before his re-election. It retained a dual structure and maintained a unitary conception of a criminal offence: in keeping with Soviet criminal law, an offence was defined as a "socially dangerous act" (article 14). However, the "social danger" of illicit behaviour was no longer exclusively associated with the state and would in future also apply to the person.[91] The new code, a more voluminous document than its predecessor, comprised 360 articles.[92] It established a new hierarchy of Russian values which placed the protection of the person at the summit, followed by economic activity, public safety, public order and state power. The revised architecture reflected the desire to sever all ties with a politically authoritarian regime.[93] Protection of the economy encompassed property crime and the old breaches of the rules of economic activity, and introduced a series of new offences. This category was designed to defend the new rules of economic activity, regulate the nascent market economy, and establish a stable normative framework for economic activity. Articles relating to corruption, however, were confined to the section dealing with offences against state power.

---

[88] Interview with Vladimir Kudryavtsev, director of the Institute of State and Law, *Izvestiya*, 26 August 1987.

[89] S.G. Kelina, 1991, pp. 3–4.

[90] L. Golovko, 1997, pp. 561–5.

[91] J. Pradel (ed.), 1998.

[92] For a formal comparison of the two texts, see S.G. Kelina, 1996, p. xxiii.

[93] "Authoritarian codes place crimes against the state above crimes against the person." J. Pradel, 1995, p. 86.

Concluding Remarks

The legitimacy the campaign against economic crime had enjoyed until the early 1980s was considerably reduced by the advent of *perestroika* and *glasnost*. The population's distress, its resentment at new wealth and growing fear of crime, were certainly enough to justify campaigns against ill-defined targets such as "economic sabotage." But offensives of this sort now had to contend with greater media coverage of insecurity, which highlighted the failure of government measures, the collective mobilisation of various groups to defend individual freedoms and entrepreneurial interests, and the widespread defiance of law enforcement agencies. Organised crime, however, seemed a case apart: the term, a recent and ill-defined addition to the Soviet vocabulary, struck a chord with the general public, which used it to label diverse forms of illegal behaviour.

Having encouraged the development of the cooperative sector, Soviet leaders began focusing on social justice, an issue which could impede economic growth if not handled correctly. But announcements that order would be restored could not disguise the incoherence of penal policy in relation to economic reforms, or its marginalisation and indeed its absence. The privatisation process implemented at the beginning of the 1990s had made this abundantly clear: there had been warnings of its effects on crime, but its proponents seemed to regard that as a relatively small price to pay. The political struggle between the Russian president and Congress of People's Deputies, which was particularly intense at that time, may explain this finding. Yet as with cooperatives, resources were specifically allocated to the campaign against "privatisation-related offences." An examination of police and judicial activity will reveal how the fight against economic crime was conducted by law enforcement agencies in this context.

PART THREE

POLICING RUSSIAN CAPITALISM

INTRODUCTION TO PART THREE

The changes I have studied in the previous part have had a strong impact on police activity. What could it mean to fight against economic crime in such a moving context? What kind of results were expected from the police? In this part, I will focus again on the everyday police struggle against changing illegal practices. Police activity is analysed wih the aid of archives available until 1991, and, for the following period, with help from multiple sources that have become available since then on this sensational issue.

Chapter 9 describes how the police crisis was publicised in the late 1980s. As I have described in the first part of this book, this crisis was not a new one, but it became a subject for public debate thanks to *glasnost*. The harsh working conditions within the police, the profession's lack of prestige, and bureaucratic shortcomings were among the issues most particularly described. In addition, opinion polls expressed the discrediting of the police among the population. In such a context, many officers chose to quit and join private security firms. At the same time, entry tests for the police became less difficult. Several political initiatives, local or national, competed to resolve those difficulties. Many new actors became involved in policing missions. In some cities, workers' militias appeared and were meant to help the police; in other towns, factory owners started to finance police forces. These often spontaneous local initiatives started conflicting with federal moves aiming at recentralising police activity. This entailed great confusion as well as the multiplication of police allegiances at the local level. The priority that was given to the fight against organised crime led to the creation of new services within the Ministry of the Interior that were highly autonomous and endowed with their own territorial organisation. The creation of a new police force specialising in the fight against tax offences further complicated the institutional landscape.

Chapter 10 allows us to grasp what the everyday fight against economic crime looked like between 1985 and 1995. Archives show the scope of police mobilisation in order to start the fight against unearned income in 1986, but they also show the never-ending need to monitor law enforcement practices, because they were either too relaxed or on the contrary too severe. From a statistical point of view, there has been a severe and longstanding increase in the number of offences since 1988. Such an increase reflects the development of differential ways of coping with illegalities. Law enforcement agencies started to focus on predatory forms of economic crime—the various forms of theft—at the expense of more fraudulent and ingenious offences, usually labelled as breaches of the rules of the Soviet economy (rules that were actually in total mutation). The strong increase in offences registered by the police from 1988 also led to renewed discourses on explanations of crime. Economic difficulties were now largely denounced as well as the shortcomings of law enforcement agencies. Regional political leaders managed to progressively impose their critique of national policies as inappropriate to local reality.

In addition to these difficulties, the police had to face new challenges linked to the privatisation of the economy. Chapter 11 shows the role played by police during the various phases of this reform's implementation. Applying legislation on individual labour activity generated some reports, but it was the development of the cooperative sector that really changed the situation for police services. Police officers were powerless in the face of new illegal private accounting practices they knew nothing about. Moreover, cooperatives created protection systems that guaranteed them great impunity. Violent entrepreneurs, specialising in extortion practices, started appearing.[1] Implementation of "spontaneous privatisations" completely eluded the police, as is shown by very interesting archives on the development of Komsomol Centres for Scientific and Technical Creativity of Youth in the region. Lastly, this Chapter describes what police did during the privatisation process, implemented in 1992. When asked to report results linked to "criminality in the sector of privatisations", law enforcement agencies followed their usual methods and privileged the most simple offences at the expense of fraud that characterised all property transfers. Agencies defended themselves by denouncing corrupt government departments in charge of property transfers and by criticising the way penal policy was conducted at the national level. Conflicts between law enforcement agencies and those in charge of economic development, as well as those between regional and federal authorities, tainted Russian political life throughout the 1990s.

[1] V. Volkov, 2002.

9

REORGANISING THE POLICING SYSTEM

The role of the police in Soviet society came under scrutiny with the advent of *glasnost*. The creation of a political issue around the "policing problem" focused on certain persistent institutional, organisational and professional difficulties that affected the maintenance of order and the fight against crime.[2] Successive Interior ministers defended very different approaches to the problem and the solutions it required: some simply called for more police resources, while others advocated a thorough overhaul of police bureaucracy.

Alexandr Vlasov, Interior Minister from 1986 to 1988, defended a position similar to that held by Mikhail Gorbachev at the beginning of *perestroika*: police forces needed to be reorganised, for their performance, skills and professionalism had been damaged by two decades of "stagnation" under Brezhnev.[3] Vlasov's successor, Vadim Bakatin,[4] seemed more willing to address the problems confronting Soviet police forces directly. His interviews changed the way the Ministry communicated on its own activities: "I would very much like to reassure you on the crime situation, but I do not have the right to do so."[5] According to Bakatin, the changing nature of crime primarily reflected shortcomings in police procedure: "In the current context of democratisation, dynamism, openness and more humane policies, the police are not prepared

---

[2] On this analytical distinction, see D. Monjardet, 1996.

[3] A. Vlasov, 1988a, pp. 46–59.

[4] Vadim Bakatin (b.1937) pursued a career in the building sector and climbed the rungs of the CPSU ladder in the Kemerovo region. Bibliography in *Komsomol'skaya Pravda*, 29 April 1989.

[5] *Pravda*, 19 January 1989.

to respond rapidly. Many police officers have failed to shoulder their responsibilities, show initiative and take risks; in fact, they have lost their way."[6] Criticism of the Brezhnev management style figured largely in the litany of explanations, but it was not the principal argument. "Like other organisations, the Interior Ministry is not immune to corruption, treachery, excessive bureaucracy, insensitivity, brutality, the compartmentalisation of services and injustice."[7] This critical view of the police was a response to public concern: "In 1988, police forces received two million letters from citizens denouncing their shortcomings."[8]

Bakatin's replacement by Boris Pugo at the end of 1990, a move condemned by the reform-minded press,[9] illustrated the desire of Party leaders for a more conservative approach. "I know people regard me as a conservative," Pugo remarked, "But I don't see how that is a sin. Reasonable conservatism is both useful and necessary."[10] Prior to his participation in the August 1991 putsch, Pugo attempted to increase the resources available to law enforcement agencies and reorganise the Ministry so that it could confront new threats and revitalise its oversight of the private sector. The service responsible for combating the theft of socialist property took charge of the campaign against economic crime, while the Interior Ministry's Sixth Directorate, tasked with fighting organised crime, saw its remit extended to drug trafficking and corruption. The powers of the KGB and MVD were strengthened following the 1991 decree on combating economic sabotage, and patrols composed of police officers and soldiers were introduced.[11] Weaknesses in the law enforcement system were attributed to inadequate resources and poor coordination of manpower.

In this chapter, I will emphasise the various aspects of the crisis that Russian police faced in the late 1980s and in the early 1990s. I will also underline the way this crisis was publicised and fostered negative social representations on the police. In such a context, many actors were involved in policing missions. Various initiatives emerged at local level in order to maintain order and fight against crime, in spite of governmental attempts to centralise police activity. Within the Interior Ministry, OBKhSS departments were renamed and

[6] *Ibid.*

[7] *Ibid.*

[8] Interview with V. Bakatin, *Agitator*, no. 20, October 1989, p. 20.

[9] *Ogonyok*, no. 52, 1990.

[10] Interview with B. Pugo, *Pravitel'stvennyi Vestnik*, no. 17, April 1997.

[11] Pugo's appointment was accompanied by that of a new vice-minister, Boris Gromov, who came from an army rather than a police or security background.

restructured. They had to secure their place between growing anti–organised crime units and the tax police, a new law enforcement body created outside of the Interior Ministry.

An Institutional Crisis

The lack of resources naturally featured at the top of the list of difficulties the police admitted they faced.[12] All ministers, including Vadim Bakatin, acknowledged the link between the state of crime (recorded and latent), police performance (the ability of police forces to deal with the crime problem) and the funds allocated to this task. The authorities showed willingness to increase crime-fighting resources. Gosplan, for example, was ordered to ensure that police forces were better equipped,[13] but there was no agreement on what was required.[14] Some sources claim that in January 1995 the police possessed one computer for every forty-six inspectors, one tape recorder and one photocopier for every hundred, and one video camera for every 231. In some cases, the number of inspectors sharing the same equipment had increased since 1993.[15]

The lack of resources was compounded by low salaries. In the mid-1980s, a police officer at the bottom of the hierarchy earned less than a skilled worker and barely more than a general medical practitioner. In theory, police officers enjoyed certain advantages—notably the right to free accommodation—but these were difficult to obtain. In 1989, 248,000 police families were looking for better accommodation, and 20 per cent of local inspectors had nowhere to live at all.[16] Certainly salaries were increased several times in the late 1980s and early 1990s—Boris Pugo claimed that a police officer earned 510 roubles a month in 1991, about as much as a soldier[17]—but the concomitant rise in prices hindered any improvement in living standards.[18]

The figures for staffing levels are confusing. In 1989, Vadim Bakatin stated that the USSR Interior Ministry employed approximately 3.5 million person-

[12] *Pravda*, 19 January 1989.

[13] USSR Supreme Soviet resolution, 4 August 1989, "On the Decisive Reinforcement of the Campaign against Crime", *Vedomosti S'ezda…*, no. 9, 9 August 1989. Article 222.

[14] Interview with Boris Pugo, *Pravitel'stvennyi Vestnik*, no. 17, April 1991.

[15] Obshchestvennyi Tsentr…, 1996, p. 22.

[16] *Izvestiya*, 8 February 1989.

[17] Interview with Boris Pugo, *Pravitel'stvennyi Vestnik*, no. 17, April 1991.

[18] The Interior Ministry's budget was increased by 14 per cent in 1989 in order to increase police pay. See the interview with V. Bakatin in *Pravda*, 17 April 1990.

nel, including 700,000 police officers.[19] According to the London-based International Institute of Strategic Studies, police numbers stood at 340,000 in 1988.[20] Mark Galeotti put the figure at 485,000.[21] According to data published in 1995, the Interior Ministry employed 540,000 police officers as well as between 260,000 and 280,000 troops.[22]

Exactly how many police were required was also a matter of uncertainty. In 1990, a leading member of the Interior Ministry's criminal research department stated the need to "recruit 10,000 uniformed police officers and 21,000 inspectors."[23] However, Boris Pugo claimed almost simultaneously that "police staffing levels had been increased by 41,000 officers" and that a further 45,000 recruits would bring forces up to "full strength."[24] These figures kept the policing problem on the political agenda and highlighted the institution's weakness in the face of rising crime.[25]

During the late 1980s and throughout the 1990s, staff turnover was notable for two trends: the departure of a considerable number of qualified police officers and their replacement by less competent individuals. By 1989, senior figures in the Interior Ministry had begun voicing concern over this exodus.[26] "Police officers, particularly cadres, are resigning and joining other sectors of activity, cooperatives in many cases."[27] Between January and May 1989, 10,000 police officers resigned and entered the private or cooperative sectors.[28] In 1989, 83,000 agents resigned; 5,000 did so for "personal reasons."[29] The haemorrhage extended to other law enforcement institutions: between 1988 and 1989, Prosecutor's Office services lost 15 per cent of their staff.[30] As one former police officer points out:

---

[19] *Tass*, 10 July 1989.

[20] A. Trehub, 1989, p. 10.

[21] M. Galeotti, 1993, p. 769.

[22] *Obshchaya Gazeta*, no. 51, 1995. See also P. Morvant, 1996, p. 23

[23] *Sovetskaya Rossiya*, 19 December 1990.

[24] Interview with Boris Pugo, *Pravitel'stvennyi Vestnik*, no. 17, April 1991.

[25] "In the MVD, they are good at counting the dollars they need, but they can't agree on the number of offences committed." In such circumstances, "everybody in Russia is afraid, but of what, exactly?" *Novoe Vremya*, no. 11, 1993. pp. 54–7.

[26] The term was frequently employed. See M. Galeotti, 1993, p. 773.

[27] Statement by Deputy USSR Interior Minister P.S. Bogdanov, head of main directorate in Moscow, quoted in Y. Gilinskii, 1995, p. 5.

[28] S. Borodin and Yu. Kudryavtsev, 1989, p. 59.

[29] A. Fatula and T. Lisitsyna, 1990a, p. 53 (and 1990b, pp. 46–9) capture perfectly the malaise felt by police officers in the late 1980s.

[30] *Pravda*, 12 August 1989.

In fact it didn't take much thought; there was no compelling reason to stay in the police. I was hated by everybody, I was poorly paid, I wasn't getting on with my family ... But on the whole, all that was bearable. The worst thing for me was that I wasn't able to do the work that had attracted me to the police in the first place, the work I was paid to do. I spent my time filling in forms, I didn't have the means to do the job properly, I was forced to compromise with various colleagues, and above all I felt powerless and useless. I found that very hard to bear.[31]

A 1989 study conducted in three Soviet republics shows that two-thirds of police officers expressed dissatisfaction with their working conditions; more than three-quarters did not want their children to follow in their footsteps. Only 56 per cent of new recruits did not openly regret their decision to join a police service. The reasons given were mostly material, but there were professional concerns—insufficient legal protection, the exasperation induced by political interference, bureaucratic constraints—and a psychological element fostered by a social context that profoundly devalued police work.[32]

Paradoxically, the widespread mistrust of law enforcement institutions was accompanied by an acknowledgement of the value of policing skills, for in a society where property rights were being transformed there was a growing need for their protection. An entrepreneur might not trust the police, but privileged access to certain officials or former officials within their bureaucracy was always useful. Given the uncertainty of the legal and social framework in which the privatisation process unfolded, there was a need to preserve and protect the rights acquired so far. At that stage, new property owners were compelled to forge alliances with what Vadim Volkov called "entrepreneurs of violence", service providers who specialised in the use of force and intimidation.[33] Various groups of social actors with the appropriate skills entered this market: former or current law enforcement agents, war veterans, army officers, and members of criminal organisations. All these actors exploited professional skills acquired in various ways (military service in Afghanistan, combat sports, etc.). The demand for renegade law enforcement officers with contacts among their former colleagues was especially high.

All police officers were tempted by the salaries offered by private security companies, which were about three times higher than Interior Ministry rates

---

[31] Interview (June 1996) with a former member of the Interior Ministry criminal investigation unit in Moscow, now head of security at a large Moscow store.

[32] A. Fatula and T. Lisitsyna, 1990a, pp. 52–4; 1990b, pp. 46–9.

[33] V. Volkov, 2002.

of pay.[34] According to the Russian Federation Chamber of Commerce and Industry, 90 per cent of the workforce in the private security sector was composed of former Interior Ministry, state security service (the KGB and, later, the FSB) and Defence Ministry employees.[35] This sector brought together three types of organisation: internal security services in large-scale enterprises and banks, private security agencies and private detective agencies. According to the head of the privately-owned Russian National Service for Economic Security, a former chief of the USSR external intelligence service, the sector employed over one million people in 1995.[36] This figure corresponded to private security companies registered with the Interior Ministry, in accordance with the 1992 law of the Russian Federation "On the Activities of Private Detective and Security Services."[37] However, many unregistered companies operated in this field.[38] Private security companies were also used by criminal organisations in order to give the relations they maintained with business a veneer of legality.[39]

Official responses to the defection of police officers were based on the commercialisation of law enforcement.[40] The police initially considered hiring out some of their officers to private enterprises. Vadim Bakatin suggested creating policing cooperatives and placing officers in businesses and shops to provide security. This proposal was not implemented, but led to the creation within the Interior Ministry of a section responsible for "extra-departmental" security (*Upravlenie po Vnevedomstvennoi Okhrany*)—that is, sites in the private sector. Private security companies claimed that the ministry had resorted to "unfair competition" by promoting its initiative at "less than the market rate."[41] However, relations between the two types of service providers were not restricted to commercial rivalry. Many ex–police officers working for private security firms still had good contacts among their former employers and facilitated various

---

[34] On police salaries, see L. Shelley, 1996, pp. 89–91.

[35] *Rossiiskaya Gazeta*, 9 September 1995.

[36] *Ibid.*

[37] V.P. Mak-Mak and M.F. Savelii, 1997.

[38] In 1995, the police mounted an operation codenamed "Shield" and dismantled 522 illegal agencies. P. Morvant, 1996, p. 26.

[39] According to Vadim Volkov, the shift to the private sector was due to a "functional crisis in law enforcement bodies", their poor public image, the reduction of financial support from the centre and the "desire to infiltrate the criminal world." V. Volkov, 1999, pp. 748–9.

[40] M. Los, 2002, pp. 165–88.

[41] *Ruskrim*, no. 2 (18), June 1997, p. 7.

forms of cooperation on a more or less official basis. In the early 1990s, some service providers acquired exorbitant powers, the "Most" security department being one example.[42] There was a risk that the commercialisation of state law enforcement agencies would lead to the privatisation of intelligence gathering: in 1994, the Interior Ministry offered banks and financial institutions the opportunity to purchase research and information on convicted individuals.[43]

By the late 1980s the reduction in police numbers had become so pronounced that the Interior Ministry was forced to mobilise all its services, including its internal troops, and adapt its recruitment policy.[44] Some commentators argued that lower standards facilitated the employment of "conformists, monsters without morals and delinquents"[45] and transformed the police into a "criminal institution."[46] The recruitment policy in force in 1990 had been authorised by the Interior Minister Vitaly Fedorchuk in 1984. It prioritised consideration of a candidate's political, professional and personal qualities, but the need for more human resources obliged department heads to ignore the guidelines in order to satisfy the hierarchy's demands.[47]

New recruits were supposed to complete a two-month local induction course, followed by six months at a training centre and a two-month probationary internship. In practice, trainee officers were often deprived of the guidance of an experienced colleague. In many cases, the fast-track training course was not followed. Instructors constantly deplored the incompetence and lack of "moral values" evinced by some of their students.[48]

According to Vadim Bakatin, criminal investigation services clearly suffered from a lack of professionalism: only 46 per cent of their personnel had received some higher education; the turnover was alarming, with 50 per cent leaving

---

[42] V. Volkov, 2002, pp. 171–3.

[43] *Ruskrim*, no. 1 (12), January 1996, p. 30.

[44] In 1989, a Supreme Soviet resolution allowed Interior Ministry troops to participate in the fight against crime ("USSR Supreme Soviet resolution, 4 August 1989: 'On the Decisive Reinforcement of the Campaign against Crime'" in *Vedomosti S'ezda Narodnykh Deputatov SSSR i Verkhovnogo Soveta SSSR*, no. 9, 9 August 1989. Article 222). In 1990 a law extended their participation to the maintenance of public order (*Vedomosti S'ezda Narodnykh Deputatov SSSR i Verkhovnogo Soveta SSSR*, no. 14, 1990. Art. 233).

[45] A. Fatula and T. Lisitsyna, 1990b, p. 46.

[46] Obshchestvennyi tsentr..., 1996, p. 23.

[47] A. Fatula and T. Lisitsyna, 1990b, pp. 46–9.

[48] See interviews with several instructors, who claimed that between a third and a half of their students lacked the qualities required of a police officer. *Ibid.*, p. 47.

within three years.[49] Bakatin's claims were supported by a study published several years later: in 1995, only 48.5 per cent of inspectors possessed a law degree, as opposed to 78 per cent in 1992; only 37 per cent were still in post after three years (58 per cent in 1992).[50] Moreover, the quality of the investigations conducted by police inspectors had deteriorated. Between 1992 and 1996, the number of cases exceeding the time-limit set by the Code of Criminal Procedure rose from 5 per cent to 7.24 per cent; cases sent back to police inspectors for further investigation rose from 1.2 per cent to 2.23 per cent.[51]

Given the working conditions, suspicion arose as to the motives of new recruits. There were fears that criminal organisations would infiltrate police forces, but in most cases becoming a police officer was regarded as the initial stage of a career strategy aimed at moving on to a private security agency. This attitude was denounced during a discussion on staffing problems at a press conference organised by the Interior Ministry in Moscow in 1995.[52] The prevalence of opportunism continued to worry the heads of the MVD Academy for several years.[53]

Public Mistrust

"Between 1986 and 1988, the press uncovered 2,500 cases of brutality, human rights violations and corruption involving police officers."[54] The police received a bad press during *glasnost*, and citizens openly admitted their lack of trust in them. Indeed, an opinion poll conducted in 1981 had already shown that the public believed the police were too slow to react to complaints, neglected crime prevention, did not mount adequate night patrols and were guilty of rudeness and "bureaucratic formalism."[55] The criticism became more virulent as time went on. According to a 1990 VTsIOM survey, two-thirds of those questioned did not trust the police; three-quarters doubted that any complaint they lodged had a chance of being cleared up. The adjectives the public most

---

[49] *Pravda*, 19 January 1989

[50] Obshchestvennyi tsentr..., 1996, p. 24.

[51] Obshchestvennyi tsentr..., 1996, p. 23.

[52] *Nezavisimaya Gazeta*, 18 January 1996.

[53] Interviews with the heads of the MVD academy, Moscow, June 2000.

[54] L. Shelley, 1996, p. 53.

[55] The poll was conducted by lawyers and used a sample of 1,500 people in Gorky *Oblast'* and the Republic of Uzbekistan. See E.P. Petrov, R.A. Safarov and S.S. Strelnikov, 1981, p. 75.

frequently applied to the police were "rude", "indifferent", and "ill-mannered."[56] Another poll revealed that less than half the respondents recently in contact with the police had been satisfied with their services.[57] Police officers were also condemned for their negligence and lack of respect.

Many respondents were reluctant to answer questions relating to police violence. Apart from the 9 per cent of respondents who thought the police physically abused everyone they arrested, most believed that physical violence occurred only in exceptional cases involving "dangerous or uncooperative" criminals. The respondents were often in favour of the police using violence, even in circumstances where it was forbidden by law: 33.8 per cent thought such practices were justified in exceptional cases and 25.3 per cent had nothing against their general application.[58] Numerous reports highlighted the violence of Russian police in the 1990s, particularly the use of torture to extract confessions.[59] Several non-governmental organisations such as the Social Centre for the Reform of Criminal Justice drew attention to these practices. The Centre possessed few resources and initially concentrated on examining cases that had gone before the courts; however, it received a large number of written complaints which, either through fear or a sense of futility, had not been communicated to the police. "By and large, cases involving police officers are quickly closed, but at least the facts have been noted. In most instances, police officers who have committed offences attempt to stop the victims lodging a complaint by threatening them with criminal proceedings."[60]

The extent of police corruption is common knowledge in Russia. In the VTsIOM survey, two-thirds of the respondents referred to it directly.[61] A large percentage of respondents to the other opinion poll refused to comment on the issue, but the general attitude to it was clear. When asked "In what circumstances is it possible to come to an arrangement with the police?" 42.5 per cent expressed no opinion on the matter; 24.3 per cent thought it possible in any circumstances and 17 per cent in all cases barring homicide and rape; while 12.4 per cent thought it could be achieved only in relation to minor offences. This image was not confined to law enforcement: 45 per cent of respondents

---

[56] Almost 3,500 people were questioned. See VTsIOM, 1990, pp. 25–9.

[57] 3,400 people, including 800 police officers, were questioned. See I.B. Mikhailovskaya (ed.), 1995, p. 55.

[58] *Ibid.*, pp. 56–63.

[59] See the 1999 Human Rights Watch report on this subject.

[60] Obshchestvennyi tsentr..., 1996, pp. 26–7.

[61] VTsIOM, 1990, p. 27.

thought that the police were "no more prone to taking bribes than officials of other public services." The tendency to regard police corruption as a fact of life remained strong throughout the 1990s and the 2000s.[62]

At the time, it was thought that such venality could be explained by poor salaries, constant exposure to sources of profit and lack of oversight at the various levels of the hierarchy. Louise Shelley suggested supplementing this traditional list with factors such as the fear of a complex legal procedure and the possibility of a harsh sentence, which encouraged bribe-giving, and also the police capacity to solve disputes or to create trouble for a competitor, which fostered bribe-taking.[63] In terms of police corruption, the public regarded the traffic police and the services combating economic crime as the worst offenders. In the 1990s, several institutional measures were introduced in a futile attempt to improve the image of the police, including the creation in late 1993 of an elite corps of state traffic inspectors to combat internal corruption in that branch. In late 1995, an internal security department was set up to monitor the conduct of all police officers.

The critique of the police often focused on bureaucratic inefficiency. By and large, the climate induced by *glasnost* was favourable to the denunciation of "excessive bureaucracy", which leaders regarded as one of the major challenges facing Soviet society. In 1989, the Interior Minister Vadim Bakatin joined the chorus and admitted that the falsification of statistics "demoralised cadres, engendered an atmosphere of deceit, and diverted the attention of police officers."[64] It also disguised the extent of criminal activity and hindered attempts to suppress it. By depicting the practice as the result of a formal constraint rather than the product of police idleness and incompetence, Bakatin diverged from the position adopted by his predecessors. However, no attempt was made to change the ways in which police performance was assessed during the 1990s, while Bakatin's successors preferred to denounce the inadequacy of resources and staffing levels. Moreover, the sociologist Yakov Gilinskii pointed out that falsification of crime statistics began to increase in 1993.[65]

The principal change concerned the redefinition of the tasks entrusted to law enforcement agencies, although no thought was given to the reorganisa-

---

[62] A study based on two polls shows that in 1993 and 1994, respectively 4 per cent and 6 per cent of respondents believed that the police could not be bought. Yu. Mazaev, 1997, pp. 68–73.

[63] L. Shelley, 1996, p. 102.

[64] *Pravda*, 19 January 1989.

[65] Obshchestvennyi tsentr..., 1996, pp. 47–8.

tion of hierarchical relations, planning of results and performance assessment. Between 1991 and 1993, the police were regulated by a Soviet law that had replaced the old statutes. According to article 2 of this law, the police were responsible for ensuring the "individual safety of the citizen, public security and the maintenance of public order, crime prevention, the rapid and thorough uncovering of offences, protection of property, participation in the provision of social and legal assistance to the population and the execution of penalties."[66] The Russian Federation Law on the Police, adopted in 1993, was similar in content but placed prevention and discovery of crime above the maintenance of order and public security.[67] This revision did not enhance the image of police forces, which were still regarded as repressive.

Opinion polls reflected the belief that the logical response to sudden changes in criminal behaviour was to enhance the ability of the police to deal with them: the most appropriate measures seemed to be more resources (salaries and equipment), more police officers and greater public involvement in the fight against crime.[68] In this respect, the Russian case is similar to that of other countries emerging from authoritarian rule. When the "fear of crime" is interpreted as a form of social pressure that justifies more repressive resources, leaders are presented with a dilemma: while defending the freedoms and values associated with the new "democratic" regime, they are also obliged to reinforce the policing apparatus in order to rise to the urgent challenges posed by new criminal threats.[69]

Recentralisation and Local Initiatives

The politicisation of the policing issue was also characterised by competing views on the way the fight against crime should be organised. The "demand for security" triggered a range of local initiatives devised by economic actors, political leaders and resident communities. Their implementation was undertaken by an equally diverse group of providers—federal police, local police, private security companies, and the internal security departments of major local plants. Many of the actors involved in the maintenance of order and/or

---

[66] "USSR Law, 16 March 1991: 'On the Soviet Police.'" *Sovetskaya Rossiya*, 16 March 1991.

[67] This law was adopted on 18 February 1993. See *Zakon Rossiiskoi Federatsii o militsii* (Russian Federation Law on the Police). Moscow, Prospekt, 1999.

[68] See VTsIOM, 1990, pp. 29–30; I.B. Mikhailovskaya (ed.), 1995, pp. 64–5.

[69] D. Bayley, 1997, pp. 59–64.

the campaign against crime advocated more privatisation and further decentralisation of policing tasks, while others took the opposite view and called for tighter federal control.[70] The proliferation of actors engaged in policing tasks conforms to the "multilateralisation" analysis of policing in modern societies, which brings together those who define security requirements and appropriate responses (auspices), and those entrusted with their implementation (providers).[71]

In the late 1980s, the search for a more coordinated policy on crime resulted in the decision to create temporary crime-fighting commissions at both national and regional level. These would be run by the heads of the Prosecutor's Offices, the Interior Ministry, the state security services, and the courts, as well as by people's deputies.[72] Leadership in the regions and republics fell to the head of the executive committee. The commissions, tasked with "mobilising all social forces in the campaign against crime",[73] were given the power to centralise information and draft recommendations.[74]

The idea of a closer alliance between police and security services had not been abandoned, however. In February 1991, a presidential decree ratified the creation of a main directorate for combating particularly dangerous crimes, organised crime, corruption and drug trafficking. Although attached to the Interior Ministry, the new entity was authorised to collaborate with security services.[75] This approach generated far more ambitious decisions. In late 1991, Boris Yeltsin signed a decree ordering the fusion of the RSFSR Interior Ministry and the RSFSR State Security Committee (KGB). In the wake of the August 1991 putsch, Yeltsin sought to secure the support of "power ministries" by founding a super-ministry: Security and Internal Affairs (MBVD).[76] The

---

[70] S. Timoshenko, 1997, pp. 117–24.

[71] D. Bayley and C. Shearing, 2001. See also F. Ocqueteau, 2004, pp. 167–9.

[72] *Vedomosti S'ezda Narodnykh Deputatov S.S.S.R. i Verkhovnogo Soveta S.S.S.R.*, no. 11, 23 August 1989. Article 257.

[73] "Presidium of the USSR Supreme Soviet resolution, 20 October 1989: 'On the Approval of the Standard Regulation of the Provisional Anti–Crime Commission'", *Vedomosti S'ezda Narodnyh Deputatov S.S.S.R. i Verkhovnogo Soveta S.S.S.R.*, no. 20, 25 October 1989. Article 375.

[74] *Ibid.*

[75] "Decree of the President of the USSR 'On Measures to Reinforce the Campaign against Particularly Dangerous Crimes and their Organised Forms'", *Vedomosti S'ezda Narodnykh Deputatov S.S.S.R. i Verkhovnogo Soveta S.S.S.R.*, no. 7, 13 February 1991. Article 180.

[76] Decree, 20 December 1991: "On the Formation of the RSFSR Security and Inte-

measure was a response to the KGB's demand for extended powers in order to combat crime, because of its worrying seriousness.[77] Yeltsin's decision caused an uproar: its opponents evoked the spectre of the NKVD and stressed the impossibility of controlling such a powerful organisation.[78] Foreign observers interpreted the decision as evidence of a "regression to dictatorship."[79] The Constitutional Council swiftly vetoed the decree.[80]

Yeltsin also wanted a body to control all law enforcement services. To this end, he created by decree an inter-departmental anti–crime-and-corruption commission inside the Security Council. Headed by Alexandr Rutskoi, then Vice-President of the Russian Federation, the new commission was responsible for coordinating the work of the Interior, Defence and Security Ministries, the state customs committee, and the federal currency and export control departments. It monitored the application of decisions taken by the president and the Supreme Soviet, organised the work of the branches specialising in combating organised crime and corruption, and prepared new legislation. The initial plan to subject the commission to parliamentary control under the vice-president of the Supreme Soviet, S. Filatov, was soon abandoned.[81] Yeltsin eventually sacked Rutskoi and took personal charge of the commission, but it was unable to break the bonds and allegiances the various law enforcement agencies had established.[82]

---

rior Ministry." The Russian term is *Ministerstvo Bezopasnosti i Vnutrennikh Del* (MBVD).

[77] "The situation in the country requires us to reinforce the participation of the KGB in the campaign against crime, and particularly its most dangerous form: organised crime. The KGB was already contributing to this task, but the level of crime is now so great that urgent measures must be adopted first to slow its increase, and then to reduce its level." Interview with Vladimir Kriyuchkov, head of the KGB, *Sovetskaya Rossiya*, 16 July 1989.

[78] See for example *Moskovskii Komsomolets*, 20 December 1991 and *Izvestiya*, 31 December 1990.

[79] W.A. Tupman, 1992, p. 23.

[80] M. Galeotti, 1993, pp. 769–86.

[81] "Decree of the President of the Russian Federation, 8 October 1992: "On Measures to Defend the Rights of Citizens, Maintain Lawful Order and Reinforce the Campaign against Crime." *Sobranie zakonodatel'stva Rossiiskoi Federatsii*, no. 42, 22 October 1992. Article 2373.

[82] "Decree of the President of the Russian Federation, 28 April 1993: "On Organisational Measures to Reinforce the Fight against Crime." *Sobranie zakonodatel'stva Rossiiskoi Federatsii*, no. 18, 3 May 1993. Article 1597.

The attempt to improve the coordination of law enforcement bodies reflected the desire to make them more efficient, but it was also designed to ensure their loyalty and reinforce the political legitimacy of Soviet leaders. In effect, a context of institutional instability and rivalry between Soviet, Russian, regional and municipal elites was conducive to the invention and diffusion of local schemes to combat crime.

Mark Galeotti has shown how the creation of the Russian Interior Ministry, not long before the collapse of the Soviet Union, represented the "triumph of localisation over centralisation."[83] Until 1990, the RSFSR was the only Soviet republic without a dedicated Interior Ministry. The Soviet version maintained direct contact with the heads of its counterparts in RSFSR regions and republics, while the Interior ministries in other republics acted as relays. The creation of the RSFSR Interior Ministry inaugurated a period of rivalry with its Soviet counterpart. Echoing Vadim Bakatin's position on the need to decentralise the campaign against crime, Viktor Barannikov, appointed to head the new ministry in September 1990, attempted to increase its autonomy by arguing that it should be accountable to the Russian Council of Ministers rather than to the Soviet ministry. After the attempted putsch of August 1991, the Soviet ministry was replaced by the Russian Interior Ministry.

The decentralisation of policing was also pursued at regional, municipal and even neighbourhood level throughout the Russian Republic.[84] On 6 April 1989, the Gorky Municipal Soviet created workers' detachments to assist the police,[85] thereby strengthening the anti–crime campaign and increasing police manpower. The manpower problem was not confined to the defections noted earlier, for many police officers had been sent to the Nagorno-Karabakh Autonomous Region, which was in the throes of war. This decision was gradually applied at national level. At the end of 1990, and "in response to massive abuse in the commercial and supply sectors and repeated requests by citizens", the central powers decided to strengthen "worker control" of the production and distribution of goods "during the stabilisation period."[86] Committees

---

[83] M. Galeotti, 1993, pp. 777–83.

[84] M. Galeotti, 1990a.

[85] *Rabochie Otryady Sodeistviya Militsii* (ROSM).

[86] Decree of the President of the USSR, 30 November 1990: "On the Reinforcement of Workers' Supervision with the Aim of Maintaining Order in the Preservation, Transport and Commerce of Standard Consumer Products and Goods." *Vedomosti S'ezda Narodnykh Deputatov S.S.S.R. i Verkhovnogo Soveta S.S.S.R.*, no. 49, 1 December 1990. Article 1074.

elected by workers' collectives were authorised to inspect establishments (including cooperatives) dealing with standard consumer goods, monitor the movement of commodities and examine accounts. They were empowered to shut down a business after notifying the appropriate Interior Ministry services, recommend the dismissal of employees found guilty of offences, and even urge the relevant services to begin legal proceedings. The right to conduct surprise inspections and shut down businesses was withdrawn within twelve months. The mobilisation of workers could be interpreted as a populist drive to tackle a serious crime situation or as part of a "conservative" offensive to undermine economic reforms.[87] Many "reformers" feared the initiative would have a negative impact, given workers' apparent hostility to *perestroika*.[88]

Another important form of decentralisation took effect in Russia in the late 1980s. The idea originated in Togliatti, an industrial city and the base of the gigantic VAZ car factory. Concerned by rising crime in the area, the factory's directors invested 6.5 million roubles, plus an annual budget of 3.5 million roubles and 200 cars, in the creation of a local police force. This was not intended as a rival force, but was designed to provide extra manpower to deal with specific tasks. Interior Ministry services retained the responsibility for investigations, but delegated the more mundane aspects of law enforcement[89] to the VAZ force. The recruits were supposed to live in the area, in order to foster closer relations with the population they were assigned to protect. The "Togliatti experiment" was an attempt by a non-repressive actor to create a "neighbourhood" police force that worked closely with existing services. The project was difficult to replicate, for economic actors with the means to finance it were not always present where needed. The experiment nevertheless inspired the Interior Minister Bakatin, who strongly supported the coexistence of a centralised policing body responsible for maintaining order and fighting crime with municipal police forces tasked with public security missions.[90]

[87] M. Galeotti, 1993, p. 775.

[88] M. Tsypkin, 1989, p. 16.

[89] Dominique Monjardet employs the term *police du sommeil* (literally, police who ensure that residents can sleep peacefully) to describe an urban (municipal, community or neighbourhood) police force which "is not equipped to track down major criminals or control riots", but is responsible for "ensuring public order (dealing with noise, disorderly conduct, littering and fly-tipping as much as controlling crime) and for intervening in disputes, pacifying inebriated, angry or foolhardy individuals, controlling traffic, etc." D. Monjardet, 1996, pp. 273–4.

[90] On the "Togliatti experiment", see M. Galeotti, 1990a, pp. 4–6. This twofold

Russian leaders believed that "weakening of social control" represented "one of the principal causes of crime", but found it difficult to devise a "democratic method of crime prevention."[91] As *druzhina*s tended to disappear during *perestroika*, numerous initiatives to revive and reinforce them were launched in the late 1980s. To some extent, the creation of workers' detachments formed part of this approach, but *druzhina*s reappeared in the country's biggest cities. In Moscow, for example, a municipal government decree issued in March 1993, followed by the municipal Duma's adoption of a bill in the summer of 1995, established the legal framework for their activity in Russia's capital city.[92] *Druzhinniki* were permitted to use handcuffs, batons and CS gas. They assisted law enforcement agencies by patrolling public places and gatherings, and provided backup in emergency situations. In practice, *druzhina*s also took part in the fight against crime by maintaining a presence in markets and checking on small shopkeepers.[93] The Moscow *druzhina* comprised 7,000 paid members, all of whom were entitled to benefits such as free public transport. Although they were supposed to act as a "bridge between the police and society", they drew criticism from police officers who resented the intrusion of outsiders and the drain on the municipal law enforcement budget.[94]

Decentralisation became an increasingly important factor in the conception and organisation of penal policy during the late 1980s, and continued to arouse debate after the collapse of the USSR. The 1990s were marked by a constant struggle between the political authorities and subjects of the Russian Federation over the allocation of resources.[95] The conflicts between all levels of territorial administration were primarily based on economic concerns, but the policing issue was also highly contentious. Regional political authorities intervened in the appointment of heads of regional Interior Ministry directorates, the funding of certain activities (patrols) and sections (maintenance of order), and the coordination of police work. In some cases, entrepreneurs made direct

---

approach was promoted throughout the 1990s and beyond, while the Interior Ministry's reform project foresaw exactly the same arrangement.

[91] "Federal Programme of the Russian Federation for Reinforcing the Campaign against Crime in 1994 and 1995." *Sobranie zakonodatel'stva Rossiiskoi Federatsii*, no. 5, 30 May 1994. Article 403, p. 671.

[92] The municipal Duma adopted a law "On the People's *Druzhina* of St Petersburg" in the spring of 1995.

[93] *Ruskrim*, no. 2 (13), February 1996, p. 13.

[94] *Ruskrim*, no. 6 (9), September 1995, p. 13.

[95] See M. Mendras (ed.), 1997.

contributions to police force funds. The growing number of sponsors helped to diversify local forms of policing but also created confusion in an institution which had to serve several masters.

New Governmental Police Forces

The principal service responsible for combating economic crime was reorganised and renamed in the early 1990s. The Interior Ministry's main directorate for "combating economic offences" was complemented by services dedicated to the repression of organised crime. Another service, the tax police, began to act independently.

In 1992, by order of the Interior Ministry, the Main Directorate for Combating the Theft of Socialist Property and Speculation (GUBKhSS) was renamed the Main Directorate for Economic Crime (GOEP).[96] Of course, a new name does not catch thieves,[97] but this change reflected the expansion of the concept of property since the late 1980s, the liberalisation of economic policy undertaken by Yegor Gaidar on 1 January 1992, and the launch of the privatisation process. A study of the directorate's organisational charts, before and after its name change, highlights some profound reforms.[98] Prior to 1992, separate departments had dealt with property theft according to the sector in which it was committed: food and agriculture, industry, services. In practice, these departments took charge of all economic offences committed in these sectors. Another department was dedicated to combating speculation and profit-driven crime in the cooperative and state sectors. Another one focused on "transregional crime" and handled major cases such as counterfeiting (production and distribution), currency trading, traffic in precious stones and metals and crime in the cooperative sector. Finally, an organisation and methodology department was tasked with analysing the results of each section's activity, conducting "economic and legal analyses" and updating resources and techniques.

After the change of name, the four deputy heads of the main directorate managed ten departments with a simultaneous focus on sectors, economic activities and categories of offences. Some of the old departments survived, such as organisation and methodology and the section combating "crime in industry, construction and the energy sector." Many forms of economic crime,

[96] *Glavnoe Upravlenie po Ekonomicheskim Prestupleniyam.*
[97] H.S. Orenstein, 1992, p. 22.
[98] These two organisational charts are reproduced in the appendix to my doctorate thesis.

including activities involving foreign countries, forgery (currency, stocks and shares) and offences involving minerals and precious metals, would in future be handled by separate specialist departments. Finally, two entirely new departments were set up to deal with corruption arising from the privatisation process and crime in the financial sector and stock exchanges. For the new main directorate, the privatisation process was exclusively associated with corruption. Other forms of crime generated by privatisation were not taken into account; the organisational chart makes no further mention of corruption despite its prevalence in the import-export and financial sectors.

The creation of police services with a capacity to tackle new criminal threats dated back to the late 1980s. The Interior Ministry services combating organised crime were reinforced in 1991.[99] Before that date only one directorate—the Sixth Directorate—had responsibility for such issues, but it lacked resources and lines of communication with the regions and republics.[100] A decree issued in February 1991 authorised the creation of a "Main Directorate for Combating the Most Serious Forms of Crime, Organised Crime, Corruption and Drug Trafficking" in all Soviet republics, although this did not happen in Moldavia, the Baltic republics and Russia. According to Alexandr Gurov, appointed as head of the Sixth Directorate in 1989 and then of the main directorate in 1991, many cadres within the Interior Ministry opposed the new structure.[101] When established in the republics it was subject to double subordination. The Sixth Directorate was dissolved following the August 1991 putsch, but it inspired the creation of new specialist services in Russia and other post-Soviet states, which started to develop quickly.[102]

By 1993, the Russian MVD's main directorate for combating organised crime[103] had become a powerful repressive institution and had acquired a greater degree of autonomy. Led by a first vice-minister, it benefited from direct contact with the head of the Interior Ministry and was therefore privileged in relation to other criminal investigation departments (criminal research unit, economic crime unit), with which it had no connection. Its twelve

---

[99] Decree of the President of the USSR "On measures to Reinforce the Campaign against the most Dangerous Crimes and their Organised Forms", signed 4 February 1991. A. Gurov, 1995, pp. 212–27.

[100] K. Maguire, 1998, pp. 245–55.

[101] A. Gurov, 1995, p. 226.

[102] *Ibid.*, pp. 235–6.

[103] In Russian: *Glavnoe Upravlenie po Bor'be s Organizovannoi Prestupnost'yu* (GUOP).

regional units[104] were spread across several regions and Russian Federation republics. The geographical structure was designed to prevent collusion between regional elites and the services fighting organised crime, which were subject to a strictly vertical hierarchy.[105] This reorganisation exacerbated the rivalry between Interior Ministry services. The new directorate, always in receipt of sizeable budgetary resource, encroached upon the work of other criminal investigation services. Moreover, its separate status and degree of independence compared with regional administrations represented a potential threat to the other criminal investigation units, which believed they were under surveillance.

The idea of forming a tax police service, fostered by the creation of a state tax department in 1991, became a reality two years later with the enactment of a law on 24 June 1993.[106] The tax police were given the power to detect, prevent and suppress tax offences, ensure the security of state tax inspections and combat corruption in these services. Their powers were enhanced once again in December 1995. Before that date they had been able to initiate proceedings, but investigations were conducted by the competent section of the Prosecutor's Office or the Interior Ministry. They thus rapidly lost all contact with a case, which meant that a large number of cases could not be followed up, as occurred with over 90 per cent of the proceedings initiated in 1994.[107] After December 1995, they were permitted to investigate cases and submit them to a court,[108] thus acquiring powers similar to those held by Interior Ministry and Prosecutor's Office services .[109] In addition to tax crime (articles 162^{-1}, 162^{-2} and

---

[104] In Russian: *Regional'noe Upravlenie po bor'be s Organizovannoi Prestupnost'yu* (RUOP)

[105] Even so, regional anti–organised crime units became involved in scandals which linked them to criminal organisations. See L. Shelley, 2000, pp. 105–6.

[106] "Russian Federation Law, 24 June 1993: 'On the Federal Organs of the Tax Police.'" *Vedomosti Verkhovnogo Soveta Rossiiskoi Federatsii*, no. 29, 1993. Article 1114.

[107] *Parlamentarizm v Rossii*, 1996, pp. 95–6.

[108] "Federal Law 'On the Introduction of Modifications and Additions to the Law of the Russian Federation on the Federal Organs of the Tax Police and the RSFSR Code of Criminal Procedure.'" *Sobranie zakonodatel'stva Rossiiskoi Federatsii*, no. 51, 18 December 1995. Article 4973.

[109] "Decree of the President of the Russian Federation, 14 February 1996, on the initial measures to apply the 'Federal Law on the Introduction of Modifications and Additions to the Law of the Russian Federation on the Federal Organs Of the Tax Police and the RSFSR Code of Criminal Procedure.'" *Sobranie zakonodatel'stva Rossiiskoi Federatsii*, no. 8, 19 February 1996. Article 739.

162⁻³),[110] they also investigated illicit businesses (162⁻⁴), illicit enterprise in the commercial sector (162⁻⁵), illicit currency transactions (162⁻⁷) and the concealment of cash resources (162⁻⁸).[111] Officers of the tax police were armed and were authorised to conduct searches, arrest suspects, place an individual under court supervision and conduct undercover investigations.

The number of tax police rose steadily from 1993 onwards, reaching 25,000 by mid-1995. The new repressive institution, a source of revenue for the state budget, constantly extended the boundaries of its remit by adding new offences to its list of prerogatives. This inevitably created tensions with other law enforcement agencies, notably the Interior Ministry services competing for a bigger slice of the crime-fighting budget. Moreover, many of its officers were former Interior Ministry employees. The tax police had a limited impact on crime, however. Recorded cases seldom resulted in charges being brought and convictions were rare: 432 offenders were convicted in 1995 and 449 in 1996.[112] Rival services frequently accused them of incompetence and corruption, for the way in which they selected the tax fraud cases that they pursued to completion raised doubts about their integrity.[113] Officers of the tax police were treated little better than those working for the Interior Ministry: their salaries, although slightly higher, were paid late.[114] Even so, they were feared by the business community for their ability to destroy an enterprise. Their motives for doing so varied and were probably often connected to the machinations of rivals.[115]

Concluding Remarks

The police crisis became public during *glasnost* and *perestroika*. The Interior Ministry services were criticised for their incompetence, their indifference to

[110] Respectively, the refusal to submit a declaration of income, concealment of income and opposition to or non-execution of the injunctions of tax services with the intention of concealing income.

[111] On the competences and organisation of the tax police, see *Pravookhranitel'nye organy Rossiiskoi Federatsii*. Moscow, Spark, 1996, pp. 168–72.

[112] *Ruskrim*, no. 5 (16), December 1996, pp. 11–2.

[113] On all these points, see O. Maes, 1999, pp. 47–52.

[114] *Ruskrim*, no. 2 (13), February 1993, pp. 10–1.

[115] In the interests of thoroughness, it should be stressed that the customs code adopted in 1993 (*Vedomosti Verkhovnogo Soveta Rossiiskoi Federatsii*, no. 31, 1993. Article 1224) enhanced the powers of customs officers to combat smuggling, illegal exports and illegal currency trading. These services could conduct investigations and initiate criminal proceedings. See *Pravookhranitel'nye organy Rossiiskoi Federatsii*. Moscow, Spark, 1996, pp. 173–9.

crime and their low probity. Public mistrust of the police encouraged local elites to get involved in policing missions. At that time, policing in Soviet society became highly multilateralised. Local governments and factory bosses became police auspices, while workers, private security firms, security departments within big enterprises were charged with providing security. This process of multilateralisation of policing has blurred the frontiers between public and private policing, between national and local interests. It has also shown that policing practices were produced by complex relations between top-down policy and local initiatives, comparable to the dialectical opposition I have emphasised in analysing economic regulation.

Mistrust of the police was also felt at governmental level. In spite of attempts to reform specialist services in the struggle against economic crime, many decisions tended to create new institutions. Anti–organised-crime departments had exceptional autonomy within the Interior Ministry, and the tax police were a completely new law enforcement institution. The emergence of these policing actors illustrated the tendency to respond to new threats with institutional innovations rather than attempt to tinker with the structure of existing services. To a certain extent, they highlighted the authorities' mistrust of traditional criminal investigation services and their ability to tackle new forms of criminality. But although these services were confronted with a crisis, the way in which they were organised and required to account for their efforts to combat economic crime was not called into question.

10

REPRESSION OF ECONOMIC CRIME

Despite the upheavals noted in the preceding chapters, the campaign against economic crime continued. Although chronically inadequate, budgets, equipment and manpower were constantly allocated to the task and results were expected. Given the circumstances, how did police officers in Sverdlovsk *oblast'* select the cases they dealt with? How did they explain the rise in crime?

This chapter provides an overview of efforts to combat economic crime in general, as a broad target. It includes the implementation of the campaign against unearned income, from 1986 to 1988, which provoked an intense mobilisation of law enforcement agencies and the population, for the last time in Soviet history. Sociologists were asked to join the fight and showed in poll results that "unearned income" was a mass phenomenon. However, never-ending debates on the definition of "unearned income" showed that the chosen target was too broad and interfered with the introduction of economic reforms on Soviet soil.

After 1988, the struggle against economic crime started to be disconnected from the implementation of economic reforms. Police results showed alarming trends in economic crime recording, but agencies focused mainly on thefts, which meanwhile became more violent. This operative priority started to reflect a new form of differential management of illegalities. Police reports still contained statements on crime explanation, but in the *glasnost* context causes started to be more directly associated with state policies.

Implementing the Campaign Against Unearned Income

The Party made high demands on police forces, at least initially. In June 1986, the CPSU Regional Committee required a daily report from the Interior Ministry's Regional Directorate.[1] By the summer of that year the flow of information had begun to diminish, although the Regional Directorate for combating the theft of socialist property still expected weekly activity reports from local departments more than a year after the campaign's launch.[2] Between May 1986 and October 1987, the campaign against unearned income generated 432 reports in the Sverdlovsk region.[3] Several Interior Ministry services took part in the offensive, including the vehicle inspectorate and the passport division. People's Control Committees were also involved, notably in the repression of *pripiski*. In 1986, the work of some 6,000 controllers resulted chiefly in administrative or disciplinary sanctions, but 197 officials were prosecuted.[4] The campaign was still a feature of administrative reports in January 1989.[5] It was also supported by intense propaganda: most regional and local daily newspapers ran columns with titles such as "Honest Rouble = Good Conscience", "The Sharp Edges of the Illegal Rouble" and "Unfair Income." Cartoons, readers' letters, articles and regular features were also employed, for the print media had been enlisted to "shape public opinion with regard to those in receipt of unearned income."[6] The Regional Committee organised "press briefing days" to this effect.[7] According

---

[1] Sverdlovsk region CPSU Committee Department of Administrative Organs, Propaganda and Agitation report, 11 September 1986: "On the Work of the Sverdlovsk Region CPSU Committee to Accomplish the CPSU Central Committee Resolution 'On Measures to Strengthen the Campaign against Unearned Income'"; 2 pages. Fond 4, opis 112, delo 219, list 2.

[2] Regional OBKhSS report, October 1987: "On the Measures Taken to Accomplish the CPSU Central Committee Resolution 'On Measures to Reinforce the Campaign against Unearned Income'"; 7 pages. Fond 4, opis 113, delo 722, list 9.

[3] *Ibid.*, list 10.

[4] Sverdlovsk region People's Control Committee report, 27 April 1987: "On the Activation of the Work of People's Control Bodies in the Framework of the Campaign against Unearned Income"; 3 pages. Fond 4, opis 113, delo 722, list 49.

[5] Regional OBKhSS report, 19 January 1989: "On the State of the Protection of Socialist Property and the Campaign against Unearned Income"; 5 pages. Fond 4, opis 118, delo 627, lists 119–23.

[6] Sverdlovsk Region CPSU Committee Department of Administrative Organs report, early 1988 "On the Measures Taken in the Campaign against Unearned Income"; 4 pages. Fond 4, opis 113, delo 722, list 19.

[7] Sverdlovsk Region CPSU Committee Department of Administrative Organs, Propaganda and Agitation report, 11 September 1986: "On the Work Carried out by the Regional Committee to Accomplish the CPSU Central Committee Resolution 'On the Measures to Reinforce the Campaign against Unearned Income'"; 2 pages. Fond 4, opis 112, delo 219, list 1.

to a report, during the first month of the campaign, 407,613 people attended meetings on "unearned income" and 29,278 people spoke at these gatherings![8]

The offensive introduced new methods for the collection and dissemination of information concerning illicit economic practices. Opinion polls were widely used and helped to raise awareness of the action undertaken. *Glasnost* highlighted the limitations of the usual sources of information and encouraged the spread of more innovative methods which enabled leaders to gain a better understanding of public expectations.[9] In January 1987, the CPSU regional committee ordered the regional OBKhSS and the head of the Sociology of Work Department at the Sverdlovsk Economic Institute to assume joint responsibility for a survey.[10] Similar initiatives had already been launched in Soviet territory. In Georgia, the daily *Zarya Vostoka* had solicited readers' views with a questionnaire on economic behaviour and personal gain.[11] On 22 August 1986, *Bakinskii Rabochii* published a questionnaire entitled "Your Opinion on the State of the Campaign against Unearned Income in the Republic."[12] Analysis of this questionnaire, set up by the Azerbaijan CP Central Committee's public opinion study centre, would help to "mobilise the population."[13]

Finding a representative sample faced an obvious difficulty, for the 2,000 respondents were selected from enterprises or establishments in sectors already regarded as vulnerable to economic crime:[14] light industry, food, public catering, commerce, public buildings and works, transport, mechanical construction[15] and agriculture.

---

[8] At the time, the population of the Sverdlovsk region was around 4.5 million. Source: *ibid.*, list 1.

[9] Particularly from 1988 onwards. See G. Mink, 1988, pp. 18–28; F. Barry, 1988, pp. 45–8.

[10] This text was adopted by the bureau of the Sverdlovsk Region CPSU Committee on 13 January 1987.

[11] *Zarya Vostoka*, 22 March 1985.

[12] *Bakinskii Rabochii*, 22 August 1986.

[13] E. Fuller, 1986, p. 1; 1987.

[14] "The sample was assembled from enterprises that were most affected by crime in various branches of the economy." See Sverdlovsk region workers' opinions on the causes and extent of unearned income in the population (a brief analysis of the results of the sociological survey conducted amongst 2,000 workers and employees, March-April 1987). Report by the Regional OBKhSS and the Sociology of Work Department of the Institute of Economy (USSR Academy of Sciences), 1987; 29 pages. Fond 4, opis 113, delo 722, list 70.

[15] The mechanical construction sector dominated the economy of the Sverdlovsk

The survey showed that the desired mobilisation was still a long way off. Most respondents had not read the resolutions and had not discussed them at work; the media, particularly the audio-visual sector, were their main source of information on the campaign. Almost half the respondents claimed they knew at least one person in their circle who concealed a certain amount of unearned income; 27 per cent knew at least ten such people. In some enterprises, the figure rose to 45 per cent. Pilfering from the workplace and speculation were the most common sources of illicit income. In the workplace, 22 per cent had witnessed the falsification of production indicators in order to obtain bonuses, 29 per cent had witnessed thefts of socialist property and 34 per cent had seen company vehicles used for private purposes.

More than half the respondents thought the measures adopted were fair; 27 per cent believed they were not harsh enough. Of those with a higher education diploma, 40 per cent favoured stricter measures. Only one third of all respondents believed the situation had improved nine months after the campaign's launch. Various explanations for its failure were advanced, including widespread flaws in accounting practices, inadequate supervision of goods and commodities, the weakness of administrative measures to combat theft, and "manifestations of social injustice in the distribution of material goods." The references to "artificial" shortages created by "profiteers" echoed the line taken by Gorbachev, but some suggestions for improving anti–crime measures diverged from the traditional explanations of crime by highlighting the difficult conditions in which workers lived and the unfair distribution of consumer goods. Respondents also called upon leaders to set an example and suggested opening shops in enterprises. One question on the survey highlighted the link between the campaign against unearned income and the law on individual labour activity revealed the suspicions engendered by the latter: "Is there a possibility that the law on individual labour activity currently being promoted by the state will partially revitalise people's attachment to private property?" Almost half the respondents said they feared such consequences.

The survey provided regional leaders with information not only on the extent of illicit economic practices, but also on the usefulness of workers' opinions and the limitations of repressive measures. Two drawbacks were apparent here: on the one hand, the information from below on crime was fragmentary and did not reflect the extent to which illicit economic practices had spread

---

region. In many cases, its factories were actually part of the military-industrial complex.

throughout society, despite the numerous agencies working to suppress them. On the other, the policy decided upon at the highest level, assuming that the decisions adopted had the desired effect, could not claim to achieve its objective as long as it ignored the reasons behind a Soviet citizen's resort to earning an illegal income. Regional authorities were now in a position to grasp the extent and complexity of the phenomenon they were up against. The survey also provided them with a scientific validation of the arguments justifying the failure of the national policy.

In practice, the campaign against unearned income encompassed all economic offences, including some that had been largely ignored in the past. The tables compiled by the regional OBKhSS directorate, for example, presented cases of private enterprise activity alongside the usual figures for theft of socialist property, speculation and corruption.[16] The regional Prosecutor's Office was quick to point out that the recording of certain forms of unearned income like the theft of petrol and the provision of labour and services did not reflect their "true extent."[17] The vagueness of the target made it easier to assess police activity: "In our town, people in receipt of unearned income go about their business openly and everybody knows about it. Our police are intensifying their efforts to deal with this scourge ... The results are not good enough ... How could they be otherwise? Five people and one car won't stop unearned income."[18]

Most of the criticism emanating from the regional Prosecutor's Office was directed at the police. Law enforcement bodies were denounced for their poor coordination, police officers for their lack of motivation and incompetence. OBKhSS officers were singled out for being "ineffective and too slow, as if the campaign was just a passing phase."[19] The way in which orders from the top

[16] Regional OBKhSS report, 18 May 1987: "On the Execution of the CPSU Central Committee Resolution 'On Measures to Reinforce the Campaign against Unearned Income'"; 7 pages plus appendix (2 tables). Fond 4, opis 113, delo 722, list 29.

[17] Regional Prosecutor's Office report, 29 April 1987: "On the Activity of Sverdlovsk Region Prosecutor's Office Services in the Execution of the CPSU Central Committee Resolution 'On Measures to Reinforce the Campaign against Unearned Income'"; 6 pages. Fond 4, opis 113, delo 722, list 45.

[18] Comments by the head of the Alapaievsk Interior Ministry department at a meeting of local law enforcement agencies "On the Application of the CPSU Central Committee Resolution 'On Measures to Reinforce the Campaign Against Unearned Income'", 16 October 1986; 4 pages. Fond 4, opis 112, delo 254, list 3.

[19] Regional Prosecutor's Office report, 29 April 1987: "On the Activity of Sverdlovsk Region Prosecutor's Office Services in the Execution of the CPSU Central Com-

were formally applied had not changed since the Brezhnev era. "Every month, we are supposed to send the regional Prosecutor's Office a report on our contribution to the campaign against unearned income. The number of recorded offences, the number of checks and raids carried out, the number of prosecutions, etc. And what do you put in the reports if there is nothing to say?"[20]

The tendency to over-record certain crimes, neglect others and focus on the most common, visible and least dangerous offences was abundantly clear. As the objectives were so vague, police officers were largely free to interpret the injunctions as they saw fit and select which cases they dealt with.

In the late summer of 1986, the CPSU Central Committee sent a telegram to all law enforcement agencies. The Committee, noting "gross distortions" in implementation of the campaign against unearned income, wanted to curb the abuses reported in the press and change current methods. The telegram resulted in meetings between the principal law enforcement agencies, "critical analyses of legislative texts", and "recommendations to halt violations of the socialist legal order."[21] The Interior Ministry's regional directorate and the regional Prosecutor's Office ordered police officers to exercise discernment, concentrate on administrative responses and restrict legal proceedings to exceptional cases.[22]

The reports produced by OBKhSS services consequently devoted much space to administrative sanctions, particularly for minor crimes against socialist property and "small-scale speculation" (*melkaya spekulyatsiya*). The hierarchy's change of tack contributed to a reduction in recorded breaches of the rules of economic activity that continued until the early 1990s. At federal level, there were 183,500 recorded cases in 1986, 136,000 the following year, and fewer than 70,000 in 1988. Overall recorded crime certainly declined during this period, but the fall was much less pronounced at federal level

---

mittee Resolution 'On Measures to Reinforce the Campaign against Unearned Income'"; 6 pages. Fond 4, opis 113, delo 722, list 44.

[20] *Pravda*, 4 March 1987.

[21] Sverdlovsk region CPSU Committee Department of Administrative Organs, Propaganda and Agitation report, 11 September 1986: "On the Work of the Sverdlovsk Region CPSU Committee to Accomplish the CPSU Central Committee Resolution 'On Measures to Reinforce the Campaign against Unearned Income'"; 2 pages. Fond 4, opis 112, delo 219, list 2.

[22] Regional OBKhSS report, 18 May 1985: "On the Accomplishment of the CPSU Central Committee Resolution 'On Measures to Reinforce the Campaign against Unearned Income'"; 8 pages. Fond 4, opis 113, delo 722, lists 21–22.

(1,340,000 cases in 1986, 1,220,000 in 1988) and barely noticeable in Sverdlovsk *oblast'* (48,840 and 47,580 cases). Property crime fell only slightly in Russia as a whole, and even began to rise significantly in the region (330,000 cases in 1986; around 430,000 in 1988). However, these figures are deceptive: the pronounced reduction in breaches of the rules of economic activity from 1987 onwards was primarily due to the repeal of the notorious "dry law" of May 1985.[23] Of the 183,500 cases recorded in 1986, two-thirds involved the "production, sale or possession of strong home-distilled alcoholic drinks"! This article covered no more than 60 per cent of recorded offences the following year and a mere 10 per cent (7,000 cases) in 1988.

Between 1986 and 1988, judicial treatment of recorded cases was marked by a fall in the number of people charged, prosecuted and convicted. More lenient penalties were applied to all categories (corrective labour, suspended sentences with or without probation, fines). While more than 300,000 people received prison sentences in 1986, less than half that number faced imprisonment in 1988. The courts, continuing a trend first noted in the mid-1970s, made increasing use of additional penalties, confiscating personal assets and removing the right to hold certain positions or engage in certain activities.[24]

Given the "distortions" observed in following the order to crack down on unearned income, ways were sought to enhance the skills of the police officers responsible for this task: "A regional seminar on investigative methods has been organised in order to improve the effectiveness and professionalism of local Prosecutor's Office agents combating the theft of socialist property, corruption, *pripiski* and other abuses of office."[25] Similar initiatives were aimed at other law enforcement bodies. In accordance with the wishes expressed in the Central Committee telegram, seminars were held to examine the 300 most significant cases of unearned income. Accountants were invited to explain the various forms of *pripiski*, and police officers were thus given the opportunity to update their knowledge.[26]

---

[23] D. Tarschys, 1993, pp. 7–25.

[24] Regional Prosecutor's Office report, 29 April 1987: "On the Activity of Sverdlovsk Region Prosecutor's Office Services in the Execution of the CPSU Central Committee Resolution 'On Measures to Reinforce the Campaign against Unearned Income'"; 6 pages. Fond 4, opis 113, delo 722, list 43.

[25] *Ibid.*, list 41.

[26] Interview with the head of the Sverdlovsk region economic crime department, an OBKhSS officer since 1973. Yekaterinburg, June 1997.

The Rise in Recorded Cases from 1988

By 1988, the parameters of the campaign against economic crime had extended beyond the repression of unearned income. Between 1989 and 1993, the statistical recording of all crime soared dramatically. While 1.2 million offences had been recorded at federal level in 1988, the figure peaked at approximately 2.8 million in 1993, with a similar increase recorded in the regions (see Table 6). Judicial repression was simultaneously intensified. The number of people charged, prosecuted and convicted increased sharply between 1988 and 1993; at the end of that period, the conviction rate was as high as it had been in 1986 (around 800,000). However, the proportion of the number of people charged vs those convicted declined—62.7 per cent in 1993—because more cases were dismissed or deferred for further investigation. In 1993, incarceration returned to its 1986 level, with more than 300,000 people receiving custodial sentences. Of the other options, suspended sentences and conditional discharges were the most popular, use of those penalties in 1993 largely exceeding the figure for 1986 (see table 18). A comparison of police and judicial statistics tells us that the increase in recorded cases was much greater than that in the conviction rate.

By and large, the campaign against predatory forms of economic crime—property theft—took precedence over the repression of more fraudulent and ingenious crimes which took advantage of radical changes in the rules of economic activity. Thefts of personal property represented less than a quarter of all recorded cases in 1986, but over half in 1993. This was matched by a spectacular increase in thefts of socialist property: in 1993, the number of recorded cases almost tripled in comparison with 1986 (see Table 7). At the beginning of this period they represented 17 per cent of recorded offences, and they amounted to 25 per cent in 1993. Most of these were simple thefts, but regional statistics also started to show a rise in the most violent forms of property crime—robbery with violence, extortion, robbery—which constituted one of the most worrying developments in crime during *perestroika*. In 1993, the federal authorities recorded more than 40,000 cases of robbery with violence, almost three times as many as in 1989, and approximately 185,000 cases of robbery, more than double the 1989 figure (see Table 8).

Property crime in all its forms was therefore the main focus of police attention from *perestroika* onwards. The clearance rate for this category simultaneously began to fall: in 1993, 64.6 per cent of thefts of state property, 63.3 per cent of robberies and 47.1 per cent of robberies with violence remained unsolved.[27]

[27] Kriminologicheskaya Assotsiatsiya, 1994, p. 131.

In a context where state resources were much sought after, false declarations of theft multiplied. The police could also use the difficulties involved in clearing up property theft as an excuse to inflate the recording of this category. The number of people officially investigated for theft of state property almost tripled between 1986 and 1993, but the conviction rate rose more slowly. In 1986, more than 88 per cent of those investigated were convicted, but the figure had fallen to 71.8 per cent by 1993. Moreover, convictions resulted in fewer prison sentences than before: in 1993, less than 30 per cent of those convicted received a prison term, as opposed to 43.4 per cent in 1986 (see Table 9). This trend also applied to the theft of personal property and robbery or robbery with violence involving state property.

These general trends were more pronounced in the Sverdlovsk region. Between 1985 and 1994, recorded crime increased by 43.1 per cent at federal level and 55 per cent at regional level; the *oblast'* accounted for 3.85 per cent of all cases recorded in Russia in 1985, rising to 4.17 per cent in 1994. The increase in thefts of socialist property exceeded the federal trend (see Table 10). In 1993, the *oblast'* topped the list of Russian Federation subordinate units in terms of recorded cases of theft of state property.[28] Between 1989 and 1993, robbery and robbery with violence increased more sharply in regional statistics than at federal level (+245 per cent and +276 per cent respectively; see Table 11). In 1993, Sverdlovsk *oblast'* recorded 6.8 per cent of the robberies committed on Russian soil and 5.65 per cent of robberies with violence. In the Russian rankings, therefore, it came second to St. Petersburg for the former crime, and took third place, behind Moscow, for the latter. Shops, warehouses, stockrooms and public catering establishments were particularly vulnerable to thefts of socialist property.[29] Recorded thefts of personal property also rose sharply. Burglary became commonplace: "two thirds of property crime involves the theft of personal property and two-thirds of these thefts are committed in the owner's home."[30] The recorded theft of vehicles and their equipment also increased.

---

[28] MVD RF *et al.*, 1994, p. 108.

[29] Sverdlovsk Region Interior Ministry Directorate report, 31 January 1990: "On Applying the Decision of the Regional Executive Committee of 27 April 1988 'On Measures to Reinforce the Campaign against the Theft of Socialist and Individual Property'"; 6 pages. Sverdlovsk Region Executive Committee archives: Fond 88p, opis 2, delo 5676, list 5.

[30] Documents prepared by the Interior Ministry Regional Directorate for the third plenum of the Sverdlovsk Regional Committee, July 1989; 8 pages. Fond 4, opis 117, delo 732, list 81. Report of the Interior Ministry Regional Directorate report,

As mentioned above, many of the reports written in 1988 and 1989 expressed concern over the rise in robbery, robbery with violence and extortion. Extortion, whether applied to socialist, cooperative or personal property, became the subject of specific reports in 1989. "Extortion is assuming increasingly organised forms. Criminal groups are characterised by the existence of strong bonds between members and the planning of their activities. Minors constitute the overwhelming majority in such groups."[31] Police forces were worried by the tendency of criminal gangs to increase in size, "structure themselves"[32] and "turn professional and reproduce by instilling in the younger members a pronounced taste for the thief's lifestyle and the cult of violence and cruelty."[33] In a very short space of time, a phenomenon that had not previously been mentioned (through lack of hard evidence or, more likely, because the hierarchy had issued no orders on the matter, thus omitting it from the agenda) had become an uncontrollable problem. While regional leaders lamented the tendency of criminal gangs to "organise", the situation was in fact far more serious, for they were already shooting at each other in broad daylight in Sverdlovsk city centre. Sverdlovsk's reputation as the "Chicago of the Urals" was based on public confrontations between the city's two largest gangs, the "Central" and the "Uralmash": "A resident of Sverdlovsk informs us that the 'situation has reached the stage where gunfire and murder are everyday occurrences. People are afraid to leave their homes." In fact, on 26 July 1989 two rival gangs exchanged fire on two occasions, first near a restaurant and then in the street, and caused a certain number of injuries.[34]

Orders issued on organised crime gave the police on the streets even more room for manoeuvre, for they were free to define the boundaries of "organisa-

---

31 January 1990: "On Applying the Regional Executive Committee Decision of 27 April 1988 'On Measures to Reinforce the Campaign against the Theft of Socialist and Individual Property'"; 6 pages. Sverdlovsk Region Executive Committee archives: Fond 88p, opis 2, delo 5676, list 5.

[31] Sverdlovsk region Prosecutor's Office report, 14 November 1989; 4 pages. Fond 4, opis 118, delo 637, list 94.

[32] Interior Ministry Regional Directorate preparatory note for the third plenum of the Sverdlovsk Region CPSU Committee, July-August 1989; 8 pages. Fond 4, opis 117, delo 732, list 84.

[33] Speech by the first Deputy Minister of the USSR Interior Ministry, L.G. Sizov, delivered at a meeting of Sverdlovsk region Party activists "On the state of Crime in the Region", 4 August 1989; 73 pages. Fond 4, opis 118, delo 7, list 60.

[34] Note from the State and Law Department of the Sverdlovsk Region CPSU Committee, September 1989; 4 pages. Fond 4, opis 118, delo 622, list 38.

tion." "Evidence of success often disguises the usual practices ... Organised crime is not a matter of three workers plotting to steal bags of cement!"[35] When ordered to step up the fight against organised crime, the police resorted to tried and tested methods in order to produce satisfactory performance indicators.

The statistical rise in theft corresponded to a rapid reduction in recorded breaches of the rules of economic activity (see Table 12). This category constituted 13.7 per cent of all recorded crime in 1986, 3.4 per cent in 1989 and 1.3 per cent in 1993. The repeal of the "dry law" was undoubtedly responsible for this decline at first, but does not explain its continuation and its culmination in the extremely low figures noted in the early 1990s. The evolution of speculation illustrates shifts in penal policy following *perestroika*: the number of recorded cases of speculation increased once again in 1990, declined rapidly in 1991, and barely received a mention in the statistics for 1992. Violations of the rules of commerce exhibited a similar tendency, although these were recorded more often, with approximately 2,800 cases in 1993. The collapse in recorded cases concerned all Chapter 6 offences with the exception of buyer and seller fraud (known as consumer fraud from 1993). As a result, this offence accounted for over half the recorded breaches of the rules of economic activity in 1993, as opposed to around 30 per cent in 1988 (see Table 13). The police were almost certain to discover breaches of this type when they checked a shop or restaurant, for shortages of consumer goods encouraged all forms of deception.

The recording of such offences did not reflect their pervasive presence in Soviet society. For example, at a time when queues at service stations were very long, fewer than one hundred cases of "illegal distribution of petrol and other fuel oils" were recorded in the late 1980s. The police tended to ignore Chapter 6 offences for a number of reasons: they lacked resources; they were reluctant to obstruct public access, even when illegal, to consumer goods; and they had not been trained to deal with innovative practices. Judicial statistics show that magistrates had taken a more lenient approach to this category of offences at a much earlier date. With regard to speculation, the number of people investigated continued to rise until 1990, but the conviction rate rapidly decreased from 1986 onwards, falling from 60 per cent of suspects in that year to less than 30 per cent in 1988. Moreover, while imprisonment accounted for a quar

---

[35] Speech by the head of the Sverdlovsk Region Department of Administrative Organs, delivered at a meeting of Sverdlovsk Region Party activists "On the State of Crime in the Region", 4 August 1989; 73 pages. Fond 4, opis 118, delo 7, list 47.

ter of the penalties inflicted in 1986, the figure began to fall in 1987, reaching 9.6 per cent in 1989 and 4.4 per cent in 1992 (see Table 14).

Despite these statistical trends, police reports repeatedly expressed alarm at the growth and diversification of breaches of the rules of Soviet economic activity. More than half the offences recorded involved trade in high-demand consumer goods.[36] The regional officials directing the campaign against economic crime were impressed by the ability of clandestine production units, which had been multiplying in the Sverdlovsk region since the mid-1980s, to respond to fluctuations in demand.

Many people remember when the price of jeans shot up in the markets, when they cost between 250 and 300 roubles a pair. Prices fell by 50 per cent when the regional executive committee and the chamber of commerce intervened, purchased wholesale imported goods and distributed them to the shops. However, because these goods did not exactly match demand, speculators supplied the markets with new brands—"Super Paris", "Super Jordan's", "Blue dollar"—and the price shot up again. Their ability to adapt and innovate was far superior to that of our commerce specialists. Most of these goods were produced not in the United States or West Germany, as it said on the label, but in a cellar in Verkhnyaya Pyshma.[37]

The exploitation of shortages encouraged the creation and maintenance of "commercial networks" composed of entrepreneurs willing to take risks with the law and local administrative and/or political officials. Practices well known in cities such as Moscow were thus replicated in provincial towns.[38] These networks highlighted the interpenetration of various forms of economic criminality. Their durability could not be guaranteed, however, for the protective arrangements they developed were dependent upon circumstances.

For several years, the manageress of clothes shop no. 40 has been creating surpluses by accounting tricks and stealing part of the takings. She has thus made over 30,000 roubles, which she has used to buy two cars and one hundred pairs of imported shoes!

[36] OBKhSS report, 19 December 1988: "On the Activity of Sverdlovsk Region Interior services in Protecting Socialist Property"; 13 pages. Fond 4, opis 117, delo 734, list 137.

[37] Verhnyaya Pyshma is a small town in the Sverdlovsk region. Source: Regional OBKhSS report, 1988: "On Offences Committed in the Commercial Sector"; 7 pages. Fond 4, opis 118, delo 627, lists 124–5.

[38] The Gastronom no. 1 or "Eliseiskii" affair comes to mind here. In 1983 the manager of this shop, which reserved its finest foods for a network of clients including Leonid Brezhnev's entourage, was sentenced to death. The extraordinary severity of the sentence is often interpreted as part of Andropov's offensive against Brezhnev and his circle (in particular I. Grishin).

She knows a great many people, especially individuals who will provide her with protection whenever she asks for it: employees of regional and municipal commerce offices, police officers, court officials and Party and Soviet members. She provides all these individuals with scarce, high-demand goods. These arrangements have created a no-go area around the criminal; she seems to be untouchable.[39]

Corruption was not a major feature of crime statistics during the *perestroika* period. Besides being difficult to prove, it was subject to overlapping legal definitions. In addition, there were extra-judicial channels for dealing with offences committed by Party members. Abuse of office accounted for slightly more than 2 per cent of all recorded cases in 1986 and a mere 0.6 per cent in 1993. The number of recorded corruption cases declined dramatically until 1989 and increased in the early 1990s, notably in 1992 following the adoption of a presidential decree on corruption (see Table 15). Most cases involved the acceptance of bribes. The legal definition of "administrative officials in positions of responsibility" meant that subordinates, as well as cadres working in privatised structures or those undergoing privatisation, were not liable to prosecution. The Sverdlovsk region recorded a slightly above-average number of corruption cases, but counted only 129 in 1993 (see Table 16). Moreover, despite an increase in the number of people investigated and convicted on corruption charges that approximately matched the number of cases recorded, the judicial approach to this form of crime was characterised by a reduction in the number of convictions in relation to the number of suspects. In 1986, three-quarters of the suspects investigated were convicted, but the figure fell to 37 per cent in 1993. During the same period, the number of people imprisoned also declined, but in this case the reduction was not as pronounced (see Table 17).

Little time was wasted in acquiring illicit skills that could be adapted to new accounting practices and forms of ownership. When faced with the sophistication of illicit economic practices like *pripiski*, OBKhSS officers expressed astonishment at the ingenuity of company accountants and admitted they were powerless to deal with the finely-crafted methods of concealment currently in use. As one 1988 report puts it, "Keeping two sets of accounts is standard practice in some businesses and organisations. Every expense is assessed twice: one example goes to the relevant ministry, the other to the internal accounts office. Accountants are seldom convicted of such practices."[40]

---

[39] Regional OBKhSS report, 1988: "On Offences Committed in the Commercial Sector"; 7 pages. Fond 4, opis 118, delo 627, list 128.

[40] Draft of a speech on economic crime to be delivered by a Department of Administrative Organs official, early 1988; 12 pages. Fond 4, opis 117, delo 734, list 5.

Developments in the Explanation of Crime

Why is there such an upsurge of criminality? Many people were satisfied by the reduction in crime between 1985 and 1987 and turned their attention to other matters.[41] Moreover, police and judicial services were ill-equipped to deal with the conditions arising from democratisation and *glasnost*. Rising crime is also linked to the particularities of the transition period—the instability we are experiencing; the growing shortages of products and commodities; the mobilisation of police forces to maintain order in other regions; and the influence of recidivists, particularly the convicts who benefited from the amnesty or received non-custodial sentences. *But the main factor* is the relaxation of discipline in the workplace and society, which stems from workers' half-hearted commitment to the maintenance of order and indifference to educational and preventive work in workers' collectives and in the home ... Let us freely admit it: we will not succeed, in the next few years, in eliminating these causes and liquidating crime.[42]

The increase in recorded crime swiftly became an issue for the regional actors involved in penal policy, for in the context of *glasnost* they were freer to find excuses for it. The reduction in breaches of the rules of the Soviet economy recorded up to 1988 reflected not "the tendency of this form of crime to decline, but the weakening of the campaign to combat it."[43] Attempts to explain the situation were noticeably pessimistic. The customary attitude gave way to acknowledgements of the problem's complexity and multiple causes; crime was no longer seen as a trace of the past that would soon disappear, but as a threat to the future. "Given the introduction of the market economy, the abrupt and significant rise in prices, the emergence of the unemployed and the democratisation of society, we must expect an increase in violent criminal acts arising from the quest for profit."[44]

---

[41] At this point, the speaker repeats the wording of the CPSU Central Committee Resolution "On the State of the Campaign against Crime in the Country and the Extra Measures Designed to Prevent Crime." *Spravochnik partiinogo rabotnika, vypusk dvadtsat' devyatyi, 1989*. Moscow, Izdatel'stvo Politicheskoi Literatury, 1989, p. 488.

[42] Speech by V.V. Andryanov, secretary of the Sverdlovsk Region CPSU Committee, at a meeting of regional CPSU activists to discuss the progress of the campaign against crime, 4 August 1989; 73 pages. Fond 4, opis 118, delo 7, lists 5–6. Emphasis added.

[43] Sverdlovsk region tribunal report, 12 July 1989: "On the State of Judicial Practice during the First Six Months of 1989 and on the Work of Regional Judges to Prevent Offences"; 5 pages. Fond 4, opis 118, delo 624, list 134.

[44] State and Law Department of the Sverdlovsk Region CPSU Committee note, 1989,

The partial change in the stance on the causes of crime could be interpreted as reflecting a desire to be seen as progressive, or as an attempt to dilute responsibility for the phenomenon. Whatever the case, it authorised a critique of the central conception of penal policy; the CPSU Central Committee decree of 2 April 1988, for example, was referred to as a "simple declaration of intent."[45] Such a reaction was allowed by the emergence of opposition at the summit of the Party-State. Regional leaders began asserting their legitimacy through a public critique of federal decisions, those taken by a "centre" which they regarded as incompetent and out of touch. One source of their anger was the wide-ranging amnesty granted in 1987 to mark the seventieth anniversary of the October Revolution: the *oblast'* contained a large number of prisons and most detainees remained in the area once they had served their sentences, although there was no reintegration policy to deal with them. Regional leaders protested at having been left to cope with the results of the generosity displayed by the Party's central leaders.[46]

However, rising crime was still attributed to the shortcomings of social control mechanisms and a lax approach to illicit economic practices. Law enforcement agencies, for example, blamed the sudden rise in thefts of socialist property on the inactivity of workers' collectives. Police reports continued to mention information about the standard figures of delinquency. Until 1990, most of these documents contained information on the number of offences committed by people under the influence of alcohol, recidivists and the unemployed. References to recidivism stressed the local context: "Every year, 15–20,000 people settle in the region after serving their sentence; a quarter of them commit an offence within twelve months."[47] By 1988, the term "parasite" had fallen out of use and had been replaced by "criminals without work." The last documents to mention "parasites" illustrated the increasing difficulty of distinguishing

---

on "Certain Assessments and Predictions on the State of Legality and Order in the Region"; 2 pages. Fond 4, opis 118, delo 622, list 33.

[45] Regional Prosecutor's Office preparatory note for a meeting of Sverdlovsk region Party activists on the state of crime in the region, 20 July 1989; 5 pages. Fond 4, opis 118, delo 625, list 27.

[46] Proposals on the anti–crime campaign by the Sverdlovsk Region CPSU Committee State and Law Department, early 1989; 8 pages. Fond 4, opis 118, delo 622, lists 43–44.

[47] Information from the Sverdlovsk region CPSU Committee State and Law Department: "On the State of Crime in the Region", early 1990; 12 pages. Fond 4, opis 118, delo 622, list 17.

between the unemployed and criminals: "Penal sanctions should not be restricted to inveterate parasites [*zlostnye tuneyadtsy*]";[48] the parasite could no longer be denounced as such, for the transformation of the rules of economic activity had altered the perception of work and "social utility." This reflected the need for new strategic distinctions such as the aforementioned one between "honest" and "dishonest" businessmen which appeared during this period. The other traditional explanatory factors, such as shortcomings in the organisation of accounting systems and monitoring of assets, were maintained until 1990. Regarding the latter, one new factor did arise from the sudden spate of thefts of personal property, particularly burglary: reports dating from 1988 onwards often referred to poor security arrangements in flats and rented accommodation. Shortcomings in recruitment policies were also noted.[49]

These "objective" causes were supplemented by the failings of law enforcement agencies. As before, the judiciary came in for relatively little criticism. The main targets were social control bodies and police forces, which were once again denounced for their incompetence, laxity, venality and bureaucracy. "The heads of local Interior departments have no priorities, are inclined to formalism and make few demands to the police officers combating the theft of socialist property."[50] The latter were attacked for their lack of discernment: "At no time between 1986 and 1988 did [they] examine the issues surrounding the protection of assets in the commercial and industrial sectors, where 64 per cent of thefts are committed."[51] Some officials pointed out that researching the causes of crime diverted police forces from their primary task—its repression. The debates that had emerged with the creation of the laboratories for the legal and economic analysis of crime in the second half of the 1970s continued to structure representations of police activity. Regional leaders, eager to demonstrate their determination to confront crime and reinforce their authority, began to advocate repression as the only foreseeable solution.

[48] Information for the political day on the theme: "The 27th CPSU Congress and the Reinforcement of Socialist Legality", 1987; 8 pages. Fond 4, opis 113, delo 161, list 209.

[49] Information from the Sverdlovsk Region CPSU Committee State and Law Department: "On the State of Crime in the Region", early 1990; 12 pages. Fond 4, opis 118, delo 622, list 17.

[50] Interior Ministry Main Directorate for Combating the Theft of Socialist Property report: "On the Activity of Sverdlovsk Region Interior Services with regard to the Protection of Socialist Property", 19 December 1988; 13 pages. Fond 4, opis 117, delo 734, list 143.

[51] *Ibid.*, list 143.

Although the idea of more humane penalties is attractive, we should not allow ourselves to be carried away by it! Our situation has nothing in common with that of the developed capitalist countries: economic and ideological crisis, high crime rates and legal nihilism.[52] In a context such as this, the action we take should be guided by the fear of the penalty ... Too much time has been devoted to examining the "objective" causes of the rise in crime: criminals are now gaining ground.[53]

The repression associated with the implementation of the "dry law" was used to support this position, for crime rates had fallen in 1986 and 1987. "The principal explanation for the increase in serious offences in twenty-three towns and districts is the relaxation of the campaign against alcoholism. The initial fear induced by repressive measures did not last."[54] Enforcement of the "dry law" had borne fruit because the "imposition of sobriety on all layers of society created a shock effect."[55]

Among other things, greater repression required extra funding for police forces. At a meeting of Party activists, the regional committee created a "Legal Order" (*Pravoporyadok*) fund for maintaining order and fighting crime. Contributors would include enterprises, organisations and citizens.[56] This innovation, suggested by the regional council of enterprise directors, stemmed from an initiative on the part of A.M. Chernetskii,[57] director general of Uralkhimmash, one of the region's largest factories. Chernetskii sought to "participate in finding solutions to the problem of funding for more police officers and improving their technical resources."[58] Plans were made to notify the central

[52] The expression was current in the Soviet Union in the late 1980s, and indicated that individuals in all sections of society were ignoring established legal rules.

[53] Speech by L.F. Bobykin, first secretary of the Sverdlovsk Region CPSU Committee, at an expanded meeting of the college of the Interior Ministry Regional Directorate, 24 January 1989; 14 pages. Fond 4, opis 118, delo 637, list 9.

[54] Preliminary speech by the head of the Department of Administrative Organs: plenum of the Sverdlovsk region CPSU Committee, early 1988; 9 pages. Fond 4, opis 117, delo 733, list 59.

[55] Information from the regional Prosecutor's Office, communicated to the Sverdlovsk Region CPSU Committee State and Law Department prior to a meeting on the anti–crime campaign, 20 September 1989; 5 pages. Fond 4, opis 118, delo 625, list 25.

[56] Resolutions taken at the conclusion of a meeting of Party activists on the state of crime in the region, 4 August 1989; 73 pages. Fond 4, opis 118, delo 7, list 71.

[57] Chernetskii was appointed mayor of Yekaterinburg in February 1992.

[58] Speech by V.V. Andryanov, secretary of the Sverdlovsk region CPSU Committee, at a meeting of Party activists to discuss the state of crime in the region, 4 August 1989; 73 pages. Fond 4, opis 118, delo 7, list 10.

authorities and ask them to draw up an appropriate legislative framework.[59] The "Legal Order" fund opened a bank account and rapidly attracted contributions.[60] The initiative was copied by other Soviet regions.[61]

The remobilisation of citizens and reinforcement of social control had to be addressed also, for the number of *druzhinniki* had fallen to 4,660 in 1989. The Interior Ministry's regional directorate suggested following the example of a town in the Kherson region, where *druzhinniki* had a "financial interest in doing their job",[62] but leaders preferred the option of creating workers' detachments to assist the police. The first detachments were created in the region's factories in April 1989, when the initiative attracted the support of the Gorky Municipal Soviet. This was long before the CPSU Central Committee turned its attention to the issue. The detachments' priorities were hooliganism and alcoholism, although they also dealt with petty theft and speculation.

When the detachments were assessed several months later, their effect was generally found to be positive, but problems were noted, especially with regard to recruitment. As they operated during working hours and members received their normal salaries, many workshop managers assigned the task to "workers nearing retirement or, conversely, to very young people who had not done their military service."[63] Police officers were hostile to the initiative: "They are integrating workers into the police, but they know nothing about this kind of work! Instead of being used to fund these detachments, the money should have been spent on strengthening police forces."[64] Opponents of the creation of workers' detachments often based their objections on financial issues. Factory

[59] Resolutions taken at the conclusion of a meeting of Party activists on the state of crime in the region, 4 August 1989; 73 pp. Fond 4, opis 118, delo 7, list 72.

[60] Sverdlovsk region CPSU Committee State and Law Department report, late 1989; 7 pages. Fond 4, opis 118, delo 622, list 24.

[61] M. Galeotti, 1990a, p. 5.

[62] Interior Ministry Main Directorate report: "On Practical Cooperation between Interior Services and Social Organisations with regard to the Defence of Public Order and the Campaign against Crime", early 1989; 4 pages. Sverdlovsk region Executive Committee archives: Fond 88r, opis 2, delo 5035, list 2.

[63] Speech by E.I. Trukhin, commander of the Vysokogorsk metal factory workers' detachment, at a meeting of Party activists on the state of crime in the region, 4 August 1989; 73 pages. Fond 4, opis 118, delo 7, list 27.

[64] Speech by V.G. Brusenkov, local inspector in the city of Sverdlovsk, at a meeting of Party activists on the state of crime in the region, 4 August 1989; 73 pages. Fond 4, opis 118, delo 7, list 32.

workers opposed them on the grounds that the task "should be left to the professionals."[65]

Despite these consensual efforts, little ground was gained in the fight against crime. The "crackdowns" launched to showcase the determination and power of the police revealed a considerable gulf between the resources deployed and the results achieved. "A major operation to combat speculation in foodstuffs and standard consumer goods was conducted in the markets. Fifty-seven police officers were ordered to raid the markets and check on the activities of the vendors ... In total, twelve fines were imposed for minor speculation and seven cases of prosecutable speculation were recorded."[66]

When local police services were confronted with orders requiring them to demonstrate their commitment to more intensive action, they reacted as they had always done: "If we had recorded every offence we noted, the regional directorate would have been scandalised! Everyone around here knew perfectly well that crime was on the increase; a reduction in the indicators would have made anyone laugh! So crime in our city increased, but only by a little! That way we avoided problems, but only the most serious ones."[67]

Efforts to reinforce the campaign against crime facilitated the production of false statistics. According to the sociologist Yakov Gilinsky, the slowdown in crime rates from 1992 onwards reflected changes in the way local police forces recorded crime. During the first few months of 1992 the Russian authorities, alarmed by the sudden increase in recorded crime, laid the blame for it directly at the door of the MVD and other law enforcement agencies:

Blaming police forces and judicial services for the sudden increase in crime is like blaming seismologists for the persistent intensity of an earth tremor. What are seismologists supposed to do in such a situation? All they can do is adjust their instruments to indicate fewer points on the Richter scale ... The MVD and other crime-fighting bodies react to the authorities' harsh demands in the usual way: as there is no real possibility of controlling crime, they focus on what they can cope with, i.e. recording crime.[68]

---

[65] Speech by V.V. Garkachev, deputy director and *druzhina* commander of a Sverdlovsk region industrial complex, at a meeting of Party activists on the state of crime in the region, 4 August 1989; 73 pages. Fond 4, opis 118, delo 7, list 56.

[66] Regional OBKhSS report: "On the Results of the Raid on Chuvakino Market and the Central *Kolkhoz* Market in the City of Sverdlovsk", January 1989; 2 pages. Fond 4, opis 118, delo 627, lists 131–132.

[67] Interview with the head of the Interior Ministry department in a small town in the Urals, in post since 1986. Yekaterinburg, June 1997.

[68] Obshchestvennyi tsentr..., 1997, p. 21.

Concluding Remarks

Soviet police practices remained fundamentally untouched by the changes ushered in by *glasnost*. The skills acquired during the Brezhnev era, the methods developed to record crime, were easily brought back into play, as the implementation of the fight against "organised crime" clearly demonstrated. The term was so vague that law enforcement bodies were able to justify their efforts by recording relatively harmless practices as long as they involved some degree of planning and teamwork. Their response to the hierarchy's orders was still guided by a concern to appear compliant. As a result, police agents contributed to a new form of differential treatment of illegalities.. Petty thefts were the most recorded offences and were associated with traditional figures of delinquency. By contrast, frauds and other breaches of the rules of economic activity sharply decreased. Associated with economic reforms in progress, they tended to be considered as illegalities. Perspectives of repression were low; they still existed however, as they depended on the way entrepreneurs were protected.

As for the explanations of crime, new factors had been introduced, but they were mentioned at local level for opportunistic reasons. Law enforcement agents tended to put the blame on consensual factors in order to satisfy regional hierarchy's expectations. The denunciation of the conception of economic policy, the incoherence of penal policy and the lack of resources devoted to law enforcement should be understood not only as a reflection of an objective situation, but also as a useful opportunity to reinterpret the results of the action undertaken. However, the evolution of police activity cannot be summarised solely by the results of its fight against economic crime as a broad target. Law enforcement agencies also had to contend with new and specific problems arising from the effects of privatisation measures and other economic reforms, problems which further weakened the capacity of the authorities to intervene in the fight against crime.

11

THE POLICE AND PRIVATISATION

In this chapter, I will try to elaborate on the hypothesis about new forms of differential treatment of economic crime during *perestroika* and after. As I have shown, local statistical results show that predatory offences were the most recorded, at the expense of frauds and other breaches of the rules of economic activity. Does this mean that the police did not intervene during the implementation of economic reforms? Archives show in fact that law enforcement bodies paid attention to these reforms: many reports mention the evolution of crime in the cooperative sector and during further privatisation stages. Designed to improve the supply of goods and services,[1] the first measures to privatise commercial activity complicated the work of the police for two reasons. First, the conception of penal and economic policy resulted in contradictory orders which police officers had to interpret and rank in order of priority. This already occurred during the implementation of the law on individual labour activity, but it was especially apparent during the development of the cooperative sector: at that time, local police services received explicit orders not to stop that sector's development. The police were isolated from spontaneous privatisations as well. They were supposed to be involved during the privatisation process, but as I will show their activity was restricted to repression of basic cases of speculation in vouchers.

Secondly, police work became more complicated because new forms of knowledge and expertise were required to deal with the effects of economic

[1] Department of Administrative Organs report, early 1988: "On the State of the Campaign against Unearned Income"; 4 pages. Fond 4, opis 113, delo 722, list 18.

reform. The police therefore faced increasing difficulties in order to tackle crime in newly privatised firms.

Practical Management of Contradictory Injunctions

A famous cartoon in the satirical magazine *Krokodil* depicts two policemen on duty in a *kolkhoz* market. One says to the other: "That old boy selling the hand-made baskets—do we congratulate him for his individual labour or punish him for unearned income?"[2] The cartoon illustrated the difficulties confronting police officers in late 1986 and early 1987. The law on individual labour activity encouraged certain economic practices which were nevertheless regarded as sources of unearned income. Regional authorities expected police forces to crack down on "major offences involving profits and unearned income" but were also anxious to avoid "tying the hands of entrepreneurs who display initiative", for their "honest labour" was "socially useful."[3] According to this position, local police forces should have "congratulated the old boy", to return to the *Krokodil* cartoon, and concentrated on major economic offences. Now given Soviet police methods, it is a reasonable assumption that local forces found it hard to ignore minor economic offences. The hierarchy swiftly resolved this dilemma by encouraging the police to adopt a more lenient approach to new forms of enterprise. On 10 April 1987, the Interior Ministry issued a special directive (*spetsial'noe ukazanie*) informing all its regional directorates that:

Police officers still do not understand the meaning of the law on individual labour activity and the resolutions on cooperatives ... Satisfying the population's consumer needs takes precedence over everything else ... Their concentration on assessing the quality of goods and services provided through such activities, or the amount of tax paid by those involved, is intolerable. They should take a more lenient approach to forms of individual labour activity and cooperatives.[4]

This position was in keeping with the spirit of the legislation, which advised control bodies to refrain from "disrupting the work rate of cooperatives."[5] The

---

[2] *Krokodil*, no. 23, August 1987.
[3] Draft of a speech by the head of the Department of Administrative Organs, to be delivered at a Sverdlovsk Region CPSU Committee meeting on the management of *perestroika*, late 1987; 7 pages. Fond 4, opis 113, delo 724, list 182.
[4] Source: Ministerstvo Vnutrennikh Del RF, 1997, p. 5. The deputy director of the Sverdlovsk region economic crime department, in post for many years, agreed to send the author this directive.
[5] In: Article 32 of the "USSR Law on Cooperation in the USSR", 26 May 1988. *Spra-*

state banking sector took a similarly indulgent approach, recommending that local agencies "treat cooperatives with maximum goodwill."[6] Individual labour activity got off to a slow start in the Sverdlovsk region, with only 2,000 people registered at the beginning of July 1987. Most of them worked in the clothing industry, but some were involved in small-scale production, photography and taxi services.[7] Cooperatives began to proliferate following the adoption of resolutions in early 1987: ninety-three establishments were registered in the region by the end of May and 646 (9 per cent of the Russian total) by January 1988. Sverdlovsk *oblast'* went on to consolidate its status as a regional pioneer in the implementation of privatisations, notably in the early 1990s. The structure of the regional economy favoured the creation of specific cooperatives:

Proceedings have begun against the director of a forestry business who, in return for bribes offered by the director of 'V' cooperative, agreed to provide timber for construction purposes. Instead of manufacturing consumer goods, the cooperative was engaged in an illegal activity: it treated the timber and shipped it to *sovkhozes* in the Kazakhstan republic.[8]

Such activities were outside the legal framework: they were speculative and did not respond to local consumer needs. Moreover, they continued a tradition of illegal trafficking between Sverdlovsk *oblast'* and the southern regions of the Soviet Union that had been observed since at least the 1960s. They illustrated the willingness of some entrepreneurs to legalise illicit commercial activities, as was reflected in a 1988 OBKhSS offensive against the theft and inter-regional trafficking of timber.[9]

Cooperatives grew rapidly in big cities like Sverdlovsk and Nizhnii Tagil, but smaller towns were often noted for an "inability to comprehend the value of

---

vochnik partiinogo rabotnika, vypusk dvadtsat' devyatyi, 1989. Moscow, Izdatel'stvo Politicheskoi Literatury, 1989, p. 415.

[6] Note from the State Bank regional bureau to the Sverdlovsk region CPSU Committee economic department, a reaction to an article in the daily newspaper *Na smenu* on the growth of individual labour activity in the region, 15 May 1987; 7 pages. Fond 4, opis 113, delo 696, lists 97–8.

[7] Information from the Sverdlovsk region CPSU Committee statistics department, July-August 1987: "On Persons Engaged in Individual Labour Activity on 1 July 1987"; 3 pages. Fond 4, opis 113, delo 696, lists 119–121.

[8] Regional OBKhSS report, 25 January 1988: "On the State and Measures of the Campaign against Unearned Income." Fond 4, opis 117, delo 734, list 11.

[9] Regional OBKhSS report, 19 December 1988: "On the Activity of Interior Services with regard to the Protection of Socialist Property"; 13 pages. Fond 4, opis 117, delo 734, list 136.

the cooperative sector. Cooperatives have been created in only half of the thirty towns in the *oblast'*, and in only ten of twenty-three districts (*raiony*)."[10] The CPSU Regional Committee's Department of Administrative Organs issued a stream of orders in an attempt to remedy the situation. Municipal committees, for example, were urged to "ask themselves" whether they were witnessing "a weakening of the campaign against unearned income because of the enactment of the law on individual labour activity and the growth of cooperatives."[11]

Throughout 1987, reports inveighed against some of the difficulties created by new forms of enterprise, problems linked to spheres of activity, price-fixing, the socio-professional background of employees and taxation. Illicit dealing in timber had already highlighted the indignation generated by speculative practices. Cooperative restaurants and cafés were regarded with particular suspicion. According to the legislation, they were free to set prices for products made on site,[12] but not for anything purchased from state-owned shops or *kolkhoz* markets. In practice, some products were 350 per cent more expensive than those sold at set prices in state-owned shops, although such profits did not appear in the accounts. Some cooperatives offered their customers alcohol, which was also illegal.[13]

The new forms of enterprise were designed to attract the inactive, although they were open to wage-earners seeking secondary employment. But many state sector employees quickly left their jobs and took up full-time employment in cooperatives. By the end of 1987, two-thirds of cooperative sector staff had previously worked for the state sector.[14] Inevitably, tensions arose:

Our most prominent photographers are resigning, finding another job (as watchman, in the fire service) and acquiring a licence. In Nizhnii Tagil, for example, sixteen of the

---

[10] *Ibid.*, p. 47.

[11] Model of the list of questions to be asked to monitor the execution of the CPSU Central Committee Resolution of 15 May 1986 "On Measures to Reinforce the Campaign against Unearned Income." The list was drawn up by the Sverdlovsk region CPSU Committee Department of Administrative Organs and addressed to CPSU municipal committees. Early 1988; 4 pages. Fond 4, opis 117, delo 734, list 48.

[12] Point 2 of USSR Council of Ministers Resolution no. 160, 5 February 1987.

[13] Sverdlovsk region Prosecutor's Office report on offences noted in the cooperative sector, 22 September 1987; 4 pages. Fond 4, opis 113, delo 722, list 157.

[14] The proportion was even higher in the public catering sector. Report by an unidentified Sverdlovsk region CPSU Committee department: "On Individual Labour Activity and Cooperatives", November or December 1987; 6 pages. Fond 4, opis 113, delo 697, lists 55–56

thirty-four photographers have already taken this course and eight more are in the process of doing so... The sixteen specialists earn a minimum of 96,000 roubles a year, with profits of more than 20,000 roubles. However, they obtain a licence for 5,400 roubles. It amounts to robbing the state![15]

Moreover, many full-time cooperative members were not registered.[16] The higher wages offered by the embryonic private sector created unfair competition and sucked in state sector workers.[17]

At first, declarations of income from individual labour activity were not closely monitored. Of the 2,000 people registered in mid-1987, police services examined only twenty-nine cases.[18] Many actors expressed anger at the gulf between profits and the revenue received by the state: "The Cocktail-Bar cooperative made 54,000 roubles but paid only 358 in tax."[19] The Finance Ministry's regional control and revision department was responsible for checking the tax returns of private enterprises and cooperatives.[20]

The difficulties noted above prompted questions concerning the legal regulation of these new sectors. Some regional committee members condemned the preference of entrepreneurs for self-regulation and called upon the state to strengthen the framework surrounding their activities. "The process of creating cooperatives is not controlled. We must learn to steer individual initiatives towards satisfying consumer needs which the state sector does not meet."[21]

---

[15] Request put to Yuri Vladimirovich Petrov, first secretary of the Sverdlovsk region CPSU Committee, by the deputy head of Sverdloblfoto, the photographers' union, 30 April 1987; 3 pages. Fond 4, opis 113, delo 697, lists 61–62.

[16] Sverdlovsk municipality Interior Ministry report, 2 November 1987: "On the Information Regarding Cooperative Activity Available to the Sverdlovsk Municipality Department for Combating the Theft of Socialist Property"; 6 pages. Fond 4, opis 113, delo 722, list 148.

[17] USSR State Bank regional bureau report, 2 April 1987: "On the Organisation of Activity Relating to the Creation of Cooperatives"; 8 pages. Fond 4, opis 113, delo 696, list 26.

[18] Information from the Sverdlovsk region CPSU Committee statistics department, July-August 1987: "On Persons Engaged in Individual Labour Activity on 1 July 1987"; 3 pages. Fond 4, opis 113, delo 696, list 121.

[19] Sverdlovsk municipality Interior Ministry report, 2 November 1987: "On the Information Regarding Cooperative Activity Available to the Sverdlovsk Municipality OBKhSS Department"; 6 pages. Fond 4, opis 113, delo 722, list 150.

[20] USSR Finance Ministry regional control and revision department report, summer 1987; 10 pages. Fond 4, opis 113, delo 693, lists 109–118.

[21] Report by an unidentified department of the Sverdlovsk region CPSU Committee,

Conflicts between the rules imposed by the legislator and those invented by entrepreneurs were already clearly apparent. The April 1988 law on cooperatives was designed to provide the sector with a proper regulatory framework.

The Police and Cooperatives

In the Sverdlovsk region, the cooperative movement gained momentum in 1988, with 646 establishments registered at the beginning of that year. Twelve months later, the number had risen to 2,661, 1,656 of which were active. At the beginning of 1990, there were 4,079 registered cooperatives in the region, 3,445 of which were active.[22] The percentage of active cooperatives in relation to the recorded number of establishments exceeded the national average.[23] Premises, equipment and raw materials seemed easier to obtain in Sverdlovsk *oblast'* than in other regions. By 1 July 1989, cooperatives were employing 1% of the regional population.[24] Six months later, this figure had almost doubled.[25] The most highly developed sectors were those involved in the production of consumer goods and the provision of basic services.[26]

The problems surrounding the identity of employees in the cooperative sector became clearer. When cooperatives were created within state enterprises, their members were often senior managers in the original structure. They

---

November or December 1987: "On Individual Labour Activity and Cooperatives"; 6 pages. Fond 4, opis 113, delo 697, lists 57–58.

[22] Information from the regional OBKhSS, July-August 1990: "On the Fundamental Developmental Tendencies of the Cooperative Movement in the Sverdlovsk Region and their Influence on Crime in the Economic Sphere"; 15 pages, p. 1. Document transmitted by the former head of the regional branch of the Union of Cooperatives (*Soyuz ob'edinennykh kooperativov*). Yekaterinburg, June 1997.

[23] M.-A. Crosnier, 1989, p. 66.

[24] Information from the OBKhSS, September 1989: "On the Measures Taken by the Interior Regional Directorate to Regulate the Activity of Cooperatives"; 5 pages. Fond 4, opis 118, delo 627, list 75.

[25] Information from the regional OBKhSS, July-August 1990: "On the Fundamental Developmental Tendencies of the Cooperative Movement in the Sverdlovsk Region and their Influence on Crime in the Economic Sphere"; 15 pages, p. 1. Document transmitted by the former head of the regional branch of the Union of Cooperatives (*Soyuz ob'edinennykh kooperativov*). Yekaterinburg, June 1997.

[26] Information from the regional OBKhSS, September 1989: "On the Measures Taken by the Interior Regional Directorate to Regulate the Activity of Cooperatives"; 5 pages. Fond 4, opis 118, delo 627, list 75.

tended to ignore their primary function and devote all their time to the more lucrative and prestigious cooperative activity. For example, one cooperative specialising in the production of micro-computers numbered among its members the chief engineer, accountant, planning and supply managers and workshop manager of the parent enterprise; these people controlled "the entire technological production chain."[27] The concern was so successful that productivity in the state-owned enterprise rapidly declined.[28] Law enforcement agencies were also worried by the employment of "delinquents" in this profitable sector. The ban on people with criminal records occupying management posts was not observed, and some cooperative workers were forced to resign for that reason.[29] Recorded cases suggest that resorting to the use of a front man was widespread in cooperatives, and indeed the most powerful criminal organisations in Yekaterinburg became increasingly involved in economic activities during the late 1980s and early 1990s.[30]

Shortages of raw materials and production goods encouraged the diversion of state property, which had a knock-on effect on prices. "In 1987, 'U' cooperative reached an agreement with one of the municipal supply agencies, which then handed over its stock of cassettes. Once recorded, they were sold at much higher prices."[31] More than 40 per cent of cooperative members claimed that shortages of essential equipment, transport and raw materials led to abuses, diversions and other offences motivated by profit.[32]

Cooperatives were forced to accept the administrative costs imposed by the officials who controlled the resources essential to the development of their commercial activities. These transactions amounted to elementary forms of

---

[27] Information drafted by the Sverdlovsk region Prosecutor's Office and Interior Directorate, early 1989: "On the Inadequacies Noted in Cooperative Activity in the Region"; 7 pages. Fond 4, opis 117, delo 734, lists121–122.

[28] *Ibid.*, lists 121–122.

[29] *Ibid.*, list 122.

[30] One researcher has traced the history of the economic development of the "Central" and "Uralmash" criminal organisations, showing that they benefited from the growth of the cooperative sector at a relatively early stage (early 1988). V.B. Zhitenev, 1993. See also V. Volkov, 2002, pp. 116–22.

[31] Information drafted by the Sverdlovsk region Prosecutor's Office and Interior Directorate, early 1989: "On the Inadequacies Noted in Cooperative Activity in the Region"; 7 pages. Fond 4, opis 117, delo 734, list 122.

[32] Interior Ministry regional directorate report, 1988: "On the Use of the Results of Sociological Surveys in the Preventive Activity of the Apparatus Combating the Theft of Socialist Property"; 3 pages. Fond 4, opis 117, delo 734, list 11.

extortion associated with registration and the allocation of premises. "According to MGU researchers,[33] 90 per cent of cooperatives in Moscow obtained premises through bribery. We have no such information for the city of Sverdlovsk, but it probably happens here as well."[34] Not all such transactions escaped attention: "The 'Yu' cooperative bought a Moskvich car and immediately 'leased' it to the district executive committee's communal services department. Now according to the executive committee accountant, there is no provision for or reference to this lease in the budget. The cooperative, which proclaims its eagerness to contribute to the electoral campaign fund, also pays for the petrol."[35]

By 1988, it was clear that the role of administrative officials in the implementation of economic policy had created considerable opportunities for the accumulation of unearned income. The living standards maintained by public officials, the way in which they accounted for their activities, and the monitoring and inspection mechanisms in bureaucratic organisations ensured that such conduct was widespread.

Price fixing and payment of taxes due were also matters of concern to police forces, which were not empowered to confiscate cooperative assets: "A cooperative's assets cannot be seized without a ruling from a court or arbitration tribunal. In reality, the competent courts refuse to handle disputes. In consequence, cooperatives believe they can act with impunity."[36] The tax issue was revived with the publication of a USSR Supreme Soviet decree on 6 June 1989. This measure increased taxes but also gave local executive committees the right to lower them, and even to exempt certain cooperatives from taxation. Local administrations thus acquired a new resource—the possibility of granting sig-

---

[33] Moscow State University.

[34] Proposals for preventing crime in the cooperative movement, put to the Sverdlovsk region CPSU Committee State and Law Department by the Yekaterinburg Legal Institute chair of civil law, summer 1989; 3 pages. Fond 4, opis 118, delo 627, list 81.

[35] This was a campaign for the election of deputies to the local Soviet. Source: report by the Department of Administrative and Military Organs inspectorate of the USSR People's Control Committee, 2 March 1989, on the application of the USSR Council of Ministers Resolution of 29 December 1989 "On the Regulation of Separate Aspects of Cooperative Activity in Accordance with the USSR Law 'On Cooperation in the USSR' in the Sverdlovsk region"; 9 pages. Fond 4, opis 118, delo 627, list 63.

[36] Information drafted by the Sverdlovsk region Prosecutor's Office and Interior Ministry Directorate, early 1989: "On the Inadequacies Noted in Cooperative Activity in the Region"; 7 pages. Fond 4, opis 117, delo 734, list 124.

nificant privileges in an arbitrary way. Warnings of the potential effects of this measure were not slow in coming: "It is quite possible that cooperatives will offer bribes in return for tax privileges or that executive committee officials will compel them to pay for this kind of service."[37] The sector swiftly devised ways to counteract the increases.[38] A cooperative in the Sverdlovsk region could go into liquidation and then register under another name in one of the Soviet republics where taxes were lower, Turkmenistan or the Baltic states, for example. As a result, the Sverdlovsk concern became a subsidiary of a cooperative registered outside the RSFSR. This procedure required the full support of administrative officials, who, as a rule, gave priority to locally-registered businesses (a proportion of whose taxes contributed to the local budget) when allocating premises.[39]

The accounting practices maintained by cooperatives attracted some sharp criticism. Given the absence of sanctions, cooperative owners had no incentive to keep rigorous accounts. "The absence of accounting documents and the accumulation of untraceable cash (no tickets or receipts) should be regarded as gross violations of the law, for they enable [cooperatives] to avoid declaring their total income. Cooperatives do not keep accounts because sanctions are restricted to warnings or, in the worst of cases, to the liquidation of the establishment."[40]

The legislation concerning cooperatives did not regulate the ways in which income was used. Cooperatives set their own wage and investment levels. No checks were made on the use of bank loans. Access to such loans was by no means guaranteed and was largely dependent on relations established with bank officials. In many cases, a cooperative's accountant was also employed by

---

[37] Proposals for preventing crime in the cooperative movement put to the Sverdlovsk region CPSU Committee State and Law Department by the Yekaterinburg Legal Institute chair of civil law, summer 1989; 3 pages. Fond 4, opis 118, delo 627, list 80.

[38] Taxes on particularly high revenues were set for cooperatives in the building, food and commerce sectors. See "Decree of the Presidium of the USSR Supreme Soviet 'On Calculating Tax on Cooperative Sector Revenues'" in *Vedomosti Verkhovnogo Soveta RSFSR*, no. 23, 8 June 1989. Article 575.

[39] Proposals for preventing crime in the cooperative movement put to the Sverdlovsk region CPSU Committee State and Law Department by the Yekaterinburg Legal Institute chair of civil law, summer 1989; 3 pages. Fond 4, opis 118, delo 627, list 81.

[40] *Ibid.*, list 82.

a bank. For the OBKhSS regional directorate, it was no accident that 28.2% of the bank loans made in 1990 went to cooperatives.[41]

The considerable opportunities for enrichment opened to cooperatives aroused the ire of local populations: "In towns like Nizhnii Tagil, cooperative workers were beaten up."[42] These incidents were often spontaneous expressions of collective anger, but public resentment was also exploited by those with scores to settle: "The pogroms[43] against cooperatives are frequently organised by racketeers."[44] The police refused to intervene: "They don't think it is their job, and do not want to waste effort on cooperative members. And the latter are unlikely to approach the police when they are targeted by racketeers."[45]

Official measures to restrict the sector's spheres of activity were met with resistance. In the Sverdlovsk region, the resolution published in December 1988 meant that more than 300 cooperatives would be required to change the kind of work for which they had been created. About 200 of these establishments specialised in screening films and videos, as well as the sale of videocassettes. Establishments were given one month to change their line of business or sign a contract with a state-owned enterprise or organisation, but this was insufficient. The restrictions proved ineffective as entrepreneurs devised various strategies to circumvent them (integrating a business into a Komsomol centre, for example). "State-owned enterprises are used by cooperatives to transform credit lines into cash. All they have to do is transfer them to cooperative accounts, acquire raw materials and goods, and then sell them on."[46]

---

[41] Information from the regional OBKhSS, July-August 1990: "On the Fundamental Developmental Tendencies of the Cooperative Movement in the Sverdlovsk region and their Influence on Crime in the Economic Sphere"; 15 pages, p. 1. Document transmitted by a former head of the regional branch of the Union of Cooperatives (*Soyuz ob'edinennykh Kooperativov*). Yekaterinburg, June 1997.

[42] Speech by V.V. Andryanov, secretary of the Sverdlovsk region CPSU Committee, at a meeting of CPSU regional activists on the state of the campaign against crime, 4 August 1989; 73 pages. Fond 4, opis 118, delo 7, list 17.

[43] "Pogrom" is the Russian term, showing that the clashes were often based on inter-ethnic feeling, as many members of restaurants and cafés' cooperatives were from Caucasus.

[44] Proposals for preventing crime in the cooperative movement put to the Sverdlovsk region CPSU Committee State and Law Department by the Yekaterinburg Legal Institute chair of civil law, summer 1989; 3 pages. Fond 4, opis 118, delo 627, list 82.

[45] *Ibid.*, list 82.

[46] USSR Finance Ministry regional control and revision department report, early 1989: "On Cooperatives"; 2 pages. Fond 4, opis 118, delo 627, list 68.

The authorities found it even more difficult to enforce the restrictions as entrepreneurs had begun to organise at local level, founding in April 1989 a regional cooperative members' union, a branch of the Union of United Cooperatives. Like the nationwide unions noted earlier, this organisation was formed to defend the interests of cooperative members. It campaigned for a crackdown on racketeering in the sector and attempted to establish a clear distinction between respectable businessmen and unscrupulous criminals. "We formed a group of civilised cooperative members—non-criminals, in other words—and mobilised all our contacts in administrative bodies and the Party."[47] The authorities were also hampered by the increase in cooperatives offering legal advice. For instance, the "Jurist" cooperative was formally registered in October 1988; six months later it had more than 3,000 clients on its books and had decided to open its first subsidiary company. According to its statutes, it "provided legal aid to the general public, cooperatives and enterprises",[48] but it also sought to participate in criminal investigations. This idea was supported by the district Prosecutor's Office and the head of the regional executive committee's justice department, but resolutely opposed by the district executive committee officials responsible for registering modifications to the status of cooperatives, who attempted to have the establishment shut down. Despite the hostility, such services were in great demand; cooperatives specialising in legal advice to the sector prospered in the Sverdlovsk region and attracted young graduates: "By the time I founded my first cooperative, it was already clear that entrepreneurs would have to join forces in order to defend their interests. The creation of a legal aid cooperative met this need by helping the entrepreneur to do his job and overcome legal and bureaucratic obstacles. There was considerable demand from the outset."[49]

In order to adapt to changes in the law, entrepreneurs needed contacts in the administration, a grasp of legal matters and a protection system. Cooperative members subjected existing legislation to close scrutiny, for their decisions were based on its provisions, contradictions and lacunae. Rather than break the law, they sought to exploit its weaknesses and incoherence in a context

---

[47] Interview with a former representative of the Sverdlovsk region League of Cooperatives, now a businessman, Yekaterinburg, June 1997.

[48] Letter from the president of the *Yurist* (Jurist) cooperative to the president of the regional executive committee and the first secretary of the Sverdlovsk region CPSU Committee, April 1989; 2 pages. Fond 4, opis 118, delo 627, list 83.

[49] Interview with a former representative of the Sverdlovsk region League of Cooperatives, now a businessman. Yekaterinburg, June 1997.

where federal authorities valued entrepreneurial inventiveness. This approach softened the impact of the blows sustained by the movement in September-October 1989, although some entrepreneurs complained about the police hostility engendered by these reversals: "Our cooperative was ransacked by district police forces, which were supposedly investigating thefts of food products and tax fraud in cooperatives."[50] The statement highlights the importance of the schemes the sector had devised to protect itself, given its lack of social legitimacy and legal vulnerability. If they were to function efficiently, they would have to shield members from the police and any other government officials who might impede their activities. A private enterprise could be protected at the behest of a leading politician or department head. The head of the CPSU Regional Committee's Department of Administrative Organs could ask for two police officers to be posted to guard a bank. Such favours revealed the extent of the collusion between Party members, government officials and business leaders.

Most of the traditional explanatory factors were not sufficient to justify the results of police activity in the cooperative sector. The police argued that they were not trained to deal with unfamiliar forms of economic crime, and were confused by federal policy.

The initial reforms implied that some of the police officers combating economic crime would receive specialised training. This concern arose with the introduction of new business legislation at the beginning of 1988. The transition to independent accounting systems and financial management meant that police officers would have to be equipped with "new professional skills",[51] and justified the need to "restructure the ways in which OBKhSS services operated."[52] Police services with direct involvement also stressed the need for change. "One police officer in six has no idea how he is supposed to deal with the greater independence in accounting and financial matters granted to cooperatives and individual labour activity; 56 per cent are unsure of their duties in these circumstances. Only one third of the officers questioned said they were capable of working effectively in the present context."[53]

---

[50] Letter to the Sverdlovsk region CPSU Committee Department of Administrative Organs, January 1990; 2 pages. Fond 4, opis 118, delo 654, list 4.

[51] *Ibid.*, list 64.

[52] Documents prepared by the regional OBKhSS for the plenum of the Sverdlovsk region CPSU, 8 July 1988; 5 pages plus appendices. Fond 4, opis 117, delo 729, lists 63–64.

[53] OBKhSS report, 19 December 1988: "On the Activity of Sverdlovsk Region Inte-

Police officers' skills had been a source of concern long before the development of the cooperative sector, but the problem was considerably exacerbated by the emergence of the private economy. There were no resources to meet new requirements; professional training was not prioritised[54] and OBKhSS officers were frequently compelled to fall back on their own limited resources. The vague wording of legislative texts and the existence of contradictory guidelines for the regulation of entrepreneurial activity meant that police officers had a purely formal knowledge of the way cooperatives worked, and were ignorant of the practices such establishments devised in order to function properly. "The first time I investigated a cooperative, I realised I knew far less than its managers. It came as a shock to me."[55] Another officer from the same service insisted that it was not "profitable" to pursue cases in the cooperative sector: "We were capable of understanding what was going on and detecting offences committed by commercial cooperatives, but it required too much time and results could not be guaranteed."[56]

The police also lacked the manpower required to deal with the new challenges. The number of officers responsible for policing the rapidly expanding cooperative sector was derisory: in September 1988, seventeen officers were tasked with monitoring the activities of the 653 cooperatives operating in the city of Sverdlovsk.[57] In 1989, alarm was expressed over inadequacy of police resources compared with those available to criminals: "The number of policemen leaving to work in other branches of the economy is not yet considerable but could soon become so, because their living standards and working conditions are not satisfactory. And criminals are now using computers!"[58] Very little effort was devoted to tackling crime in the cooperative sector. It was extremely

---

rior Services with regard to the Protection of Socialist Property"; 13 pages. Fond 4, opis 117, delo 734, list 142.

[54] *Ibid.*, list 142.

[55] Interview with the current deputy director of the Sverdlovsk region office for combating economic crime. Yekaterinburg, June 1997.

[56] Interview with a former regional OBKhSS cadre, in post until 1990 and since working for a private company. Yekaterinburg, June 1997.

[57] Regional OBKhSS report, October 1988: "On the Activity of Sverdlovsk Municipality Department for Combating the Theft of Socialist Property with regard to the Prevention of Offences against the Economic System and Abuses of Office"; 6 pages. Fond 4, opis 117, delo 734, list 96.

[58] Proposals by the Sverdlovsk region CPSU Committee State and Law Department with regard to the campaign against crime, early1989; 8 pages. Fond 4, opis 118, delo 622, list 44.

rare for a cooperative member to stand trial or be convicted of an offence. At the very most, proceedings were initiated. At the end of 1988, federal OBKhSS cadres, instructed by the Interior Ministry to monitor the regional directorate, found that no cooperative member had as yet been tried in a criminal court for property theft, breaches of the rules of economic activity or abuse of office.[59] The principal sanction applied to cooperatives was closure, with 300 establishments closed down on health or economic grounds by the end of 1988.[60] Police forces seemed uninterested in the sector's development that year: no cooperative sector offences were recorded in Nizhnii Tagil between January and October 1988. This aroused the ire of the Interior Ministry's regional directorate, which decided to sanction the head of the local OBKhSS service.[61]

In such a context, "the few offences recorded were not particularly dangerous to society. On the other hand, no attempt is being made to dismantle dangerous criminal groups."[62] While the hierarchy tried to encourage the development of cooperatives and at the same time step up the campaign against large-scale economic crime, it did not address the methods used to monitor the activities of subordinate agencies. OBKhSS services, which were keen to convey the impression that they were complying with orders, swiftly restricted their targets to cafés and restaurants. They also pounced on *shashlik* (grilled meat) vendors, for it was easy to detect whether they were falsifying accounts, avoiding tax or selling sub-standard products. The less visible cooperatives operating within large-scale enterprises—specialists in the timber and metal trades, for example—were much more difficult to monitor.

Police officers often reacted to the situation by "exit" or "voice" strategies.[63] Defection could be a matter of giving priority to opportunistic practices during working hours: negligence, idleness, corruption, theft, participation in criminal undertakings. "The corruption case involving an OBKhSS inspector in the city of Sverdlovsk is still fresh in our minds ... We are now confronted

---

[59] Main OBKhSS Directorate report, 19 December 1988: "On the Activity of Sverdlovsk region Interior Services to Protect Socialist Property"; 13 pages. Fond 4, opis 117, delo 734, list 141.

[60] *Ibid.*, list 141.

[61] Order of the Interior Ministry Main Directorate, October 1988: "On the Serious Inadequacies Noted in the Activities of Services Combating the Theft of Socialist Property in the Municipalities of Sverdlovsk, Nizhnii Tagil, Berezovskii and Nevyansk, and on the Sanctions Applied to the Guilty"; 4 pages. Fond 4, opis 117, delo 734, lists 111–112.

[62] *Ibid.*, list 111.

[63] A. Hirschman, 1970.

with something far worse: another agent of the same service, motivated by the taste for money, is accused of murder. This is the dénouement of a long-standing relationship with recidivist speculators."[64] Many officers resigned: according to the head of the OBKhSS, more than half of his staff did so between 1988 and 1993.[65] "Qualified specialists are leaving us because they are disoriented: businessmen enrich themselves with impunity and nothing is done to stop them."[66] Police officers were confused and tended to "kowtow to businessmen and abandon most of their principles."[67] While their colleagues in other services took jobs as watchmen, OBKhSS officers readily accepted employment in the economic intelligence and internal security departments run by major enterprises.

Some police officers chose to speak out, openly criticising the government's penal policy and highlighting the contradictions in CPSU Central Committee resolutions.[68] They also complained about the amount of time required to "clarify legal difficulties."[69] These officers readily portrayed themselves as the victims of central decisions, claiming that they were given no notification of imminent changes to the law, and were forced to adapt their work to policies that they did not understand and over which they had no influence. Such resentment was also expressed in other Soviet cities.[70]

---

[64] Preliminary speech by Yuri Petrov, first secretary of the Sverdlovsk region, at an expanded meeting of the college of the regional Interior Ministry directorate, 22 January 1988; 5 pages. Fond 4, opis 117, delo 730, list 50.

[65] Interview conducted in Yekaterinburg, June 1997.

[66] Speech by V.V. Andryanov, secretary of the Sverdlovsk region CPSU Committee, at a meeting of Party activists on the state of crime in the region, 4 August 1989; 73 pages. Fond 4, opis 118, delo 7, lists 21–22.

[67] Speech by V.I. Vinokurov, first secretary of the Verhnyaya-Salda municipality CPSU Committee, at a meeting of Party activists on the state of crime in the region, 4 August 1989; 73 pages. Fond 4, opis 118, delo 7, list 25.

[68] The Resolution of 2 April 1988 "On the State of the Campaign against Crime in the Country and Additional Measures to Prevent Crime" aroused a great deal of criticism. Source: preparatory note by the Sverdlovsk region Prosecutor's Office for a meeting of Party activists on the anti–crime campaign, 20 July 1989; 5 pages. Fond 4, opis 118, delo 625, list 27.

[69] Proposals by the Sverdlovsk region CPSU Committee State and Law Department with regard to the campaign against crime, early 1989; 8 pages. Fond 4, opis 118, delo 622, list 45.

[70] In April 1989 in Leningrad, policemen even dared to organise a public demonstration asking for improvement of their working conditions. Some of the leaders were rapidly arrested. See: *Literaturnaya Gazeta*, no. 19, 1989; *Pravda*, 5 May 1989.

The Observation of Spontaneous Privatisation

The hierarchy within the Interior Ministry did not request regular reports on the various forms of spontaneous privatisation. The information available on illicit practices in TsNTTMs (Centres for Scientific and Technical Creativity of the Youth)[71] and "Komsomol enterprises" confirms that no penal policy was implemented with regard to these structures. In 1987, TsNTTMs were seen as pioneer initiatives in the process of economic reform. Encouraging the creativity of young Komsomol members was a duty, a means of assisting the "democratisation of the economy", the "development of the self-financing principle" and the "initiative of young people."[72]

According to an assessment conducted by the socio-economic department of the CPSU Regional Committee, TsNTTM turnover exceeded 25 million roubles, while Komsomol enterprises generated 20 million roubles . Over one-fourth of the registered income earned by TsNTTMs was transferred to executive committee budgets and allocated to scientific and technological research and development. Among other things, this money funded equipment for a hospital treating troops fighting in Afghanistan, the construction of a zoological park and the creation of crèches. There were 36 TsNTTMs and 133 Komsomol enterprises operating in the Sverdlovsk region at the beginning of 1990. TsNTTMs were engaged in a variety of tasks: they adjusted equipment; drew up project estimates; manufactured machinery and instruments for scientific, medical and other purposes; produced consumer goods and construction materials; and equipped classrooms with computer hardware.[73]

The CPSU Regional Committee's socio-economic department, responsible for checking the accounts of these enterprises, criticised their book-keeping: "The most characteristic accounting practices are unwarranted payment of travelling expenses and the padding of expenses."[74] Given the poor quality of available accounting documents, the supervisory body found it difficult to track and verify the movement of capital.[75] Moreover, these commercial structures often engaged in speculative activities connected to shortages of con-

---

[71] *Tsentry Nauchno-Tekhnicheskogo Tvorchestva Molodyozhi* (TsNTTM). See chapter III, A, 1, b.

[72] Sverdlovsk region CPSU Committee socio-economic department report, early 1990: "On New Forms of Economic Activity Arising from Komsomol Committee Initiatives in the Region"; 5 pages. Fond 4, opis 118, delo 527, list 47.

[73] *Ibid.*, lists 47–48.

[74] *Ibid.*, list 49.

[75] *Ibid.*

sumer goods. "The 'Universal' union created by the Komsomol committee in the town of Kushva made over 35,000 roubles from the sale of televisions, calculators and computers, its prices being 88 per cent higher than those set by the state."[76]

Staging of concerts and screening of videocassettes were particularly troublesome for the authorities: there was no control over the kind of films shown; videos were sold unofficially; entry to screenings was on a cash only basis; no tickets were issued and the takings did not appear in the accounts. According to supervisory bodies, these activities facilitated the concealment of large amounts of money.[77] Banned cooperatives sometimes used TsNTTMs as fronts: "It is worrying to note that many of the film and videocassette cooperatives closed down by local services are continuing to operate within TsNTTM or other Komsomol organisations."[78]

The socio-economic department expressed outrage at the practices it uncovered and their immunity from punishment. "All kinds of wheelers and dealers are attracted by the highly advantageous working conditions in these structures. The legal basis is weak and the training of cadres non-existent ... Greater supervision is urgently required."[79] These structures benefited from political and administrative protection and were able to rebuff attempts by financial control bodies to meddle in their affairs. "It is time to eliminate the specific privileges enjoyed by Komsomol-sponsored enterprises, particularly with regard to the state's financial control services. They should not be allowed to prevent these services from monitoring their activities in future."[80] However, the authorities' concerns were limited to the ability of the socio-economic department to deal with the situation; on very few occasions were the police or courts involved. "I knew exactly what was going on in that Centre, but it was untouchable. When I began to take a close look at it, I swiftly realised that

---

[76] *Ibid.*

[77] *Ibid.*, list 50.

[78] Report by the inspectorate of the Military and Administrative Services Department of the USSR People's Control Committee, 2 March 1989, on the application of the USSR Council of Ministers Resolution of 29 December 1988 "On the Regulation of Certain Aspects of Cooperative Activity in Accordance with the USSR law 'On Cooperation in the USSR' in the Sverdlovsk region"; 9 pages. Fond 4, opis 118, delo 627, lists 61–62.

[79] Sverdlovsk region CPSU Committee Socio-Economic Department report, early 1990: "On the New Forms of Economic Activity Arising from Komsomol Committee Initiatives in the Region"; 5 pages. Fond 4, opis 118, delo 527, list 50.

[80] *Ibid.*, list 51.

I was making a mistake. A top-ranking regional politician phoned my boss and explained that the Centre in question should be left alone."[81]

In practice, TsNTTM managers were not troubled by sanctions; when accused of economic offences, they were treated in the same way as CPSU members. Disciplinary sanctions constituted the chief threat, but their impact was diminishing by the day.

The archives consulted for this book contain virtually no information on other methods of privatising commercial activity. Leasing procedures were regarded in a rather positive light.[82] Even so, there were warnings that this reform might have detrimental effects. Of particular concern was the arbitrary way in which sale prices were calculated, as well as the vulnerability of property rights: "The procedure for setting the sale price, which is activated when the lease is signed, is not adequately regulated. The evaluation of the leased asset relies on subjective criteria."[83] With regard to vulnerability: "Guaranteeing a lease with an option to purchase is problematic. How can a workers' collective be assured that it will indeed assume ownership after three years?"[84]

The CPSU Regional Committee ordered legal and economic research institutes to compile reports on the potential effects of the economic reforms under consideration. Their predictions were often disturbing and highly accurate in their assessment of the possible criminal consequences of forthcoming reforms. "Share ownership will erode citizens' savings. There is little doubt that only those with significant means will buy shares, and that most of their resources will come from the shadow economy. By introducing share ownership, we are creating a mechanism for money-laundering."[85]

This prediction is significant for the very fact of its existence, although the influences behind its formulation are highly ambiguous. It could reflect objective expertise, but it could also express the willingness to give scientific ground to political opinions. Indeed, political opposition had begun to crystallise

---

[81] Interview with a former Sverdlovsk region OBKhSS officer, in post from 1985 to 1990 and now employed in the security department of a regional bank, Yekaterinburg, June 1997.

[82] Note on the involvement of the Sverdlovsk region CPSU Committee socio-economic department in drafting and realising economic reforms, 1989; 8 pages. Fond 4, opis 118, delo 527, list 56.

[83] Socio-Economic Department report compiled from studies conducted by the Economic Institute (USSR Academy of Sciences) on the problems relating to economic reform, late 1989; 16 pages. Fond 4, opis 118, delo 527, list 18.

[84] *Ibid.*, list 18.

[85] *Ibid.*, list 22.

around the speed and extent of programmes for economic reform. The text cited above contributed to this debate by advocating a gradualist approach, given the risks involved. However, observation of the privatisation process confirms the relevance of the forecast.

Repression of 'Crime in the Sphere of Privatisation'

The inability of penal policy to cope with the effects of privatisation was reflected in police activity at local level. However, at some point in 1992–93 police services created a new operational category—"offences in the sphere of privatisation"[86]—which comprised property crime, breaches of the rules of economic activity and abuse of office. But a close examination of the cases pursued as part of this new mission suggests that when compared to the scale of the illicit practices arising from *prikhvatizatsiya*, police efforts were minimal.[87] Results of the fight against "offences in the sphere of privatisation" were obtained through the recording of petty cases of vouchers' speculation and swindles.

Prikhvatizatsiya. The anonymity of the vouchers facilitated their circulation and misappropriation. Every institutional actor with access to vouchers could try to amass them. Investment funds were at the forefront of this activity and often resorted to a variety of underhand methods. Some funds suddenly wound up their business, leaving the clients who had entrusted their vouchers to them with nothing.[88] Such cases often attracted wide media coverage, shocked the public and contradicted the political discourse which emphasised the "popular" or "mass" aspect of this phase of the privatisation process. The savings banks (*sberbank*), tasked with distributing vouchers to the general public, sometimes padded the list of beneficiaries with the names of people who

---

[86] See, for example, Z. Korneva, 1993; S. Alyabin, A. Bochkov and Z. Korneva, 1994.

[87] The neologism is a play on words from the substantive *privatizatsiya* and the verb *prikhvatit'*, meaning to monopolise, corner or capture.

[88] Two notorious cases involved, for instance, the St Petersburg investment funds *Amaris* and *Revansh*. "Between October 1992 and February 1993, the founders of the joint-stock company *Amaris* amassed more than 190,000 vouchers and attempted to steal them by winding up the business. At the same time, the founders of the limited liability company *Revansh* swindled a large number of people out of 150,000 vouchers. Other massive investment fund swindles took place in St Petersburg. In total, more than one million of the city's inhabitants were swindled." *Kriminogennye faktory...*, 1993.

had recently left the area or had died before the enactment of the presidential decree on privatisation cheques.[89] The Property Funds, which operated until late 1993, and the Committees for the management of State Property, sometimes ignored their obligations, "forgot" to cancel vouchers that had already been used at auctions and competitive tenders, and used them again.[90] Offences were also noted in relation to deposit centres and the destruction of used vouchers. The list of offences related to trafficking in vouchers extended to forgery, four cases of which were recorded in the Sverdlovsk region.[91] All citizens in possession of vouchers were vulnerable to a variety of swindles, particularly if they sold them in the street or to the agencies set up in factories by investment funds,[92] where the rate fluctuated.

Other offences noted during the first phase of privatisation were linked to the various methods of ownership transfer: auctions and public tenders, shares sales and leasing an enterprise with an option to purchase.

Auctions and public tenders. Offences arising from auctions and public tenders for privatisation of shops, catering businesses and small-scale enterprises could involve three types of actor: officials of the department overseeing the transaction, buyers and managers of the enterprise undergoing privatisation.

Administrative officials were in a position to modify auction and public tender procedures. An auction was supposed to be advertised in the press, but such information might be conveyed only to a single interested party. On occasion, procedure was abandoned completely and the asset was transferred directly. Favouritism of this kind went hand-in-hand with a predatory attitude: "Staff often supplement their salaries with the returns from privatisation operations."[93]

---

[89] Interior Ministry Regional Directorate report, 1994: "On the Fundamental Principles and Perspectives of Privatisation in Russia", p. 4.

[90] Louise Shelley describes one case in which an agent of the St Petersburg State Property Committee was arrested on suspicion of recycling 90 per cent of the eight million vouchers used at the auctions and competitive tenders organised at municipal level. L. Shelley, 1995, p. 250.

[91] *Prestunost' v sfere privatizatsii* (Crime in the Sphere of Privatisation). Document produced by the Sverdlovsk region economic crime department, June 1994, 9 pages.

[92] In one of Yekaterinburg's largest factories, an investment fund installed agencies offering scarce food products in exchange for vouchers. Interview with the director of one of the largest investment funds, Yekaterinburg, September 1994.

[93] Interview with the director of the Sverdlovsk regional Committee for the Manage-

Buyers committed offences by bending the rules in order to gain an advantage or eliminate potential rivals. The most common practices involved using contacts in the administration to monopolise access to information, sideline competitors or obtain unwarranted advantages. I personally attended three auctions at which shops were sold off, all of which were characterised by a flagrant disregard for procedure. In the first instance, the asset went to the single bidder present. Two individuals attended the second auction, but one dropped out almost immediately. The third was attended by several bidders, one of whom, surrounded by scowling bodyguards,[94] persuaded his rivals to withdraw. In all three cases, the asset was acquired for a sum close to the starting price. Several studies confirm the existence of such practices: "according to information from police sources, the acquisition of 70 per cent of the assets up for auction is negotiated before the adjudication process."[95] Intimidation was not confined to the auction room and sometimes occurred at an earlier stage, when information on rivals was obtained from banks. According to the existing legislation, all bidders had to demonstrate their solvency by depositing a certain sum in an agreed bank. It was therefore a simple matter for bidders with contacts in this bank to discover the identity of potential rivals and force them to withdraw.[96]

Regarding managers of enterprises undergoing privatisation, the case is more complex, for their manoeuvres to underestimate the assets' value and acquire part of the capital cheaply were not always illegal. Fraudulent bankruptcy, which was not covered by criminal legislation at the time, enabled managers to seize certain means of production or avoid repaying bank loans. The people who eventually bought the enterprise were usually accomplices or front men from the former management team. Finally, managers ostensibly acting for an outside investor would buy shares, at auctions or public tenders for example, benefiting from conditions normally reserved for the workers' collective.

The creation of joint-stock companies and the distribution of shares. The practices associated with this method of ownership transfer were equally hard to define, for the border between legitimate and illegitimate economic behaviour was superimposed on the line between the licit and the illicit. While the behaviour

---

ment of State Property investment department, November 1994. This interviewee was appointed director of the committee shortly afterwards.

[94] A uniformed police officer was present in the room. Observation at an auction organised by the Yekaterinburg Property Fund, September 1993.

[95] Citation from a press article in: L. Shelley, 1995, p. 250.

[96] Interview with an employee of the Yekaterinburg Property Fund, September 1993.

of many entrepreneurs aroused public indignation, it was not always clearly illicit.[97] For example, the managers of an enterprise could take a hand in drawing up the list of employees with shares priority, create a company to purchase shares or, as mentioned earlier, exploit the legal loophole concerning bankruptcy. This ambiguity extended to buyers' behaviour. If, for instance, someone bought shares but failed to implement an investment programme—one of the conditions of the sale—was he then guilty of an offence? The services combating economic crime in the Sverdlovsk region believed it amounted to a swindle or an abuse of trust, but the regional Prosecutor's Office refused to cancel such transactions. The indignant letters received by the representative of the president of the Russian Federation[98] in the Sverdlovsk region denounced practices that were illegitimate rather than illicit. One letter, written by the employees of a sand-refining plant, expressed outrage at the way a "handful of criminals" were being allowed to "plunder resources." In fact, it appeared that the plant's privatisation had divided the workforce: some employees remained loyal to the senior managers, while others sided with an outside investor. The latter group had proved stronger during the public tender process, despite goals that did not extend beyond selling the sand to foreign markets. The new owners invested nothing, but raked in the foreign currency.[99] In other cases, buyers resorted to clearly illicit practices, including the extortion of shares. For example, Louise Shelley records that criminal organisations used violence and false documents to gain control of fifty-three enterprises in St Petersburg and Murmansk. Their members would visit an enterprise, pretend to be distributing humanitarian aid, and request the addresses of all those who had retired from the enterprise, all the shareholders. They subsequently contacted these people and forced them to hand over their shares.[100]

Exercising the option to purchase. The main issue arising from privatisations conducted on the basis of a lease with an option to purchase was the determi-

---

[97] E. L. Feige, 1997, pp. 21–34.

[98] Boris Yeltsin created this position following the August 1991 putsch in order to have a personal line to information on events in the regions. In the Sverdlovsk region, the president's representative received numerous letters from citizens who were scandalised by the economic and political practices they were witnessing.

[99] Letter to V.V. Mashkov, the president's representative in the Sverdlovsk region, from representatives of the workers' collective of the Peschannyi kar'er factory, 27 September 1993. V.V. Maskov produced this letter when interviewed on 1 October 1993.

[100] L. Shelley, 1995, p. 252.

nation of the asset's value and its eventual purchase price. For example, buyers sought to reach an agreement with the competent administrative body in order to obtain a pre-dated document and reduce the price of the asset. Outside investors generally attempted to acquire the rights reserved for employees. Contracts could be exchanged between the responsible administration and an outside purchaser without the employees being informed. Such deals often involved the most profitable parts of the business. Moreover, employees would be pressurised into ceding their rights to the leased asset. These practices were especially prevalent in small towns in the Urals, where communities were built around a single factory and the absence of opposing force facilitated agreements between the factory director, the mayor, the official handling municipal privatisations and their allies. Nevyansk, a small town of 50,000 inhabitants, was a case in point. In 1993, the Sverdlovsk regional soviet's control committee noted that thirty-one out of thirty-three procedures were marked by irregularities. The body responsible for the transfer of ownership could not provide documents attesting to their legality. The new owners benefited from privileges that were theoretically reserved for employees; in many cases they had not even signed the lease contract. All the new owners were linked in one way or another to the factory director's clique and the mayor. Similar practices were noted when property was privatised by auction.[101]. The Nevyansk case was far from unique: in such small towns of the Urals, privatisation was characterised by a patron-client approach to the allocation of resources.

The beneficiaries of the reform were clearly those with the necessary financial and administrative resources. Access to information and close contacts with members of the agencies controlling the privatisation process were of crucial importance. The principal actors in this scenario were economic (factory directors, young entrepreneurs), political, administrative and, sometimes, criminal. The active participation of criminals in the privatisation process was in no doubt, for at least two reasons. On the one hand, the funds they had acquired through protecting and running cooperatives, not to mention their solid contacts with public officials and politicians, had enabled them to prepare for the opportunities afforded by the reforms. On the other, the history of organised crime in Yekaterinburg tells us that score-settling and the murder of business leaders and directors of shops, banks and insurance companies were at their height between 1992 and 1994.[102] Demonstrations of support organised

[101] Dossier compiled in June 1993 by the Sverdlovsk region Soviet Control Committee. Documents consulted in the committee's office by permission of the director, A. Matrosov, in October 1993.

[102] V.B. Zhitenev, 1993, pp. 20–34. See also *Syshchik* (The Sleuth), a journal specialis-

by businessmen when their "protector" was arrested or murdered highlighted the involvement of major criminal organisations in the implementation of economic reforms. The best example of this is the way in which entrepreneurs reacted to the arrest of Konstantin Tsyganov. They organised press conferences and stressed the stability that Tsyganov had brought to the area. In response to a question on the effects of collaborating with Tsyganov, an entrepreneur declared: "He helped us to feel secure... Thanks to his support we could solve certain problems, examine others calmly, and influence the course of events. We felt confident when meeting businesses with which we might form partnerships; we felt we had much more freedom during delicate negotiations."[103]

Differential treatment of illegalities during the privatisation process. A criminal investigation officer exclaimed in 1994, "Deal with offences being committed in the privatisation process? I'd love to. But how? The crooks pillaging our country are unscrupulous and audacious because they are allowed to get away with it. Nothing is asked of us. We are spectators; we are watching the blooming of the market economy."[104]

Observers of *prikhvatizatsiya* frequently denounced the ability of criminals to operate with impunity.[105] In such a context, what were the police charged with combating "crime in the sphere of privatisation" actually doing about it? This category represented in fact a negligible—and decreasing—proportion of the crime recorded in the region, partly because some of the illicit practices linked to privatisation were defined as property crime or corruption. The results may have been poor, but the services fighting economic crime in the Sverdlovsk region were still praised for their professionalism, given that many of Russia's regions had recorded no privatisation-related offences at all.[106]

---

ing in criminal issues. The crime reporting in the local daily newspapers of the period is equally convincing.

[103] *Na Smenu*, 28 May 1993.

[104] Interview with a criminal investigation officer in Yekaterinburg, October 1994.

[105] S. Fish notes that these policies (the liberal economic reforms of 1992) "inadvertently created a climate of what Russians call *beznakazannost'*. The word, which may be translated as 'impunity' but which actually carries an even stronger connotation, captures a situation in which there are practically no disincentives to extortion, theft, and murder, simply because anyone who cares to plan his crimes with a modicum of care faces no threat of being apprehended." S. Fish, 1998, p. 92.

[106] Report by the Interior Ministry of the Russian Federation Main Directorate for

At both national and regional level, figures declined by 50 per cent between 1993 and 1994, and fell even more steeply between 1994 and 1995 (see Table 19). This trend may be explained by the fact that almost all the offences recorded in 1993 involved trafficking in vouchers. This accounted for 98 per cent of offences recorded at national level![107] In 1994, such offences still accounted for between 70 per cent and 80 per cent of privatisation-related crime at both central and regional levels. The campaign against crime in the sphere of privatisation therefore almost ground to a halt in 1995, when the vouchers were withdrawn from circulation. Given the need to produce results, trafficking in vouchers was a natural target, for it occurred in the streets and was perceived as speculation, and dealers often lacked protection. More discreet types of privatisation-related offence, as well as those committed by less vulnerable individuals, were ignored.

The selection of other cases from 1994 onwards was based on two factors: suspicion (aroused by observation or denunciation) and more or less official authorisation from the hierarchy and corresponding political authorities. "The major cases our services handle correspond to a combination of circumstances ... Every time we envisage taking action, we inform our hierarchy. I suppose that in turn, it informs other people, but regional or local political authorities usually interfere after the intervention and demand explanations."[108]

As a rule, the decision to take up a case was triggered by orders recommending investigation of a certain investment fund, business or administrative body. For example, a scandal broke out in September 1993, when an investigation uncovered collusion between officials of the Yekaterinburg property fund and bidders attending auctions of city-centre shops. The fund's director was eventually forced to resign.[109] The scandal unfolded against a background of hostility to the soviets, which were dissolved shortly afterwards, in October 1993, following the confrontations in Moscow—a decision which supported the theory that scores were being settled in the Yekaterinburg case. The affair illustrated

---

Economic Crime "On Crime in the Sphere of the Privatisation of State and Municipal Enterprises in 1995", January 1996; 5 pages.

[107] Text of a response by the Interior Minister to a parliamentary question, December 1994: "On Assessing the Privatisation of State and Municipal Enterprises in 1994, and on Measures to Increase the Efficiency of Privatisations in the Context of Russian Federation Economic Reforms", 5 pages.

[108] Interview with the deputy director of the Sverdlovsk region economic crime department, Yekaterinburg, June 1997.

[109] *Vechernyi Ekaterinburg*, 18 September 1993.

not only the confrontations between executive and legislative powers, but also the rivalry between the regional administration and the largest municipal authority in the *oblast'*.

In 1994, specialist law enforcement services investigated cases linked to swindles, corruption, the diversion of state assets immediately prior an enterprise's privatisation, tax fraud, forgery and use of forged accounting documents, and violation of anti–monopoly laws.[110] The traditional catalogue of explanations for the causes of crime did not encompass "crime in the sphere of privatisation." As we have noted with regard to offences committed in the cooperative sector, it was not possible to mobilise the traditional figures of delinquency, although the depredations of criminal organisations were denounced. Similarly, technical factors (accounting practices, surveillance) had little relevance in the context of privatisation, apart from shortcomings in the recruitment of personnel responsible for the transfer of property. In the main, causal factors suggested were problems within the policing apparatus, tensions with the agencies managing privatisations, and the weakness of the legislative framework on which law enforcement bodies relied.

As we have seen, 1988 marked the beginning of a decline in the competence of the police officers specialising in combating economic crime. The gulf between their knowledge of illicit practices and their ability to suppress them continued to expand. In 1994, services fighting economic crime in the Sverdlovsk region were still struggling to obtain the computers they needed to analyse the accounts of suspect enterprises. Further operational difficulties arose in the early 1990s. "Services combating economic crime are receiving less and less information on the commission of offences. The sources they once had in enterprises—peoples' control committees, labour inspection bodies, etc.—have been dissolved or radically transformed. Illicit practices are now occurring in private enterprises, which do not allow state services to monitor their activities."[111]

During the Soviet period, the authority of law enforcement agencies derived more from their ability to obtain and deal with inside information about enterprises than from the manpower they deployed. When this means of control

[110] Interview with the deputy director of the Sverdlovsk region economic crime department, Yekaterinburg, June 1997.

[111] Regional economic crime department report, December 1992: "On the Activity of the Regional Economic Crime Department with regard to the Transformation of the Economy of the Russian Federation"; 15 pages. Report consulted in the offices of the regional economic crime department during an interview with the deputy director, Yekaterinburg, June 1997.

disappeared, they were isolated from the business world and became dependent on their own observations and on possible whistleblowers' initiatives from private enterprises.

In 1994, privatisation often highlighted confusion over the remits of anti–economic-crime units and criminal investigation departments. Before that time, anti–economic-crime units had handled crimes against state property, while criminal investigation departments had dealt with crimes against individual property. As soon as all property crimes were grouped together in a single chapter (July 1994), both services could claim responsibility for their investigation. "If the offence arises from an economic activity involving accounting, banking or other documents, the anti–economic crime services are competent. Other cases should be dealt with by criminal investigation services."[112]

Given the implacable struggle over allocation of resources, these rivalries reduced the powers of the police even further. Specialist services believed they had been sidelined, for they could no longer benefit from external sources of information and had to compete against services with far greater manpower. The creation of the tax police reinforced their feeling of marginalisation.

The police attempted to justify their poor performance, primarily by denouncing the agencies charged with implementing the reform. The committees for the management of state property and the short-lived property funds were accused of ignoring their duties and failing to monitor the legality of transactions. "The right to alert judicial services to the illegality of a privatisation transaction was never exercised."[113] Moreover, they had resisted attempts by law enforcement bodies to monitor their activities. The police condemned their "self-sufficiency" (*samodostatochnost'*) and preference for working behind closed doors.[114] Secrecy impeded the detection of "abuses of position for personal gain", although the existence of such behaviour could not be doubted.[115]

Finally, the services combating economic crime criticised the existing legal framework for its incoherence. The way economic reforms were being imple-

---

[112] Russian Federation Interior Ministry internal directive addressed to all Interior Ministry regional departments, November 1994. Document consulted during an interview with the deputy director of the Sverdlovsk region economic crime department. Yekaterinburg, June 1997.

[113] *Ibid.*

[114] Regional economic crime department report, December 1994: "On the Criminal Situation with regard to the Privatisation Process"; 23 pages. Report consulted on the premises of the regional economic crime department. Yekaterinburg, June 1997.

[115] *Ibid.*

mented reinforced hostility to government policy that dated back to the late 1980s. The political climate was conducive to the use of this particular argument: the leaders of Sverdlovsk *oblast'* were demanding autonomy, which they saw as essential to the defence of regional interests, and denouncing central economic policy. The governor[116] attacked the "centre" for decisions that were ill-suited to the region's economic and social problems, and argued that privatisation, industrial restructuring and conversion of armaments factories should be left to regional bodies. Regional police extended the argument to the anti–crime campaign by calling for the decentralisation of penal policy.

The Constitution of the Russian Federation stipulated that the organisation of the judiciary, criminal procedure, criminal and prison legislation, civil legislation, civil procedure and arbitration procedure were federal or joint matters.[117] The struggle for the allocation of resources that characterised relations between the Russian Federation and its subjects from 1992 onwards encouraged certain regional politicians to contest this arrangement and call for more power.[118] One of the most prominent figures in this dispute was Eduard Rossel, governor of the Sverdlovsk region. Rossel had plans to transform the region (*oblast'*) into a Urals republic (*respublika*), and announced his intention to adopt a specific criminal code.[119] Apart from the drafting of annual programmes to intensify anti–crime activity, initiated in 1995, nothing ever came of this ambition.[120] However, the declaration of intent reflected the desire to mobilise symbols of sovereignty to emphasise the determination of regional leaders. There was even talk of creating a regional currency, the Ural franc, which was equally unacceptable to the federal authorities.[121]

The deterioration of relations between the "centre" and the regions tended to reinforce the bond between the *oblast'*'s police chiefs and political leaders.

---

[116] Eduard Rossel, governor until autumn 1993, was replaced by A. Strakhov. Rossel was returned to power in 1995.

[117] Articles 71 and 72 of the Russian Federation Constitution, approved by referendum on 12 December 1993.

[118] Claims were advanced in the context of the construction of the Russian federal system, an asymmetrical and differential process (the central power negotiated the rights granted to each subordinate unit of the Russian Federation on a case by case basis). "Russie: qui gouverne les régions?" (dossier compiled by Jean-Robert Raviot), *Problèmes Politiques et Sociaux*, no. 783, 18 April 1997, p. 3.

[119] Obshchestvennyi tsentr..., 1997, p. 51.

[120] *Oblastnaya Gazeta*, 3 March 1995.

[121] On the plan for a Ural Republic, see G. Favarel-Garrigues, "La région de Sverdlovsk et le pouvoir du gouverneur" in M. Mendras (ed.), 1997, pp. 161–92.

By controlling the appointment of the head of the Interior regional directorate, almost always a "native son", governors were able to use coercion to defend their economic and electoral interests, and contributed by doing so to the differential treatment of illegalities. While they did not always participate in defining the priorities of the anti–crime campaign, they actively contributed to the maintenance of public security and continued to intervene directly in judicial matters, which now encompassed the privatisation of regional assets. During the 1990s, this collusion prompted federal government initiatives to bring criminal investigation departments back under central control. For example, "inter-regional" services for combating organised crime, created in 1993, were designed to monitor political and law enforcement elites in all federal subordinate units. Furthermore, federal inspection teams began stepping up visits to the regions in the mid-1990s. In the summer of 1998, a control commission set up by Vladimir Putin, then head of the FSB, was dispatched to Yekaterinburg. The head of the Interior Ministry regional directorate, suspected of maintaining close contacts with one of the city's two main criminal organisations, was removed from his post despite the support of Governor Rossel. Other leading figures in the regional police suffered a similar fate.[122] The inspection, a politically motivated attempt to curb the governor's ambitions, was portrayed as an emergency measure, a necessary move to re-establish the state's authority in a "particularly criminalised" region which was subject to the violence of "powerful mafias" and the "wheeling and dealing" of local elites.[123] The attempt to impose a new set of rules on political, economic and law enforcement elites prefigured the "dictatorship of the law" policy which Russia's new president, Vladimir Putin, would ceaselessly refine in the first years of the twenty-first century.

Concluding Remarks

During *perestroika* and afterwards, differential treatment of economic illegalities has adapted to social and economic changes but has maintained its main features. At national level, priority to economic reforms led to marginalising of penal policy in this field. At the same time, growing fear of crime in Soviet society called for some results. An emphasis was put on the struggle against organised crime and predatory forms of economic crime. The distinction

[122] *Nezavisimaya Gazeta*, 20 April 1999.
[123] *Ibid.*

251

between them and frauds and other business offenses perpetuated the traditional Soviet distinction between illegalities and delinquency. Regional leaders gained more autonomy in their contribution to policing missions. First, they took part in the financing and development of local initiatives in order to improve law enforcement policy. Secondly, they still did not define the main priorities of the fight against economic crime, though they intervened more often in personal cases, as governors also took an active part in the struggle for ownership of state enterprises' property rights.

Street-level police having to deal with an overflow of economic illegal practices reacted as they used to do before. Petty thieves were their favourite target. Most of their activity in the struggle against economic crime was devoted to the defence of state or personal property. First, this answered expectations from above, even if most of the registered cases might be considered as low-scale cases. Secondly, it was easier than tackling frauds in the new private sector. Indeed, police staff were held back at that time by their incompetence and by the lack of resources to deal with new forms of economic offences. This imbalance between petty thieves as delinquents and economic illegalities that occurred during the implementation of privatisation was to be observed throughout the 1990s. Police results were justified by local officers' growing critique of national economic and law enforcement policies.

CONCLUSION

This research has shown that certain continuities can be distinguished in the evolution of economic crime recorded by Russian police services since 1965: the general increase in recorded cases, the sharp rise in property theft and growth of "breaches of the rules of economic activity" were of concern to governing bodies long before the advent of *perestroika*, and especially from the mid-1970s onwards. Many institutional changes were introduced at that time in law enforcement activity in order to deal better with economic crime: penalties for petty economic offences were slightly softened, specialised training for anti–economic-crime officers emerged, clearance rate became one of the main criteria to assess police activity, some attempts were made to use criminological knowledge in order to better understand crime causes. However, these changes did not improve the situation as they hardly dealt with shortcomings in the Soviet economic system.

From 1985, *perestroika* and *glasnost* began to modify some of the characteristics of economic crime, notably by encouraging the almost complete change in breaches of the rules of economic activity, the spread of their more violent forms, and the growing concern for protection of private property. They also influenced the perception of insecurity, a phenomenon which would attract increasing media coverage and political slogans.

By the late 1980s, political leaders had begun to base their legitimacy on determination to address the increasing fear of crime in a society disoriented by an ongoing process of change.[1] This was reflected in programmes for the reform of penal policy and the "democratisation" of the policing apparatus[2] which, from that period on, focused as much on personal safety in public

[1] M. Los, 2002, pp. 165–88.
[2] D. Bayley, 1997, pp. 59–64.

places as on the protection of private property. The protean fear of crime contributed to the emphasis the Soviet regime placed on its ability to guarantee security. Aware of the need to commit themselves to re-establishing order, Russian leaders responded to new threats by decreeing emergency measures that owed much to the conventional logic of repression. Following the tradition of Soviet campaigns against delinquency, new targets, as menacing as they were all-encompassing, replaced "hooliganism" and "parasitism", as was shown by the campaign against "organised crime" launched during the *glasnost* period, becoming a priority of penal policy.

The idea that crime reduction was automatically linked to a greater capacity for repression continued to hold sway. Police manpower was increased; elite departments were created and their powers extended. In particular, the new services dedicated to combating "organised crime" were rapidly granted budgets, prerogatives and investigative powers that far exceeded those of other criminal investigation services. However, they were still obliged to meet the strict performance targets that characterised the bureaucratic organisation of policing in the USSR.

The period of emergence from communism did little to foster criticism of the administrative evaluation principle. Beyond the case of the Interior Ministry, we have also seen that in the early 1990s the services responsible for privatising state assets—structures that embodied the break with the Soviet economic order—paradoxically operated according to the logic of central planning, for they were required to submit quantified results on a regular basis in order to comply with the hierarchy's objectives. In the case of the police, the continuing obligation to produce results[3]—the role of indicators of recorded cases and clearance rates in the evaluation of police performance—had two main effects: it encouraged police officers to carry on as before, and thus enabled them to benefit from the opportunities for personal gain afforded by *perestroika*.

Indeed, the failure to reform the bureaucratic organisation of police activity favoured the return to tried and tested procedures when complying with orders from above: falsification of performance indicators, juggling of penal definitions, extortion of confessions to boost the clearance rate, etc. These methods encouraged police officers to concentrate on the least socially harmful offences and the most vulnerable targets. This happened during the development of the

---

[3] The Interior Ministry produced a new list of police performance indicators in 2005 (Prikaz MVD Rossii, no. 650, 5 August 2005).

cooperative sector from 1987, as well as during the privatisation process, from 1992 to 1994, when basic cases of voucher speculation were the only ones recorded by the police. The focus throughout the 1990s on combating "organised crime" resulted in Russia's prisons being packed with recidivist petty thieves who had committed their offences in groups; it contributed significantly to the rise in the incarceration rate, which reached US levels in 2000.[4] By the late 1980s, the police had adopted a similar approach to economic crime, and were concentrating on its predatory forms such as thefts of low-value goods while ignoring the "shrewder" offences that inevitably emerged from privatisation measures and other reforms, such as the accounting, commercial and tax fraud committed by actors with better protection. Such a distinction between predatory delinquency and frauds or other business offences has perpetuated the traditional Soviet differential management of economic illegalities.

The pioneers of capitalism effectively gambled on flaws in the regulatory framework by committing offences and inventing new rules. For entrepreneurs, the chances of avoiding police repression depended on their ability to gain access to protection systems and thus counter the threat of prosecution. By accumulating "administrative resources" (a Russian term that appeared later, to denote privileged links with an administrative official who could facilitate the development of a business), they were able to acquire unwarranted privileges and reduce their vulnerability. Collusion of this sort was observed at regional level in the agencies responsible for property transfers, economic development and commercial matters, and also in law enforcement bodies. Entrepreneurs developed ambivalent relations with the latter: while fearing them, they were obliged to establish personal contacts with it in order to pursue their economic goals.

A job as a police officer also acquired a market value. Some officers took advantage of this by resigning from the Interior Ministry and placing their expertise and professional contacts at the service of private interests. Others remained in post and exploited the latitude paradoxically afforded by the obligation to produce results. As they themselves provided the indicators that formed the basis for their assessment, they could use their jobs to serve their own interests once they had fulfilled the stated requirements. The growth of such opportunistic behaviour, which had been noted as far back as the Brezh-

---

[4] In Russia, there were 729 detainees for every 100,000 inhabitants in 2000. See G. Favarel-Garrigues, 2003, pp. 121–36.

nev era, now depended less on the police officer's ability to obtain access to scarce goods and services than on finding clients with whom he could exploit his professional expertise. Several studies have highlighted the importance of lucrative activities in the exercise of a policing role, either while on duty or in an extraprofessional capacity.[5] In many cases, officers acted within the law, given the commercialisation of police surveillance and the search for private sector sponsors to support the work of local Interior Ministry departments. More broadly, officers actively contributed to the formation of a private security sector to protect the business world. They often benefited also from opportunities to set up so-called foundations for "veterans of criminal investigation services" or "widows and orphans of ex–police officers." Despite the defections observed in the late 1980s, a policeman's job was still an attractive proposition, and the relaxation of recruitment standards made it easier to obtain. Authentic criminal organisations—to retain the definition used in current Russian legislation—were thus able to develop within criminal investigative branches, as illustrated by several scandals.[6] In the final analysis, the continuities observed in law enforcement practices are the product of governmental choices that have facilitated resort to tried and tested skills and methods, and of renewed opportunities for personal gain linked to the exercise of a policing role.

Such a finding brings knowledge to the understanding of the protection business in Russia during the 1990s,[7] by focusing on police supply. Archives help to understand how an ambivalent relation to professional responsibility has developed in the Soviet anti–economic-crime units since 1965. Motives for working in such services were linked to professional expectations, but also to more opportunistic considerations. The way police activity was assessed allowed local officers to respond to expectations from above while fulfilling

---

[5] L. Kosals *et al.*, 2002.

[6] The biggest scandal—"werewolves in epaulettes"—made headlines in 2003. The principal lesson of this affair was not that the officers of Moscow's criminal investigation department—the legendary MUR—enthusiastically used their position to run rackets, but that they were distinguished by exemplary professional trajectories. The inquiry revealed that their outstanding operational efficiency was achieved mainly by planting weapons and/or drugs on homeless and marginalised people, an activity that enabled them to obtain bonuses and promotion. This scandal was clearly triggered by political motivations, as showed by the role played by A. Khinstein, journalist, deputy and member of the pro-presidential party, in the actual denunciation of the scandal. See his book, A. Khinstein, 2005. Despite the political connection, the facts presented by the journalist's investigation seem credible.

[7] F. Varese, 2001.

personal goals, and this way has not changed during the post-Soviet period. Such skills allowed them to benefit from the new opportunities that appeared in the late 1980s. Indeed, from the time of *perestroika*, working as a "violent entrepreneur" became compatible with an official police job. Like their counterparts in organised crime groups described by Volkov, police-based "violence-managing agencies" also challenged state capacity to monopolise the use of force, but they did it from within.[8]

Against this background, the conception and implementation of policing tasks have become stakes in the rivalry among those who hold the reins of power in Russian society. Many actors have invested in the definition of policing, not only in the business world, but also among regional and local political elites. Since the late 1980s, regional leaders with a desire for greater autonomy have attempted to respond to demands for security by supporting the work of local law enforcement services and denouncing the inability of the "centre" to address the problem of crime. These political confrontations have helped to diversify local policing configurations, according to the degree of input from regional political authorities and local business figures, and to blur the definition of policing authorities and tasks. The determination of federal leaders throughout the 1990s to prevent collusion between local political, law enforcement and criminal actors reflected these power relations, which characterised the making of Russian federalism.

This willingness has also been observed after the period studied. Attempts to recentralise law enforcement policy developed after Vladimir Putin's accession to the presidency in 2000.[9] Public security missions were delegated to the city level while control of criminal investigation departments was reinforced. All police staff were put under surveillance. The new president kept on criticising police departments' activity, sometimes rather vehemently: "Citizens should be proud of the work of law enforcement agents, rather than crossing the street when they see a uniform. Those who aim at getting richer rather than defending the law have no place in these services."[10] Government management of this issue therefore consisted less in reforming the institution than in controlling agents better.

[8] V. Volkov, 2002.
[9] On the recentralisation of law enforcement services since 2000, see N. Petrov, 2005.
[10] http://president.kremlin.ru/appears/2005/04/25/1123_type63372type82634_87049.shtml (Accessed in October 2007).

In a manner similar to Yuri Andropov's taking-over of the Interior Ministry, many executives were ousted. This was the policy already adopted by Vladimir Putin when he directed the Russian state security service back in 1998. In 2003, more than half of the managers of regional directorates of the Interior had already been dismissed. The new appointment rules aim to limit the influence of governors, in favour of the federal administration. Whereas in the 1990s such positions were granted to executives who had had their entire career on the spot, new rules of "intensive horizontal rotation" designate people who have nothing to do with the region they are to administer.

At the same time, and pursuing Yuri Andropov's policy, many FSB (former KGB) executives have been placed at management positions in police departments. Though it is impossible to know the exact number of cases, Rachid Nurgaliev's career is emblematic of the tendency: after working for more than twenty years (1981–2002) in state security services, he was nominated assistant to the Interior Minister in 2002 and Interior Minister two years later. Several assistants of his followed the same trajectory. The FSB is also present in the seven federal district services created in 2003. These new institutions are in charge of coordinating and controlling application of federal decisions in the regions, notably in law enforcement policy. However, the results of such a recentralisation policy are not decisive, either in the fight against criminality, or in the improvement of police practices. At best it produces police corruption scandals and exploits the negative image of police within the population. Real visibility exposes the police more than other law enforcement agencies (which are less present in the Russian population's everyday life) to resentment.

Finally, this study has showed that defining economic crime and dealing with illegalities have always been valuable political resources in Soviet and post-Soviet Russia. Although in practice the police approach to economic crime has focused on predatory crime, the Russian government has never abandoned the idea of imposing its rules on the business world. Exploitation of the legal vulnerability of entrepreneurs is a mode of government to which all Russian leaders, from Mikhail Gorbachev to Vladimir Putin, have resorted with varying degrees of success. After encouraging cooperative members to develop their businesses, and even exhorting police services to treat them with indulgence, Soviet leaders attempted to bring them to heel before launching a final offensive against "economic sabotage", yet another in a long line of traditional repressive campaigns. The controversy this measure aroused helped to justify another U-turn by governing bodies at a time when carrying out the privatisation process by all means became a political priority, and law enforcement policy in this field was considered secondary. But the subsequent indulgence towards illicit entrepreneurial practices did not definitively shut down debate on the rights and wrongs of personal enrichment: the determination to punish "economic criminals" emerged as one of the main sources of political legitimacy during the 1990s. While many political figures like General Lebed and Yevgeny Primakov echoed popular resentment by denouncing the criminalisation of the economy and the state and calling for ruthless repression, advocates of economic reform endeavoured to play down the issue, depicting it as regrettable but essential to wealth creation, and sometimes even recommending an "amnesty" for illicitly acquired capital.

Twenty years after *perestroika*, the Russian government's relations with the business world illustrate the fundamental role of these confrontations in shaping the political legitimacy of post-Soviet leaders. Once in power, Vladimir Putin, just like his predecessors, has had to reconcile two conflicting perceptions of government duty when taking official action: allow the unbridled growth of the economy and re-establish order by combating crime in all its forms. After some hesitation,[11] the new government has stood on a hard line by maintaining pressure on entrepreneurs' legal vulnerability in order to obtain their loyalty. The most famous case was Mikhail Khodorkovsky's trial in 2005: an exemplary sanction was to serve as a signal to the entire profession. Beyond this spectacular scandal, the whole institutional design of surveillance and repression of "economic crime" has been reshaped. Since 2000, the government has showed a growing concern for offences that were formerly known as "breaches of the rules of economic activity." Institutional changes have touched, for example, the departments dealing with economic crime. In 2003, the Russian government finally decided to abolish the tax police and create a single entity for combating economic, financial and fiscal offences within the Interior Ministry. But the quick creation of a whole set of rules against money laundering has certainly been the most striking example of this trend.

Following international norms, the Russian government funded a financial intelligence unit in 2001. It has used the financial intelligence unit as a tool to

[11] For instance, in June 2002 the government revealed a plan aimed at encouraging Russians who had capital abroad to repatriate it to Russia; while the funds would be liable to tax, there would be no need to justify their origin. At the same time, Putin declared: "The state should not clutch [every entrepreneur] by the sleeve and ask him to justify the origin of his resources if it has been unable to guarantee normal investment conditions in the past." (*Kommersant*, 20 June 2002).

crack down on certain banks or enterprises for political reasons, and more broadly to intimidate the business world by centralising information on private enterprises and banks. Between 2003 and 2006, the number of cases of money laundering submitted to the criminal justice system increased from 618 to 7,957, while the number of convictions rose from 14 to 532. This policy is above all a major aspect of the "dictatorship of the law" that has guided Russian policy since 2000. In fact, the government's project has aimed at disciplining political, administrative and economic elites by exploiting their legal vulnerability, and thus forestalling attempts to form an opposition group that might contest its authority. Control of the main media, intelligence units and judicial services could be used to weaken them and bully them into supporting the ruling elite. Campaigns against corruption and money laundering, which are as vague as Soviet economic crime categories were, have played a far-reaching role in this offensive.

Defining criteria for the "legal", "legitimate" or "moral" acquisition of wealth has generated incessant political confrontations in Russia since the mid-1980s. These battles often took the form of periodic revelations of compromising documents (*kompromaty*) on adversaries, a brutal form of "naming and shaming" that reached its peak in the late 1990s. The adoption of international recommendations on money laundering has helped make it possible for the team currently in power to centralise intelligence relating to practices of the business world and to monopolise the use of *kompromaty*. Notable examples of the value of this resource for political domination are the 2006 murder of Andrei Kozlov, who was vice-president of the Russian Central Bank in charge of combating money laundering, and the 2007 appointment of Viktor Zubkov as Prime Minister of the Russian Federation following five years of faithful service as director of the financial intelligence unit, and just before Vladimir Putin took his place in 2008. Fixing the border between "clean" and "dirty" money—that is, managing the distinction between delinquency and economic illegalities—remains a permanent key feature of political power in post-Soviet Russia.

APPENDIX

TABLES

Table 1. Economic crime in the RSFSR Criminal Code

Criminal Code Chapter	Criminal Code Article
Chapter I: crimes against the state	**article 87**: manufacture or sale of counterfeit banknotes or securities
	article 88: infractions of the rules regarding currency transactions
Chapter II: crimes against socialist property	**article 89**: theft of state property
	article 90: robbery of state property
	article 91: robbery with violence of state property
	article 92: theft of state property by embezzlement, misappropriation or abuse of power
	article 93: theft of state property by deception
	article 93¹: major theft of state property
	article 94: causing material damage by fraud or abuse of trust
	article 95: extortion of state property
	article 96 (from 1965): minor theft of state property
	article 97: appropriation of state property either found or acquired by chance by the guilty party
Chapter VI: breaches of the rules of economic activity	**article 152**: production of poor quality, non-standard or incomplete merchandise
	article 152¹: falsification of account or production statistics (*ochkovtiratel'stvo*)
	article 153: private enterprise activity and brokerage
	article 154: speculation
	article 154² (from 1970 to 1977): small-scale purchase, sale or exchange of currency or securities

261

	article 156: buyer or seller fraud
	article 156[1]: violation of the rules of commerce regarding alcoholic drinks
	article 156[2] (from 1981): obtaining illicit remuneration for work linked to services rendered to the population
	article 156[3] (from 1981): violation of the rules of commerce
	article 156[4] (from 1983): illicit sale of petrol or other fuel oils
	article 157: sale of a poor quality, non-standard or incomplete product
	article 162 (from 1962): exercise of a forbidden professional activity
	article 167 (from 1962): breach of the rules relating to the exploitation of underground resources and the handing over of gold to the state
	article 169 (from 1962): illicit tree felling
Chapter VII: abuses of office	article 170: abuse of power
	article 171: exceeding power
	article 173: passive corruption (acceptance of a bribe)
	article 174: active corruption (offer of a bribe)
	article 174[1]: mediation of a corrupt transaction
	article 175: misconduct by a state official in a position of responsibility

Source: *Ugolovnyi kodeks RSFSR*, 1983.

Table 2. Economic crime in the RSFSR Code of Administrative Offences (1984)

Chapter	Article
Chapter VI: Crimes against state property	article 46: violation of the law on socialist property on mineral resources
	article 47: violation of the law on socialist property on the water
	article 48: violation of the law on socialist property in the forests
	article 49: minor misappropriation of state property
Chapter X: Crimes in the sphere of transport and communications	article 125: use of means of transport for monetary gain
	article 128: fraud in the sphere of public transport

Chapter XII: crimes in the sphere of commerce and finance	**article 146**: violation of the rules of commerce by workers in commercial enterprises and public catering establishments
	article 147: violation of the rules of commerce regarding alcoholic drinks
	article 149: violation of the rules of commerce regarding *kolkhoz* markets
	article 150: illicit street selling
	article 151: minor speculation
	article 153: illegal foreign currency and payment document transactions
	article 154: illegal sale of payment documents acquired in foreign currency without the right to convert them into currency
	article 155: illegal issue or acquisition of petrol and other fuel oils
	article 156: violation of the rules regarding the exercise of small-scale production activities
	article 157: exercise of a banned small-scale production activity

Source: *Vedomosti Verkhovnogo Soveta RSFSR*, no. 27, 1984, article 909.

Table 3. Institutions responsible for investigating economic crimes
in accordance with the Soviet Code of Criminal Procedure

Investigative responsibilities	*Articles*
Police and Prosecutor's Office (according to the gravity of the offence committed)	– most crimes against socialist property (articles 89, 90, 91, 93, 94, 96², 98, 99, 100); certain economic crimes (articles 153, 154, 156, 157, 162, 167)
Prosecutor's Office	– some economic crimes (article 152, 152¹) – all abuse of office (articles 170–175)
KGB	– counterfeiting (article 87), currency trading (article 88) – some crimes against socialist property (articles 92, 93¹)

Source: L. Shelley, 1996, pp. 71–72 (table based on a Soviet Code of Criminal Procedure published in 1972).

Table 4. Comparison in absolute values and percentages of the evolution of recorded cases in the RSFSR and the Sverdlovsk region (1965–84)

Year	Number of offences recorded in the RSFSR	Increase or decrease in relation to the previous year (%)	Number of offences recorded in the Sverdlovsk region	Increase or decrease in relation to the previous year (%)
1965	483,550	+ 0.1 (% to 1964)	15,917	– 5.2 (% to 1964)
1966	582,965	+ 20.6	19,455	+ 22.2
1967	572,884	– 1.7	20,191	+ 3.7
1968	618,014	+ 7.9	21,428	+ 6.1
1969	641,385	+ 3.8	21,262	– 0.8
1970	693,552	+ 8.1	23,311	+ 9.6
1971	702,358	+ 1.3	23,939	+ 2.6
1972	706,294	+ 0.6	23,821	– 0.5
1973	695,647	– 1.5	23,620	– 0.9
1974	760,943	+ 9.4	25,849	+ 9.4
1975	809,819	+ 6.4	37,953	+ 46.8
1976	834,998	+ 3.1	35,493	– 6.5
1977	824,243	– 3.1	33,776	– 4.9
1978	889,599	+ 7.9	38,004	+ 12.5
1979	970,514	+ 9.1	42,265	+ 11.2
1980	1,028,284	+ 6.0	43,119	+ 2
1981	1,087,908	+ 5.8	44,579	+ 3.3
1982	1,128,558	+ 3.7	44,622	+ 0
1983	1,398,239	+ 23.9	56,671	+27
1984	1,402,694	+ 0.3	55,565	– 2

Source for the RSFSR: Kriminologicheskaya Assotsiatsiya, 1994, pp. 15–16. For the Sverdlovsk region: Sverdlovsk region Interior Ministry Department report, 6 January 1978: "On the Activity of Interior Ministry Services in the Fight against Crime and Offences in the Sverdlovsk Region in 1977." Fond 4, opis 89, delo 158, list 59. From 1978, the figures are from the annual activity reports compiled by police forces: Sverdlovsk region Interior Ministry Department report, October 1984 "On the Data Illustrating the State of Crime in the Region between 1979 and 1983"; 1 page. Fond 4, opis 107, delo 201, list 49.

Table 5. Comparison in absolute values of the evolution of the recording of three categories of economic offences in the RSFSR and the Sverdlovsk region (1966–84)

	Theft of socialist property (art. 89)		Speculation (art. 154)		Corruption (art. 173, 174, 174¹)	
	RSFSR	Sverdlovsk region	RSFSR	Sverdlovsk region	RSFSR	Sverdlovsk region
1966	43,830	1,464	5,184	86	1,422	20
1967	39,889	1,457	6,543	100	1,427	28
1968	44,285	1,333	7,026	79	1,506	21
1969	44,384	1,216	7,593		1,534	
1970	49,329	1,382	7,983	94	1,755	18
1971	52,895	1,475	8,480	118	1,725	23
1972	50,378	1,431	9,015	131	1,837	22
1973	52,469	1,606	9,073	183	2,037	38
1974	59,533	1,640	9,220	285	1,939	37
1975	65,697	2,725	9,559	285	2,124	39
1976	70,623	2,825	10,031	297	2,215	26
1977	74,519	2,691*	10,838	364*	2,222	51*
1978	79,987	2,900	12,039	516	2,447	45
1979	88,431	3,328	13,264	506	2,902	42
1980	97,192	3,434	14,569	545	3,268	70
1981	102,511	3,320*	16,127		3,753	
1982	104,883	3,223	16,971	607	4,244	72
1983	138,412	4,652	16,410	577	4,704	87
1984	130,615	4,601*	17,048		5,334	

Sources: Federal statistics to 1982 and regional statistics to 1976 are taken from the General Prosecutor's Office archives in Moscow. Considerable cross-checking with the regional archives suggests that they are reliable. Between 1978 and 1980: Sverdlovsk region Prosecutor's Office report, 21 October 1981: "On the State of Legality in the Fight against Theft, Speculation and Corruption"; 9 pages. Fond 4, opis 100, delo 214, lists 73–81. The data are presented in gross figures. For 1981 to 1983, the figures are taken from the annual activity reports compiled by police forces: Sverdlovsk region Interior Ministry department report, October 1984: "On the Data Illustrating the State of Crime in the Region between 1979 and 1983"; 1 page. Fond 4, opis 107, delo 201, list 49. The asterisk (*) indicates non-available data calculated from various indirect sources.

Table 6. Comparative evolution of the number of recorded cases in Russia (RSFSR, then Russian Federation) and the Sverdlovsk region between 1985 and 1994

	Number of offences recorded in Russia (RSFSR, then RF)	*Number of offences recorded in the Sverdlovsk region*
1985	1,416,935 (+1.0%)	54,546 (– 1.9%)
1986	1,338,424 (– 5.5%)	48,839 (– 10.5%)
1987	1,185,914 (– 11.4%)	46,046 (– 5.7%)
1988	1,220,361 (+2.9%)	47,580 (+3.3%)
1989	1,619,181 (+32.7%)	63,108 (+32.6%)
1990	1,839,451 (+13.6%)	70,992 (+12.5%)
1991	2,167,964 (+17.9%)	89,331 (+25.8%)
1992	2,760,652 (+27.3%)	109,651 (+22.7%)
1993	2,799,616 (+1.4%)	108,123 (– 1.4%)
1994	2,632,708 (– 6%)	109,987 (+1.7%)

The percentages in brackets indicate the increase or decrease in the number of recorded offences in relation to the previous year. Source: Kriminologicheskaya Assotsiatsiya, 1994, pp. 8–9. For 1994, and for the period 1990–94 in the Sverdlovsk region: MVD R.F. *et al.*, 1995, p. 20. For the period 1985–1989 in the Sverdlovsk region: "Information on the State of Crime in the Region by the Sverdlovsk region CPSU Committee State and Law Department", early 1990; 12 pages. Fond 4, opis 118, delo 622, list 11.

Table 7. Evolution of the number of property crimes recorded in Russia (RSFSR, then Russian Federation) between 1986 and 1993

	Number of crimes against state property	*Increase or decrease (% in relation to the previous year)*	*Number of crimes against personal property*	*Increase or decrease (% in relation to the previous year)*
1986	229,945		330,027	
1987	209,138	– 9.1	322,159	– 2.4
1988	215,673	+ 3.1	428,611	+ 33.0
1989	294,097	+ 36.4	672,609	+ 56.9
1990	365,924	+ 24.4	779,188	+ 15.8
1991	497,157	+ 35.9	992,116	+ 27.3
1992	686,542	+ 38.1	1,330,661	+ 34.1
1993	642,597	– 6.5	1,367,417	+ 2.7

Source: Crimes against state and socialist property are covered by articles 89–101 of the Criminal Code. Crimes against personal property are covered by articles 144–151. Kriminologicheskaya Assotsiatsiya, 1994, pp. 99 & 124.

Table 8. Evolution of the various forms of crime against state property recorded in Russia between 1988 and 1993

	1988	1989	1990	1991	1992	1993
Art. 89	119,265	195,211	262,825	395,534	540,984	497,457
		(+63.6%)	(+34.6%)	(+50.4%)	(+36.7%)	(− 8.1%)
Art. 90	1,981	3,261	3,682	5,588	10,347	10,771
		(+64.6%)	(+12.9%)	(+51.7%)	(+85.1%)	(+4.0%)
Art. 91	421	797	827	951	2,707	3,637
		(+89.3%)	(+3.7%)	(+15%)	(+184.6%)	(+34.3%)
Art. 92	51,676	47,106	43,368	39,070	36,867	33,114
Art. 93	3,119	3,008	3,846	3,302	3,772	6,061
Art. 93[1]	623	1,277	2,624	6,818	16,732	25,797
Art. 94	2,047	1,820	1,729	1,632	2,440	2,950
Art. 95	14	189	139	167	359	588
Art. 96	28,278	30,462	34,277	30,750	54,027	42,492

Source: Kriminologicheskaya Assotsiatsiya, 1994, pp. 127–8.

Table 9. Evolution of convictions for the theft of state property (art. 89) in Russia between 1986 and 1993

	1986	1987	1988	1989	1990	1991	1992	1993
Number of people investigated	77,068	63,939	69,971	78,925	95,512	139,920	200,164	216,735
Number of people convicted	68,420	47,804	40,481	44,646	59,540	87,641	121,630	155,739
Number of people sentenced to prison	33,447	23,913	24,350	28,334	34,002	40,017	56,046	64,370

Source: Kriminologicheskaya Assotsiatsiya, 1994, pp. 234–5.

Table 10. Comparative evolution of the theft of state and personal property recorded in Russia and the Sverdlovsk region between 1985 and 1993

	Recorded thefts of state property		Recorded thefts of personal property	
	Russia	*Sverdlovsk region*	*Russia*	*Sverdlovsk region*
1985	107,947	4,343	272,376	13,613
1986	96,045 (-11.0%)	3,212 (-26.1%)	268,285 (-1.6%)	11,527 (-15.4%)
1987	119,265 (+24.1%)	2,868 (-10.7%)	359,464 (+34.0%)	11,639 (+1%)
1988	195,211 (+63.6%)	3,677 (+28.2%)	558,959 (+55.5%)	14,400 (+23.7%)
1989	262,825 (+34.6%)	6,440 (+75.1%)	648,496 (+16%)	22,514 (+56.3%)
1990	395,534 (+50.5%)	8,070 (+25.3%)	839,880 (+29.5%)	27,163 (+20.6%)
1991	540,984 (+36.7%)	13,108 (+62.4%)	1,096,882 (+30.6%)	39,355 (+44.8%)
1992	497,457 (-8.1%)	18,528 (+41.3%)	1,063,829 (-3.0%)	49,573 (+25.9%)
1993		16,200 (-12.6%)		44,481 (-10.3%)

Sources: For the Russian figures: Kriminologicheskaya Assotsiatsiya, 1994, pp. 102 & 127. For the period 1985–89 in the Sverdlovsk region: "Information on the State of Crime in the Region by the Sverdlovsk Region CPSU Committee State and Law Department", early 1990; 12 pages. Fond 4, opis 118, delo 622, list 138. For the period 1990–93 in the Sverdlovsk region: MVD R.F. *et al.*, 1994, pp. 94, 101 & 108.

Table 11. Comparison of the evolution of the number of robberies and robberies with violence recorded in Russia and the Sverdlovsk region between 1985 and 1993

	Recorded cases of robbery		Recorded cases of robbery with violence	
	Russia	Sverdlovsk region	Russia	Sverdlovsk region
1985		2,378		356
1986		1,773 (− 25.4%)		240 (− 22.6%)
1987		1,840 (+3.7%)		251 (+4.5%)
1988		2,702 (+46.8%)		346 (+37.8%)
1989	75,220 (+71.6%)	4,277 (+76.5%)	14,551 (+79.2%)	673 (+94.5%)
1990	83,306 (+10.7%)	5,398 (+26.2%)	16,514 (+13.5%)	746 (+10.8%)
1991	101,956 (+22.4%)	6,904 (+27.8%)	18,311 (+10.9%)	978 (+31.1%)
1992	164,895 (+61.7%)	10,705 (+55.0%)	30,407 (+66.1%)	1,542 (+57.6%)
1993	184,410 (+11.8%)	12,530 (+17.0%)	40,180 (+32.1%)	2,271 (+47.2%)

Sources: For the period 1985–89: "Information on the State of Crime in the Region by the Sverdlovsk Region CPSU Committee State and Law Department", early 1990; 12 pages. Fond 4, opis 118, delo 622, list 138. For the period 1990–93: MVD R.F. *et al.*, 1994, pp. 108 and 115.

Table 12. Evolution of the number of breaches of the rules of economic activity recorded in Russia between 1986 and 1993

	Number of recorded cases (chap. 6)	Increase or decrease (% in relation to previous year)	Proportion of total number of recorded cases
1986	183,476		13.7
1987	135,927	– 26	11.4
1988	69,161	– 49.2	5.7
1989	64,179	– 7.2	3.4
1990	70,656	+ 10.1	3.8
1991	59,742	-15.4	2.8
1992	41,421	-30.7	1.5
1993	37,065	-10.5	1.3

Source: Kriminologicheskaya Assotsiatsiya, 1994, p. 144.

Table 13. Evolution of the number of cases of speculation, buyer and seller fraud (consumer fraud from July 1993) and violations of the rules of commerce recorded in Russia between 1986 and 1993

	Article 154	Increase or decrease (%)	Article 156	Increase or decrease (%)	Article 156³	Increase or decrease (%)
1986	21,321		19,131		10,351	
1987	22,671	+ 6.3	20,083	+ 4.9	10,039	– 3.0
1988	24,325	+ 7.2	19,826	– 1.3	11,332	+ 12.8
1989	23,644	– 2.8	21,091	+ 6.3	11,458	+ 1.1
1990	26,800	+ 13.3	19,842	– 6.0	15,890	+ 38.6
1991	18,988	– 29.2	18,934	– 4.6	14,674	– 7.7
1992	3,959	– 69.2	23,131	+ 22.1	7,693	– 47.6
1993	843	– 68.8	19,846	– 14.2	2,796	– 63.7

Source: Kriminologicheskaya Assotsiatsiya, 1994, pp. 145–6.

Table 14. Evolution of convictions for speculation in Russia (1986–1993)

	1986	1987	1988	1989	1990	1991	1992	1993
Number of people investigated	18,993	20,630	24,819	22,867	25,158	19,445	4,902	1,252
Number of people convicted	11,951	8,557	7,217	4,523	7,275	5,463	1,216	466
Proportion of people sentenced to prison*	24.1%	17.9%	11.1%	9.6%	11%	7%	4.4%	

* In relation to the number of those convicted. Source: Kriminologicheskaya Assotsiatsiya, 1994, pp. 234–5.

Table 15. Evolution of the number of corruption cases recorded in Russia between 1986 and 1993

	Number of recorded cases of corruption (art. 173, 174, 174¹)	*Increase or decrease (% in relation to previous year)*	*Share in the number of recorded abuses of official position*
1986	6,562		23.6
1987	4,155	– 36.7	17.8
1988	2,462	– 40.8	13.2
1989	2,195	– 10.8	13.0
1990	2,691	+ 22.6	15.7
1991	2,534	– 5.8	16.4
1992	3,337	+ 31.7	21.2
1993	4,511	+ 35.0	27.0

Source: Kriminologicheskaya Assotsiatsiya, 1994, p. 163.

Table 16. Evolution of the number of corruption cases recorded in the Sverdlovsk region between 1989 and 1993

	Number of cases recorded in the Sverdlovsk region	Increase or decrease in relation to the previous year (%)
1989	51	
1990	77	+ 51.0
1991	46	– 40.3
1992	90	+ 95.6
1993	129	+ 43.3

Source: MVD RF *et al.*, 1994, p. 128.

Table 17. Evolution of convictions for corruption in Russia (1986–93)

	1986	1987	1988	1989	1990	1991	1992	1993
Number of people investigated	4,600	2,846	1,994	1,308	1,510	1,266	1,543	2,278
Number of people convicted	3,454	2,008	812	451	649	612	686	843
Proportion of people sentenced to prison*	34.1%	45%	33.1%	28.4%	34.5%	26.6%	32.1%	29.9%

* In relation to the number of those convicted.
Source: Kriminologicheskaya Assotsiatsiya, 1994, pp. 234–5.

Table 18. Evolution of the judicial treatment of recorded cases in Russia, 1986–1993

	1986	1987	1988	1989	1990	1991	1992	1993
Number of people investigated	1,128,439	969,388	834,673	847,577	897,299	956,258	1,148,962	1,262,566
People prosecuted	827,173	593,369	459,705	505,089	589,092	654,808	782,453	967,181
People convicted	797,286	580,074	427,039	436,988	537,643	593,823	661,392	792,410
Prison Sentences	305,427	196,640	149,113	162,033	203,359	207,489	225,926	292,868
Corrective Labour	195,262	150,332	112,702	103,513	116,979	129,209	120,917	143,464
Conditional discharge (uslovno)	85,553	65,125	53,990	60,825	80,551	59,738	73,896	124,198
Suspended sentence (otsrochka)	79,563	64,697	54,562	56,560	72,065	83,270	95,107	142,592
Fines	124,623	97,177	54,030	51,961	62,271	72,292	62,931	70,906

Source: Kriminologicheskaya Assotsiatsiya, 1994, pp. 220–6.

Table 19. Evolution of the number of privatisation-related offences recorded in
Russia and the Sverdlovsk region, 1993–95

	1993	1994	1995
Russian Federation	3,387	1,749	1,086
Sverdlovsk Region	202	110	77

Source: data submitted by the Sverdlovsk region service for combating economic
crime. Interview with the head of this service, June 1997.

SOURCES

I was able to consult only a limited number of relatively uninteresting declassified documents during my visits to the CPSU Central Committee archives in Moscow. However, when in Yekaterinburg between 1995 and 1997 I was granted full access to archives covering the organisation of the fight against crime at regional level from the 1960s to the end of 1991. The Sverdlovsk region Centre for the Documentation of Social Organisations (*Tsentr Dokumentatsii Obshchestvennykh Organizatsii Sverdlovskoi Oblasti*, TsDOOSO) houses the archives of the Sverdlovsk region CPSU Committee up to the dissolution of the Soviet Union, that is, those of the Regional Committee secretariat, its various departments, and CPSU control bodies. The archives also contain personal files on leading figures and activists as well as citizens' letters to the committee. I consulted seventy-seven files (delo) of varying length (180 pages on average) collected in twenty-one inventories (opics). These documents, dealing mainly with the campaign against crime and the activities of administrative organisations, were composed of reports and other texts sent by law enforcement services to the Party's regional leadership. I consulted more than 400 texts ranging from two to eighty pages, but was unable to establish what proportion of all documents produced by these services during the period under review this volume amounted to. I selected 252 for their representative quality and wealth of information. Most of the texts used are reports (*spravki*): 214 documents generally written and dispatched by regional police and judicial services and by departments of the administrative organisations of the CPSU regional committee. Further material came from Party control committees, other regional committee departments dealing with economic crime, *druzhinas*,[1] local branches of *Gossnab* (state committee for material technical supply) and Party municipal committees.

Activity reports compiled by law enforcement bodies (police, Prosecutor's Offices and courts) and by Party municipal committees were presented in three different forms. Some described the fight against crime in all its forms. Others reported on the action taken by the services that specialised in combating economic offences. The third form contained information on the implementation of the CPSU Central Committee resolutions which provided the basis for the campaigns against economic crime. In addition, inspection reports, generally written by Prosecutor's Office services, control committees or other organisations mandated by the CPSU Regional Committee, assessed the performance of local law enforcement agencies.

Among the other files scrutinised, the minutes of meetings organised by the CPSU Regional Committee to discuss crime in the region and the work of law enforcement bodies were particularly informative. These meetings usually brought together the CPSU Regional Committee's Department of Administrative Organs and representatives of the various bodies involved in fighting economic crime. A reading of these minutes provides an insight into the relations among penal policy actors and confirms that the information presented in the administrative reports formed the basis for the discourse and representations of crime adopted by regional political leaders. Finally, I examined documents that, in the context of *glasnost*, reflected among other things the desire to assess "public opinion" in relation to illicit sources of income, as well as regional economic department reports on individual labour activity, the cooperative sector and "spontaneous privatisations."

Other written sources appear in the footnotes to each chapter. The generosity of some of the people I spoke to enabled me to gain access to valuable private archives, notably the specialised library in the Moscow flat of Viktor Sokirko and Lidia Tkachenko, founders of the Society for the Defence of Convicted Businessmen, where I consulted many judicial files, *samizdati* and documents collected since *perestroika*. The documentation also owes much to meetings with researchers and experts including O. Anyanin, M. Belanovskii, B.Bolotskii, L. Drapkin, Ya. Gilinskii, V. Zhitenev, S. Kelina, V. Kolesnikov, T. Kuznetsova, G. Sinilov, M. Voronin, G. Zabryanskii and M. Zatsepin, as well as with journalists like V. Ivanidze, S. Plotnikov, V. Smirnov and Yu. Shchekochikhin. Further information was gleaned from Soviet and Russian press files in France, at the Institute for Comparative Research on Institutions and Law (IRCID) at Ivry-sur-Seine and the Bibliothèque de Documentation Internationale Contemporaine (BDIC) at Nanterre. The thematic catalogue of press articles preserved by Radio Free Europe/Radio Liberty in Budapest was also of great assistance. I finally succeeded in collecting policing and judicial statistics at national and regional level with the help of the General Prosecutor's Office, although the information held does not provide a complete picture of the "results" of penal policy.

The oral sources used in the book play a supporting role. The subject matter made it difficult to envisage series of descriptive interviews with police officers and judges, during which they could be questioned about their professional practices. All the operational police officers I spoke to agreed to be interviewed after recommendations by a third party. These encounters were not always fruitful from a sociological point of view, either because they were too short or because the interviewee was very careful in his choice of words (when surrounded by colleagues, for example). Former police officers and those I met outside their places of work talked more freely, but it was still difficult to record their contributions. The text contains extracts from interviews, conducted mainly in Yekaterinburg in 1997, with five operational officers of the regional service combating economic crime (including two senior, long-serving officers); four former officers (two of whom worked for private security companies); the chief of police of a small town in the region; two prosecutors; two arbitration tribunal judges and two regional pioneers of the cooperative movement. Material was also obtained from several officials of the regional and municipal services responsible for property transfers, whom I had the good fortune to meet in 1993 when doing work placement at the Regional Committee for the Management of State Property, an excellent opportunity to observe the implementation of the privatisation process.

BIBLIOGRAPHY

The list is confined to references cited in the text. A more exhaustive bibliography accompanies my doctorate thesis (Favarel-Garrigues, 2001). This bibliography includes general references, books and articles on contemporary Russia and literature on policing and criminal issues in Russia. French and English publications are separated from those in Russian.

Publications in English and French

Ancel, M. and Y. Marx, *Les codes pénaux européens. Tome IV*, Paris, Centre Français de Droit Comparé, 1971.

Andreff, W., *La crise des économies socialistes. La rupture d'un système*, Grenoble, Presses Universitaires de Grenoble, 1993.

Aslund, A., *Gorbachev's Struggle for Economic Reform. The Soviet Reform Process, 1985–1988*, Ithaca (NY), Cornell University Press, 1989.

—— *How Russia Became a Market Economy*, Washington, The Brookings Institution, 1995.

Bardach, E., *The Implementation Game: What Happens After a Bill Becomes a Law*, Cambridge, Mass., MIT Press, 1977.

Barry, D., G. Ginsburgs and P.B. Maggs, *Soviet Law after Stalin. Part I: The Citizen and the State in Contemporary Soviet Law*, Leiden, Sijthoff, 1977.

Barry, D., G. Ginsburgs and P.B. Maggs (eds), *Soviet Law after Stalin. Part II: Social Engineering through Law*, Alphen aan den Rijn, Sijthoff & Noordhoff, 1978.

Barry, F., "De l'utilité des sondages d'opinion en URSS", *Le Courrier des Pays de l'Est*, n° 334, November 1998, pp. 45–8.

Baumol, W.J., "Entrepreneurship: Productive, Unproductive and Destructive", *Journal of Political Economy*, vol. 98, no. 5, 1990. pp. 893–921.

Bayart, J.-F. (ed.), *Les trajectoires du politique, 1. La réinvention du capitalisme*, Paris, Karthala, 1994.

Bayley, D., "Who are we Kidding? Or Developing Democracy Through Police Reform" in *Policing Emerging Democracies*, Washington, National Institute of Justice, October 1997, pp. 59–64.

BIBLIOGRAPHY

Bayley, D. and C. Shearing, *The New Structure of Policing: Description, Conceptualization and Research Agenda*, Washington, National Institute of Justice, 2001.

Berelowitch, A. and M. Wieworka, *Les Russes d'en bas*, Paris, Seuil, 1996.

Berliner, J.S., *Factory and Manager in the USSR* (1957), Cambridge, Mass., Harvard University Press, 1968.

Boycko, M., A. Schleifer and R. Vishny, "Privatizing Russia", *Brookings Papers on Economic Activity*, no. 2, 1993, p. 147.

—— *Privatizing Russia*, Cambridge, Mass., MIT Press, 1995.

Brodski ou le procès d'un poète, Paris, Le Livre de Poche, 1988.

Brokhin, Y., *Hustling on Gorky Street*, New York, Dial Press, 1975.

Brown, A., *The Gorbachev Factor*, Oxford, Oxford University Press, 1996.

Brown, A. and M. Kaser, *Soviet Policy for the 1980's*, London, Macmillan, 1982.

Bunce, V., "Quand le lieu compte: spécificités des passés autoritaires et réformes économiques dans les transitions à la démocratie", *Revue Française de Science Politique*, vol. 50, no. 4–5, 2000, pp. 633–56.

Burawoy, M. and K. Hendley, "Between Perestroika and Privatisation: Divided Strategies and Political Crisis in a Soviet Enterprise", *Europe-Asia Studies*, vol. 44, no. 3, 1992, pp. 371–402.

Carbonnier, J., *Sociologie juridique* (1978), Paris, PUF, 1994.

Carothers, T., "The End of the Transition Paradigm", *Journal of Democracy*, vol. 13, no. 1, 2000, pp. 5–21.

Cartier-Bresson, J. (ed.), *Pratiques et contrôle de la corruption*, Paris, AEF et Montchrestien, 1997.

Cartier-Bresson, J. "Causes et conséquences de la délinquance financière 'grise'. Le cas de la corruption", *Les Cahiers de la sécurité intérieure*, no. 36, 2nd quarter 1999, pp. 63–90.

—— "Etat, marchés, réseaux et organisations criminelles entrepreneuriales" in Institut de Sciences Pénales et de Criminologie, *Criminalité organisée et ordre dans la société*, Aix–en-Provence, Presses Universitaires d'Aix–Marseille, 1997, pp. 65–93.

Chalidze, V., *Le crime en Union soviétique*, Paris, Olivier Orban, 1978.

Chavance, B., "Réformer le système économique soviétique: l'histoire d'un échec" in J. Sapir (ed.), *Retour sur l'U.R.S.S. Economie, société, histoire*, Paris, L'Harmattan, 1997, pp. 153–4.

—— *Le système économique soviétique de Brejnev à Gorbatchev*, Paris, Nathan, 1989.

Chmatko, N. and M. de Saint Martin, "Les anciens bureaucrates dans l'économie de marché en Russie", *Genèses*, no. 27, June 1997, pp. 88–108.

Clark, W.A., *Crime and Punishment in Soviet Officialdom. Combating Corruption in the Political Elite (1965–1990)*, Armonk, M.E. Sharpe, 1991.

Colas, D., *Le léninisme* (1982), Paris, PUF, 1998.

—— *Les Constitutions de l'URSS et de la Russie (1905–1993)*, Paris, PUF, 1997.

Commaille, J. and B. Jobert (eds), *Les métamorphoses de la régulation politique*, Paris, L.G.D.J., 1998.

Commaille, J., *L'esprit sociologique des lois. Essai de sociologie politique du droit*, Paris, PUF, 1994.

BIBLIOGRAPHY

Connor, W.D., *Deviance in Soviet Society. Crime, Delinquency and Alcoholism*, New York, Columbia University Press, 1972.

Cox, T., *From Perestroika to Privatization. The Politics of Property Change in Russian Society, 1985–1991*, Aldershot and Brookfield, Avebury, 1996.

Crosnier, M.-A., "Le mouvement coopératif mis au pas", *Le Courrier des Pays de l'Est*, January 1989, no. 336, pp. 66–9.

Debuyst, C. *et al.*, *Histoire des savoirs sur le crime et la peine. Volume 2. La rationalité pénale et la naissance de la criminologie*, Brussels, De Boeck, 1998.

Delmas-Marty, M., *Les grands systèmes de politique criminelle*, Paris, Presses Universitaires de France, 1992.

Delmas-Marty, M. (ed.), *Criminalité économique et atteintes à la dignité de la personne. Tome I: Europe*, Paris, Maison des Sciences de l'Homme, 1997.

Delorme, M.-H., *Krokodil. Ivan Ivanovitch s'amuse*, Paris, Seghers, 1964.

Dobry, M., *Sociologie des crises politiques* (1986), Paris, Presses de la FNSP, 1992.

Dobry, M. (ed.), "Les transitions démocratiques: regards sur l'état de la 'transitologie'", *Revue Française de Science Politique*, vol. 50, no. 4–5, 2000, pp. 579–764.

Doig, A. and M. Levi, "Délinquance économique et justice pénale. Le cas du Royaume-Uni", *Déviance et Société*, vol. 20, no. 3, September 1996, pp. 238–54.

Duchêne, G., "L'analyse de la seconde économie" in Marie Lavigne (ed.), *Travail et monnaie en système socialiste*, Paris, Economica, 1981, pp. 256–87.

—— *L'économie de l'URSS*, Paris, La Découverte, 1987.

Duhamel, L., "La criminalité économique en Sibérie de Brejnev à Gorbatchev", *Revue d'Etudes Comparatives Est-Ouest*, vol. 22, n°4, 1991, pp. 21–48.

—— "La criminalité économique en U.R.S.S., ses formes et son ampleur", *Revue d'Etudes Comparatives Est-Ouest*, vol. 20, no. 3, 1989, pp. 71–92.

Edelman, M., *Constructing the Political Spectacle*, Chicago University Press, 1988 (translated into French by C. Cler as *Pièces et règles du jeu politique*, Paris, Le Seuil, 1991).

Fainsod, M., *Smolensk Under Stalin's Rule*, New York, Random House, 1958. (French translation: *Smolensk à l'heure de Staline*, Paris, Fayard, 1967.)

Favarel-Garrigues, G., *La lutte contre la criminalité économique en Russie soviétique et post-soviétique*, Paris, Institut d'Etudes Politiques, January 2001.

—— "Priorités et limites de la politique pénitentiaire en Russie", *Critique Internationale*, no. 16, July 2002, pp. 121–36.

—— "La bureaucratie policière et la chute du régime soviétique", *Sociétés Contemporaines*, no. 57, 2005, pp. 63–82.

Feige, E.L., "Underground Activity and Institutional Change: Productive, Protective and Predatory Behaviour in Transition Economies" in Task Force on Economies in Transition, Commission on Behavioural and Social Sciences and Education, National Research Council, *Transforming Post-Communist Political Economies*, Washington, National Academy Press, 1997, pp. 21–34.

Feldbrugge, F.J.M., "Government and Shadow Economy in the Soviet Union", *Soviet Studies*, vol. 36, no. 4, October 1984, pp. 528–43.

Fish, S., "The Roots and the Remedies for Russia's Racket Economy" in S.S. Cohen, A. Schwarz and J. Zysman (eds), *The Tunnel at the End of the Light. Privatization,*

Business Networks and Economic Transformation in Russia, Berkeley, University of California Press, 1998, pp. 86–138.

Fitzpatrick, S., *Le stalinisme au quotidien. La Russie soviétique dans les années 1930*, Paris, Flammarion, 2002.

Fortescue, S., "The Restructuring of Soviet Industrial Ministries since 1985" in Aslund (ed.), *Market Socialism or the Restoration of Capitalism*, Cambridge University Press, 1992, pp. 15–18.

Foucault, M., *Discipline and Punish: the Birth of the Prison*, translated by Alan Sheridan, London, Allen Lane, 1977. (French original: *Surveiller et punir. Naissance de la prison*, Paris, Gallimard, 1975.)

Frisby, T., "The Rise of Organised Crime in Russia: its Roots and Social Significance", *Europe-Asia Studies*, vol. 50, no. 1, 1998, pp. 27–48.

Fuller, E., "Azeri Press Publishes Opinion Poll on Nonlabor Incomes", *Radio Liberty Research*, no. 341, 4 September 1986, pp. 3–6.

—— "The Campaign against Nonlabor Incomes in Azerbaidjan", *Radio Liberty Research*, no. 26, 14 January 1987, pp. 4–7.

Galeotti, M., "Perestroika, Perestrelka, Pereborka: Policing Russia in a Time of Change", *Europe-Asia Studies*, vol. 45, no. 5, 1993, pp. 769–86.

—— "From Gorky to Tol'yatti: New Models for the Police", *Radio Liberty Report on the USSR*, vol. 2, no. 35, 31 August 1990, pp. 4–6.

Gatto, D. and J.-C Thoenig, *La sécurité publique à l'épreuve du terrain*, Paris, l'Harmattan and IHESI, 1993.

Gilinskii, Y., *The Police in Russia: From Totalitarianism to Democracy?* St Petersburg, 1995.

Golovko, L., "Le nouveau code pénal de la Russie", *Revue de Science Criminelle et de Droit Pénal Comparé*, no. 3, July-September 1997, pp. 561–77.

Grabher, G. and D. Stark (eds), *Restructuring Networks in Post-Socialism*, Oxford, Oxford University Press, 1997.

Grossman, G., "The 'Second Economy' of the USSR", *Problems of Communism*, XXVII, September-October 1977, pp. 25–40.

—— "Notes on the Illegal Private Economy and Corruption" in Joint Economic Committee, *Soviet Economy in a Time of Change*, vol. 1, Washington, 1979, pp. 834–55.

—— "The Second Economy in the USSR and Eastern Europe: a Bibliography", *Berkeley-Duke Occasional Papers on the Second Economy in the USSR*, no. 1, Sept. 1985, pp. 12–24.

—— "Roots of Gorbachev's Problems: Private Income and Outlay in the Late 1970's" in Joint Economic Committee (Congress of the U.S.), *Gorbachev's Economic Plans*, vol. 1, Washington, 1987.

Grossman, G. and V. Treml, "Introduction to the Series", *Berkeley-Duke Occasional Papers on the Second Economy in the USSR*, no. 1, September 1985, pp. 1–9.

Hewett, A. and C.G. Gaddy, *Open for Business. Russia's Return to the Global Economy*, Washington, The Brookings Institution, 1992.

Hewett, E.A., *Reforming the Soviet Economy. Equality versus Efficiency*, Washington, The Brookings Institution, 1988.

Hibou, B. (ed.), *Privatising the State*, London, C. Hurst & Co., 2004 (French original *La privatisation des Etats*, Paris, Karthala, 1999).

Hirschman, Albert O., *Exit, Voice, and Loyalty: Responses to Decline in Firms, Organizations, and States*, Cambridge, Mass., Harvard University Press, 1970.

—— *Shifting Involvements. Private Interest and Public Action*. Princeton University Press, 1982. (Translated into French by M. Leiris and J-B. Grasset as *Bonheur privé, action publique*, Paris, Fayard, 1983.)

Hoffman, D., *The Oligarchs: Wealth and Power in the New Russia*, New York, Perseus Book Group, 2002.

Hoffman, E.P., "Information Processing in the Party: Recent Theory and Experience" in K.W. Ryavec (ed.), *Soviet Society and the Communist Party*, Amherst, University of Massachussets Press, 1978.

Holmes, L., *The End of Communist Power*, Cambridge, Polity Press, 1993.

Human Rights Watch, *Confessions at Any Cost. Police Torture in Russia*, New York, Human Rights Watch, 1999.

Ioffe, O.S., "Soviet Law and the New Economic Experiment" in O.S. Ioffe and M.W. Janis, *Soviet Law and Economy*, Dordrecht, Martinus Nijhoff (ed.), 1986, pp. 3–28.

Jobert, V., *La satire soviétique contemporaine. Société et idéologie*, Paris, Presses Universitaires de Paris-Sorbonne, 1991.

Johnson, S. and H. Kroll, "Managerial Strategies for Spontaneous Privatization", *Soviet Economy*, vol. 7, no. 4, 1991, pp. 281–316.

Johnson, S.K. Kroll and S. Eder, "Strategy, Structure and Spontaneous Privatization in Russia and Ukraine" in V. Milor (ed.), *Changing Political Economies: Privatization in Post-Communist and Reforming Communist States*, Boulder, Lynne Rienner, 1994.

Johnston, M., "A la recherche de définitions: vitalité politique et corruption", *Revue Internationale des Sciences Sociales*, no. 149, September 1996, pp. 371–88.

Jones, A. and W. Moskoff, *Ko-ops: The Rebirth of Entrepreneurship in the Soviet Union*, Bloomington, Indiana University Press, 1991.

Juviler, P.H., *Revolutionary Law and Order*, New York, Macmillan, 1976.

Katsenelinboigen, A., "Coloured Markets in the Soviet Union", *Soviet Studies*, vol. 29, no. 1, January 1977, pp. 62–85.

—— "Corruption in the USSR: Some Methodological Notes" in M. Clarke (ed.), *Corruption. Causes, Consequences and Control*, London, Frances Pinter, 1983, pp. 220–38.

Katz, Z., "Insights from Emigrés and Sociological Studies on the Soviet Economy" in *Soviet Economics Prospects for the Seventies*, Washington, U.S. Congress, Joint Economic Committee, 1973, pp. 87–120.

Kelina, S.G., "On Drafting New Criminal Legislation in the USSR", *Coexistence*, no. 28, 1991, pp. 3–12.

Klebnikov, P., *Godfather of the Kremlin. Boris Berezovsky and the Looting of Russia*, New York, Harcourt, 2002.

Knight, A., *The KGB, Police and Politics in the Soviet Union*, Boston, Unwin Hyman, 1990.

Kornai, J., *Le système socialiste: l'économie politique du communisme*, Grenoble, Presses Universitaires, 1996.

Kott, S. (ed.), "Pour une histoire sociale du pouvoir en Europe communiste", *Revue d'Histoire Moderne et Contemporaine*, vol. 49, no. 2, 2002, pp. 5–254.

Kourilsky-Augeven, Ch., *Cours de terminologie juridique russe*, Université Paris-X Nanterre, roneo, 1998.

Kouznetsov, V., "La privatisation en Russie, 1992–1995", *Le courrier des pays de l'Est*, no. 400, June 1995, pp. 21–27.

Kramer, J.M., "Political Corruption in the USSR", *Western Political Quarterly*, vol. 30, no. 2, June 1977, pp. 213–24.

Kruzhin, P., "Political Organs Created in the MVD", *Radio Liberty Research Bulletin*, 30 December 1983, pp. 22–9.

Lagrange, H., *Demandes de sécurité: France, Europe, Etats-Unis*, Paris, Le Seuil, 2003, p. 54.

Lagroye, J., *Sociologie politique*, Paris, Presses de la FNSP and Dalloz, 1993.

Lampert, N., *Whistleblowing in the Soviet Union. Complaints and Abuses under State Socialism*, London, Macmillan, 1985.

Lapina, N., "Le secteur privé en URSS de 1986 à 1991: structures et acteurs du marché", *Le Courrier des Pays de l'Est*, no. 400, June 1995, pp. 14–19.

Lascoumes, P., "Normes juridiques et mise en oeuvre des politiques publiques", *L'année Sociologique*, 40, 1990, pp. 43–71.

——— *Les affaires ou l'art de l'ombre. Les délinquances économiques et financières et leur contrôle*, Paris, Le Centurion, 1985.

Lascoumes, P. and A. Depaigne, "Catégoriser l'ordre public: la réforme du code pénal français de 1992", *Genèses*, no. 27, June 1997.

Lascoumes, P., P. Poncela and P. Lenoel, *Au nom de l'ordre. Une histoire politique du code pénal*, Paris, Hachette, 1989.

——— *Les grandes phases d'incrimination. Les mouvements de la législation pénale 1815–1940*, Paris, G.A.P.P.-C.N.R.S.-Paris X, Ministère de la Justice, 1992.

Ledeneva, A., *Russia's Economy of Favours: Blat, Networking and Informal Exchange*, Cambridge University Press, 1998.

Le Huérou, A., *Les pratiques de sécurité locale dans la Russie post-soviétique*, Paris, IHESI, 2003.

Lesage, M., "La loi sur la coopération du 26 mai 1988 en URSS. Analyses et commentaires", *Le Courrier des Pays de l'Est*, November 1988, no. 334, pp. 49–60.

——— *L'administration soviétique*, Paris, Economica, 1981.

——— *Les régimes politiques de l'U.R.S.S et de l'Europe de l'Est*, Paris, P.U.F, 1971.

Levada, Y., *Entre le passé et l'avenir. L'homme soviétique ordinaire. Enquête*, Paris, Presses de la FNSP, 1993. (Translated from Russian by J. Tordjman and A. Berelowitch.)

Lewin, M., *The Gorbachev Phenomenon: a Historical Interpretation*, Berkeley, University of California Press, 1988. (French translation: Lewin, M., *La grande mutation soviétique*, Paris, La Découverte, 1989.)

——— *Le siècle soviétique*, Paris, Fayard, 2003.

Linz, J. and A. Stepan, *Problems of Democratic Transition and Consolidation*, Baltimore, Johns Hopkins University Press, 1996.

Lipsky, M., *Street-Level Bureaucracy. Dilemmas of the Individual in Public Services*, New York, Russell Sage Foundation, 1980.

Los, M., "Crime and Economy in the Communist Countries" in P. Wickman and T. Dailey (eds), *White Collar and Economic Crime*, Lexington, Lexington Books, 1982. pp. 121–37.

—— "Economic Crimes in Communist Countries" in I.L. Barak-Glantz and E.H. Johnson (eds), *Comparative Criminology*, Beverley Hills, Sage, 1983, pp. 39–57.

—— *Communist Ideology, Law and Crime. A Comparative View of the USSR and Poland*, London, Macmillan, 1988.

Los, M. (ed.), *The Second Economy in Marxist States*, Basingstoke & London, Macmillan, 1990.

Los, M., "Post-Communist Fear of Crime and the Commercialization of Security", *Theoretical Criminology*, vol. 6, no. 2, 2002, pp. 165–88.

Lotspeich, R., "Crime in the Transition Economies", *Europe-Asia Studies*, vol. 47, no. 4, 1995, pp. 555–89.

Maes, O., "La collecte de l'impôt en Russie. L'invention d'une politique publique (1990–1998)", *Cahiers Anatole Leroy-Beaulieu*, no. 3, January 1999, p. 47.

Maggs, P.B., "Improving the Legal Mechanisms for Economic Change" in Barry, D., G. Ginsburgs and P.B. Maggs (eds), *Soviet Law after Stalin. Part II: Social Engineering through Law*, Alphen aan den Rijn, Sijthoff & Noordhoff, 1978. pp. 117–38.

Maguire, K., "Policing the Russian Mafia", *The Police Journal*, vol. 71, no. 3, July-September 1998, pp. 245–55.

Marx, K. and F. Engels, *The German Ideology*, London, Lawrence & Wishart, 1970. (French version: *L'idéologie allemande (1845–1846)*, Paris, Editions Sociales, 1982, translation by H. Auger, G. Badia, J. Baudrillard and R. Cartelle, supervised by G. Badia)

Mayntz, R., "Les bureaucraties publiques et la mise en oeuvre des politiques", *Revue Internationale des Sciences Sociales*, vol. 31, no. 4, 1979, pp. 677–90.

Medvedev, Z.A., *Andropov*, New York, Norton, 1983.

Mendras, M., "La Russie: administrations sans foi ni loi" in D. della Porta and Y. Meny (eds), *Démocratie et corruption en Europe*, Paris, La Découverte, 1995, pp. 117–30.

Mendras, M. (ed.), "Russie: le gouvernement des provinces", *Nouveaux Mondes*, no. 7, winter 1997.

Mink, G., "La réhabilitation des sondages d'opinion en URSS, Pologne et Hongrie", *Le Courrier des Pays de l'Est*, no. 329, May 1988, pp. 18–28.

Monjardet, D., "Professionalisme et médiation de l'action policière", *Les Cahiers de la Sécurité Intérieure*, no. 33, third quarter 1998, pp. 21–50.

—— *Ce que fait la police. Sociologie de la force publique*, Paris, La Découverte, 1996.

Morvant, P., "Corruption Hampers War on Crime in Russia", *Transition*, 8 March 1996, pp. 23–31.

Nelson, L.D. and I.Y. Kuzes, *Radical Reform in Yeltsin's Russia. Political, Economic, and Social Dimensions*, Armonk and London, M.E. Sharpe, 1995.

Nivat, A., *Quand les médias russes ont pris la parole*, Paris, L'Harmattan, 1997.

Ocqueteau, F., *Polices entre Etat et marché*, Paris, Presses de Sciences Po, 2004.

Ofer, G. and J. Pickersgill, "Soviet Households Savings: A Study of Soviet Emigrant Families", *Quarterly Journal of Economics*, vol. 94, no. 3, August 1980, pp. 121–43.

Ofer, G. and A. Vinokur, "The Labor-Force Participation of Married Women in the Soviet Union: a Household Cross-Section Analysis", *Journal of Comparative Economics*, vol. 7, no. 2, June 1983, pp. 158–76.

Offe, C., "Vers le capitalisme par construction démocratique? La théorie de la démocratie et la triple transition en Europe de l'Est", *Revue Française de Science Politique*, vol. 42, no. 6, December 1992, pp. 923–42.

Orenstein, H., "Crime and Punishment: Old Problems and New Dilemmas for an Emerging Eastern and Central Europe", *Low Intensity Conflict and Law Enforcement*, vol. 1, no. 1, summer 1992, pp. 14–41.

Orland, L., "Perspectives on Soviet Economic Crime" in O.S. Ioffe and M.W. Janis, *Soviet Law and Economy*, Dordrecht, Martinus Nijhoff, 1986, pp. 169–212.

Peck, M.J. and T. Richardson (eds), *What is to be Done? Proposals for the Soviet Transition to the Market*, New Haven, Yale University Press, 1992.

Petrov, N., "Siloviki in Russian Regions: New Dogs, Old Tricks", *Power Institutions in Post-Soviet Societies*, 2, 2005 [http://www.pipss.org/document331.html]

Picca, G., *La criminologie*, Paris, PUF, 1993.

Pomorski, S., "Crimes against the Central Planner: 'Ochkovtiratel'stvo'" in D.B. Barry, G. Ginsburgs and P.B. Maggs, *Soviet Law after Stalin. Part II: Social Engineering through Law*, Alphen aan den Rijn, Sijthoff & Noordhoff, 1978, pp. 291–317.

——— "Criminal Law Protection of Socialist Property in the USSR" in D.B. Barry, G. Ginsburgs and P.B. Maggs, *Soviet Law after Stalin. Part I: The Citizen and the State in Contemporary Soviet Law*, Leyden, Sijthoff, 1977, pp. 223–58.

Pradel, J., *Droit pénal comparé*, Paris, Dalloz, 1995, p. 86.

Pradel, J. (ed.), *Le code pénal russe de 1997*, Travaux de l'Institut de Sciences Criminelles de Poitiers, vol. XIX, Paris, Cujas, 1998.

Pressman, J.L. and A. Wildawsky, *Implementation. How Great Expectations in Washington are Dashed in Oakland*, Berkeley, University of California Press, 1973.

Queloz, N., "A-t-on encore des raisons de distinguer criminalités économique et organisée?", *Les Cahiers de la Sécurité Intérieure*, no. 36, second quarter 1999, pp. 21–39.

Quinton, B., "Des petits entrepreneurs en URSS: les patrons des coopératives", *Le Courrier des Pays de l'Est*, no. 360, May-June 1991. pp. 25–44.

Reiner, R., "Policing and the Police" in M. Maguire, R. Morgan and R. Reiner, *The Oxford Handbook of Criminology*, Oxford, Clarendon Press, 1997, pp. 997–1049.

Revuz, Ch., *Ivan Ivanovitch écrit à la Pravda*, Paris, Editions Sociales, 1980.

Reynaud, J.-D., *Les règles du jeu et la régulation sociale* (1988), Paris, Armand Colin, 1997.

Rigby, T.H. and F. Feher (eds), *Political Legitimation in Communist States*, New York, St Martin's Press, 1982.

Robert, Ph. *et al.*, *Les comptes du crime. Les délinquances en France et leurs mesures* (1985), Paris, L'Harmattan, 1994.

Robertson, M., "The Impact of Crime in Eastern Europe on the European Union", *Low Intensity Conflict and Law Enforcement*, vol. 3, no. 1, summer 1994, pp. 135–49.

Rose-Ackerman, S., *Corruption: a Study in Political Economy*, New York, Academic Press, 1978.

Rutland, P., "Economic Crisis and After" in S. White, *Gorbachev and After*, Cambridge University Press, 1992, pp. 37–49.

Sachs, J.D., "Spontaneous Privatization: a Comment", *Soviet Economy*, vol. 7, no. 4, July-September 1991, pp. 317–21.

Sakwa, R., *The Quality of Freedom. Khodorkovsky, Putin and the Yukos Affair*, Oxford, Oxford University Press, 2009.

Sapir, J. (ed.), *Retour sur l'URSS. Economie, société, histoire*, Paris, L'Harmattan, 1997.

Schumpeter, J., *Capitalism, Socialism and Democracy (1942)*, London, Allen & Unwin, 1976. (Translated into French by G. Fain as *Capitalisme, socialisme et démocratie*, Paris, Payot, 1963.)

Shelley, L.I., "The Second Economy in the Soviet Union" in M. Los, *The Second Economy in Marxist States*, Basingstoke & London, Macmillan, 1990 (1990a), pp. 11– 26.

—— "The Soviet Militsiia: Agents of Political and Social Control", *Policing and Society*, no. 1, 1990 (1990b), pp. 39–56.

—— "Privatization and Crime: the Post-Soviet Experience", *Journal of Contemporary Criminal Justice*, vol. 11, no. 4, December 1995, pp. 244–56.

—— *Policing Soviet Society. The Evolution of State Control*, London & New York, Routledge, 1996.

—— "Is the Russian State Coping with Organized Crime and Corruption?" in V. Sperling, *Building the Russian State. Institutional Crisis and the Quest for Democratic Governance*, Boulder, Westview, 2000, pp. 105–6.

Shlapentokh, V., "Privatization Debates in Russia: 1989–1992", *Comparative Economic Studies*, no. 2, summer 1993, pp. 19–31.

Simis, C., *La société corrompue*, Paris, Robert Laffont, 1982.

Simis, K., "The Machinery of Corruption in the Soviet Union", *Survey: a Journal of East and West Studies*, vol. 23, no. 4, Autumn 1977, pp. 35–55.

Slider, D., "Embattled Entrepreneurs. Soviet Cooperatives in an Unreformed Economy", *Soviet Studies*, vol. 43, no. 5, 1991, pp. 797–821.

Smith, G.B., "Procuratorial Campaigns against Crime" in D.B. Barry, G. Ginsburgs and P.B. Maggs, *Soviet Law after Stalin. Part III: Soviet Institutions and the Administration of Law*, Alphen aan den Rijn, Sijthoff & Noordhoff, 1979, pp. 143–67.

—— "The Struggle over the Procuracy" in P.H. Solomon, Jr. (ed.), *Reforming Justice in Russia, 1864–1996: Power, Culture and the Limits of Legal Order*, Armonk, M.E. Sharpe, 1997, pp. 348–73.

Solomon Jr, P.H., "Specialists in Policymaking: Criminal Policy, 1938–1970" in K.W. Ryavec (ed.), *Soviet Society and the Communist Party*, Amherst, University of Massachusetts Press, 1978 (1978a), pp. 153–76.

—— *Soviet Criminologists and Criminal Policy: Specialists in Policymaking*, New York, Columbia University Press & Macmillan, 1978 (1978b).

—— "The Persistence of Judicial Reform in Contemporary Russia", *East European Constitutional Review*, vol. 6, no. 4, fall, 1997, pp. 50–6.

Solomon Jr, P.H. (ed.), *Reforming Justice in Russia, 1864–1996: Power, Culture and the Limits of Legal Order*, Armonk, Sharpe, 1997.

Solnick, S., *Stealing the State. Control and Collapse in Soviet Institutions*, Cambridge, Mass., Harvard University Press, 1998.

Soulier, G., "Les institutions judiciaires et répressives" in M. Grawitz and J. Leca, *Traité de science politique. Volume 2*, Paris, PUF, 1985, pp. 510–52.

Stark, D. and L. Bruszt, *Postsocialist Pathways. Transforming Politics and Property in East Central Europe*, Cambridge University Press, 1998.

Tarschys, D., "The Success of a Failure: Gorbachev's Alcohol Policy, 1985–1988", *Europe-Asia Studies*, vol. 45, no. 1, 1993, pp. 7–25.

Tchkhikvadze, V. (ed.), *L'Etat soviétique et le droit*, Moscow, Editions du Progrès, 1971.

Tikhomirov, V., "Capital Flight from Post-Soviet Russia", *Europe-Asia Studies*, vol. 49, no. 4, 1997, pp. 591–615.

Timoshenko, S., "Prospects for Reform of the Russian Militia", *Policing and Society*, vol. 8, no. 1, 1997, pp. 117–24.

Trehub, A., "Hard Times for Soviet Policemen", *Radio Liberty Report on the USSR*, vol. 1, n° 23, 9 June 1989, pp. 18–21.

Tsypkin, M., "Workers Militia: Order Instead of Law?" *RFE/RL Research Report*, 17 November 1989, pp. 14–17.

Tupman, W., "La démocratisation des services de police dans la nouvelle Communauté des Etats Indépendants", *Les Cahiers de la Sécurité Intérieure*, no. 8, February-April 1992, pp. 23–38.

Vaksberg, A., *La mafia russe*, Paris, Albin Michel, 1992.

Van de Kerchove, M., "Les différentes formes de baisse de la pression juridique et leurs principaux enjeux", *Cahiers de Recherche Sociologique*, no. 13, autumn 1989, pp. 11–29.

Varese, F., *The Russian Mafia. Private Protection in a New Market Economy*, Oxford, Oxford University Press, 2001.

Volkov, V., "Violent Entrepreneurship in Post-Communist Russia", *Europe-Asia Studies*, vol. 51, no. 5, July 1999, pp. 741–54.

—— *Violent Entrepreneurs. The Use of Force in the Making of Russian Capitalism*, Ithaca, Cornell University Press, 2002.

Voslensky, M., *La nomenklatura. Les privilégiés en URSS*, Paris, Pierre Belfond, 1980. (Translated from German by C. Nugue.)

Wädekin, K.-E., *The Private Sector in Soviet Agriculture*, Berkeley & Los Angeles, University of California, 1973.

Weber, M., *Economie et société. Tome 2. L'organisation et les puissances de la société dans leur rapport avec l'économie* (1924), Paris, Plon, 1995. (Translated from German by J. Freund *et al.* under the supervision of J. Chavy and E. de Dempierre.)

Weinberg, E.A., *The Development of Sociology in the Soviet Union*, London & Boston, Routledge and Kegan Paul, 1974.

Werth, N., *Histoire de l'Union soviétique* (1990), Paris, PUF, 1992.

BIBLIOGRAPHY

Publications in Russian

Alyabin, S., A. Bochkov and Z. Korneva, "Prestupleniya v sfere privatizatsii" (Offences in the Sphere of Privatisation), *Vestnik MVD RF*, no. 4, 1994, pp. 24–36.

Animitsa, E.G. and N.M. Ratner, *Regional'nyi aspekt privatizatsii* (Regional Aspects of Privatisation), Yekaterinburg, Institut Ekonomiki, 1993, p. 36.

Aslakhanov, A., *Prestupnost'v sfere ėkonomiki* (Crime in the Economic Sphere), Moscow, Moskovskii Yuridicheskii Institut MVD Rossii, 1997.

Aslund, A., "Novykh russkikh obogatili tri osnovnykh istochnika" (Three Fundamental Sources have Enriched the New Russians), *Izvestiya*, 20 June 1996.

Bolotskii, B.S., "Problemy legalizatsii (otmyvanii) dokhodov ot nelegal'noi ėkonomicheskoi deyatel'nosti" (Problems of Legalisation (Laundering) of the Proceeds of Illegal Economic Activity), in *Tenevaya ėkonomika. Ekonomicheskie, Sotsial'nye i Pravovye Aspekty* (The Shadow Economy. Economic, Social and Political Aspects), Moscow, Nezavisimyi Blagotvoritel'nyi Fond Kul'tury "Foros", 1996, pp. 12–19.

Borodin, S. and Yu. Kudryavtsev, "Prestupnost': ne panikovat', a razobrat'sya" (Crime: React and Don't Panic), *Kommunist*, no. 14, September 1989, p. 59.

Chalidze, V., *Ugolovnaya Rossiya* (Criminal Russia) (1977), Moscow, Terra, 1990.

Churbanov, Yu., *Ya rasskazhu vsyo, kak bylo...* (I Will Tell Everything about my Past...), Moscow, Izdatel'stvo Nezavisimoi Gazety, 1993. (The confessions of Leonid Brezhnev's son-in-law.)

Dolgova, A.I. and S.V. D'Yakov (eds), *Organizovannaya prestupnost'* (Organised Crime), Moscow, Yuridicheskaya Literatura, 1989.

Dubov, Yu., *Bolshaya Paika* (The Big Slice), Moscow, Vagrius, 2002.

Dudenkov, B., "Malye predpriyatiya—shag k rynku" (Small Businesses—a Step Towards the Market), *Voprosy Ekonomiki*, no. 8, 1991, p. 70.

Fatula, A. and T. Lisitsyna, "Proshu uvolit' menya" ("I Request my Dismissal..."), *Sovetskaya Militsiya*, no. 4 & no. 5, 1990, pp. 49–54 & 46–9.

Felzenbaum, V., T. Kuznetsova and L. Nikiforov, "Tenevaya ekonomika: osnovy vozniknoveniya, evolyutsii i oslableniya" (The Underground Economy: the Basis of its Emergence, Evolution and Weakening), *Voprosy Ekonomiki*, no. 1, January 1991, pp. 100–11.

Freinkman, L., "Finansovyi kapital i formirovanie promyshlennoi struktury v Rossii" (Financial Capital and the Formation of an Industrial Structure in Russia), *EKO*, no. 10, 1994, p. 6.

Gilinskii, Ya (ed.), "Organizovannaya prestupnost' v Rossii: teoriya i real'nost'" (Organised Crime in Russia: Theory and Reality), *Trudy Sankt-Peterburgskogo filiala Instituta Sotsiologii RAN. Serie III*, no. 4, August 1996, p. 96.

Golovin, S. and A. Shokhin, "Tenevaya ekonomika: za realizm otsenok" (For a Realistic Evaluation of the Underground Economy), *Kommunist*, no. 1, 1990, pp. 51–7.

Gorbachev, M., *Politicheskii doklad Tsentral'nogo komiteta KPSS XXVII S'ezdu Kommunisticheskoi Partii Sovetskogo Soyuza* (Political Report of the CPSU Central Committee to the 27th CPSU Congress), Moscow, Izdatel'stvo Politicheskoi Literatury, 1986.

Goryainov, K., V. Ovchinskii and L. Kondratyuk, *Uluchshenie vzaimootnoshenii gra-zhdan i militsii* (To Improve Relations between Police and Citizens), Moscow, Infra-M, 2001.

Goryanovskii, A., "Ukrast' mozhno vsyo. Rezul'taty vklyuchennogo nablyudeniya" (You can Steal Anything. Results of a Participitative Observation), *Sotsiologicheskie Issledovaniya*, 1990, no. 2, pp. 56–64.

Govorukhin, S., *Strana vorov na doroge v svetloe budushchee* (Country of Thieves on the Road to a Radiant Future), Narva, Firma "Shans", 1994.

Gurov, A., *Krasnaya mafiya* (The Red Mafia), Moscow, Samotsvet, MIKO "Kommercheskii vestnik", 1995.

—— *Professional'naya prestupnost'* (Professional Crime), Moscow, Yuridicheskaya Literatura, 1990.

Gurov, A. and Y. Ryabinin, *Ispoved' vora v zakone* (Confessions of a Thief-in-Law), Moscow, Samotsvet, 1995.

Gutsenko, K.F., *Pravookhranitel'nye organy v SSSR* (Organs of Repression in the USSR), Moscow, Izdatel'stvo Moskovskogo Universiteta, 1991.

Ispravnikov, V.O., "Tenevaya ekonomika: èkspropriatsiya, otmyvanie ili legalizatsiya?" (The Shadow Economy: Expropriation, Laundering or Legalisation?) in *Tenevaya èkonomika. Ekonomicheskie, sotsial'nye i pravovye aspekty* (The Shadow Economy: Economic, Social and Political Aspects), Moscow, Nezavisimyi Blagotvoritel'nyi Fond Kul'tury "Foros", 1996, pp. 4–11.

Ivanov, L.O. and L.V. Il'ina, *Puti i sud'by otechestvennoi kriminologii* (Pathways and Future of Criminology), Moscow, Nauka, 1991.

Kelina, S.G., "Vstupitel'naya stat'ya" (Introductory Article) in *Ugolovnyi kodeks Rossiiskoi Federatsii* (Russian Federation Criminal Code), Moscow, BEK, 1996, pp. 12–26.

Kharkhordin, O., *Oblichat' i litsemerit'*, St Petersburg, Evropeiskii Universitet v Sankt-Peterburge, 2002.

Khinstein, A., *Okhota na oborotnei* (Hunt for Werewolves), Moscow, Detektiv Press, 2005.

Khokhryakov, G., "Mafiya v SSSR: vymysly, domysly, fakty" (The Mafia in the USSR: Fiction, Supposition and Fact), *Yunost'*, no. 3, 1989, pp. 11–18.

Kipman, N., "O kompetentnosti i professionalizme" (On Competence and Professionalism), *Sovetskaya Militsiya*, no. 4, 1990, p. 19–24.

Kirichenko, N. *et al.*, "Pobeditelei ne sudyat" (We Don't Judge the Winners), *Kommersant*, 13 June 1995, pp. 16–24.

Kleimenov, M.P. and O.V. Dmitriev, "Rèket v Sibiri" (Racketeering in Siberia), *Sotsiologicheskie Issledovaniya*, no. 3, 1995, pp. 81–7.

Klyamkin, I., "Oktyabr'skii vybor prezidenta" (The October Choice of the President), *Ogonyok*, n° 47, Nov. 1990, pp. 4–7.

Kolesnikov, V.V., *Ekonomicheskaya prestupnost' i rynochnye reformy. Politiko-ekonomicheskie aspekty* (Economic Crime and Market Reform. Political and Economic Aspects), St Petersburg, Izdatel'stvo Sankt-Peterburgskogo Universiteta Ekonomiki i Finansov, 1994.

Korneva, Z., "Prestupleniya v sfere privatizatsii" (Offences in the Sphere of Privatisation), *Vestnik MVD RF*, no. 4–5, 1993, pp. 22–9.

BIBLIOGRAPHY

Koryagina, T., "Tenevaya ekonomika v SSSR" (The Underground Economy in the USSR), *Voprosy Ekonomiki*, 3, 1990, pp. 110–19.

Kosals, L. *et al.*, *Ekonomicheskaya aktivnost' rabotnikov pravookhranitel'nykh organov postsovetskoi Rossii* (The Lucrative Activities of Law Enforcement Officers in Post-Soviet Russia), Moscow, 2002.

Kostyukovskii, Ya., "Organizovannaya prestupnost' glazami eyo uchastnikov" (Organised Crime as Seen by its Members), in Gilinskii, Ya. (ed.), *Organizovannaya prestupnost' v Rossii: teoriya i real'nost'*, St Petersburg, Sankt-Peterburgskii Filial Instituta Sotsiologii RAN, 1996, pp. 26–41.

Kriminologicheskaya Assotsiatsiya, *Izmenenie prestupnosti v Rossii. Kriminologicheskii kommentarii statistiki prestupnosti* (The Evolution of Crime in Russia. Criminological Commentary on Crime Statistics), Moscow, Kriminologicheskaya Assotsiatsiya, 1994.

Kryshtanovskaya, O., "Nelegal'nye struktury v Rossii" (Illegal Structures in Russia), *Sotsiologicheskie Issledovaniya*, no. 8, 1995, pp. 94–106.

—— "Finansovaya oligarkhiya v Rossii" *Izvestiya*, 10 January 1996.

Kudryavtsev, V.N., *Prichinnost' v kriminologii* (The Study of Causes in Criminology), Moscow, Yuridicheskaya Literatura, 1968.

Larin, Yu., *Chastnyi kapital v SSSR* (Private Capital in the USSR), Moscow & Leningrad, Gosudarstvennoe Izdatel'stvo, 1927. One chapter republished in *Antologiya Èkonomicheskoi Klassiki. Toma 2*, Moscow, Ekonov, 1993, pp. 435–83.

Lar'kov, A., "Kriminalizatsiya ekonomiki" (The Criminalisation of the Economy), *Rossiiskaya Federatsiya*, 13, 1994, pp. 36–9.

Luneev, V., "Korruptsiya, uchtyonnaya i fakticheskaya" (Corruption, Recorded and Real), *Gosudarstvo i Pravo*, no. 8, 1996, pp. 79–80.

Marx, K. and S.F. Engels, *Sochineniya. Izdanie vtoroe. Tom 2* (Works, 2nd. edn., vol. 2), Moscow, Gosudarstvennoe Izdatel'stvo Politicheskoi Literatury, 1955.

Mazaev, Yu., "Kak izmenyaetsya otnoshenie naseleniya k militsii" (How the Relation Between the Population and the Police Changes), *Sotsiologicheskie Issledovaniya*, no. 11, 1997, pp. 68–73.

Medvedev, Zh., *Neizvestnyi Andropov* (The Unknown Andropov), Rostov–on–Don, Feniks, 1999.

Mikhailovskaya, I.B. (ed.), *Prestupnost': chto my znaem o nei. Militsiya: chto my dumaem o nei* (Crime: What we know about it. The Police: What we Think of them), Obninsk, INTU, 1995.

Ministerstvo Vnutrennih Del RF, Ministerstvo Yustitsii RF, Mezhgosudarstvennyi statisticheskii komitet sodruzhestva nezavisimykh gosudarstv, *Prestupnost' i pravonarusheniya. 1992. Statisticheskii sbornik.* (Crime and Violations of the Law. 1992. A Compendium of Statistics), Moscow, 1993. [Same publication for crime statistics for 1993, 1994 and 1995].

Mishin, G., *Problema èkonomicheskoi prestupnosti. Opyt mezhdistsiplinarnogo izucheniya* (The Problem of Economic Crime. Sketch for an Interdisciplinary Study), Moscow, VNII MVD Rossii, 1994.

MVD Rossii, *Izuchenie obshchestvennogo mneniya o sostoyanii pravoporyadka i effektivnosti deyatel'nosti organov vnutrennih del* (Study of Public Opinion on the State of the Order and Efficiency of the Activity of Interior Ministry Organs), Moscow, MVD Rossii, 1995.

Myslovskii, E., "Mafiya: organizatsiya ili obraz zhizni" (The Mafia: an Organisation or a Way of Life?), *Sovetskaya Bibliografiya*, no. 1, 1989, pp. 4–12.

Neizvestnyi Rutskoi: politicheskii portret (Rutskoi, an Unknown Quantity: a Political Portrait), Moscow, Obozrevatel', 1994.

Nikolaeva, M.I. and A. Yu. Shevyakov, *Tenevaya ekonomika: metody analiza i otsenki* (The Shadow Economy: Analytical and Evaluative Methods), Moscow, TsEMI AN SSSR, 1987.

Obshchestvennyi Tsentr Sodeistviya Reforme Ugolovnogo Pravosudiya, *Materialy prilozheniya k informatsionnoi zapiske "Nekotorye voprosy realizatsii ugolovnoi politiki v sovremennykh usloviyakh"* (Documents appended to the informative note on "Some Questions Concerning the Realisation of Penal Policy in Current Conditions"), Moscow, Obshchestvennyi Tsentr Sodeistviya Reforme Ugolovnogo Pravosudiya, 1997.

—— *Poiski vykhoda. Prestupnost', ugolovnaya politika i mesta zaklyucheniya v postsovetskom prostranstve* (Crime, Penal Policy and Prisons in the Post-Soviet Environment), Moscow, Prava Cheloveka, 1996.

Osipenko, O.V., "Tenevaya eëkonomika: popytka politiko-ekonomicheskogo analiza" (The Shadow Economy: Sketch for a Political and Economic Analysis), *Ekonomicheskie Nauki*, no. 8, 1989, pp. 12–8.

—— *Labirinty tenevoi ekonomiki* (The Labyrinths of the Shadow Economy), Moscow, Znanie, 1990.

—— *Svoyo delo. Ob individual'noi trudovoi deyatel'nosti.* (One's Own Business. On Individual Labour Activity), Moscow, Izdatel'stvo Politicheskoi Literatury, 1991.

Parlamentarizm v Rossii. Federal'noe sobranie 1994–1995 (Parliamentarism in Russia. Federal Assembly, 1994–1995), Moscow, Fond Razvitiya Parlementarizma v Rossii, 1996.

Perekhod k rynku. Kontseptsiya i programma (The Transition to the Market. Conception and Programme), Moscow, Arkhangel'skoe, 1990.

Perestyuk, B.V., "Arenda: shag vperyod ili nazad?" (Leasing: A Forward or Backward Step?), *EKO*, n° 7, 1990, pp. 137–9.

Petrov, E.P., R.A. Safarov and S.S. Strelnikov, "Obshchestvennoe mnenie i sovetskaya militsiya" (Public Opinion and the Soviet Police), *Sovetskoe Gosudarstvo i Pravo*, no. 7, 1981, pp. 71–77.

Pokhmelkin, A.V. and V.V. Pokhmelkin, *Ideologiya i ugolovnaya politika* (Ideology and Penal Policy), Moscow, Moskovskii Institut Psikhologo-Pravovykh Issledovanii, 1992.

Prestupnost'—ugroza Rossii (Crime—a Threat to Russia), Moscow, 1993, p. 31.

Razinkin, V.S., *Vory v zakone i prestupnye klany* (Thieves-in-Law and Criminal Clans), Moscow, 1995.

Rogov, I.I. *Ekonomika i prestupnost'* (The Economy and Crime), Alma-Ata, Kazakhstan, 1991.

Rutgaizer, V., "Tenevaya ekonomika SSSR. Obzor literatury i issledovanii" (The Shadow Economy in the USSR. A Review of Publications and Research), *Svobodnaya Mysl'*, no. 17, 1991, pp. 119–25.

Satarov, G., M. Levin and M. Tsirik, "Rossiya i korruptsiya: kto kogo?" (Russia and Corruption: Who Will Get Who?), booklet published in *Rossiiskaya Gazeta*, 19 February 1998.

Shatalin, S., "Sotsial'noe razvitie i èkonomicheskii rost" (Social Development and Economic Growth), *Kommunist*, no. 14 (1294), September 1986, pp. 59–70.

Shokhin, A., *Social'nye problemy perestrojki* (The Social Problems of Perestroika), Moscow, Ekonomika, 1989.

Sinilov, G. K., *Ekonomiko-pravovye issledovaniya v sisteme sotsial'noi profilaktiki khozyaistvennykh pravonarushenii* (Economic and Legal Research on the System for the Social Prevention of Economic Offences), Moscow, Mimeo, 1980.

Sirotkin, V., *Mark Masarskii. Put' naverkh rossiiskogo biznesmena* (Mark Masarsky. The Rise of a Russian Businessman), Moscow, Mezhdunarodnye Otnosheniya, 1994.

Struchkov, N.A., "Izuchenie obstoyatel'stv obuslovlivayushchikh prestupnost' v SSSR" (The Study of the Circumstances that Condition Crime in the USSR), *Sovetskoe Gosudarstvo i Pravo*, no. 12, 1971, pp. 98–105.

Tenevaya ekonomika (The Shadow Economy), Moscow, Ekonomika, 1991.

Tikhonov, V., *Khronika stremitel'nykh let* (Chronicle of the Impetuous Years), Moscow, Respublika, 1996.

—— *Kooperatsiya: za i protiv* (Cooperatives: For and Against), Moscow, Pik, 1991.

Tolkachenko, A. *Ekonomicheskaya prestupnost'. Ugolovno-pravovye voprosy* (Economic Crime. Legal and Penal Issues), Moscow, Mezhdunarodnyi Nezavisimyi Ekologo-Politologicheskii Universitet, 1994.

Trubin, V.V., *Prestupnost' v sfere privatizatsii* (Crime in the Sphere of Privatisation), Yekaterinburg, Yuridicheskii Institut, 1993.

Vasilev, D., "Rossiiskaya programma privatizatsii i perspektivy eyo realizatsii" (The Russian Privatisation Programme and Perspectives on its Realisation), *Voprosy Ekonomiki*, no. 9, 1992, pp. 8–15.

Vlasov, A.V. (ed.), *Sovetskaya militsiya. Istoriya i sovremennost'. 1917/1987* (The Soviet Police Then and Now, 1917/1987), Moscow, Yuridicheskaya Literatura, 1987.

Vlasov, A.V., "Na strazhe pravoporyadka" (The Preservation of Legal Order), *Kommunist*, no. 5, 1988, pp. 46–59.

Vodolazskii, B. and Yu. Vakutin, *Prestupnye gruppirovki: ikh obychai, traditsii, "zakony"* (Criminal Goups: Customs, Traditions, 'Laws'), Omsk, 1979.

VTsIOM, *Issledovanie otnosheniya obshchestvennogo mneniya naseleniya RSFSR k probleme prestupnosti i rabote pravookhranitel'nykh organov* (A Survey of Public Opinion in the RSFSR with Regard to the Problem of Crime and the Work of Law Enforcement Services), Moscow, VTsIOM, 1990.

Yakovlev, A.M., "Prestupnost' v sfere èkonomiki" (Crime in the Economic Sphere), *Sovetskoe Gosudarstvo i Pravo*, 1986, 4, pp. 48–55.

—— "Preduprezhdenie èkonomicheskoi prestupnosti" (The Prevention of Economic Crime), *Sovetskoe Gosudarstvo i Pravo*, 1987, 1, pp. 62–9.

—— *Sotsiologiya èkonomicheskoi prestupnosti* (Sociology of Economic Crime), Moscow, Nauka, 1988.

—— *Ekonomicheskaya prestupnost': zakon i zhizn'* (Economic Crime: Law and Life), Moscow, Znanie, 1990.

Yarochkin, V., *Organizovannaya prestupnost'. Otkuda ukhodit ugroza* (Organised Crime. Where Does the Threat Come From?), Moscow, "Os'-89", 1995.

Yeltsin, B., *Ispoved' na zadannuyu temu* (Confession on a Given Theme), Riga, Rukitis, 1990.

Yur'ev, L., "Mesto v teni. Podpol'nyi biznes" (A Place in the Shadows. Underground Business), *Biznes*, 1991, no. 3, pp. 4–7.

Zaslavskaya, T., "Chelovecheskii faktor razvitiya èkonomiki i sotsial'naya spravedlivost'" (The Human Factor in Economic Development and Social Justice), *Kommunist*, vol. 63, no. 13, September 1986, pp. 61–73.

Zhitenev, V.B., *Mafiya v Ekaterinburge. Obshchestvennoe mnenie i pressa ob organizovannoi prestupnosti* (The Mafia in Yekaterinburg. Public Opinion and the Press on Organised Crime), Yekaterinburg, 1993.

INDEX